DISCARD

The Individual

Income Tax

Studies of Government Finance

TITLES PUBLISHED

Federal Fiscal Policy in the Postwar Recessions
by Wilfred Lewis, Jr.

Federal Tax Treatment of State and Local Securities
by David J. Ott and Allan H. Meltzer

Federal Tax Treatment of Income from Oil and Gas
by Stephen L. McDonald

Federal Tax Treatment of the Family
by Harold M. Groves

The Role of Direct and Indirect Taxes in the Federal Revenue System
A Report of the National Bureau of Economic Research and the Brookings Institution*

Federal Tax Treatment of Foreign Income
by Lawrence B. Krause and Kenneth W. Dam

The Individual Income Tax
by Richard Goode

* Published by the Princeton University Press. All other titles published by the Brookings Institution.

The Individual

Income Tax

RICHARD GOODE

Studies of Government Finance

THE BROOKINGS INSTITUTION

WASHINGTON, D.C.

THE BROOKINGS INSTITUTION is an independent organization devoted to nonpartisan research, education, and publication in economics, government, foreign policy, and the social sciences generally. Its principal purposes are to aid in the development of sound public policies and to promote public understanding of issues of national importance.

The Institution was founded December 8, 1927, to merge the activities of the Institute for Government Research, founded in 1916, the Institute of Economics, founded in 1922, and the Robert Brookings Graduate School of Economics and Government, founded in 1924.

The general administration of the Institution is the responsibility of a self-perpetuating Board of Trustees. The Trustees are likewise charged with maintaining the independence of the staff and fostering the most favorable conditions for creative research and education. The immediate direction of the policies, program, and staff of the Institution is vested in the President, assisted by the division directors and an advisory council, chosen from the professonal staff of the Institution.

In publishing a study, the Institution presents it as a competent treatment of a subject worthy of public consideration. The interpretations and conclusions in such publications are those of the author or authors and do not purport to represent the views of the other staff members, officers, or trustees of the Brookings Institution.

Foreword

THE FEDERAL INCOME TAX was adopted more than half a century ago. During that half century numerous changes in rates, inclusions, exclusions, and deductions have been made and many more have been proposed. Alternative sources of revenue, such as consumption and wealth taxes, have also been urged, and many proposals have been made for lower and less progressive rates.

This study is an appraisal of the experience with the income tax. It also analyzes various suggested modifications in this tax and considers alternative taxes. The author's analysis will be helpful in clarifying many of the issues involved in these proposals. It is the most comprehensive appraisal of the income tax that has yet been made.

As in all Brookings publications, the author here expresses his own conclusions. The trustees, officers, and staff of the Brookings Institution no less than others may disagree with some of the author's analysis or conclusions. Such are the differences which must be reconciled in the political process of policy making. The treatment here makes a notable contribution toward both a better understanding of many of the underlying issues and toward more informed policy making.

The author has had the benefit of criticisms and suggestions from a number of professional specialists. The Reading Committee consisted of Douglas H. Eldridge, Lawrence H. Seltzer, Louis Shere, and Herbert Stein. In addition, the author had helpful comments from

Joseph A. Pechman, Director of Economic Studies, and from John A. Brittain, E. Cary Brown, Walter J. Blum, Donald J. Daly, Arthur Fefferman, Gary Fromm, Harold M. Groves, Reed R. Hansen, Bert G. Hickman, C. Harry Kahn, Robert J. Lampman, Leif Mutén, Raymond L. Richman, Carl S. Shoup, Richard E. Slitor, William S. Vickrey, Melvin I. White, and others. The author also wishes to acknowledge the research assistance that he received, at different stages, from M. Leon Askren, Peter M. Gentilini, and Sunder Dass Magun and, for briefer periods, from Jean-Pierre Poullier and Eleanor Steinberg. The manuscript was edited by Herbert C. Morton and Medora Richardson. Sheau-eng Lau prepared the charts. Adele Garrett prepared the index.

This study is part of a special program of research and education on taxation and public expenditures, supervised by the National Committee on Government Finance and financed by a special grant from the Ford Foundation.

The views expressed in this study do not purport to represent the views of the National Committee on Government Finance or the advisory committee, or the staff members, officers, or trustees of the Brookings Institution, or the Ford Foundation.

Robert D. Calkins
President

July 1964
The Brookings Institution
1775 Massachusetts Ave., N.W.
Washington, D.C.

Studies of Government Finance

Studies of Government Finance is a special program of research and education in taxation and government expenditures at the federal, state, and local levels. These studies are under the supervision of the National Committee on Government Finance appointed by the Trustees of the Brookings Institution, and are supported by a special grant from the Ford Foundation.

MEMBERS OF THE ADVISORY COMMITTEE

Contents

Text Tables

Charts

Appendix Tables

CHAPTER I

Introduction

ON FEBRUARY 25, 1913, the Secretary of State proclaimed the ratification of the Sixteenth Amendment to the U.S. Constitution, giving Congress "power to lay and collect taxes on incomes, from whatever source derived. . . ." This amendment, the first to be adopted in forty-three years, overturned a Supreme Court decision[1] that had blocked the individual income tax for almost two decades, and opened a new chapter in the fiscal history of the United States.

Within less than two months, the House Ways and Means Committee reported the bill that became the first permanent individual income tax law in the United States. The bill was approved October 3, 1913, with effect from March 1, 1913. At that time the income tax was already well established elsewhere. It had been in effect in Great Britain during most of the nineteenth century, and a super tax on large incomes had been adopted there in 1909. In 1913, income taxes were also in use in Prussia, the Netherlands, the Swiss cantons, Australia, New Zealand, Japan, and other countries and in the State of Wisconsin.

The Ways and Means Committee described its 1913 income tax

[1] *Pollock* v. *Farmers' Loan and Trust Co.*, 157 U.S. 429 (1895), 158 U.S. 601 (1895). This decision declared unconstitutional an income tax law enacted in 1894. An income tax had been levied during the Civil War but was allowed to lapse in 1872.

1

bill as a response to "the general demand for justice in taxation, and to the long-standing need of an elastic and productive system of revenue." The committee made clear that it considered the income tax permanent and an important innovation. The report predicted that, once established, the tax would "meet with as much general satisfaction as any tax law" and—more sanguinely—that "All good citizens . . . will willingly and cheerfully support and sustain this, the fairest and cheapest of all taxes. . . ."[2]

Growth of the Income Tax

The act of 1913 set up an income tax system which remains in effect in the United States today, despite numerous revisions. It includes an individual income tax, applying to natural persons and trusts, and a corporation income tax. The individual tax is a global tax assessed against taxable income from all sources; however, long-term capital gains have been subject to special treatment since 1921 and earned income was taxed at preferential rates for a number of years. Corporations are generally taxed as separate entities, and dividends received by shareholders are subject to the individual income tax. Unincorporated enterprises are generally not taxed as entities; their proprietors and partners pay the individual income tax on total profits regardless of whether withdrawn or retained in the business.[3]

The taxes on income fulfilled the expectation that they would be elastic and productive revenue sources, responding both to changes in tax rates and to changes in national income. The individual income tax alone accounted for almost one-fifth of federal revenue during World War I. Its relative contribution rose in the

[2] H. Rept. 5, 63 Cong. 1 sess., April 22, 1913, reprinted in *Internal Revenue Bulletin,* Cumulative Bulletin 1939-1, Pt. 2 (January-June 1939), pp. 1-3.

[3] When certain conditions are met, closely held corporations may elect to be taxed as partnerships and owners of unincorporated businesses may elect to be taxed as corporations (Internal Revenue Code of 1954, as amended, secs. 1361, 1371-77), but only a small minority have chosen these options. My practice is to give citations of statutory provisions, regulations, and rulings that I judge not to be well known but to omit citations of familiar and easily accessible provisions. Readers whose needs are met by a reliable and rather detailed secondary source will find convenient the annual issues of Commerce Clearing House, *U.S. Master Tax Guide* (Chicago: Commerce Clearing House) or the Harvard Law School, World Tax Series, *Taxation in the United States* (Chicago: Commerce Clearing House, 1963).

1920's, despite sharp rate reductions, and fell in the early 1930's despite rate increases. In response to the fiscal demands of World War II, the income tax was transformed into a mass tax and became the leading revenue source of the federal government. The yield increased spectacularly. During World War II the individual income tax provided one-third of total cash receipts (including social insurance contributions and other nonbudget receipts). After the war, the proportion of revenue provided by the individual income tax continued to grow, reaching 42 percent in the fiscal years 1946-63 (Appendix Table A-1).[4]

The rise in yield of the income tax was made possible by increases in rates going far beyond early expectations and by a great broadening of coverage. The 1913 act set rates ranging from 1 percent, on the first $20,000 of taxable income, to 7 percent, on taxable income in excess of $500,000. The professor of public finance at Harvard found the maximum rate "clearly excessive" on the grounds that Congress at one stroke had appropriated for the use of the federal government "about seventy percent of the total possible proceeds of direct taxation upon large incomes," which, "as the experience of all countries" showed, was subject to a limit of safety of "probably ten percent" and certainly not more than 12 percent.[5] By 1917, the top rate had reached 67 percent. During World War II and most postwar years up to 1964, rates ranged from 20 percent or more in the first bracket to a maximum of more than 90 percent (Appendix Table A-9). Rates scheduled to apply in 1965 will begin at 14 percent and rise to a top of 70 percent.

The 1913 act was expected to apply to only about 1 percent of the population, including taxpayers and their dependents,[6] and

[4] The income tax share of federal government cash receipts, cited above and in Tables A-1 and A-2, is somewhat smaller than its share in "budget receipts" since the latter exclude certain items that are included in cash receipts (particularly excise tax and employment tax receipts transferred to social security and highway trust funds). The World War I period is taken as fiscal years 1917-20, fiscal year 1920 being the year of peak revenue and reflecting the highest tax rates.

[5] Charles J. Bullock, "The Federal Income Tax," in *Proceedings of Eighth Annual Conference under the Auspices of the National Tax Association, 1914* (Madison, Wis., 1915), p. 277.

[6] Derived from estimate of House Ways and Means Committee (H. Rept. 5, reprint p. 3) on the assumption that the average number of persons covered on each taxable return was 2.5.

the actual number was smaller. As recently as 1939, only 5 percent of the population were subject to the income tax. In 1960, almost three-fourths of the population were covered. (See Table 1 and Appendix Table A-3.)

By 1918, individual income tax liabilities surpassed $1 billion and approached 2 percent of total personal income. Twenty-seven years later, in another wartime year, the tax absorbed 10 percent of personal income (Table 1). In 1960, the fraction was almost as high.

TABLE 1. Growth of the Federal Individual Income Tax, 1913-60[a]

Calendar Year	Percentage of Population Covered	Tax as Percentage of Personal Income
1913	Less than 1.0[b]	0.1[c]
1918	7.7	1.8[c]
1926	4.2	0.9
1939	5.0	1.2
1945	74.2	10.0
1950	58.9	8.0
1960	73.1	9.8

[a] Derived from the same sources as Appendix Tables A-3 and A-4; footnotes to those tables also apply here.
[b] My rough approximation.
[c] The underlying personal income estimate for 1913 is the average for 1912-16; that for 1918 is the average for 1917-21.

Although the individual income tax has been widely used by the states, it has never attained as much prominence at the state level as at the federal level. Until the mid-1930's the tax spread rapidly among the states, but thereafter it was adopted by only a few states. In 1960, individual income taxes were levied by 33 of the 50 states. They produced 12 percent of total state tax revenue, a substantially smaller share than general sales taxes or motor fuel taxes.[7] State income taxes have been held back by state constitutional restrictions and the fear of driving out residents and business. Since about 1940, the heavy use of the income tax by the federal government has discouraged the states from relying more on this revenue source.

[7] Advisory Commission on Intergovernmental Relations, *Tax Overlapping in the United States, 1961* (1961), pp. 16, 23.

Why Study the Income Tax?

The pre-eminence of the individual income tax in the federal revenue system reflects its productivity and, more basically, a widespread belief that it is the fairest means of meeting national government costs. Moreover, as the federal government has assumed greater responsibility for moderating economic fluctuations, the quick response of the income tax to changes in business activity has come to be recognized as a valuable stabilizing force as well as a fiscal convenience.

Criticisms of the income tax, nevertheless, have persisted throughout the past half century and lately have intensified. These criticisms differ in sophistication and vehemence and, being advanced from various points of view, are often inconsistent with each other. Some of the objections reflect little more than dissatisfaction with heavy taxation of any kind and concentrate on reduction of tax rates. This dissatisfaction was aggravated in the 1950's and early 1960's by the more-than-proportionate increase in income tax liabilities that automatically accompanied the growth of total income and average personal income. But other critics argue that the income tax is more objectionable than alternative taxes and should be partly or wholly replaced.

An income tax with high, graduated rates is said to inhibit private saving and investment and thus to slow capital formation and the rate of economic growth. It is also said to discourage initiative and enterprise in business ventures and to lessen the willingness to accept new and more responsible employment or to work long hours. Moreover, the income tax is alleged to cause business executives and individual investors to divert time and ingenuity from productive activities to tax compliance and minimization. Efforts to avoid taxation are thought to reduce economic efficiency because they distort decisions with respect to forms of business organization, contracts, and portfolios. Critics note that the United States has been growing less rapidly than West Germany, France, Italy, and Japan, which rely less heavily on income taxes and more heavily on indirect consumption taxes.

Many supporters of the income tax have become less enthusiastic. They are disturbed by special provisions allowing much income to escape taxation, the ingenuity of taxpayers in finding loopholes, the reluctance of Congress to repair the erosion of the tax base, and incomplete compliance with the law. In 1960, for example, the amount of income actually taxed equaled only about two-fifths of total personal income (Chart 1). Economists have concluded that the income tax is less neutral in its effects than was often supposed in the past. Egalitarians are asking whether progressive taxation of income is the best means of attaining their objectives. Suggestions for new forms of taxation have received far more attention from experts in the recent past than they did ten or twenty years ago.

CHART 1. Derivation of Individual Income Tax Base, 1960

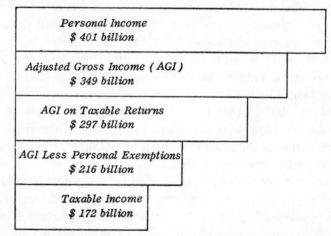

Source: Appendix Tables A-4, A-5, and A-6.

Some of these criticisms reflect disillusionment with a revenue system which has moved in the direction that many experts wished it to go but which clearly is still far from ideal. Some tax experts are suffering from having got what they wanted, a fate that cynics have asserted is at least as sad as not getting what one wants. Other criticisms reflect renewed emphasis on the classical objective of growth and diminished interest in problems of income distribution.

Suggestions for improvement are numerous and varied. They call for actions ranging from minor technical amendments to abolition of the tax. A favorite program among supporters of the income tax includes broadening the base by ending unjustified omissions and deductions from taxable income and reducing nominally high tax rates to offset the revenue gained from base-broadening. As originally conceived, this approach was designed to maintain, or enhance, the role of the income tax in the federal revenue system. Base-broadening and rate adjustments, however, may be combined in a program that diminishes the percentage of total revenue obtained from the income tax.

Other programs call for de-emphasis of the income tax and partial substitution of sales taxes and excises or other indirect taxes. These proposals usually are concerned more with tax rates than with structural reforms but often include some provisions of the latter kind. In the United States, they are sponsored mainly by business groups and conservatives, but in Sweden a Social Democratic government imposed a retail sales tax in 1959 and raised the rate in 1962 while reducing income taxes.

More extreme programs contemplate the elimination of the income tax and its replacement by a sales tax, turnover tax, or value-added tax. Usually these proposals are rooted in a persistent conservative opposition to progressive taxation. Paradoxically, however, the income tax is also disliked on the far left. In 1960, Chairman Nikita Khrushchev announced, and the Supreme Soviet adopted, a program for the elimination of the individual income tax in Soviet Russia over a period of years. Since the U.S.S.R. had always relied mainly on turnover taxes, the program was less extreme than it would have been in the United States or most other Western countries; nevertheless, the Soviet government suspended the plan in 1962, attributing the step to the need for resources to strengthen defenses against "imperialists."[8]

Recently the range of alternatives has been extended by suggestions for graduated taxes on personal consumption expenditures and personal wealth as a major supplement to the income tax or a complete substitute. Some economists think that the expenditure tax and the wealth tax would avoid disadvantages of the income tax without sacrifice of progressivity. Although personal taxes on consumption and wealth are not really new ideas, they have so far had only limited application and are novel elements in a program

[8] N. S. Khrushchev, *Raising the Soviet Standard of Living* (New York: Crosscurrents Press, 1960), pp. 19-33, 96-99; *Manchester Guardian Weekly*, Sept. 27, 1962.

for action. The expenditure tax and the wealth tax merit attention because fresh proposals on taxation are scarce and because their analysis gives perspective on the income tax.

Scope of the Book

This book presents a general appraisal of the individual income tax and considers possible revisions of the tax. Emphasis is on the equity and economic effects of the income tax and alternative revenue sources, but attention is also given to administration and compliance and to certain other aspects of taxation. The focus is on the federal income tax in the United States, but many points that must be examined are relevant for state income taxes and for income taxes in other countries.

Only incidental references are made to the special problems of taxing business profits. Although technical provisions relating to the measurement of profits, such as depreciation and depletion allowances, generally apply to both the corporation income tax and the individual income tax, they can be more conveniently treated in connection with the taxation of corporations, which account for the major part of business profits in the United States. The present book also omits the intricate questions arising out of the relationship between the taxation of corporations and their shareholders.

The book appears soon after the fiftieth anniversary of the modern income tax in the United States. Fifty years may not seem a long time in the history of the republic or in the life of a form of taxation. But the period since 1913 has seen a huge increase in taxation and the development of new fiscal-policy doctrines. Interesting and enlightening as it might be, a detailed history of the income tax is not presented.[9] The subject is the contemporary tax and the tax of the future. Where does the United States stand in income taxation after half a century of experience? Where should the country try to go in the years ahead?

As in any survey, the task of selection is difficult. The income tax is imposed by a complex statute accompanied by detailed

[9] For historical reviews, see Roy G. Blakey and Gladys C. Blakey, *The Federal Income Tax* (New York: Longmans, Green, 1940) and Randolph E. Paul, *Taxation in the United States* (Boston: Little, Brown, 1954).

regulations. Even to ascertain exactly what the law provides, one cannot rely only on the Internal Revenue Code and official regulations but must refer to a mountain of congressional committee reports, court decisions, handbooks, treatises, and legal journals. In order to explain how the law came to be what it is, one would have to sift through published committee hearings, records of congressional debates, memoirs and biographies, and newspaper reports, and to supplement the printed record by interviews with many persons who have influenced legislation. When one proceeds to the appraisal of the economic effects of the income tax, the volume of literature, although still large, drops off rapidly. This is particularly true of topics of intermediate scope, involving neither the great issues, such as whether the income tax retards saving, or the minutiae, such as the measurement of the taxable yield of securities bought at a discount. This book discusses the great issues and touches on some of the technical details but concentrates on other questions.

The next chapter deals with the suitability of income as a tax base from the standpoints of fairness and practicality and examines the case for other tax bases. In Chapters III and IV, the economic effects of the income tax are broadly compared with those of direct and indirect taxes on consumption and wealth. Three chapters on the definition and measurement of the income tax base follow. These treat certain costs of earning income that present special problems, income items that are excluded from taxable income, and personal deductions which are allowed even though they are not costs of obtaining income. A special effort is made to ascertain the influence of these provisions on the yield of the tax, its progressivity, and its influence on economic decisions. Capital gains and losses are the subject of a separate chapter because of their strategic importance and because of marked differences of opinion respecting the extent to which they should be reflected in taxable income and the tax rates that should apply to capital gains. Chapter IX surveys topics relating to the level and structure of personal exemptions and income tax rates. The effects of the income tax on the distribution of income and wealth and on the severity of the business cycle are examined in Chapters X and XI. The book concludes with a chapter on income tax reform and the place of the individual income tax in the revenue system.

Taxes are never pleasant to those who pay them, and taxation seldom brings about an increase in production. Ignoring the benefits of government expenditures and looking only at a particular tax or tax provision, it is easy to find harmful economic effects or inequities. A grave shortcoming of this approach is the failure to take account of the undesirable consequences of other taxes that might be substituted for the one under consideration or of a budget deficit or reduction in government expenditures. An opposite error, occasionally encountered, is to excuse the defects of the income tax on the grounds that it finances essential government services, without considering the possibility of obtaining revenue from a revised income tax or from another source.

These biases cannot be wholly avoided, but they can be minimized by frequent comparisons between alternative revenue sources and tax provisions. The comparative approach is followed to the extent feasible within the limits of a book on the individual income tax. No attempt is made to determine whether taxation is too heavy or too light relative to social needs or government expenditures. It is assumed in this study that any change in revenue due to income tax revision or the introduction of a new tax would not affect the government's total receipts because it either would be offset by changes in the rates of the income tax or other taxes or would prevent tax rate increases or decreases that would otherwise occur.

The objective of the book is to increase understanding of the individual income tax and alternative taxes with the hope that in the long run this will help in policy formulation. On many economic issues—perhaps the majority of important questions—definitive conclusions cannot be provided. Theory and data are inadequate, and experts disagree. On other points, disagreements arise from conflicts of social values and political preferences. Nevertheless progress seems possible toward a better public understanding of alternatives. I have not refrained from expressing opinions on controversial subjects but have tried to warn the reader of uncertainties and differences of opinion.

CHAPTER II

Income as a Tax Base

THE BELIEF that the individual income tax is the fairest of all taxes arises from the conviction that it accords best with ability to pay. Net income is a measure of a person's capacity to command economic resources, and, intuitively, it seems to be a good indicator of ability to help finance government.

The income tax has also gained approval because of its directness and adaptability to graduated rates. It is a direct tax in the sense that legislators expect those who pay it will be unable to shift it to others. A direct tax can take account of taxpayers' family circumstances and other individual conditions in a way that is not possible under a sales tax or other indirect tax which is collected from producers or distributors in the expectation that they will pass it on to customers. By providing for personal exemptions and graduated rates, the income tax may cause an individual's tax to increase faster than his income, with the result that the percentage of income absorbed by the tax rises with income. Because of this characteristic, the income tax is called a progressive tax, a term that should be understood in a technical rather than a political sense. The principle of tax progressivity has been accepted to some degree in nearly every country, and the income tax has won support as the primary instrument of progressivity.

The case for the income tax has elicited controversy as well

11

as support. Ability to pay is subject to diverse interpretations; critics have called it a slogan rather than a principle. Progressivity has never been universally accepted as desirable; even its supporters disagree about its rationale. Income taxation, moreover, is not the only means of achieving progressivity. Taxes on estates, inheritance, and gifts contribute to progressivity, although their coverage is limited, and it is doubtful that they could be made a major source of revenue. Direct, progressive taxes could also be assessed against personal consumption and wealth.

Whether personal income is indeed the fairest tax base and the best base for progressive taxation is ultimately a question of taste and political values. But this does not mean that the issues cannot be illuminated by analysis, that one set of preferences is as good as· another. The implications of tax doctrines can be clarified and preferences examined for consistency with other values. The feasibility of correctly assessing alternative taxes can be considered. These questions are the subject of this chapter.

Fairness and Progressivity of Alternative Taxes

The significant alternatives to income as a basis of personal taxation are wealth and consumption. Taxes on personal wealth or net worth are in effect in Sweden, Norway, the Netherlands, Germany, and a few other countries. The yield of these taxes is much less than that of the income tax in the same countries. The wealth taxes differ from the American general property tax in that they require the aggregation of all, or most, items of property owned by the individual and allow deductions for debts; personal exemptions are provided and rates may be graduated. Lately there has been discussion of the possibility of a direct tax on personal consumption expenditures. Unlike sales taxes and excises, this tax would be assessed on the basis of individual returns, with provision for personal exemptions and graduated rates. Personal expenditure taxes were introduced on a limited scale in India in 1957 and in Ceylon in 1959, but these taxes have been rescinded. Throughout this book, the terms "wealth tax" and "expenditure tax" refer to personal taxes of the kind just identified rather than to more familiar forms of taxation of property and consumption.

The United States Constitution may bar the federal government from imposing a wealth tax. Taxes on property have been held to be direct taxes which cannot be levied by Congress unless apportioned among the states according to population.[1] The status of an expenditure tax is also uncertain. Perhaps it would be upheld as an income tax with a deduction for saving, or possibly the courts would decide that it is not a direct tax within the meaning of the Constitution. Doubts about constitutionality, however, should not preclude the discussion of innovations. When the country was convinced that the income tax should be adopted, the Constitution was amended.

Definition of Income

Many American students have accepted as an ideal starting point for tax purposes an income definition usually associated in the United States with the names of Haig and Simons but which was anticipated by Schanz in Germany and apparently also by Davidson in Sweden.[2] In Haig's language, income is "the increase or accretion in one's power to satisfy his wants in a given period in so far as that power consists of (*a*) money itself, or, (*b*) anything susceptible of valuation in terms of money."[3] Simons equates per-

---

[1] Art. 1, sec. 9; *Pollock* v. *Farmers' Loan and Trust Co.*, 157 U.S. 429, 558 (1895); *Brushaber* v. *Union Pacific Railroad Co.*, 240 U.S. 1, 14 (1916).

[2] Georg Schanz. "Der Einkommensbegriff und die Einkommensteuergesetze," *Finanz-Archiv*, Vol. 13 (1896), pp. 1-87. Henry C. Simons acknowledged Schanz's contribution and included a review of the German literature in his book, *Personal Income Taxation* (Chicago: University of Chicago Press, 1938), pp. 59-102. An extended treatment of the history of the discussion appears in a three-part article by Paul H. Wueller in *Political Science Quarterly* under the general title "Concepts of Taxable Income": "The German Contribution," Vol. 53 (March 1938), pp. 83-110; "The American Contribution," Vol. 53 (December 1938), pp. 557-83; "The Italian Contribution," Vol. 54 (December 1939), pp. 555-76. See also Fritz Neumark, *Theorie und Praxis der modernen Einkommensbesteurung* (Bern: A. Francke, 1947), pp. 34-50.

For the reference to David Davidson, I am indebted to Professor Leif Mutén of Uppsala, who cites Davidson's monograph *Om beskattningsnormen vid inkomstskatten* (Uppsala, 1889).

[3] Robert Murray Haig, "The Concept of Income—Economic and Legal Aspects," in *The Federal Income Tax*, Haig, ed. (New York: Columbia University Press, 1921), p. 7, reprinted in American Economic Association, *Readings in the Economics of Taxation*, Richard A. Musgrave and Carl S. Shoup, eds. (Homewood, Ill.: Irwin, 1959), p. 59.

sonal income with the algebraic sum of consumption and change in net worth.[4]

Most experts believe, however, that it is not feasible to take into account all accrued changes in the value of assets and liabilities and that the income tax should be limited to realized income as reflected in transactions or conventional accounting statements.[5] Many think that it would not be desirable to tax unrealized capital gains even if it were feasible to do so. A number of writers favor a definition of taxable income more restricted than that of Haig and Simons in other respects.

The U.S. statutes do not attempt a general definition of income; they rely mainly on the enumeration of items to be included, excluded, or deducted. However, the statutory listing is not exhaustive. The Internal Revenue Code, quoting the language of the Sixteenth Amendment, refers to income "from whatever source derived" and states that taxable income includes "but [is] not limited to" the enumerated items. The limits of the income concept have to be determined by administrators and the courts on a case-by-case basis. Although the courts have tended to become more permissive and to allow a broadening of the concept,[6] many important items that qualify as realized income are omitted from the tax base in the United States. Initially, nevertheless, it will be convenient to compare income, consumption, and wealth as tax bases on the assumption that each is defined as comprehensively and accurately as would be feasible in a new system devised without regard to political commitments to the present income tax law or vested interests in its provisions.

Conceptual as well as practical difficulties are involved in following through the definition of income. One group of problems relates to the definition of personal consumption and turns mainly on the distinction between goods and services that yield direct satisfactions and intermediate goods and services that are used to produce final goods and services. Other difficulties relate to the meas-

[4] Simons, *Personal Income Taxation*, p. 50.
[5] Simons conceded this. See his posthumous book, *Federal Tax Reform* (Chicago: University of Chicago Press, 1950), pp. 48, 74.
[6] Harvard Law School, World Tax Series, *Taxation in the United States* (Chicago: Commerce Clearing House, 1963), pp. 366-67.

urement of changes in net worth or capital gains and losses when the price level and interest rates vary.

The distinction between consumption and intermediate goods and services depends more on individual attitudes and convention than on physical characteristics. An automobile, a restaurant meal, or a scholarly book may be a source of personal gratification or a means of enabling its buyer to earn more income. Or it may serve both purposes. Simons acknowledges that the measurement of consumption "presents insuperable difficulties to achievement of a rigorous conception of personal income"[7] but concludes that, in practice, income can be measured well enough for tax purposes.

Nicholas Kaldor, on the other hand, gives little attention to the definition of consumption but stresses the difficulties of measuring changes in net worth.[8] Because of these difficulties, Kaldor concludes that "the problem of *defining* individual Income, quite apart from any problem of practical measurement, appears in principle insoluble." This leads him to argue that consumption is a better measure of taxable capacity than income and to recommend an expenditure tax as an important supplement to the income tax.

In Kaldor's view, "the ideal definition of Income, as a measure of taxable capacity, is to be thought of . . . as Consumption plus *Real* Capital Accumulation . . ." and the insoluble problem is to distinguish between real and nominal capital accumulation. Real capital accumulation, he says, occurs when an individual secures "increased command over both consumption goods and income yielding resources. . . ."[9] Fictitious gains that are due merely to an increase in the price level can be approximately eliminated by deflating by an index of consumer prices. But there is a second kind of rise in asset prices which Kaldor considers a fictitious gain for which a proper correction cannot be made.

The value of income-yielding assets will rise if there is a general fall in interest rates. If, for example, the relevant interest rate falls from 5 percent to 4 percent, the capital value of a perpetual

---

[7] *Personal Income Taxation*, p. 110.

[8] *An Expenditure Tax* (London: Allen and Unwin, 1955), pp. 54-78. The quotation is from p. 70.

[9] *Ibid.*, pp. 69-70.

stream of income of $100 a year will rise from $2,000 to $2,500; the value of a twenty-year stream of $100 per year, from $1,246 to $1,359. Kaldor argues that this kind of appreciation is also spurious because it does not make the investor better off relative to other capitalists and because it does not give him increased command over capital assets. He points out that a correction for changes in interest rates is not possible because the relevant interest rate cannot be inferred from the market; when share prices rise it is not possible to say how much of the rise is due to a lower interest (capitalization) rate and how much to expectations of improved earnings.

Kaldor's criterion seems to be overly exacting. Why should income be considered real only if it affords increased command over both consumption goods and capital assets, that is, increased power to consume now *and* in the future? Why not say that increased power to consume is a sufficient condition and that income accrues when an increase occurs regardless of whether the power is exercised? To be sure, an increase in capital values due to a fall in interest rates is less advantageous to a property owner than an increase due to the expectation of higher yields. If income is defined merely as an increase in the power to consume, this difference will not be taken into account immediately, but, if the expectation proves to be correct, the difference will be reflected in future income.[10] It is incorrect to say that an appreciation of asset values due to a general decline in interest rates does not make the owners better off relative to other capitalists. Owners of long-term securities gain relative to holders of short-terms and cash and relative to those who aspire to accumulate wealth in the future.[11] If income is

[10] For example, when a twenty-year income stream rises in market value from $1,246 to $1,359, the Haig-Simons definition indicates that $113 of income has accrued to the owner. If annual yield is the fixed amount of $100 per year, the capital appreciation is due to a fall in the interest rate from 5 percent to 4 percent. The total taxable income over twenty years is $113 + 20 ($100) = $2,113. If, on the other hand, the interest rate is constant at 5 percent, the capital appreciation reflects the expectation that the annual yield will rise from $100 to $109. If this expectation proves correct, the total taxable income, according to Haig-Simons, will be $113 + 20 ($109) = $2,293. It is true that the present value of the $2,293, discounted at 5 percent, is equal to the present value of the $2,113, discounted at 4 percent.

[11] See the Memorandum of Dissent by the Minority of the United Kingdom Royal Commission on the Taxation of Profits and Income in *Final Report*, Cmd. 9474 (London, 1955), p. 367.

interpreted each year as the power to command consumption goods, a consistent and logical pattern will emerge over the years.

It is highly doubtful, moreover, that the income tax would be fairer if all incomes were corrected for changes in the price level. This question is postponed for consideration in the chapter on capital gains and losses.

Since the conceptual difficulties of defining income arise from ambiguities in the definition of consumption and changes in net worth, replacement of the income tax by an expenditure tax *and* a wealth tax would resolve none of these difficulties. Substitution of one of the two alternative taxes would eliminate some of the conceptual problems. The literature on the definition of personal consumption and personal wealth is less extensive than that on the definition of income, and the problems of defining these items are less widely appreciated, because the expenditure tax and the wealth tax have been used much less than the income tax.

Ability to Pay

Fairness is generally recognized as comprising equal treatment of equals and reasonable differences in the treatment of unequals. In regard to taxation, capacity or ability to pay is the relevant aspect of equality and inequality. Income and competing tax bases derive their appeal from their relation to capacity or ability to pay.

In the crudest sense, ability to pay means only the possession of resources that can be turned over to the state. A pauper can pay little in taxes whereas a millionaire can pay much. Most people fall between the extremes. But the idea of ability to pay, if it has any value as a tax criterion, must convey something more.

The doctrine of ability to pay can be given meaning without reviving the pseudo-scientific, and now discredited, interpretations of it that flourished in the past.[12] While I agree that the sacrifices

---

[12] For criticisms of the hedonistic interpretation of ability to pay, particularly of its use as an argument for progressive taxation, see Simons, *Personal Income Taxation*, pp. 5-19; Elmer D. Fagan, "Recent and Contemporary Theories of Progressive Taxation," *Journal of Political Economy*, Vol. 46 (August 1938), pp. 457-98, reprinted in *Readings in the Economics of Taxation*, pp. 19-53; M. Slade Kendrick, "The Ability-to-Pay Theory of Taxation," *American Economic Review*, Vol. 29 (March 1939), pp. 92-101; and Walter J. Blum and Harry Kalven, Jr., *The Uneasy Case for Progressive Taxation* (Chicago: University of Chicago Press, 1953).

of taxpayers cannot be precisely measured and summed, as many earlier writers assumed, I do not think that it is necessary or wise to abandon the idea of appraising and comparing, in a rough way, the burdens that taxes impose.

Ability to pay taxes is the capacity of paying without undue hardship on the part of the person paying or an unacceptable degree of interference with objectives that are considered socially important by other members of the community. If A has more income than B, it seems reasonable to say that A has greater ability to pay taxes in the sense that the payment of a given amount will hurt A less and will be less likely to force a cut in socially desirable consumption. In judging what A and B will give up, one makes an estimate of what they would do and how they would feel if they were representative of others in similar relevant circumstances. The doctrine of taxation according to ability to pay is not destroyed by the undoubted fact that others do not know how A and B actually feel as individuals. Debaters' points can easily be scored by supposing that, although A is a rich bachelor and B a poor widow, A is so sensitive that he will suffer more by forgoing an extra bottle of champagne than B will from giving up milk for her children. But most sensible people will consider this an implausible case, and, if pressed, will say that, even in the assumed circumstances, milk for B's children should have priority over champagne for A.

The ability-to-pay principle supports progressive taxation only if taxpaying capacity increases faster than income, which is a stronger assertion than the general argument made above. The assertion has appeal because it is plausible to suppose that people first satisfy their most urgent needs and then use additional income to meet less urgent wants and because, in civilized communities, public or private assistance is given to those who lack the means to provide for themselves the items that are customarily bought with small incomes. It is widely agreed, even by severe critics of extensive progression, that people below a certain level of poverty should not be expected to pay taxes. Acceptance of a personal exemption necessarily implies endorsement of at least a limited degree of progression, since tax liability will rise faster than income immediately above the exemption, even if rates are not graduated. In my judgment, the reasoning that approves this limited degree of progression can also justify much wider progressivity. To deny this would imply that there is a sharp discontinuity in the sacrifices made in paying taxes or in the social importance of successive increments of income, consumption, or wealth. It seems more plausible to suppose that the private and social importance of additional units diminishes gradually over a very wide range. This can be recognized by granting a variable exemption or, more effectively, by applying graduated tax rates.[13]

If this seems distressingly imprecise, it is because ability to pay is being regarded as the name of a numerical formula rather than a term of ethics or politics, as it should be. Ability to pay is no more imprecise than concepts such as the national interest, general welfare, due process of law, morality, and duty. It is as susceptible of objective evaluation as are intelligence, social adjustment, prudence, and many other personal characteristics.

Basic ethical and political judgments can better be taken from political leaders or public consensus than from experts. My observation is that the majority of citizens and legislators in the United States and other democratic countries accept ability to pay as a guiding principle of taxation and interpret it as justifying progressivity. They talk and act as if they believe that progressive taxation is needed to maintain a proper relation between the sacrifices of individual taxpayers and to give recognition to social priorities in the use of income and wealth. Without assuming that some such beliefs are widely accepted, I find it hard to account for political discourse on taxation or for revenue legislation. Even if one concedes that many participants in the debates use the language of ability to pay and progressivity as a cloak for personal or class interests,[14] it is still significant that they think it advantageous to appeal to these ideas.

Generalizations about ability to pay provide no formula for tax allocation. In democratic countries, legislators are delegated the responsibility of choosing taxes and rate schedules in the light of

[13] Early in this century, Gustav Cassel proposed a progressive income tax consisting of a single statutory rate and personal exemptions which would increase with income but less rapidly than income. The exemptions were intended to cover the cost of "the necessaries of efficiency," which Cassel thought increased with income "but more slowly. . . ." See "The Theory of Progressive Taxation," *Economic Journal,* Vol. 11 (December 1901), pp. 481-91.

[14] Louis Eisenstein, *The Ideologies of Taxation* (New York: Ronald Press, 1961).

their judgment about ability to pay and other criteria. Economists
and sociologists can aid them by trying to develop indirect measures of the consequences of unequal income distribution, employ-
ing indicators such as life expectancy, health, crime rates, educational attainments, and voter participation in elections.[15]

Reduction of Economic Inequality

Critics of the ability-to-pay theory do not always reject progressive taxation. Many of them advocate progressivity but try to
support it without resort to utilitarian arguments. They assert that
progressive taxation is desirable because it will reduce economic
inequality, which they treat as an objective in itself. Henry Simons,
for example, urged that the discussion be reduced "frankly to the
level of ethics or aesthetics" and, in a much-quoted sentence, said,
"The case for drastic progression in taxation must be rested on the
case against inequality—on the ethical or aesthetic judgment that
the prevailing distribution of wealth and income reveals a degree
(and/or kind) of inequality which is distinctly evil or unlovely."[16]

The discard of pretensions to numerical exactness in the measurement of personal sacrifices and satisfactions is a step forward. I
find it difficult, however, to accept the reduction of inequality as an
ultimate objective in the same sense that the minimization of sacrifices and the maximization of happiness may be considered as
ends.[17] To be sure, reduction of economic inequality or the prevention of excessive growth of inequality has long been regarded as
desirable as a means of avoiding concentration of political power,
envy, and unrest and as helpful in the maintenance of a democratic
society. But much of the reasoning in support of this policy seems
closely related to the ability-to-pay theory.

Furthermore, the Simons' statement and similar ones may go

---

[15] Fagan, in *Readings in the Economics of Taxation*, pp. 50-53; Robert J.
Lampman, "Making Utility Predictions Verifiable," *Southern Economic Journal*,
Vol. 22 (January 1956), pp. 360-66; Harold M. Groves, "Toward a Social Theory
of Progressive Taxation," *National Tax Journal*, Vol. 9 (March 1956), pp. 27-34.

[16] *Personal Income Taxation*, pp. 18-19.

[17] Bertrand Russell takes the position that, although "there are strong arguments for approximating to an even distribution" of material goods, "they are
nevertheless arguments as to means," and an equal distribution should not be
regarded "as something having intrinsic value on its own account." See *Human
Society in Ethics and Politics* (New York: New American Library for World
Literature, Mentor Book, 1962), p. 109. See also Richard A. Musgrave, *Theory
of Public Finance* (New York: McGraw-Hill, 1959), p. 222.

too far in rejecting the possibilities of reasoned evaluation of tax schemes. They are open to the interpretation that there are no objective standards for allocating taxes, but only personal preference or caprice. To recognize the element of ethics or aesthetics—or, one should add, politics—is not to say that choices do not also involve analytical questions. The ability-to-pay formulation impresses me as more fruitful than that of Simons because it suggests more lines of inquiry concerning the consequences of different distributions of taxes and disposable income. Finally, I do not think that the reduction of inequality has received anything like the degree of popular support that has been accorded to ability to pay.

These considerations lead me to the conclusion that the reduction of economic inequality is a valid objective of progressive taxation but that it is secondary to the objective of allocating taxes according to ability to pay.

Measures of Ability to Pay and Inequality

Income is an incomplete measure of the quantity of resources at the disposal of a person since it does not take account of wealth which also represents command over resources. Wealth, to be sure, can be resolved into income because it arises either from the accumulation of past income or the expectation of future income. But this does not alter the fact that the possession of wealth gives economic power additional to that attributable to current income. A person with, say, an income of $4,000 a year and net worth of $100,000 is certainly better off than one with the same income and no property.

Nevertheless, wealth has a claim for consideration only as a supplementary index of ability to pay. It does not rival income as the primary index. The principal reason is that wealth, as usually defined, does not include the expectation of future income from personal effort. In modern legal and accounting systems, the capital value of personal earnings is not wealth because the right to receive all such income cannot be bought and sold; long-term labor contracts are commonly barred, and short-term contracts usually cannot be freely transferred. Wealth is a seriously incomplete index of taxable capacity because it takes no account of economic resources of persons who depend on earnings from personal services.[18]

[18] Earl R. Rolph and George F. Break suggest in *Public Finance* (New York:

Consumption is a genuine rival to personal income as an index of ability to pay taxes and as a basis for the assessment of progressive taxes. Citing Hobbes, Kaldor has contended that it may be just and expedient to tax people with reference to what they take out of the common pool (the national product) rather than what they contribute and has suggested that consumption may be a better tax base than income.[19]

Although Kaldor's argument has merit, his metaphor is not very enlightening. Investment, no less than consumption, is a withdrawal from the common pool in the sense that it is an exercise of a claim on the use of resources. In this respect, there is no difference between the purchase of, say, food-processing machinery and a household refrigerator. Taxes are levied because it is necessary to compel people to relinquish their claims on resources and thus to allow the government to use them. Whether consumption claims or investment claims should give way is a question of policy.

The most important difference between income and consumption as tax bases resides in the differences in allocation of the base among individuals and over time for any one person. In the aggregate, the difference cannot be great because most disposable personal income is consumed. From 1950 to 1963, personal consumption expenditures in the United States were never less than 92 percent nor more than 94 percent of disposable personal income in any year.[20] For particular families and individuals, of course, the difference is greater than for the aggregate, since the total includes units with consumption and income ratios above and below the average. But for a large fraction almost the same arithmetic result would be obtained by applying an income tax and an expenditure tax schedule that would yield the same total revenue.[21]

The majority of families have little opportunity to consume

Ronald Press, 1961), pp. 196-200, that human capital should be included in the base of a wealth tax, but I do not think that human capital can be measured with the degree of accuracy that is properly demanded for taxation. Furthermore, I see dangers of infringement on personal liberties in applying a tax on the present value of potential earnings: Would a person with great earning capacity who refused to work enough to earn the money to pay his tax be sent to jail?

[19] *An Expenditure Tax*, p. 53.

[20] *Economic Report of the President, January 1964*, p. 226.

[21] For cross-classifications of income and consumption, 1946-50, see 1951 Survey of Consumer Finances, *Federal Reserve Bulletin*, Vol. 37 (September 1951), p. 1062.

much more than their income over their lifetime because they start with little inherited wealth and could not find creditors who would allow them to pile up large debts if they chose to borrow continuously. (This assertion is based on the Haig-Simons definition, which includes in income gifts received, social security and public assistance payments, and similar items which are often not regarded as income; if these items were excluded from income, the number with lifetime consumption in excess of income no doubt would be considerably increased.) Furthermore, most people's lifetime saving seems to be small relative to their lifetime income; this is indicated by the small fraction of persons who die with enough wealth to be required to file estate tax returns and by scattered information on net worth.

For the majority whose lifetime consumption and disposable income are about equal, there are nevertheless stages of the life cycle and occasional years in which consumption is considerably more or less than disposable income. There are reasons for expecting both young married couples and elderly persons to spend more than their current income, the young couples going into debt to cover the expenses of setting up households and rearing children and the elderly drawing down savings accumulated during their most productive years. Superficially viewed, statistical data seem to confirm these expectations, but the apparent relation may be misleading because both the young and the old tend to have lower incomes than the middle-aged.[22] At any income or age level, consumption tends to exceed income in years when family income declines because of unemployment or illness of the wage earner, poor business conditions, or other adversity.

For the majority of the population, the substitution of an expenditure tax for an income tax would involve mainly a rearrangement of the timing of tax payment, with more taxes being paid in years of dissaving and less in years of saving. There seems to be no principle of justice, nor even any popular prejudice, holding that taxes should be relatively heavy in periods of youth and age and years of temporary adversity and relatively light at other times. Arguments have been advanced in favor of averaging out short-term fluctuations in the tax base and even variations over the life cycle,

[22] See Sidney Goldstein, *Consumption Patterns of the Aged* (Philadelphia: University of Pennsylvania Press, 1960), pp. 58, 240-42.

regardless of whether income or consumption is taxed. If averaging over a long period of time were allowed, the difference between an expenditure tax and an income tax would be greatly reduced.

There remains the difference in treatment of the relatively small number of people who build up or draw down their wealth by significant amounts over their lifetime. Under a flat-rate expenditure tax, Richard Spender and John Keeper would have the same total liability if their lifetime consumption were the same, even though Spender financed himself by using up inherited wealth while Keeper saved two-thirds of his income and built up a fortune. Under an income tax, Keeper would pay more tax than Spender.

Since the satisfactions obtained by Keeper and Spender cannot be directly measured, it is impossible to be sure whether they are equally well off and in a subjective sense have equal taxable capacity. If, however, a common standard of evaluation is used, Keeper clearly is better off because he enjoys the same amount of consumption as Spender plus whatever satisfactions are associated with the making of additions to wealth. Spender is worse off, on these terms, because he enjoys no more consumption and suffers whatever pains are associated with giving up wealth. Consumption does not reflect these differences, but income does; income plus net worth, with some weighting, reflects them better. A person who could look into the psyches of the two might find that Keeper's low consumption ratio is due to poverty of imagination rather than to the positive attractions of wealth accumulation and that Spender attaches little significance to the dissipation of his wealth. But those who cannot do that kind of analysis must be content with the application of a common standard derived from general observation and market data—and from introspection. On that basis, the relation between the liabilities of Keeper and Spender seems more just under an income tax than under an expenditure tax.

When progressivity is viewed simply as a means of reducing economic inequality, personal income seems clearly superior to either consumption or wealth as a sole tax base. Economic inequality has two dimensions, differences in consumption and differences in power associated with wealth accumulation. Up to a high level, differences in consumption may be the most noticeable feature of inequality, but toward the top of the pyramid wealth accumulation usually attracts more attention. Wealth accumulation surely has a more direct relation to the concentration of political influence than lavish consumption does. An income tax strikes accretions to economic power, whether devoted to consumption or other purposes. An expenditure tax is less effective than an income tax as a check on the accumulation of fortunes; a wealth tax does not affect consumption financed out of income from personal effort. A combination of an income tax and a wealth tax or a personal expenditure tax and a wealth tax might be superior to either the income tax or the expenditure tax alone as a means of reducing economic inequality. (This comparison is based on the assumption that the three taxes are equally well designed and administered—a condition which, as explained below, may be hard to satisfy.)

The superiority of the income tax over the expenditure tax is narrowed when the income tax applies to capital gains only as they are realized rather than to income including accrued but unrealized gains. A tax on realized income is less effective as a barrier to wealth concentration than a tax on accrued income but more effective in this respect than an expenditure tax.

The considerations that have convinced most experts that it would not be feasible to tax capital gains in advance of realization are equally relevant to a wealth tax. In the United States and other countries where a wealth tax is not levied, a tax on realized income of individuals is supplemented by taxes on corporate profits and on estates, inheritances, and gifts. This system, although less potent than a combination involving a wealth tax, can be an effective means of redistribution.

"Double Taxation of Saving"

A long-standing argument in favor of taxing consumption rather than income is the contention that a tax on income results in unfair double taxation of saving. John Stuart Mill asserted, "No income tax is really just from which savings are not exempted. . . ."[23] This amounts to saying that no income tax can be as fair as an expenditure tax. This view was endorsed by Marshall, Pigou, Einaudi, and other distinguished economists. Most of them, however, thought that a direct tax on consumption was not feasible and regarded the criticism as a theoretical nicety rather than an argument for tax

[23] *Principles of Political Economy*, Bk. V, chap. ii, sec. 4, W. J. Ashley, ed. (London: Longmans, Green, 1929), p. 814.

revision. Irving Fisher argued strongly for a direct tax on consumption in preference to a tax on personal income, although he confused the issue by insisting that the consumption tax should be called an income tax. He refused to concede that a direct tax on personal consumption (which he called income) was impracticable.[24]

Although it has been expressed with varying degrees of refinement, the double-taxation-of-saving argument is basically simple. Suppose that all income is taxed when it accrues. For the person who consumes his income that is the end of the story. But the saver must pay another tax on the return from his investments when that return accrues. He is taxed twice. Assume, for example, a proportional income tax of 50 percent and a market interest rate of 4 percent on safe investments. Suppose that John Keeper receives $100 of additional income, pays the tax on it, invests the remaining $50 in high-grade bonds, and thus obtains a gross annual yield of $2. His total taxes will be $50 in year 1 plus $1 a year in later years. If Keeper and his heirs permanently maintain the investment, the present value of the taxes, discounted at 4 percent, is $75 ($50 + $1/.04). Richard Spender, who also receives an additional $100 of income, saves nothing, and the present value of his total taxes with respect to this incremental income is $50.[25]

Under a flat-rate expenditure tax of 100 percent, Keeper would pay nothing in year 1 but would pay $2 a year in future years if he consumed the yield from his new investment. As under the income tax, Spender would pay $50 in year 1. Again assuming a perpetual investment on the part of Keeper and his heirs and discounting at 4 percent, the present value of the expenditure tax payments is $50 for both Spender and Keeper.

A little consideration, however, will show that something is wrong with this illustration. In the income tax case, Keeper is supposed to pay $50 for an asset with a net yield after tax of $1 a year. If this yield is treated as a perpetuity and discounted at 4 percent,

[24] Fisher's great theoretical work on income is *The Nature of Capital and Income*, originally published in 1906 (New York: Macmillan); his views on taxation appear in "Income in Theory and Income Taxation in Practice," *Econometrica*, Vol. 5 (January 1937), pp. 1-55, and in a book by him and Herbert W. Fisher entitled *Constructive Income Taxation* (New York: Harper, 1942).

[25] Cf. A. C. Pigou, *A Study in Public Finance*, 3d ed. (London: Macmillan, 1949), pp. 118-19.

its present value is $25. This $25 is what is left to Keeper out of the $100 of income received in year 1 when the present value of all income taxes is deducted. But surely Keeper would be foolish to pay $50 for an asset with a present value of only $25. Would he not rather keep the $50 in his mattress or safe deposit box?

This objection to the illustrative computations calls attention to a fundamental defect of the double-taxation argument. It is not literally true that saving is taxed twice under the income tax. The income tax reaches the income from which saving is made and investment yields, but saving is not taxed as such. A decision to save is not necessarily a decision to invest and hence not necessarily a decision to incur future income tax liabilities. If an investment is in fact made, its yield represents new income quite distinct from the income that was originally saved. In the illustration, Keeper pays more income tax than Spender because he has more income. Furthermore, the same discount rate should not be applied when a general income tax is in effect and when it is not. A general income tax of 50 percent, by cutting all yields in half, would reduce the net discount rate from 4 percent to 2 percent. At a 2 percent discount rate, a net yield of $1 a year in perpetuity is worth the $50 that Keeper is supposed to pay for it. In year 1, the income tax allows both Keeper and Spender the alternatives of buying consumption goods worth $50 or income-yielding assets worth $50.[26]

The income tax curtails opportunities to obtain additional income (power to consume) by investment or work. If the tax is uniform it curtails all such opportunities equally. An expenditure tax, on the other hand, applies to the exercise of power to consume rather than to its acquisition; if the tax is uniform, it applies equally to all consumption. The double-taxation-of-saving argument does not show that consumption is a fairer basis for judging equal treatment than income is. It is true that an income tax reduces the percentage gain in consumption that can be enjoyed by postponing consumption and investing one's savings, whereas an expenditure tax leaves the ratio between present and future consumption opportunities (but not the absolute amounts of consumption) the same as it would be with no tax. In my opinion, this characteristic does

[26] See C. W. Guillebaud, "Income Tax and 'Double Taxation,'" *Economic Journal*, Vol. 45 (September 1935), pp. 484-92.

not pose a question of justice, but it does raise economic issues that will be considered in the next chapter.

Administration and Compliance

To assess a tax on accrued income in literal conformity with the Haig-Simons definition would require information on both personal consumption and net worth (wealth). An income tax administered in this way would be more demanding than either an expenditure tax or a wealth tax, and if it were practicable to assess the income tax it would be easy to assess either of the other two taxes.

General Problems

The Haig-Simons definition is a conceptual guide rather than an assessment formula, and its authors did not suggest that taxable income actually be measured by adding together personal consumption and the change in the taxpayer's net worth. Nevertheless, the information required to assess a comprehensive tax on accrued income could also be used to assess taxes on wealth and personal consumption. Direct information on the value of capital assets would be necessary, and a figure for consumption could be derived indirectly, as the difference between income and net saving.

Even under an expenditure tax, direct measurement of personal consumption would be unnecessary. The usual proposal is that consumption be measured as a residual rather than by adding up its components. Personal consumption expenditures would equal net income minus (positive or negative) additions to net worth or saving. This approach has been recommended because few families keep comprehensive records of consumption expenditures. When records are available they would be harder to verify than records of income receipts since most families have a larger number of consumption transactions than of income transactions and deal with more suppliers of consumer goods and services than payers of income. Accounting conventions and practices are concerned mainly with the measurement and reporting of income and net worth and only incidentally with consumption.

An income tax conforming to the Haig-Simons concept, which

may be called a tax on accrued income, would be assessed on net income calculated as: gross current income *minus* costs of obtaining income *plus* realized net capital gains *plus* unrealized net capital gains (realized and unrealized capital losses being regarded as negative capital gains). Both gross income and costs would include cash items and certain imputed and accrued items. Conceptual and practical difficulties arise with respect to each of the principal items entering into the assessment. What receipts shall be included in gross income? How shall costs of obtaining income be distinguished from personal consumption expenditures and from new investment? How shall capital gains be measured? Must "true" gains and losses be distinguished from nominal gains and losses?

The peculiar difficulty with respect to accrued but unrealized capital gains and losses is administrative. To take account of unrealized gains and losses would require the detailed listing of taxpayers' assets and liabilities and annual valuations. The lists would be long, and for many items market quotations would not be readily available. Considerable difficulty is encountered in valuing certain securities and many business properties for purposes of the estate tax, despite the fact that these valuations need to be made only once for each of a relatively small number of taxpayers. Most experts agree that annual appraisals would not be feasible under the income tax.[27]

The omission of accrued but unrealized capital gains and losses from the assessment results in a tax which may be called a tax on realized income, even though its base includes certain accrued and imputed items. Efforts have been made to justify the omission on theoretical grounds by supporting a realization requirement usually on the basis of a harvest analogy.[28] Income is likened to a fruit that cannot be enjoyed until it is severed from the tree. This line of argument is unconvincing for two reasons. First, the growth of unharvested fruits, or unrealized gains, surely constitutes an increase

[27] A limited plan for taxing accrued capital gains was proposed in 1937 in the Twentieth Century Fund report, *Facing the Tax Problem* (New York, 1937), pp. 413, 431, 477-80, 490-91.

[28] On the legal and economic origins of the realization criterion, see Lawrence H. Seltzer, *The Nature and Tax Treatment of Capital Gains and Losses* (New York: National Bureau of Economic Research, 1951), pp. 25-46; for critical comments on the criterion, see Simons, *Personal Income Taxation*, pp. 80-100.

in economic power and is often a source of direct satisfactions, even though the accrued gain may be difficult to measure. Second, it seems inconsistent to require realization, in principle, with respect to nonbusiness assets but to accept conventional accounting practices with respect to depreciation and depletion and other accruals.

This omission of accrued gains and losses makes the income tax a duller instrument than it would be if all gains and losses could be reliably determined and included as they accrue. But if provision is made for constructive realization of capital gains and losses when the taxpayer dies or gives away his property, this partly compensates for the failure to take account of the gains and losses as they accrue.

In practice, taxable income under U.S. law is not identical with realized net income, broadly defined. Taxable income does not include certain items of realized income. In computing taxable income, some costs are not allowed as deductions and certain personal expenditures that are not costs of obtaining income are deducted. The consequences of the departures from a comprehensive measure of income will be considered in later chapters.

A tax on personal consumption could be assessed by subtracting net saving from realized income (or adding net dissaving to realized income). A country that levies an expenditure tax, while avoiding certain difficulties peculiar to the measurement of capital gains and losses, would encounter most of the conceptual and practical problems that are met in assessing a tax on realized income and the further problem of verifying net saving.

The measurement of net saving involves not only subtle theoretical issues relating to the definition of capital and capital maintenance—which are encountered also in the measurement of realized income—but major difficulties of administration. In practice, most of the subtleties no doubt would be disregarded under an expenditure tax, as they are under an income tax, but the administrative difficulties could not be avoided.

Saving could be measured on a flow basis as: outlays for capital assets *minus* proceeds of sales of capital assets *plus* repayment of debt *minus* proceeds of borrowing *plus* additions to bank accounts and other cash balances *minus* reductions in bank accounts and other cash balances. Or saving could be determined by comparing stocks at the beginning and end of year and thus ascertaining the net increase in holdings of capital assets and cash balances and the reduction of indebtedness. All of the items, of course, can have negative or positive signs; the total of saving is the algebraic sum.

Both flow and stock information would be useful, but balance sheets would be needed to make sure that saving was properly measured. If complete balance sheets were not available to the authorities, unscrupulous persons could evade the expenditure tax by failing to report proceeds from the disposal of assets and using the proceeds to finance consumption or to acquire items that are deductible as saving. They might also merely overstate their gross acquisitions of assets. This kind of evasion would be inhibited if a wealth tax were combined with the expenditure tax, but the need for balance sheets would not thereby be eliminated.[29]

Although complete balance sheets would be helpful for checking evasion of the income tax, they have not been generally demanded of individuals in the United States or other countries with well-developed income taxes. Balance sheets are less essential for enforcement of a tax on realized income than for assessment of a personal expenditure tax. Under the income tax, balance sheet data are useful for verifying capital gains and losses and for ascertaining whether changes in net worth are consistent with reported income. The latter purpose can be served only by reasonably complete balance sheets; the former requires information on the realization proceeds and acquisition costs of those assets that are likely to produce capital gains or losses. For income tax assessment, information is not essential on several items which are particularly hard to uncover and which seldom give rise to taxable gains or deductible losses, including cash balances, personal debt, jewelry, and consumer durables. For expenditure tax purposes, it is not necessary to know the original cost of old assets disposed of in the current year, but it is essential to know the realization proceeds of all disposals, the cost of all newly acquired assets and changes in cash

[29] Nicholas Kaldor stresses the interlocking features of the expenditure tax and wealth tax in his *Indian Tax Reform, Report of a Survey* (New Delhi: Ministry of Finance, Government of India, 1956). For skeptical comments, see my paper "Taxation of Saving and Consumption in Underdeveloped Countries," *National Tax Journal,* Vol. 14 (December 1961), pp. 305-22 (Brookings Institution Reprint No. 55, 1962).

balances and debt. Omission or incorrect reporting of any of these capital items can affect the expenditure tax assessment by the full amount of the error, whereas for income tax purposes only the gain or loss is at issue.

Complete accounting for assets and liabilities would of course be indispensable for the administration of a wealth tax. Furthermore, current valuations would be highly desirable. If items were assessed at book value or original cost until a transaction occurred, as has been suggested,[30] the wealth tax would lose much of its advantage as a supplementary measure of economic capacity. Failure to take account of unrealized appreciation or decreases in the value of assets would be a more serious defect in a wealth tax than in an income tax. Any particular gain or loss affects wealth in all subsequent years but affects income of only one year, hence later actual or constructive realization will do more to make up for the earlier omission of accrued gains and losses under the income tax than under the wealth tax. A wealth tax on book value, like a tax on realized income, imposes an additional liability when appreciated assets are sold and hence may deter economically desirable switches of investments.

American experience with the general property tax reveals the gravest difficulties in discovering and valuing intangibles and household property. Granted that the federal government might be more efficient than local assessors, and that there would be advantages in linking wealth tax and income tax assessments, it still does not seem realistic to contemplate a wealth tax with low exemptions and broad coverage. A tax limited to a small number of rich persons might be feasible, and the tax could be extended to a somewhat larger group if it were thought to have great social and economic advantages. As an instrument for checking the concentration of wealth, an annual tax on net worth does not seem to have great advantages over an integrated system of income, estate, and gift taxes, and it might be easier to improve the existing income and transfer taxes than to introduce a new tax on wealth.

In summary, it seems that neither a tax on income including

[30] By Kaldor in his report on India (*Indian Tax Reform*, p. 25). The Indian statute, however, provides for annual valuations; see Harvard Law School, World Tax Series, *Taxation in India* (Boston: Little, Brown, 1960), pp. 411-12.

accrued but unrealized capital gains nor a broad personal wealth tax could be successfully applied without extraordinary administrative cost. Of the two, the wealth tax would be the more demanding because the exact timing of unrealized gains would have more influence on the cumulative amount of liability for this tax. A personal expenditure tax would be less difficult to administer than either a tax on accrued income or a personal wealth tax but more difficult than a tax on realized income. Assessment and enforcement of the expenditure tax would involve nearly all the steps necessary for the successful application of a tax on realized income and in addition the special problem of measuring net saving. The verification of net saving would require complete balance sheet data, including information on cash balances, personal debts, and other items that are particularly difficult to discover.[31]

American Experience with the Income Tax

The enforcement of the income tax has been greatly aided by withholding of tax on wages and salaries. In the United States, the major portion of the total individual income tax is collected in this way. Withholding could be extended to dividends, interest, and certain other periodic income payments, as in many countries, but Congress has rejected recent proposals for doing so.

Although compliance with the income tax is incomplete, there is no evidence of widespread evasion in the United States. Comparison with national income estimates, which are derived mainly from data from sources other than individual income tax returns, indicates that about nine-tenths of estimated total adjusted gross income

---

[31] A more formal comparison of the items entering into the various tax bases can be presented as follows: Let G = gross income receipts, E = costs of obtaining income receipts, S = proceeds of sales of capital assets, P = purchases of capital assets, K = cost or other basis of capital assets sold, A = accrued but unrealized capital gains, B = cash balance, D = debt, and the subscripts 1 and 2 denote, respectively, the beginning and end of the year. Then accrued income is

$$G - E + S - K + A$$

Realized income is

$$G - E + S - K$$

Personal consumption is

$$G - E + S - P - (B_2 - B_1) - (D_1 - D_2).$$

(AGI) appears on tax returns.[32] (AGI is income net of business costs but before personal deductions and personal exemptions.) Part of the remaining AGI belongs to persons who are not taxable because their income is less than their personal exemptions. In 1960, it appears that a sum equal to about 7.5 percent of total AGI was illegally omitted from individual income tax returns owing to failure to file returns or understatement of AGI on returns.[33] A further, unknown amount of income escaped taxation because of under-reporting of capital gains and improper claims of personal exemptions and deductions which were not discovered by the Internal Revenue Service.

Administrative costs are moderate. In the fiscal year ended June 30, 1962, total administrative expenses of the Internal Revenue Service amounted to less than 0.5 percent of tax collections. An allocation of expenses among taxes is not available; however, even on extreme assumptions concerning other taxes, the expenses for administering the individual income tax were less than 1 percent of collections from it.[34]

Indirect Taxation

Excise taxes, sales taxes, and other indirect taxes still have an important role in the American federal-state-local revenue system and in other countries. Proposals are made from time to time for the adoption of a federal sales tax in the United States. Indirect taxes cannot be considered close substitutes for well-administered direct taxes on income or consumption since the indirect taxes are ordinarily less broad in coverage, are less easily adaptable to the individual circumstances of taxpayers, and usually lack progressivity. Do the indirect taxes nevertheless satisfy other tests of equity?

[32] Joseph A. Pechman, "What Would a Comprehensive Income Tax Yield?" in House Ways and Means Committee, *Tax Revision Compendium* (1959), Vol. 1, p. 256; U.S. Department of Commerce, Office of Business Economics, *Survey of Current Business*, May 1963, p. 3.

[33] Estimated total AGI not appearing on tax returns was $33 billion (derived from Table A-6). Of this amount, I roughly estimate that $7 billion consisted of the AGI of nontaxable individuals (see footnote 2, Chapter IX), leaving $26 billion of illegally unreported income out of aggregate AGI of $349 billion.

[34] Commissioner of Internal Revenue, *Annual Report for Fiscal Year Ended June 30, 1962*, pp. 16, 82.

Aside from economic considerations, which are to be discussed later, the main argument in favor of broad sales taxes or production taxes is that they would strike those who legally or illegally escape the income tax. Since the indirect taxes are simpler and require less information than the income tax, illegal evasion would be more difficult; furthermore, those who benefit from legal loopholes or other unjustifiable preferences under the income tax would be reached by the sales tax. Partial substitution of a sales tax for an income tax, therefore, would transfer some of the tax load to those who successfully escape the income tax.[35] Those who improperly escape the income tax, however, would still pay less taxes in the aggregate than other citizens, and the adoption of the sales tax would introduce new inequities. Might not justice be better served by devoting to the improvement of the income tax the political and administrative resources that would be required to adopt and collect a federal sales tax?

Where income tax evasion is more widespread than in the United States or where administrative capacity is limited, simplicity and enforceability may be overriding advantages of indirect taxation. Most of the underdeveloped countries cannot now successfully apply the income tax on a wide scale. The authorities cannot recruit either the technicians or the clerks that are needed. In business and the professions modern accounting is not commonly practiced, many people are illiterate, and a large part of output originates in small-scale agriculture and shops. There is no tradition of voluntary compliance with tax laws. In these circumstances, an income tax may be so poorly and erratically applied that it will lack the characteristic advantages that are usually associated with the tax. Most countries in this position wish to make some use of the income tax in recognition of demands for social justice and in order to gain experience that will enable them to apply the tax more widely. But these countries cannot be expected to place primary reliance on the income tax in the near future; indirect taxes are better suited to the environment.

In all countries, selective excises are regarded as appropriate for financing government services that specially benefit sections of

[35] Harold M. Somers, "Theoretical Framework of Sales and Use Taxation," *Proceedings of Fifty-fourth Annual Conference on Taxation,* National Tax Association (Harrisburg, Pa., 1962), pp. 615-16.

the community but which cannot be conveniently sold to consumers. Gasoline taxes and other automotive taxes that are used to pay for highways are an important example. Excises also may be used to facilitate the regulation or discourage the production and consumption of goods that are thought to involve social costs that are not covered by market prices. Taxes on alcoholic beverages and tobacco are sometimes supported on this basis, but in practice these taxes ordinarily are not designed to carry out a coherent regulatory policy.

There is support for excises on luxuries or nonessentials on the grounds that consumption of these items is optional and indicates taxpaying ability. In fact, however, the excises with large yields are on commodities that are widely consumed and whose demand is relatively insensitive to price. If many consumers chose not to buy the taxed commodities, the yield would suffer. Economists have often condemned the excises because they discriminate on the basis of taste. The popular emphasis on the voluntary character of excises on nonessentials, nevertheless, may not be completely unfounded. These taxes do allow consumers an additional dimension of flexibility in that a drastic reallocation of spending in response to illness or other emergencies can bring with it a reduction in the amount of taxes paid. The excises, however, seem a clumsy means of dealing with such situations compared with a deduction for medical expenditures under the income tax or other special allowances. A more important element in the public attitude may be what one writer has called a "perversion" that leads people to feel guilty about smoking, drinking, and luxurious spending and to think it right that they should be taxed on their indulgences.[36]

A more prosaic explanation of the continuation of the excises is that they have been used for a long time, and consumers seem to be less conscious of them and less resentful of them than they are of the income tax or a retail sales tax. Many do not know the excise tax rates, and others seem to have a kind of myopia that keeps them from seeing that small items in time add up to significant totals. Opinion leaders, whose income is usually above the average, may be less vexed by excises than by the progressive income tax.

These considerations may help explain the persistence of in-

[36] David Walker, "Some Comments on the Taxation of Personal Income and Expenditure in the United Kingdom, 1945-53," *Public Finance*, Vol. 9 (1954), p. 206.

direct taxes and cause one to doubt that they will be dispensed with in the foreseeable future. But I do not think that they indicate that the American tax system could be made fairer by increasing the proportion of revenue obtained from indirect taxes.

Conclusion

The income tax emerges well from this examination of the issues of equity and administration. Personal income seems to be the best single index of taxable capacity and the best single basis of progressive taxation. Income, however, is not a complete measure of ability to pay. There are strong arguments for supplementing an individual income tax with taxes on accumulated wealth in the form of estate and gift taxes; an annual tax on net worth also has appeal but may not be feasible. A good case can be made for a few excise taxes.

CHAPTER III

Effects of Taxes on Income, Consumption, and Wealth

THE INCOME TAX, like other taxes, is intended to divert resources from private consumption and investment to public use. Taxation will also have the unintended effect of curtailing total output if it reduces investment and discourages work. An important question is how the income tax compares in this respect with alternative taxes. The comparison is important because it will help show whether the benefits of government expenditures could be obtained at less social cost by modifying the tax system.

In this chapter and the next one, the principal economic effects of the income tax and other taxes are compared on the assumption that the amount of revenue raised and the size and composition of government expenditures would be approximately the same under different tax systems. This assumption, though necessary in my opinion to allow isolation of questions of tax policy, is not free of ambiguities and difficulties. Alternative tax schemes that would yield equal revenues under certain economic conditions might yield unequal amounts under other conditions; there is no one set of equivalent-yield rates for the different taxes.[1] However, for analytical purposes it seems legitimate to defer for separate consideration the response of tax yields to cyclical fluctuations in business activity and to assume that tax rates would be adjusted from time to time as might be required to maintain equal revenues over longer periods of time.

Three analytical issues are involved in the comparison of taxes: (1) the significance of the choice of the tax base; (2) the influence of the degree of progressivity; and (3) the difference, if any, between direct and indirect or impersonal taxes, given the base and the degree of progressivity. To simplify a presentation that is unavoidably complex at certain points, I shall discuss the choice of the tax base in this chapter and shall combine the treatment of the other issues in Chapter IV.

The analysis of different tax bases is conducted in this chapter by comparing direct taxes on income, consumption, and wealth. Despite the practical difficulties in applying a direct expenditure tax and a wealth tax, I consider a further analysis of them useful because it may indicate whether a great effort to overcome the difficulties would be worthwhile and because it tells something about indirect and impersonal taxes on consumption and wealth. In an attempt to isolate the economic significance of the tax base, this chapter deals mainly with flat-rate taxes, with only passing attention to effects due to rate graduation. Although flat-rate taxes on consumption and wealth would not be proportional to income, owing to differences in the average ratios of consumption and wealth to income at high and low income levels, the analysis abstracts from possible differences in economic effects due solely to the distribution of the taxes among income groups.[2] The effects of rate graduation and of different distributions among income groups will be considered in Chapter IV.

[1] Bent Hansen, *Economic Theory of Fiscal Policy*, trans. P. E. Burke (Cambridge, Mass.: Harvard University Press, 1958), pp. 34-37, 90-100.

[2] This chapter draws on my papers "Income, Consumption, and Property as Bases of Taxation," *American Economic Review*, Vol. 52, Papers and Proceedings (May 1962), pp. 327-34 (Brookings Institution Reprint No. 60, 1962), and "Taxation of Saving and Consumption in Underdeveloped Countries," *National Tax Journal*, Vol. 14 (December 1961), pp. 305-22 (Brookings Institution Reprint No. 55, 1962).

Influence on Saving

Much of the interest in the expenditure tax can be traced to a belief that its substitution for the income tax would favor saving and therefore capital formation and growth. In examining this proposition, I shall consider first the influence of different forms of taxation on incentives and capacity to save, deferring to the next chapter comments on the relation between saving, capital formation, and growth.

Incentives to Save

Under an expenditure tax, a person who forgoes a given amount of present consumption and lends or invests his savings can enjoy a greater increase in future consumption than would be possible under an equal-yield income tax. The gain in future consumption may be regarded as a reward for saving or, more accurately, as a reward or incentive for saving-and-lending or saving-and-investing, since the gain is made possible by the interest obtained by lending or investing the savings.

Consider the alternatives open to a person subject to a 50 percent income tax or a 100 percent expenditure tax. If in year 1 he receives $100 of income he will be liable for $50 of tax under the income tax. He can either consume the remaining $50 immediately or save and invest it and, at a market rate of interest of 4 percent, realize a net return of $1 in one year ($2 gross return minus $1 of income tax). Thus, by giving up $50 of present consumption he can enjoy $1 of additional consumption each year in the future, or he can exchange $50 of present consumption for $51 of consumption one year later. Under the consumption tax, he can save and invest $100 in year 1 and obtain a yield of $4, which will allow him to consume an additional $2 a year, or he can exchange $50 of present consumption for $52 of consumption one year later. Under the expenditure tax, the interest reward for saving-and-investing—computed with respect to the amount of present consumption forgone—remains unimpaired at 4 percent, whereas the reward is cut in half by the 50 percent income tax.

The saver is better off under the expenditure tax because postponement of consumption also postpones tax payment, permitting him to earn interest on the postponed tax. In the illustrations above, the saver receives twice as large an increment to his future consumption power under the expenditure tax as under the income tax because he has twice as much to invest under the expenditure tax. By parallel reasoning, it can be shown that an expenditure tax increases the cost of anticipatory consumption financed by borrowing. Under the expenditure tax, advancing the date of consumption also advances the date of tax payment and requires additional borrowing, to cover the tax, and greater interest payments.

If aggregate net saving by taxpayers were zero each year, the opportunity for tax postponement by individual savers would not affect the yield of a flat-rate expenditure tax compared with that of a flat-rate income tax. In any year, savers would pay less than under an income tax but dissavers would pay more, and the negative and positive differences would be exactly offsetting. On the more realistic assumption that aggregate personal saving is positive, an allowance has to be made in setting equivalent-yield rates for the two taxes. For example, if personal saving equals 5 percent of total income, an expenditure tax of 111 percent would be required to yield as much revenue as a 50 percent income tax, whereas with zero aggregate saving a 100 percent expenditure tax would suffice.[3]

With a high expenditure tax rate, the absolute amount of consumption that one can enjoy immediately or in the future is smaller than with a low tax rate, but the relation between present and future consumption opportunities is not affected if the tax rate is uniform. Whatever the relation between the expenditure tax rate and the income tax rate and regardless of whether the two taxes yield equivalent revenue, the interest reward for saving-and-investing always equals the market rate of interest under the expenditure tax; it is always less than the market rate of interest under the income tax. This is true if the reward is measured by relating the net increment in future consumption power to the amount of present consumption that the saver forgoes.[4]

---

[3] Suppose that income is 100 and income tax yield 50. With zero saving, consumption will be 50, and the required expenditure tax rate will be $50/50 = 100$ percent. With saving of 5, consumption will be 45 and the required expenditure tax rate $50/45 = 111$ percent. For a general statement concerning equivalent-yield rates of income tax and expenditure tax, see Appendix B.

[4] See Appendix B.

A wealth tax of course falls directly on accumulated savings. It will more sharply restrict opportunities to add to future consumption power by saving than will a general income tax of equal yield because the wealth tax is concentrated on recipients of property income, which constitutes only 15 to 20 percent of all personal income.[5] A comprehensive wealth tax will absorb five to seven times as great a fraction of property income as will an equal-yield general income tax (both taxes assumed to be non-graduated, to lack personal exemptions, and to be equally well enforced). Since the average rate of return on total personal wealth usually does not exceed 4 to 5 percent,[6] a 1 percent general tax on wealth would take about one-fifth to one-fourth of all property income.

The rate of return on saving-and-investing will be higher under an expenditure tax than under an equal-yield income tax and much higher under either of these taxes than under an equal-yield wealth tax. There is, I think, a presumption that the propensity to save will respond to some degree to the rate of return and therefore will be highest under an expenditure tax, lowest under a wealth tax, and intermediate under an income tax.[7] Deductive reasoning does not indicate whether differences in thriftiness will be great or small, nor is there satisfactory statistical evidence on the question.

In addition to the effects operating through the current rate of return, the taxes may influence the amount of wealth that people wish to hold in relation to income. Adoption of an expenditure tax

[5] Irving B. Kravis, "Relative Income Shares in Fact and Theory," *American Economic Review,* Vol. 49 (December 1959), p. 933.

[6] The average rate of return on the net worth, exclusive of consumer durables, of nonfarm households was 5.1 percent in 1929 and 3.6 percent in 1946-58. For purposes of these calculations, property income is represented by the sum of rental income of persons, dividends, and personal interest (personal income components, as estimated by the Office of Business Economics, U.S. Department of Commerce, in *Economic Report of the President, January 1964,* p. 225); the net worth estimates are from Raymond W. Goldsmith, Robert E. Lipsey, and Morris Mendelson, *Studies in the National Balance Sheet of the United States* (Princeton, N.J.: Princeton University Press for National Bureau of Economic Research, 1963), Vol. II, pp. 78, 118-19. Both the income and asset figures include owner-occupied houses and exclude unincorporated business enterprises.

[7] This conclusion differs from the agnostic position that many economists have taken regarding the influence on thrift of a change in the interest rate and represents a revision of my own earlier position with respect to the effect of different taxes. For an elaboration, see Appendix B.

will reduce the amount of real consumption that can be financed by using up a given amount of wealth and, in this sense, may be viewed as a capital levy on existing wealth held for future consumption. Wealth-holders may save more in an effort to restore the desired relation between wealth and income.[8] (Those who plan to accumulate in the future will not have to cut their consumption to build up additional wealth to cover the expenditure tax because the tax will be deferred until the wealth is used.) On the other hand, the payment of the expenditure tax may cause people who are already living off capital to use it up at a faster rate, which will partly offset any additional saving undertaken by those who are induced to build up their wealth. Since a wealth tax is an annual tax on past and future accumulations, rather than a one-time levy on wealth in existence at the time of its adoption, introduction of this tax seems more likely to cause a downward revision than an increase in the desired ratio of wealth to income.

Capacity to Save

Many popular discussions stress not the adverse effect of the income tax on incentives to save but its influence on the capacity to save. Income taxpayers simply have less left out of which they can save. But, of course, any other tax of equal yield would take the same amount of resources from the private sector and would also tend to decrease private saving. The income tax can be said to reduce capacity to save more than other taxes of equal yield if those who pay the income tax are more disposed to save than those who bear the other taxes. The usual version of this argument depends on differences in progressivity, a subject which is discussed in Chapter IV.

There is also a more subtle version of the capacity-to-save argument, holding that aggregate saving can be increased by transferring taxation in each income class from those who are most inclined to save to those who are least inclined to do so; the capacity to save is increased where the inclination to save is strongest. Furthermore, the argument does not require that the form of taxation influence attitudes toward present and future consumption or

---

[8] Nicholas Kaldor, *An Expenditure Tax* (London: Allen and Unwin, 1955), p. 96.

accumulation. The community's saving ratio can be raised without altering the ratio of saving to disposable income of any individual, provided high savers are given command over a larger fraction of the resources available to the private sector.

This reasoning suggests that an expenditure tax will be more favorable to private saving than an equal-yield tax on income because the expenditure tax will leave a larger proportion of real disposable income in the hands of those with higher-than-average saving rates. The implicit assumption is that people who have high ratios of total saving to total income will also save a large fraction of a small increment to their disposable income, that is, that a high marginal propensity to save is associated with a high average propensity to save. Although exceptions can be imagined, the assumption is plausible. Average saving ratios reflect age and family composition, tastes, habits, opportunities, and other factors which change slowly, and presumably these influences also determine marginal saving ratios.

It is easy, nevertheless, to form an exaggerated impression of what can be accomplished by reallocating taxes between high and low savers. Differences between the impacts of alternative tax formulas will not be as great as differences between the marginal propensities to save of high and low savers, provided that the choice of tax formula does not itself influence individual propensities to save. This is true because all feasible measures impose taxes on both high and low savers; hence the effect on saving is a weighted average of high and low marginal propensities to save, with the weights depending on the amounts of tax paid. To illustrate, consider A and B, who have equal incomes but different saving behavior. Assume that A's average and marginal propensities to save are zero and that B's are 20 percent and that these propensities are not affected by the form of taxation. If A is taxed while B goes free, private saving is unaffected; if B is taxed and A is not, saving is curtailed by 20 percent of the revenue. There is, however, no feasible and socially acceptable means of taxing A while exempting B, unless they differ in characteristics other than saving behavior. The alternatives are to tax both A and B on income, total consumption, selected items of consumption, or property. Under a general income tax A and B will pay equal amounts, and private saving

will be reduced by 10 percent of the revenue. If A and B are subjected to a flat-rate expenditure tax, A will pay 5/9 of the aggregate
tax and B 4/9; private saving will be reduced by approximately
8.9 percent of the revenue.[9]

It is not clear whether the substitution of a wealth tax for an
income tax or an expenditure tax (with rates set to distribute the
total tax among income classes in the same proportions) would
involve a reallocation of the tax load between persons with different
saving propensities. The most widely accepted hypothesis is that
saving is inversely related to the ratio of wealth to income because,
as the ratio rises, further accumulation satisfies progressively less
urgent wants. Even if this is true at a given time for any one individual, it is not necessarily a reliable indicator of differences
between individuals. Wealthy persons may have relatively high
propensities to save because they have a taste for accumulation or
at least have the habit of accumulation.

Morgan reports that his studies indicate that high assets tend to
be associated with high marginal propensities to save. He finds that
budget studies show that high-asset families save more than other
families at high income levels and less at low income levels and
that, when the influence of income is statistically controlled, high-
asset families save more when they have an increase in income and
dissave more when they have a decrease in income than low-asset
families experiencing similar changes in income. He attributes
differences at lower income levels to the fact that assets facilitate
dissaving and at higher incomes to the persistence of individual
attitudes. Morgan concludes, ". . . we can interpret public policy
in terms of what it does to people who have many assets or few
assets, on the general assumption that the people with large amounts
of assets are the people who want to save, have always saved, will
continue to do so, and are most likely to save any increments in
income or assets."[10] However, other statistical analyses, based on

[9] If A and B each have income of 100, their consumption expenditures in the
absence of tax will be 100 and 80 respectively. Their payments under a flat-rate
expenditure tax will be divided in approximately the same proportions, with A paying 100/180 = 5/9 and B paying the remaining 4/9. The tax-induced reduction
in private saving will be (5/9 × 0%) + (4/9 × 20%) = 8.9%.

[10] James Morgan, "The Motivation of Savers," in *Savings in the Modern
Economy*, Walter W. Heller and others, eds. (Minneapolis: University of Min-

aggregates, support the hypothesis of an inverse relation between saving rates and the ratio of wealth to income.[11]

Conclusion with Respect to Saving

It appears that both incentives to save and capacity to save on the part of those who are most eager to do so will be greater under an expenditure tax than under an income tax and least under a wealth tax. Abstracting from difference in the distribution of these taxes among income classes, it follows that the propensity to save will be highest under an expenditure tax, intermediate under an income tax, and lowest under a wealth tax. The considerations on which this conclusion is based, however, neither reveal whether the range of differences in the propensity to save is wide or narrow nor allow a statement about the amount by which private saving will be affected by an increase or decrease in taxation.

A rise in the national propensity to save will contribute to growth only if accompanied by rising investment. The composition of investment, moreover, affects the growth rate and the social acceptability of any level of output. Consideration must be given to the influence of taxation on investment.

Influence on Investment

Whereas advocates of the expenditure tax or indirect consumption taxes often imply that the rate of capital formation is limited by the propensity to save, those who favor a wealth tax usually stress the inducement to invest as the limiting factor. Advocates of a wealth tax attach great importance to the fact that wealth tax liability is largely a fixed charge in the short run. Hoarders, bond-holders, and owners of valuable works of art and furniture pay as much tax as equally wealthy investors in highly productive business ventures (provided all these forms of wealth are equally well assessed for taxation). Investment of cash balances, conversion of high-grade bonds into shares in risky enterprises, or borrowing in

---

nesota Press, 1953), p. 214. See also University of Michigan, Survey Research Center, *Contributions of Survey Methods to Economics,* Lawrence R. Klein, ed. (New York: Columbia University Press, 1954), pp. 184-86, 245-48.

[11] William Hamburger, "The Relation of Consumption to Wealth and the Wage Rate," *Econometrica,* Vol. 23 (January 1955), pp. 1-17.

order to undertake a business venture increases wealth tax liability only if the yield is added to net worth. Income tax liability will be increased by any successful investment, and expenditure tax liability will go up if part of the yield is consumed.

As an illustration, consider the alternatives faced by a person with $1,000 of cash at the beginning of the year under an income tax of 50 percent or a wealth tax of 2 percent. For simplicity, assume initially that he will not consume any additional income obtained by investing the cash and that the wealth tax is assessed on net worth at the end of the year. The results of hoarding and of investing in an asset with a gross yield of 4 percent will be as follows:

	With Income Tax	*With Wealth Tax*
Hoarding		
Gross yield	0	0
Tax liability	0	$ 20.00
Balance, end of year	$1,000	980.00
Investment		
Gross yield	40	40.00
Tax liability	20	20.80
Balance, end of year	1,020	1,019.20
Net gain due to investing	20	39.20

The wealth tax imposes an annual carrying charge on net assets and in a sense makes the financial yield of hoarding negative rather than zero. (This refers to the immediate financial yield; hoarders presumably derive other satisfactions from their cash balances or expect to obtain income from investing them in the future.) The gain from investing, with the wealth tax, is the difference between the balance that would be left at the end of the year if the owner hoarded and the balance he will have if he invests. In the above illustration, the net gain is the difference between a balance of $980.00 and one of $1,019.20. This gain falls short of the gross yield only by the amount of the wealth tax on the gross yield, which is assumed to be saved. Under the 50 percent income tax, of course, the net yield is only half the gross yield. Paradoxically, the net gain from investing is greater under the wealth tax than under the income tax, even though the gross yield is the same and the wealth tax liability is greater than the income tax liability.

The difference between the wealth tax liability associated with a high-yield investment and a low-yield one is, at most, the wealth tax on the yield. There is no difference in wealth tax liability when the additional investment yield is consumed. Under an income tax, liability varies directly with investment yield, regardless of the proportion consumed. Since, for equal revenue, the wealth tax rate will be much lower than the income tax rate, the wealth tax always cuts much less deeply than the income tax does into the gain that can be realized by choosing a high-yield investment rather than a low-yield one.

Expenditure tax liability, like wealth tax liability, depends on the proportion of investment yield which is consumed, but in this case the maximum tax liability occurs when the whole yield is consumed and no additional liability arises so long as none of the yield is consumed. The expenditure tax is more favorable than an income tax or wealth tax to those who strive for rapid accumulation by seeking high-yield investments. On the other hand, the expenditure tax offers less opportunity to increase one's current consumption by selecting high-yield assets. This is clearly true when the comparison is with the wealth tax but is also true in comparison with the income tax because, with tax rates yielding equal revenues, the expenditure tax will bear more heavily on one who consumes all of his income than on the average person, who saves part of his income.

Before drawing conclusions about the influence of the different taxes on investment incentives, it is advisable to consider the function of high yields. The traditional view is that high yields—or, more accurately, prospects of high yields—are necessary to induce investment in especially risky enterprises. If the difference between high and low yields is narrowed by taxation, will not this result in a bias against venturesome investments, such as those associated with the introduction of new products, and in favor of conservative investments? And may not the tax discourage even conservative investments compared with hoarding? Contrary to first impressions, close analysis indicates that the answer to these questions is not clearly "yes" and may, indeed, be "no."

The key to the problem is the interpretation of the reward for risk. It seems that the reward should be measured, not in absolute amount nor in relation to the total investment, but in relation to the net amount of capital at risk. Now, the reward for assumption of risk will not be impaired relative to the net amount of capital at risk by a proportional income tax, provided all losses from unsuccessful investments can be fully offset against taxable income.[12] To illustrate, suppose that, in the absence of taxation, an investor would be willing to commit $1,000 to a risky venture if he expected, in addition to the normal return on safe investments, a further 10 percent or $100 a year to compensate for the assumption of risk. A proportional income tax of 25 percent will reduce the risk premium to $75 after tax; but, if the loss can be fully offset against other taxable income in the event that the venture is wholly unsuccessful, the net amount at risk will be reduced to $750, and the risk premium will still be 10 percent of this sum. With no loss offset or an imperfect offset, the reward for risk assumption will be cut relatively more than the amount at risk, and the venture may become unacceptable.

Under the U. S. income tax, loss offsets are liberal for business operating losses but less so for losses on worthless securities. An operating loss of an unincorporated business may be deducted against any other current income of the proprietor or partners; if the loss exceeds income, the deficit may be carried back and deducted against taxable income of the three preceding years, and any balance not offset in this way may be carried forward for five years. Capital losses are generally deductible only against capital gains, but adverse incentive effects are mitigated by the low tax rates on long-term gains and the option of timing realized gains to offset losses (Chapter VIII). Even for operating losses, offsets are imperfect because sometimes losses are too large to be offset against income over a nine-year period and because tax rates are graduated. Under graduated rates, the reward for a successful investment tends to be taxed in a higher rate bracket than the income

[12] The classic statement is that of Evsey D. Domar and Richard A. Musgrave in their paper "Proportional Income Taxation and Risk-Taking," *Quarterly Journal of Economics*, Vol. 58 (May 1944), pp. 387-422, reprinted in American Economic Association, *Readings in the Economics of Taxation*, Richard A. Musgrave and Carl S. Shoup, eds. (Homewood, Ill.: Irwin, 1959), pp. 493-524. See also Richard A. Musgrave, *Theory of Public Finance* (New York: McGraw-Hill, 1959), pp. 312-36.

against which a loss is offset; hence possible rewards are cut more deeply than possible losses.

An expenditure tax allows no loss offset as such but permits the investor to set aside whatever premium he thinks appropriate to cover his risk and to recoup his investment as quickly as market conditions allow. The investor's own behavior, rather than formal accounting requirements and legal rules, defines the return that is subject to taxation. An expenditure tax, therefore, is more favorable to investment than an income tax that lacks loss offsets; the difference may be small, however, between an expenditure tax and an income tax incorporating as liberal loss offsets as are provided by the U. S. law.[13]

A wealth tax automatically allows losses to be offset against taxable wealth up to the full extent of the investor's net worth. Thus, within this limit, the tax does not alter the relation between the amount of resources that the investor risks and the gain that he may realize, even when the gain would all be added to taxable wealth.

Taxation, it seems, is much less damaging to the reward for risk-taking than it may appear to be when loss offsets are neglected. Indeed, a tax with full loss offsets may actually stimulate investors to be more venturesome than they would be in the absence of taxation. The tax will not cut the reward for risk in relation to the amount at risk but will cut investors' disposable incomes and may induce them to take more risk in an effort to restore their income.[14] (On the other hand, feeling poorer, investors may consider a more conservative portfolio appropriate to their reduced station.)

This line of reasoning should not be pressed to the point of saying that investment incentives are immune to heavy taxation. Loss offsets are likely always to be less than perfect under the income tax, and their significance may not be fully appreciated by investors. The reward for assumption of risk is not the only socially necessary part of the return on investment. The prospective return

[13] E. Cary Brown is right, in my opinion, in criticizing Kaldor's treatment of risk. See "Mr. Kaldor on Taxation and Risk Bearing," *Review of Economics Studies*, Vol. 25 (October 1957), pp. 49-52. Nevertheless, Kaldor's judgment that an expenditure tax is more favorable to risk bearing than an income tax may be correct when the comparison is between an expenditure tax and an income tax with seriously incomplete loss offsets. See his book, *An Expenditure Tax*, p. 121.

[14] Domar and Musgrave, in *Readings in the Economics of Taxation*, pp. 513-15.

must include compensation for the discovery and supervision of new investment opportunities. It must be more attractive than the nontaxable returns that can be obtained by purchasing art objects, furniture, automobiles, and other items that yield direct satisfactions to their owners.[15] (This competition becomes the more severe the wider the range of imputed and monetary returns from property that are excluded from taxable income.) The existence of loss offsets does not prevent the income tax from encroaching on the part of ordinary investment returns that is necessary to overcome inertia and the attractions of owning property yielding nontaxable returns.

Furthermore, the separation of incentives for saving from incentives for investment, although analytically useful, may become misleading if too rigorously maintained. To the extent that saving is undertaken for the explicit purpose of financing a particular investment, say an expansion of the saver's own business enterprise or the purchase of a house, the motives and incentives cannot be disentangled. The absolute amount of the possible net gain, not merely the reward for risk-taking, is relevant in such cases. The interaction of incentives for saving and investment can also be seen in connection with the wealth tax. Although a wealth tax is approximately neutral with respect to the form in which property is held, it is not neutral with respect to the amount of wealth held. The wealth tax would be more favorable to investment than a tax on property income, but it does not follow that it would be more favorable than a general income tax or general expenditure tax.

On balance, it seems that, of the three taxes, the expenditure tax is most conducive to private investment because it treats saving liberally and also infringes only slightly on the reward for risk-taking. The wealth tax is the least favorable to the growth of private capital but appears to have the minimum effect on the composition of financial portfolios and presumably also on the composition of real investment. The income tax seems to occupy an intermediate position. The margin of difference between the taxes is uncertain. It is important to remember that the attainment of a rapid rate of

[15] I am indebted to Leif Mutén for calling my attention to the competition between ordinary investment and the purchase of art objects and other personal property yielding direct satisfactions. The point is analogous to the effect of income taxation on the relative attractiveness of working for wages and of performing services for oneself discussed in Chapter VI.

capital formation depends on monetary and fiscal policy and many other forces which, in the aggregate, are likely to be more influential than the form of taxation.

Special considerations, for example, apply to an important form of investment which will be treated in Chapter V—investment in human beings in the form of outlays for education and other items that increase earning capacity. The income tax discriminates against this kind of capital formation because it does not allow the investment outlays to be amortized against taxable income. This discrimination likely would continue under an expenditure tax inasmuch as all educational expenditures are commonly classified as consumption despite the investment character of some of these outlays. The discrimination would be intensified in so far as educational investment financed by borrowing was treated as taxable consumption. Wealth taxes and property taxes, on the other hand, discriminate in favor of human capital inasmuch as the value of expected future earned income is not considered property.

Factual Evidence on Investment Incentives

Doubts about the effect of the income tax on investment incentives, unfortunately, cannot be resolved by the simple procedure of asking investors how they feel. Investors do not necessarily analyze clearly their own behavior, and their self-interest inclines them to overstate the adverse effects of taxation. Nevertheless, carefully devised surveys may be worth something if the results are cautiously used.

The most extensive survey of individual investors' attitudes was carried out by a Harvard Business School group in 1949.[16] They interviewed 746 "active investors," most of whom had large incomes. On the basis of explicit statements about taxation by the persons interviewed and the investigators' interpretation of the respondents' more general statements about their investments, the research group made the following findings with respect to the influence of the income tax on investment decisions:

1.   Whereas only about one-third of the whole sample group

[16] J. Keith Butters, Lawrence E. Thompson, and Lynn L. Bollinger, *Effects of Taxation: Investment by Individuals* (Boston: Graduate School of Business Administration, Harvard University, 1953).

were influenced by the tax, the majority of those with incomes above $25,000 were influenced.

2. Among those whose decisions were influenced, 71 percent were induced to shift to more conservative investments and 29 percent to shift to more venturesome investments.

3. Much of the shifting to more venturesome investments was motivated by a desire to take advantage of preferentially low tax rates on long-term capital gains.

4. The investors who were interviewed appeared to attach little significance to loss offsets; apparently the presence of loss offsets did not compensate in their minds for a reduction in after-tax yields and limitations on the deductibility of capital losses were not an important deterrent.[17]

Statistical data on the volume and composition of investment and investment yields shed little light on the effects of taxation on investment incentives because of the virtual impossibility of isolating taxation from the many other forces that influence investment and investment yields.

Influence on Work

The income tax clearly reduces the net compensation for work; the expenditure tax does so only a little less obviously. Immediate or future consumption is presumably the principal reward that motivates work, insofar as economic considerations are controlling. The expenditure tax and the income tax will have the same kind of impact on current consumption capacity but, for equal revenues, the expenditure tax will fall somewhat more heavily on this part of the reward. Future consumption capacity is greater under the expenditure tax if part of the salary or wage is saved and invested, but it seems more meaningful to ascribe this gain to saving-and-investing than to count it as part of compensation for work. If one merely hoards his wages, the additional wealth that he can build up under a flat-rate expenditure tax is illusory because it consists entirely of the postponed tax; future consumption capacity in this case is reduced as much as current capacity. Only to the extent that

[17] *Ibid.*, pp. 36-43 *et passim.*

work is motivated by a desire to accumulate wealth for the sake of power and prestige rather than to augment consumption capacity can it be said that the expenditure tax infringes less than the income tax does on rewards for working.[18] The drive for accumulation may be significant for some business executives and professional men.

√ A reduction in the net rate of compensation due to taxation does not necessarily cause people to work shorter hours, to retire earlier, or to refuse promotions. One reason is that much work, including a great part of the most highly paid, provides satisfactions in itself. Even with respect to the more strictly economic side of working, the effect is uncertain. Taxation may cause some persons to work less and others to work more in an effort to maintain or achieve a desired standard of living. Deductive reasoning does not indicate which reaction will predominate. (As discussed in Chapter IV, a judgment can be made about the influence of tax progressivity as distinguished from the average weight of taxation.)

The available evidence, although inconclusive and to some extent contradictory, offers more support for the hypothesis that the supply of labor as a whole is either insensitive or negatively related to the wage rate than for the hypothesis that it is positively responsive to a high degree. Historically, the work week has shortened as real wages have risen; however, social and economic developments other than the improvement of wages may have been mainly responsible. Several empirical studies have found inelastic or negatively sloping supply curves for labor in certain occupations or population groups.[19] Many of these studies are old, and the coverage of high-income groups is scanty. The recent studies relate

[18] With graduated tax rates, the taxpayer can more easily minimize lifetime tax liability under the expenditure tax than under the income tax because he usually has more control over the timing of his consumption than over the timing of his income.

[19] For a tabular summary, see George F. Break, "Income Taxes, Wage Rates, and the Incentive to Supply Labor Services," *National Tax Journal*, Vol. 6 (December 1953), pp. 350-51. Of the 19 studies tabulated by Break, only one (an opinion survey of a sample of executives) reported a positive slope for the whole group; two studies reported positive slopes for certain subgroups and negative slopes for other subgroups. A recent study based on a field survey of 2,997 spending units in 1959 found a negative relation between hours of work and wage rates (James N. Morgan, Martin H. David, Wilbur J. Cohen, and Harvey E. Brazer, *Income and Welfare in the United States* [New York: McGraw-Hill, 1962], pp. 76-77).

to an environment in which a graduated income tax plays an important role but in which there are opportunities for avoiding the full impact of the tax. The survey evidence is relevant to the effects of any kind of taxation that reduces real compensation rather than to the difference, if any, between income tax and consumption taxes.

For a study completed in 1950, Sanders interviewed 160 business executives and professional men of the type who act as advisers or consultants to executives concerning the effect of taxation on executives' incentives and behavior.[20] He supplemented the interviews with group meetings and other evidence. He concluded that taxation had not caused a serious loss of executive services, except in certain areas. The great majority of those interviewed thought that effort was not being abated because of taxation; one small group thought that taxes drove executives to work harder, and another small group thought that the reaction was more often a relaxation of effort. Taxes in general appeared to dispose executives to postpone their retirement, but the effect was limited by formal retirement plans and other factors. Sanders found a considerable number of cases in which executives had refused promotions or transfers when the change would have increased their work load without greatly increasing after-tax earnings. Withholding of effort for tax reasons appeared to occur chiefly among executives who were also business owners and who were free of the discipline imposed by the corporate hierarchy. Sanders concluded that, although taxation had, or was likely to have, important effects on executive behavior, "popular generalizations about the repressive effects of taxation on executive incentives" were not borne out by his study.[21]

Another careful study of the influence of the income tax was conducted in England in 1956 by Break, who interviewed a sample of 306 solicitors and accountants. These persons should be more sensitive to taxation than the average because they are self-employed, are well informed about taxation, and are subject to relatively high marginal tax rates. About half of the respondents

[20] Thomas H. Sanders, *Effects of Taxation on Executives* (Boston: Graduate School of Business Administration, Harvard University, 1951).

[21] *Ibid.*, pp. 1, 8-9, 12-14, 17, *et passim*.

indicated no tax influence on hours of work or date of retirement; the others indicated incentive and disincentive effects in varying degrees, with no clear preponderance of positive or negative reactions. Break summarized his conclusions from the data as follows:

> The fact that neither the qualitative nor the quantitative dimension of the problem can be measured with any precision . . . means that . . . any estimate of the magnitude of the net effect . . . is almost purely speculative. It can be stated with considerable certainty, nonetheless, that this net effect, be it disincentive or incentive, is not large enough to be of great economic or sociological significance.[22]

A British survey covering a lower income group was carried out in 1952, at the request of the Royal Commission on the Taxation of Profits and Income, by the Social Survey, a sociological research division in the Central Office of Information.[23] In order to concentrate on persons who might have most opportunity to adjust their effort to income tax, the study was restricted to operative and supervisory workers who could or did work overtime and who received incentive pay; clerical, distributive, and professional workers were excluded as were all self-employed persons. Although nearly all respondents grumbled about the income tax, "few . . . had any detailed knowledge of the way they were affected by income tax" and few seemed to adjust their behavior to the existence of the tax. A major conclusion was that "There was no evidence from this enquiry of productive effort being inhibited by the income tax structure within its present limits." There was some indication that respondents "having strong anti-income tax views tended slightly more often than others to work less than average hours," but this attitude was not associated with accurate knowledge of the amount of tax that would be paid on additional earnings. Among those who said that the income tax affected their own productivity, those who said it was an incentive were almost as numerous as those who said it was a deterrent.[24]

Theoretical considerations and the empirical evidence suggest

---

[22] George F. Break, "Income Taxes and Incentives to Work: An Empirical Study," *American Economic Review*, Vol. 47 (September 1957), pp. 529-49, quotation from p. 543.

[23] Royal Commission on the Taxation of Profits and Income, *Second Report*, Cmd. 9105 (London, 1954), Appendix I, pp. 91-124.

[24] *Ibid.*, pp. 92, 110, *et passim*.

three points that are worth emphasizing. First, the influence of taxation on the amount of work done is uncertain and may be weaker than popular discussions imply. Second, whatever the net influence is, it is likely to be much the same for the bulk of the labor force when the tax base is income as when it is consumption, provided the taxes yield equal revenue and are proportional or progressive to the same degree. Third, the allocation of labor among employments may be more sensitive to taxation than the total labor supply is. A man who would work no less if real wages were generally reduced may change jobs in order to get a better wage. Even a carefully devised and fully enforced income tax or expenditure tax would not affect all employments equally because of differences in the degree to which total compensation consists of nonpecuniary advantages which are immune to both taxes. In addition to these unavoidable differences, there are also non-uniformities due to imperfections of tax law and varying opportunities for tax evasion. With high tax rates, labor can be expected to flow toward occupations and working arrangements that are subject to relatively light taxation and away from sectors that are subject to relatively heavy taxes. People may also be induced to do more house repairs, gardening, and other chores for themselves and less work for pay.[25]

Conclusion

Aside from any differences in progressivity or special features, the taxation of income seems likely to be less favorable to private saving and investment propensities than the taxation of consumption but more favorable than the taxation of personal wealth. Income taxes and consumption taxes both reduce the reward for work, but it is uncertain whether, on balance, they increase or decrease the willingness to work. A wealth tax has no direct effect on earnings from personal effort and presumably has little if any influence on the supply of effort. Neither deductive reasoning nor the factual evidence now available clearly shows whether the economic differences between the three tax bases are great or small.

[25] See my paper, "The Income Tax and the Supply of Labor," *Journal of Political Economy,* Vol. 57 (October 1949), pp. 428-37, reprinted in *Readings in the Economics of Taxation,* pp. 456-69.

CHAPTER IV

Economic Effects
of Progressivity

THE ECONOMIC ANALYSIS of tax progressivity can be conveniently combined with a comparison between direct and indirect taxes, since direct taxes are generally progressive and indirect taxes regressive or proportional. The income tax and the other direct personal taxes need not be progressive; if a consensus could be reached in favor of proportional or regressive taxation, it could be carried out more exactly by direct taxation than by indirect taxes. Prevailing sentiments, however, demand progressivity in direct taxes, for its own sake and as an offset to the regressivity of excises and other indirect taxes. Both supporters and opponents of progressivity rightly feel that their objective is associated with the extent to which revenue is raised by indirect taxes. Direct taxes on income, consumption, and wealth, moreover, are likely to differ in distribution among income classes and in progressivity, a point which was held to one side in the preceding chapter.

Progressivity is here measured with respect to income. A progressive tax or tax system takes a larger fraction of large incomes than of small incomes. A regressive tax or tax system takes a smaller fraction of large incomes than of small incomes, and a proportional one takes the same fraction of all incomes. Taxes that are progressive over certain ranges of income often are proportional or regressive over other ranges.[1]

Who Pays Indirect Taxes?

Indirect taxes are collected from producers or sellers in the expectation that they will be passed on to consumers as a separate charge or as an unidentified part of the price. Forward shifting is assumed to occur because, if it did not, producers would switch to untaxed activities. Even with full shifting to the consumer, some productive resources will be forced out of the industry because a smaller quantity of the taxed item will be consumed at the higher price.

Economists have always conceded that, in certain cases, producers may have to bear a large part of a new tax for a time because they are specialized in the production of the taxed item and cannot readily move to other industries. Some theorists go further, contending that absorption by the factors of production is the general rule even in the longer run. They argue that, when producers try to switch from taxed to nontaxed industries, earnings will be driven down in the latter. They conclude that factor incomes (wages, profits, interest, and rent) will be generally reduced and that the average price of goods will remain unchanged, with any rise in the prices of taxed goods being offset by a fall in the costs and prices of other goods.

The traditional theory does neglect some difficult points, particularly when applied to a sales tax, turnover tax, or other broad-based tax or to a large group of selective excises considered jointly. Since the taxed activities comprise a large part of the total, producers' attempts to move to untaxed fields are likely to have repercussions on factor incomes throughout the economy. Moreover, the prices of taxed goods can rise without a compensating fall in

[1] Another usage is to define progressivity, regressivity, and proportionality with respect to the tax base, rather than with respect to income. The two usages may result in different classifications of taxes on consumption or wealth. My practice is to refer to consumption or wealth taxes that are proportional with respect to their bases as "flat-rate" taxes and taxes that are progressive with respect to their bases as "graduated" taxes.

other prices only if total expenditures increase, which may be prevented by monetary restrictions or other conditions. The absolute price level is itself an influence on behavior rather than a neutral statistic.

Adjustment to a massive change in taxation is likely to be a more complex, time-consuming, and far-reaching process than the simple forward-shifting theory contemplates. Whatever happens to the general price level and to economic activity as a whole, however, the relative prices of goods which are subjected to sales or excise taxes can be expected to rise compared with other prices. In this sense, the taxes can be said to fall on buyers according to the part of their incomes that they spend for taxed items.

The hypothesis that excises and sales taxes are passed on to buyers seems to me the most plausible simple statement that can be made about the incidence of these taxes; nevertheless, I am not prepared to rule out the possibility of absorption by producers.[2] Later in this chapter, primary attention is given to statistical estimates based on the assumption that the indirect taxes are fully passed on to buyers, but the implications of absorption by recipients of factor incomes are also noted. Since the indirect taxes are largely, although not exclusively, on consumer goods and services, the assumption of forward shifting treats them as general or selective consumption taxes. The alternative assumption equates the indirect taxes with taxes on income, which, in the absence of knowledge to the contrary about producers of a particular item, may be considered approximately proportional to factor income (personal income other than transfer payments).

The usual view is that direct taxes on personal income, consumption, or wealth cannot be shifted. While there are no doubt exceptional circumstances in which short-run shifting does occur,

[2] For support of the forward-shifting hypothesis, see Richard A. Musgrave, "On Incidence," *Journal of Political Economy*, Vol. 61 (August 1953), pp. 306-23, and *Theory of Public Finance* (New York: McGraw-Hill, 1959), pp. 211-31, 287-311. The hypothesis that indirect taxes are fully absorbed by the factors of production is developed by Earl R. Rolph, *Theory of Fiscal Economics* (Berkeley and Los Angeles: University of California Press, 1954), pp. 123-71. A succinct review of the controversy, with the conclusion that sales taxes fall mainly on consumers and are usually shifted through higher prices, can be found in John F. Due, "Sales Taxation and the Consumer," *American Economic Review*, Vol. 53 (December 1963), pp. 1078-84.

the assumption that in general the personal taxes rest on those who pay them seems reasonable.

Taxpayers are less aware of the amount paid in the form of many indirect taxes than they are of the income tax or other direct taxes. Even when a sales tax or excise is quoted as a separate addition to commodity prices, as it customarily is when levied at the retail stage, consumers may underestimate the total that they pay in the course of a year. When the tax is absorbed by producers it is still harder to identify. Income tax withholding, however, reduces the difference in the degree to which people are aware of the amount which they pay under that tax and under indirect taxes.

Tax consciousness may have important political implications, but it does not appear to condition the economic consequences of taxation to any great extent. Economists generally assume, for example, that a 1 percent tax on wages will have the same influence on labor supply and consumption as a 1 percent cut in the wage rate. Although this simplification abstracts from possible differences in the immediate reactions of organized labor, it does not seem misleading as regards the more lasting effects of taxation.

More questionable is the assumption, also commonly made, that the effects of taxation depend mainly on changes in real income and relative prices rather than on money income and nominal prices. This means, for example, that workers will react in the same way to a reduction in money wages and to an increase in the prices of the things that they buy which cuts their real wages equally. There is evidence that this is not true in the short run; a change in money income is more quickly felt than a change in the purchasing power of a constant income. People have a money illusion that obscures changes in the real value of financial tokens. This illusion must have been weakened by the experience of rising prices during the 1940's and 1950's, increased familiarity with price indexes, and the explicit introduction of the cost of living into wage negotiations. Adjustment lags due to the money illusion are probably shorter than they formerly were, and in the long run the illusion does not seem significant.

If tax consciousness is economically unimportant and if the money illusion is weak and temporary, indirect taxes that raise the price of consumer goods will have approximately the same consequences as an expenditure tax that is distributed in the same way among population groups. Excises or sales taxes which were generally conceded to depress producers' earnings by a calculable amount would be equivalent to direct taxes on income, but, as argued below, the uncertainty of the incidence of the indirect taxes may condition their effects on business operations and investment.

Consumption and Wealth Tax Bases in Relation to Income

The available information indicates that a tax on consumption—either a flat-rate direct tax on expenditures or a fully shifted sales tax—would be regressive with respect to income. A flat-rate tax on personal wealth or net worth apparently would be regressive with respect to income over lower income ranges and progressive

CHART 2. Ratios of Alternative Taxes to Money Income, 1949-50[a]

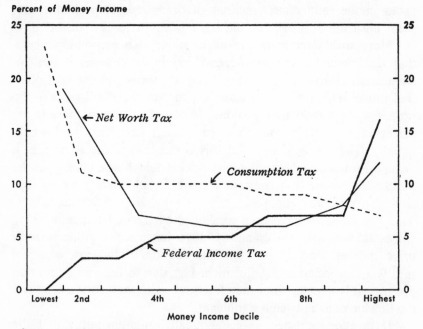

Percent of Money Income

Money Income Decile

[a] Federal individual income tax (excluding tax attributable to net capital gains) compared with flat-rate taxes of equal yield on net worth and personal consumption. For sources and explanation, see Appendix C.

over high income ranges. This can be seen from Chart 2, which shows, for deciles or quintiles of money income, the ratio of tax liability to income of flat-rate taxes on consumption and net worth that would have yielded about the same amount of revenue as the federal income tax in 1950. A curve showing effective rates of the federal income tax (exclusive of the tax attributable to capital gains) is included for comparison.[3]

The broadest retail sales taxes do not cover all consumption expenditures, and they usually apply to certain capital outlays and business expenses. Studies by Reed R. Hansen, based on 1950 expenditure patterns, point to the following conclusions: (1) For lower income classes, the "typical retail sales tax" in the United States is slightly less regressive than a flat-rate tax on all consumption expenditures. (2) At higher income levels the two forms of tax are almost equally regressive (Appendix C). (3) The sales tax tends to be heavier on large families than on small families with the same income and heavier on city families than on rural families. (4) These inequalities and regressivity can be lessened by exempting from tax food consumed at home.[4]

Excises differ greatly depending on their base and rate structure. The ones that raise the greatest revenue, such as those on alcohol and tobacco, appear decidedly regressive. The federal excise taxes in the United States, as a group, seem to be as regressive as the typical state sales tax or perhaps slightly more regressive.[5] The

[3] Later survey data, which became available after the completion of the estimates given in this chapter, tend to corroborate the general pattern of relationships among income, consumption, and net worth that underlie Chart 2. Earlier surveys also showed the same general kind of relationship between consumption and disposable income. The more recent data on consumer expenditures in relation to disposable income are from a Bureau of Labor Statistics field survey of urban families and single consumers in 1960-61; for comments, see Appendix C. The later data on net worth of consumers are from the Survey of Consumer Finances for 1962 but differ somewhat in coverage from the adjusted 1950 survey data used in making the estimates for Chart 2; see Appendix C. Information on net worth of high income groups appears in George Katona and John B. Lansing, "The Wealth of the Wealthy," *Review of Economics and Statistics*, Vol. 46 (February 1964), pp. 1-13.

[4] Reed R. Hansen, "An Empirical Analysis of the Retail Sales Tax with Policy Recommendations," *National Tax Journal*, Vol. 15 (March 1962), pp. 1-13.

[5] Richard A. Musgrave and others, "Distribution of Tax Payments by Income Groups: A Case Study for 1948," *National Tax Journal*, Vol. 4 (March 1951), p. 43.

excises could be revised to make them less regressive, but it does not seem feasible to achieve a significant degree of progressivity through excise taxation in a country such as the United States, where there are few sharply drawn class lines in consumption patterns. Progressive excises and customs duties may be feasible in underdeveloped countries because of wider differences between items consumed by high-income and low-income families.

The statistics on the relation between consumption and income and net worth and income are unsatisfactory in several respects. The data are believed to be least adequate for high income groups because the rich are often reluctant to give information to interviewers and because their financial affairs are complex.[6] The omission from the statistics underlying Chart 2 of capital gains and losses and imputed rent of owner-occupied dwellings and other nonmonetary items of income and consumption clouds the picture. The estimates of net worth are particularly inadequate because they had to be pieced together from different sources and because they omit several kinds of asset (see Appendix C).

Even if the statistics were highly accurate, their significance for tax policy would be debatable because they show a cross section for a single year rather than a continuous record, a snapshot instead of a moving picture. The high ratios of consumption to income and of net worth to income at the lower end of the income array suggest that the current year's income may not be a good indicator of the longer-term economic status of families in these brackets. All budget surveys show consumption expenditures in excess of income in the lowest income classes, but it is hard to see how many families can go on spending more than their income for a long period of years (provided the measure of income includes public assistance payments and other transfers, as is the practice in most surveys). The high consumption ratio in the lowest income

[6] See Raymond W. Goldsmith, "Statistics of Saving in the United States," American Statistical Association, *Proceedings of the Business and Economic Statistics Section,* Dec. 27-30, 1959, p. 247. The Board of Governors, with the aid of the Census Bureau, and the Survey Research Center of the University of Michigan are making special surveys of high-income families which may augment knowledge of their portfolios. For early reports of findings, see "Survey of Financial Characteristics of Consumers," *Federal Reserve Bulletin,* Vol. 50 (March 1964), pp. 285-93, and Katona and Lansing, *Review of Economics and Statistics,* Vol. 46, pp. 1-13.

classes appears to be explained partly by the presence in these classes of families whose income is temporarily depressed and of retired persons whose previous income was greater. The high ratio of aggregate net worth to aggregate income in these classes may have a similar explanation, with retired persons exercising an especially great influence on the ratio. On the other hand, in high income classes the ratios of aggregate consumption to aggregate income and of aggregate net worth to aggregate income may be held down by the presence of families whose incomes are higher than usual. Both low income classes and high income classes include families who are regularly in these classes and families who are temporarily there, but the low income classes include proportionately more of those whose income is below normal than of those whose income is above normal, whereas the reverse is true of high income classes.

Statistics for any one year probably make a consumption tax appear more regressive with respect to income than would statistics in which the cumulative or average income and consumption for a period of several years, or for a lifetime, were compared. The cross-section statistics make a flat-rate tax on net worth appear more regressive in lower income classes and less progressive in higher income classes than would a longer-term comparison for identical families. Suitable data are not available to measure the difference between the two kinds of ratio. A hypothesis that has received attention from specialists in recent years is that the average ratio of consumption to families' normal or "permanent" income is the same at all income levels.[7] If this is true, a flat-rate tax on all consumption will be proportional with respect to normal or permanent income, although regressive with respect to current income in any one year.[8] While the hypothesis has not been dis-

[7] Milton Friedman, *A Theory of the Consumption Function* (Princeton, N.J.: Princeton University Press for National Bureau of Economic Research, 1957).

[8] David G. Davies has made estimates suggesting that a general consumption tax would be proportional with respect to "permanent income" ("Progressiveness of a Sales Tax in Relation to Various Income Bases," *American Economic Review*, Vol. 50 [December 1960], pp. 987-95, especially p. 993). These estimates, however, do not provide a test of the permanent income hypothesis but are illustrations of certain implications of Friedman's hypothesis if valid. Lacking a direct observation of permanent income, Davies derived an estimate of permanent income in each measured income class by dividing mean measured consumption by a constant. This, of course, produces a constant ratio of consumption (and of a general consumption tax) to estimated permanent income.

proved, I think that it goes farther than is warranted.

The most appropriate time period for judging progressivity or regressivity is not obvious. In general, short periods are subject to more erratic fluctuations than long periods. A day, a week, or a month seems too short a period to reveal significant relations, and in many respects a year is also too short. But a long period of years, or a whole lifetime, is not necessarily ideal. Past prosperity mitigates the hardship of paying a tax that is high in relation to current income, and previous indigence helps excuse a low ratio of tax to current income, but there are limits to the degree to which the past should be allowed to dominate the present. The future, being unforeseeable in detail, simply cannot be brought into calculations of the tax burden.

Until better statistics are compiled, tax progressivity and regressivity can justifiably be measured on the basis of available single-year data, but with the qualification that the estimates for the lowest and highest incomes are probably less representative than those for a wide range of middle incomes.

Impact on Saving and Consumption

If high-income families tend to increase or decrease their saving by a larger fraction of any change in their disposable income than low-income families do—that is, if the marginal propensity to save increases with income—a progressive tax will be paid at the expense of private saving to a greater extent than a proportional or regressive tax. Although direct evidence on the marginal propensity to save in different income classes is not available, the marginal propensity can be approximated from statistics of disposable income and net saving. On the basis of such approximations, I have estimated the impact on net saving of the federal individual income tax in 1950 (exclusive of the tax attributable to net capital gains) and of a proportional income tax and a fully shifted flat-rate tax on consumption that would have yielded enough revenue to replace the graduated income tax. The proportional income tax is included in order to show the influence of rate graduation and as a proxy for a sales tax that is fully absorbed by the factors of production. The estimates reflect solely the distribution of tax liability among income groups and do not allow for any difference in saving propensities under consumption taxes and income taxes.

The estimates indicate that, under 1950 conditions, the proportion of revenue coming out of potential private saving would have been as follows:

Federal individual income tax (exclusive of
    tax on net capital gains) ....33 percent;
Proportional income tax ....28 percent;
Flat-rate consumption tax ....27 percent.

The derivation of the estimates is described in Appendix C.

The estimates confirm the expectation that the progressive income tax falls more heavily on saving than would a proportional income tax or a flat-rate consumption tax, but the difference is smaller than seems to be implied by many comments. Differences between the two flat-rate taxes, due solely to their distribution among income classes, appear to be minor.[9]

For reasons mentioned in the discussion of progressivity and regressivity, cross-section budget data may not be a reliable indicator of the relation between income and expenditures of identical families for a period of years. If families determine their consumption partly with reference to their normal or permanent income rather than their current income, marginal propensities to save derived from cross-section data will overstate the impact on saving of a permanent tax.[10] This may be one reason why marginal saving propensities derived from consumer budget studies usually exceed statistical estimates based on time series. My estimates conform to this pattern; the cross-section estimates given here imply a substantially greater marginal propensity to save than the time-series esti-

[9] Estimates by Richard A. Musgrave for 1957 were published while my work was in progress. His estimates show the following reductions of personal saving in relation to tax revenue: federal individual income tax, 31 percent; proportional income tax, 22 percent; sales tax, 18 percent ("Effects of Tax Policy on Private Capital Formation," in *Fiscal and Debt Management Policies,* Research Studies for the Commission on Money and Credit [Englewood Cliffs, N.J.: Prentice-Hall, 1963], pp. 65, 68). For comments, see Appendix C.

[10] Friedman, *Theory of the Consumption Function;* Franco Modigliani and Richard Brumberg, "Utility Analysis and the Consumption Function: An Interpretation of Cross-Section Data," in *Post-Keynesian Economics,* Kenneth K. Kurihara, ed. (New Brunswick, N.J.; Rutgers University Press, 1954), pp. 383-436.

mate of the marginal propensity to consume used in the analysis of countercyclical effects in Chapter XI and Appendix E.[11]

Estimates based on budget surveys for a single year may also exaggerate the difference between the effect of progressive and regressive taxes, but this is not necessarily true. The budget studies indicate a marginal propensity to save which is much greater for both low incomes and high incomes than for middle incomes; for the low incomes this reflects a reduction in negative saving as income increases whereas for the high incomes it reflects an increase in positive saving.[12]

If the limitations of the data and methods are overlooked, my estimates indicate that the difference between the impact on saving of the progressive income tax and that of a flat-rate consumption tax is an unimpressive 6 percent of the yield (33 percent for the income tax compared with 27 percent for the consumption tax). On the assumption that this relation was still applicable a decade later, replacement of the entire individual income tax by a flat-rate consumption tax would have increased private saving by only about $2.4 billion in 1960 (6 percent of individual income tax liabilities of $39.5 billion).[13] This sum is equal to about 11 percent of actual personal saving of 1960, to about 8 percent of net private domestic investment, and to about 3 percent of gross private domestic investment.[14] A comment on the possible contribution to growth of such an increase in saving and investment appears at the end of the chapter.

[11] For a review of the subject, see Jean Crockett, "Income and Asset Effects on Consumption: Aggregate and Cross Section," in *Studies in Income and Wealth*, Conference on Research in Income and Wealth, Vol. 28 (Princeton, N.J.: Princeton University Press for National Bureau of Economic Research, 1964), pp. 97-132.

[12] If the saving function were linear, the bias would cause the slope (the over-all marginal propensity to save) to be overstated, but the marginal propensity to save would be the same at all income levels. For curvilinear functions, it is not certain whether the marginal propensity will be more overstated for low incomes or for high incomes.

[13] This estimate reflects only the difference in distribution of tax payments among income groups and does not allow for any influence of the form of taxation on individual propensities to save. I have not adjusted income tax liability to exclude the tax attributable to net capital gains. Musgrave's estimates indicate a substantially greater effect from the substitution (*Fiscal and Debt Management Policies*, p. 65).

[14] *Economic Report of the President, January 1963*, pp. 180, 186.

Investment Incentives

Since investors in unincorporated enterprises and purchasers of corporate stock tend to have above-average incomes, they pay less under a proportional or regressive tax than under a progressive tax and have more resources to put into their own businesses or into the acquisition of shares. Furthermore, as explained in Chapter III, offsets of business losses may be more complete under a proportional or regressive tax than under a progressive one. In these respects, nonprogressive taxes are more favorable to business investment than a progressive income tax is.

Although indirect taxes ordinarily qualify as nonprogressive, they impose an obstacle to business operations and investment that is not raised by a net income tax. Producers and distributors must advance funds to cover taxes levied prior to the retail stage, which increases their working-capital requirements and exposes them to the risk that they may not be able to recover the advance if sales volume or prices prove to be lower than expected. Retail taxes are less troublesome but still must be paid on unprofitable sales as well as profitable ones. From the point of view of producers, the indirect taxes constitute an inescapable increase in costs of doing business. In many industries, even a moderate-rate sales tax or excise will increase costs by an amount that is large relative to the margin of profit on sales. Even when they are generally reflected in higher prices, indirect taxes are not innocuous with respect to investment.[15]

The actual volume of investment depends on both the willingness to invest under given market conditions and the expected state of demand for final output. If the substitution of indirect taxes for progressive income taxes significantly narrowed the market for consumer goods, this would partly or wholly offset any beneficial effect on investment incentives. The foregoing analysis suggests that such a substitution would indeed reduce the propensity to consume but that the difference may not be great.

While, in my judgment, common opinion is probably correct in

[15] I am indebted to Carl S. Shoup for calling my attention to the risk elements in indirect taxation.

considering the present individual income tax more injurious to investment incentives than indirect taxes or a less progressive income tax would be, the extent of the difference is conjectural. Because of the large portion of private investment that is carried out by corporations, the corporation income tax may influence investment decisions more than the individual income tax does.

Work Incentives

While the net influence of taxation is uncertain, it seems likely that people will choose to work more under a regressive or proportional tax system than under a progressive system. As pointed out in Chapter III, the net influence is the unpredictable result of two effects that are thought to be partly offsetting in the normal case. One effect is a reduction in taxpayers' real disposable income, which tends to stimulate them to work more in an effort to restore their position. The other effect, which tends to discourage work, is a cut in net earnings per unit of work. Technically, the second effect is called the price or substitution effect, because economists view wages as the price of labor or a measure of the rate at which free time can be substituted for the goods and services purchasable with one's earnings. Regressive, proportional, and progressive taxes have similar income effects but different price or substitution effects.

To isolate the influence of progressivity, consider a person who would pay the same amount under alternative progressive, proportional, and regressive taxes, provided his money income was the same. The income effect of the three taxes will be the same, but the price effect will be different. Whereas the progressive tax reduces the net price received for successive units of free time, the proportional tax leaves the net earnings rate constant, and the regressive tax allows it to increase. Although the net balance remains uncertain, the price effect is clearly most adverse under the progressive tax. This conclusion is reinforced by the presumption that the attractiveness of free time increases relative to that of wage income as the work week lengthens and that a person who has control over the number of hours he works will insist on an increasing wage rate for hours above some minimum.

As an illustration, consider a man who is working 40 hours a week at an hourly rate of $2.50 and earning $100. A 10 percent proportional tax will reduce the net wage to $2.25; if hours of work are constant, income after tax will fall to $90. A progressive tax with an exemption of $50 per week and a rate of 20 percent on income above the exemption will also reduce the man's income to $90 after tax if his hours of work are unchanged, but the net wage rate will now be $2.50 for the first 20 hours and $2.00 for additional hours. Without knowing more about the person, we cannot predict whether he will try to maintain his after-tax income by working longer hours, but this course is clearly less feasible and less likely to be taken under the progressive tax. Under the proportional tax, income can be restored to the pretax level by working 4.44 hours more; under the progressive tax, 5.00 hours of additional work are required.

The force of this argument is diminished by virtue of the fact that most individuals do not have the opportunity of working exactly the number of hours that they wish. Unless they are self-employed, they must conform to their employer's requirements. But there is flexibility through absenteeism, selection among jobs, and part-time supplementary jobs. Employers are likely to respond to the preferences of the majority of their workers; the length of the work week is a standard subject of collective bargaining.

Although the same difference between progressive taxes and proportional or regressive taxes exists for business executives, independent businessmen, and professional persons, the alternatives faced by such persons are more complex than those presented to wage earners. Power, prestige, interest in one's work, and nontaxable emoluments may be more important. The salary that the ABC Corporation must pay to entice an executive to work for it rather than the XYZ Corporation is surely much greater than the net compensation that society must offer to induce him to work as an executive rather than a clerk. Nevertheless, some men may be discouraged from becoming executives or transferring to more responsible jobs because progressive taxation reduces the net earnings attainable by assuming responsibility.

A qualification that could be significant arises from the differences in amounts of tax payable by various social and economic groups under progressive, proportional, and regressive systems. High income groups will pay more and low income groups less under progressive rates than under the other systems. If it could be shown that high income groups are less sensitive than low income groups to a change in their marginal rate of compensation and more inclined to work more to try to make up for a cut in their average compensation rate, this would offset to some degree the greater discouragement offered by progressive tax rates to work by members of each income group. But this is a speculative matter on which it would be hard to obtain reliable information.

Cost of Tax Compliance—and Avoidance

A recurrent criticism of the income tax, applicable with even greater force to the expenditure tax and wealth tax, is that its complexity causes much time and energy to be diverted to the socially unproductive activity of complying with the tax. Individual investors and business executives give much attention to the income tax, with the aid of a large and talented group of tax lawyers and accountants. Surely, the argument runs, there are more useful things for these people to do.

Although the choice of word is a matter of semantics, most efforts seem to be devoted toward tax avoidance rather than compliance literally understood. A person who conducted his affairs without regard to opportunities for minimizing income tax would no doubt be somewhat inconvenienced by requirements for record-keeping and the filing of returns but would escape worry about many subtleties of law and accounting. It would be unrealistic, of course, to expect taxpayers to neglect possibilities of tax avoidance or to refrain from complaining about the trouble and expense to which they must go to take advantage of them.

A less conspicuous, but perhaps more important, form of economic waste is the alteration of investment and employment choices in order to avoid income taxes—the selection of investments whose before-tax yield is lower than that of others but whose after-tax yield is higher, the choice of jobs on the basis of the degree of tax shelter enjoyed by the compensation, and many other such decisions.

Although these are valid criticisms of the income tax or any other refined direct tax, something can be said on the other side. Many efforts at tax avoidance are provoked or invited by the existence of exclusions, deductions, and other provisions that are questionable from the standpoint of equity and social policy. Removal of these provisions would improve the equity of the income tax and at the same time lessen the wastes and distortions attributable to it. Other complexities of the income tax are due to efforts to achieve equity and neutrality in a complex environment. If these refinements are not considered worth their cost in complexity and distortions, they could be eliminated within the income tax framework without going so far as to substitute indirect taxes for the income tax. Even though such a simplification of the income tax would sacrifice some of its characteristic advantages, the results might be preferable to those attributable to massive substitution of indirect taxes.

Although efforts at tax avoidance and complexities of the statutes, regulations, and administrative procedures depend to some extent on the height of tax rates, the exact relationship is unclear. Many of the practices that have grown up might not be eliminated or even greatly abated if income tax rates were simply reduced, without other reforms, and the revenue were replaced by indirect taxation.

Finally, indirect taxes are not without complications, and their effects on patterns of investment and production can be great. Selective excises will discourage production of the taxed items, to an extent depending on the elasticity of demand. Although the traditional view that this inevitably results in a less efficient use of resources has been properly questioned, the probability that inefficiency will occur seems no less than it is with respect to changes induced by the income tax.

Concluding Remarks

Many discussions have, I think, greatly exaggerated the possible differences in the influence of alternative taxes on work incentives, private saving, and investment. Careful theoretical analyses and factual evidence on the subject are inconclusive. Moreover, the contribution that additional saving and investment can make to the growth of an economy such as that of the United States may be less than is commonly supposed. According to Denison's estimates, it would be necessary to increase net investment by an amount equal to 1.4 percent of national income each year in order to raise the rate of growth of national income by 0.1 percentage point over the next 20 years.[16] (This assumes that labor inputs and the quantity of land are the same as they would have been without the additional investment.) To finance this investment by additional personal saving would require a saving rate almost one-fourth higher than that of 1960-62.[17] My tentative estimates indicate that as drastic a change in tax progressivity as would be involved in replacing the progressive income tax by a flat-rate tax on consumption would have increased personal saving in 1960 by less than half this fraction.[18] If Denison is right about the role of capital, the possibility of speeding growth by tax revisions that will stimulate saving is unimpressive, even with liberal allowance for possible errors in my estimates and for incentive effects. Other scholars attribute more of growth to additional capital formation than Denison does, mainly because they believe that technological progress must be "embodied" in new capital goods.[19] Their models allow more scope for stimulating growth by tax measures that increase saving.

A tax revision that would cause the number of hours worked to increase by x percent (with capital inputs constant) would increase total output much more than a revision that stimulated an x percent increase in the annual amount of new investment (with labor inputs constant). One reason is that the contribution of capital is made by the stock, of which new investment in any year is

[16] Edward F. Denison, *The Sources of Economic Growth in the United States and the Alternatives Before Us,* Supplementary Paper No. 13 (New York: Committee for Economic Development, 1962), pp. 115-16.

[17] Personal saving in 1960-62 averaged 6.1 percent of national income (*Economic Report of the President, January 1964,* pp. 221, 226).

[18] Musgrave's estimates indicate a greater increase in personal saving (*Fiscal and Debt Management Policies,* p. 65).

[19] See, for example, Robert M. Solow, "Technical Progress, Capital Formation, and Economic Growth," *American Economic Review,* Vol. 52, Papers and Proceedings (May 1962), pp. 76-86; a further comment by Denison appears in "The Unimportance of the Embodied Question," *American Economic Review,* Vol. 54 (March 1964), pp. 90-93.

only a small fraction. Another reason is that the value of labor inputs—measured, as it must be, by labor's share of national income—is much greater than the value of capital inputs. But too little is known about the influence of taxation on work to allow an economist to confidently prescribe a tax system that would increase the amount of work done by x percent, even if he felt free to disregard other objectives.

The preceding remarks about saving are based on the tacit assumption that an increase in the propensity to save would immediately be translated into additional investment. The assumption implies that capital formation is limited by the propensity to save rather than by the willingness to invest. This may be true in many underdeveloped countries and in the United States in buoyant periods, but it does not seem to have been true in the United States during the late 1950's and early 1960's. During that period, the American economy suffered from a tendency toward chronic deficiency of aggregate demand. In these conditions, an attempt to save more may prove abortive and may depress income and output. This hard-learned lesson of the 1930's has been forgotten in many discussions of tax policy and growth.

Predictions of demand over long periods of time are hazardous, and I shall not attempt one here. Rather I shall content myself with the assertion that there is no guarantee that demand will press so hard against available resources that an increased propensity to save would automatically increase private investment. If conditions similar to those of the past several years persist, minimum discouragement of investment will be a more important criterion of tax policy than minimum effects on saving.

CHAPTER V

Treatment of Certain Costs
of Earning Income

A NET INCOME TAX should allow the deduction from gross receipts of all costs of obtaining income. The U.S. tax makes adequate provision for the deduction of most business costs, as reflected in accounting statements, and for most costs of obtaining investment income. Provisions are less complete for deducting costs of earning income as a self-employed person or employee.

Even with respect to earned income, most of the obvious costs are deductible. A professional person or salesman, for example, can claim deductions for all the usual expenses of maintaining an office, operating an automobile in connection with his work, and travel away from home, as well as many outlays for entertaining clients and customers. An employed person is allowed to deduct nonreimbursed expenses of travel away from home in connection with his job, union and professional association dues, the cost of specialized work clothing and necessary tools, and other items.

The difficulties arise mainly in connection with items that may combine consumption and cost elements. Items of this nature, which are considered in this chapter, include the expenses of traveling between home and place of employment, additional household expenses of working wives, educational expenses, and travel and entertainment expenses. Also discussed is the question whether a depreciation or depletion allowance should be deducted to reflect the loss of earning capacity with the passage of time.

The American income tax is more generous than the British but less liberal than the Swedish and German taxes with respect to deductions by employed persons. In the United Kingdom, deductions from employment income are limited to those which the person "is necessarily obliged to incur . . . wholly, exclusively, and necessarily in the performance" of his duties, and this rule is narrowly interpreted. Nondeductible items include expenses of obtaining employment and dues for membership in professional organizations.[1] The rules are more liberal for self-employed professional persons and appear to permit the deduction of most of the items that are deductible in the United States. In Sweden and the Federal Republic of Germany, deductions appear to be allowed for much the same items as in the United States; however, in Sweden membership dues are generally not deductible even when they are necessary expenses, and practices may be more rigid than in the United States in regard to entertainment expenses. Sweden and Germany both allow the deduction of commuting expenses within limits.[2]

As will appear more vividly in the discussion of individual items, there are no fully satisfactory criteria for distinguishing between consumption and costs of earning income. Although the distinction is customarily made in household budgets and the social accounts, it is less firmly based than is usually supposed. In a sense, a large proportion of all consumption may be considered a cost of production—not only subsistence costs, but also conventional necessities and amenities, which vary greatly with occupation and social station. For example, a junior executive in a large firm who spent no more for clothing than is provided by the Bureau of Labor Statistics standard budget for a clerical worker would not long keep his position. It is a commonplace that law-

[1] Harvard Law School, World Tax Series, *Taxation in the United Kingdom* (Boston: Little, Brown, 1957), p. 238.

[2] Harvard Law School, World Tax Series, *Taxation in Sweden* (Boston: Little, Brown, 1959), pp. 314-19, and *Taxation in the Federal Republic of Germany* (Chicago: Commerce Clearing House, 1963), pp. 266-68, 401.

yers and brokers often meet prospective clients at the country club. An acceptable address may be almost as important as respectable conduct in gaining admittance to circles in which new clients can be found.

Property income is defined, generally and for the income tax, on a more nearly pure net basis than income from personal effort. In principle, property income is measured net of all current costs of using the property and net of depreciation allowances covering the cost of capital assets whose value is exhausted with use or the passage of time.

It is unlikely that a rigorous measurement of net income from personal effort can be developed which is quite comparable with net property income. Human beings cannot be treated merely as productive agents. Consumption is both the end of production and an intermediate good that induces further productive activity and makes it possible. All that can be hoped is that marginal refinements can be made in the measurement of taxable income, where this can be done without excessive burdens of compliance and administration.

Commuting and Moving Expenses

The costs of commuting to one's regular place of work are not deductible; deductions are allowed for travel to places of temporary employment away from home. Difficulties of interpretation arise in marginal cases with respect to the location of a person's home, the meaning of being away from home, and the distinction between temporary and indefinite periods of employment. These problems of tax administration are not at issue here. The question is whether the long-standing rule against the deduction of regular commuting expenses is proper. It has been contended that commuting expenses are costs of employment and should be deducted if they can be properly identified and distinguished from other personal expenditures for local transportation.

In Sweden, costs of daily travel between home and place of work are deductible by an employee who lives far enough away to need transportation. Generally, the deduction covers only the cost of the cheapest means of transportation. Thus, a person who drives his car to work ordinarily may deduct the cost of bus or train transportation; however, if the saving in time resulting from the use of a private car is more than an hour and a half per day, a deduction may be taken for the cost of operating the car.[3]

It is true that, given one's place of residence, commuting expenses may be necessary. But it does not follow that these expenses are primarily costs of earning income rather than consumption. A great part of commuting expenses may be regarded as the consequence of a consumption preference exercised in choosing a place of residence. Those who live in the suburbs because they like trees and grass clearly are making a consumption decision which entails commuting expenses as well as the costs of maintaining a lawn. Commuting expenses and housing expenses, moreover, are often close substitutes. Other things equal, an easily accessible dwelling sells or rents for more than one in a remote location. A part of the difference in price reflects lower costs of commuting. If a person chooses to spend $100 a month traveling to and from his home in a distant suburb, this expenditure is similar in function to that of another who pays $100 a month more rent in order to live close to his place of work. While it is not feasible for everyone to live within walking distance of his work, there is nearly always a wide range of choice of exact location.

The income tax already favors home-owning suburbanites over apartment-renting residents of central cities because of the treatment of owner-occupied dwellings; commuters by automobile are favored by the deductibility of state and local gasoline taxes. The addition of a deduction for ordinary commuting expenses would accentuate existing inequities and would constitute an additional mild encouragement to decentralization. It would stimulate extravagant means of travel. The rule against the deduction of commuting expenses seems justified.

The cost of moving to a new place of residence may be regarded as a consumer expenditure when the move reflects personal preference, or it may be considered a cost of earning income when it is dictated by employment requirements or opportunities. Often it is hard to classify moves on an objective basis. The acceptance of a job in a new location is not enough to prove that the costs of moving were incurred primarily for the purpose of earning income. The

[3] *Taxation in Sweden,* p. 316.

change of jobs may equally well have been prompted by a desire to change residences. Motives may be mixed or obscure even to a person who moves.

Prior to the Revenue Act of 1964 no deduction was allowed for moving expenses; reimbursements for the cost of moving to a new place of work for the same employer were not included in adjusted gross income, but reimbursements received from a new employer were treated as income. The 1964 act granted a deduction for employees' nonreimbursed moving expenses and for reimbursed expenses of moving to accept a job with a new employer, while continuing the old treatment of expenses connected with transfers for the same employer. Certain safeguards were included to prevent the deduction of outlays that are predominantly personal consumption.[4] Deductions will not be available to persons who move in an unsuccessful effort to find a new job, to those who remain for only short periods of time at any one job location, or to the self-employed.

Neither the old law nor the new one satisfactorily distinguishes work-related costs from personal consumption. While the old provisions undoubtedly denied deductions for some moving expenses that were genuine costs of earning income, the new provisions will allow deductions for the costs of some moves that are motivated by considerations other than employment opportunities. In support of the new provision, it can be argued that, since an exact classification of moving expenses is not feasible, it is desirable to resolve doubts in favor of deductibility in order to avoid deterring mobility.

Housekeeping and Child-Care Expenses

Persons who go to work outside the home often incur expenditures for services that would otherwise be done at home. Not only working wives, but also single people and to a lesser extent husbands

---

[4] The main safeguards are the requirements that (a) the new place of work be at least 20 miles farther from the former residence than was the former place of work; and (b) in the case of nonreimbursed moves, the person moving work full time as an employee in the new location for at least 39 weeks during the first 12 months after the move (Internal Revenue Code of 1954, as amended, sec. 217). At the fringes of the 20-mile zone there seems to be an inconsistency in the treatment of moving expenses and commuting expenses, and the full-time employment rule involves questions of interpretation and possible hardships for those who fail to meet it through no fault of their own.

whose wives remain at home, incur additional expense. The failure to allow the deduction of these costs in the computation of taxable income constitutes a bias against outside employment. To be sure, the tax system has not prevented a great increase in the proportion of married women in the labor force. But complaints are heard, particularly from upper-middle class women who are articulate and tax conscious.

The absence of deductions for additional costs of working is a defect of the income tax that cannot be fully corrected. The costs in question are diverse and indistinguishable from ordinary consumption. They include the wages of domestic servants, additional expenditures for quickly prepared food and restaurant meals, part of expenditures for clothes and personal care, and perhaps even part of the cost of household appliances. Outlays for all of these items are incurred by families in which the wife does not work outside the home as well as by those in which she does. It would be impossible to draw a satisfactory distinction between ordinary consumption and additional expenditures that are costs of earning income. Even if certain expenses could be identified as costs, a deduction for them would be unfair to families—usually those with low and low-middle incomes—in which the household work is done by the working wife or other family members in the evenings or on weekends compared with families which hire household help and enjoy more leisure. The practical effect of an allowance for expenses for household help would be discrimination in favor of upper-middle income groups.

These objections apply, but with less force, to the present limited deduction for child care expenses (Chapter VII).

The discrimination against working wives could be mitigated by a special earned income credit or a special minimum standard deduction (discussed in Chapter IX). The credit or deduction would be allowed regardless of whether additional expenditures were actually made because of the wife's employment. This would be much simpler than a deduction for actual expenditures and more favorable to families which do the household work themselves instead of hiring others to do it or buying the services in the form of more highly processed goods. A minimum deduction would not satisfy professional women and others with above-average earnings, nor would an earned income credit unless it was a liberal one.

Educational Expenditures

Expenditures for education that increases earning capacity or that is intended to do so are a strategically important cost of earning income but are deductible to only a limited extent.[5] Those who invest in themselves are discriminated against compared with persons who have spent little in preparation for their occupations and investors in physical assets. The tax provisions are paradoxical at a time when the country is becoming increasingly conscious of the need for highly trained persons and of the contribution of education to economic progress.[6]

Present Regulations

Treasury regulations are highly restrictive. They deny deductions, not only for expenses incurred "primarily for the purpose of fulfilling the general educational aspirations or other personal purposes of the taxpayer," but also for expenditures for "education undertaken primarily for the purpose of obtaining a new position or substantial advancement in position." Deductions are allowed only for

Expenditures . . . for education (including research activities) undertaken primarily for the purpose of:
(1) Maintaining or improving skills required by the taxpayer in his employment or other trade or business, or
(2) Meeting the express requirements of a taxpayer's employer, or the requirements of applicable law or regulations, imposed as a condition to the retention by the taxpayer of his salary, status, or employment.[7]

[5] This section is based on my paper "Educational Expenditures and the Income Tax," in *Economics of Higher Education*, Selma J. Mushkin, ed. (U. S. Department of Health, Education, and Welfare, Office of Education, Bulletin 1962, No. 5; Brookings Institution Reprint No. 64, 1962). For a general treatment of economic aspects of education, see Theodore W. Schultz, *The Economic Value of Education* (New York: Columbia University Press, 1963).

[6] Edward F. Denison estimates that increased education was responsible for 23 percent of the growth of real national income in 1929-57 and 42 percent of the growth of real national income per person employed in that period. See *The Sources of Economic Growth in the United States and the Alternatives Before Us*, Supplementary Paper No. 13 (New York: Committee for Economic Development, 1962), p. 73.

[7] Treasury Regulations, sec. 1.162-5.

The regulations state that deductions will ordinarily be allowed for the cost of education for the purpose of maintaining or improving skills "if it is customary for other established members of the taxpayer's trade or business to undertake such education." Deductions for required education are restricted to expenditures "for the minimum education required by the taxpayer's employer, or by applicable law or regulations, as a condition to the retention of the taxpayer's salary, status, or employment." Deductions are not allowed for expenses of "education . . . required of the taxpayer in order to meet the minimum requirements for qualification or establishment in his intended trade or business or specialty therein. . . ."[8]

Illustrating the meaning of the rules, the authors of the regulations mention the case of A, who is employed by an accounting firm and who takes courses to enable him to qualify as a certified public accountant. Expenditures for these courses are not deductible, as they were made before A became qualified as a CPA. B, a general practitioner of medicine, takes graduate courses in order to become a specialist in pediatrics and is allowed no deductions for his expenses. C, a less ambitious general practitioner, takes "a 2-week course reviewing developments in several specialized fields, including pediatrics, for the purpose of carrying on his general practice" and is entitled to deductions for his expenses. D is a schoolteacher who is required by her employer or by law "either to read a list of books or to take certain courses" in order to hold her job. After completing the prescribed courses, she receives a master's degree and is given an automatic salary increase. D can deduct her educational expenses. E, a graduate student at a university, aspires to become a professor and therefore must obtain an advanced degree. While working toward the degree, E is a part-time teacher at the university. His educational expenses are not deductible since he has not completed the education required to become qualified as a regular faculty member.

The present regulations represent a liberalization of previous provisions, made by the Treasury Department in 1958 in response to a series of court decisions holding that educational expenditures may sometimes be costs of earning income. In attempting to prevent deductions for general education, however, the authors of the

[8] *Ibid.*

regulations excluded educational outlays that contribute to future earning capacity and that have great economic significance for the individual and the community. If a similar attitude were taken toward physical capital, deductions from taxable income presumably would be allowed for maintenance expenses and capital replacement costs, but would be denied for depreciation of capital used to establish new firms, to enlarge existing enterprises, or to introduce new products. The regulations concerning educational expenditures are less favorable to the new man and the ambitious than to the established and the timeserver.

Unsatisfactory as the regulations may seem, the difficulties of devising better rules should not be underestimated. In many other countries, the tax treatment of educational expenses is less liberal than in the United States; however, university students often pay little or no tuition and, in certain European countries at least, may receive subsidies to cover living expenses. In Canada, students in full-time attendance at a university or other post-secondary educational institution are allowed to deduct tuition fees in computing taxable income; the deduction may be taken even when the fees are paid by parents or others.[9]

Possible Revisions

By analogy with the treatment of investment in physical capital, it seems that persons who make expenditures for education that increases their earning power, or that is intended to do so, should be permitted to capitalize these outlays and write them off against taxable income through depreciation or amortization allowances. Income-producing educational expenditures are investments with a limited life and, if it is feasible, they should be given the same tax treatment as other investments. Failure to allow tax-free recovery of educational outlays means that the income tax falls in part on the return of capital rather than on net income.

In order to bring out significant issues, I shall attempt to give the broad outlines of a suitable plan. The suggestions are intended

[9] CCH Canadian, Ltd., *Canadian Master Tax Guide*, 18th ed. (Don Mills, Ont., 1963), para. 505a. In his budget speech in March 1964, the Minister of Finance proposed that the deduction be allowed also for part-time students and for tuition fees for secondary education. See *House of Commons Debates*, 26 Parliament 2 sess., Vol. 109 (1964), p. 981.

to serve as a basis for discussion rather than as recommendations for immediate legislation. The plan, in brief, is that part of the personal costs of college education and professional, technical, and vocational education should be capitalized and written off against the student's future earned income over a period of ten to twenty years or more. Minor costs of part-time study would be currently deducted. Provisions limiting deductions to expenses relating to the taxpayer's current position would be dropped.

If the amortization of educational expenditures is justified as a refinement in the definition of income, the deductions should be taken against the income attributable to the education. The deduction should be taken by the student, rather than his parents, even when the latter pay the educational expenses. Expenditures by parents, relatives, or friends may be considered as gifts to the student. He would be allowed to recover free of income tax the value of these gifts just as he can now write off against income the cost of a depreciable asset acquired as a gift. The privilege of writing off the value of gifts in the form of education probably should not extend to scholarships and other aid received from educational institutions, governments, corporations, or other organized bodies.

The personal costs of education are far less than total costs because of heavy expenditures by governments and nonprofit institutions. Personal costs are those met by students, parents, and other private individuals. They include (1) money outlays for tuition and fees, books and supplies, and travel; (2) any additional living expenses of the student; and (3) earnings forgone while studying. Forgone earnings are by far the largest component of the costs of college and graduate education, and they constitute an important part of high school costs. This part of costs is already excluded from the tax base, and no special deduction is necessary or appropriate. Although living expenses above those that would be incurred by a person who was not a student should be deductible, it would be difficult to distinguish these additional expenses from ordinary living costs; therefore, as a practical matter, no allowance is suggested for additional living expenses. The costs to be capitalized and amortized would be those listed under item 1 above.

In principle, expenditures for education should be classified as costs of earning income when incurred for that purpose, regardless of whether they could clearly be shown to result in additional income. The taxpayer's intention is the dominant factor governing the distinction between other "ordinary and necessary" business and professional expenses and personal expenses. Mixed motives are especially common, however, with respect to education, and there is no body of accounting and administrative rules to distinguish one kind of educational outlay from another.

As a practical possibility, the current deduction or amortization of educational expenditures might be allowed with respect to: (1) any courses creditable toward a degree at an accredited college or university, regardless of whether a degree is earned; (2) vocational training at a recognized trade school, business college, or similar institution; and (3) a supplementary, continuation, or refresher course of a predominantly professional or vocational nature taken at a recognized or accredited institution. Part-time studies and correspondence courses as well as full-time resident study should be eligible. Expenditures for ordinary high school studies and elementary school would be classified as personal expenses rather than costs of earning income.

As regards college and university studies, this plan would err on the side of liberality, because it would cover some educational expenditures that are predominantly consumption, as judged by presumed motivation or apparent influence on income. Most college and university education, however, seems to add to earning capacity, and it is difficult to rule out the possibility of economic motivation in connection with any part of it. The rate of private monetary return on total private costs of college education appears to be high—about 12½ percent net of income tax in 1940 and 10 percent in 1950, according to Becker's estimates.[10] If a large fraction of college costs were classified as consumption expenditures, the calculated rate of return on the remaining outlays would be high indeed. The imperfection due to a liberal allowance for college costs seems less objectionable than the present practice of permitting

[10] Gary S. Becker, "Underinvestment in College Education?" *American Economic Review*, Vol. 50, Papers and Proceedings (May 1960), pp. 346-54. Becker's estimates are for urban white males. His figures on costs include forgone earnings, and returns are adjusted for differential ability. The decline in the rate of return between 1940 and 1950 is due almost entirely to higher income tax rates.

virtually none of these expenditures to be charged against taxable income.

The diversity of trade schools, business colleges, and similar institutions and the absence of a comprehensive accrediting system for them would complicate the application of administrative checks to assure that the expenses of study at these institutions were legitimate educational expenditures. A difficulty in connection with supplementary training and continuation or refresher courses would be to identify vocational courses. Many extension courses, evening classes, and correspondence courses are almost entirely consumption, dealing with subjects such as hobbies, arts and crafts, current events, and music appreciation. Courses cannot always be distinguished on the basis of their content. A music course, for example, may be vocational training for one person but avocational for another. It seems that the best rule would be to allow current deductions or amortization charges only for expenses relating to education which the taxpayer represents as being primarily vocational or professional and which the authorities consider reasonably related to his occupation or occupational plans. This standard would be harder to apply than the present rule respecting education but little if any more difficult than the rules on a number of other deductions. The amounts involved may be smaller and many may feel that it is better public policy to be liberal with respect to educational expenses than with respect to some of the items now deductible.

The suggestion that no income tax allowance be made for ordinary high school education is debatable. There is considerable overlap between high school courses and the training offered by trade schools and business colleges, on the one hand, and by liberal arts colleges, on the other. For pupils in public high schools, however, the amount that could be written off would be small even if the plan were extended to them. Since most young people now go to high school, the principal effect of an income tax allowance for the personal costs of secondary education would be to encourage attendance at private schools.

It would seem reasonable to limit the deductions or amortization charges to taxable earned income, without insisting that a direct link be shown between the education and the taxpayer's occupation. Although education may make one a better investor, the relation between property income and education is tenuous. If educational expenditures could be written off against property income, persons with inherited wealth might gain an undue advantage. Even with the earned-income limitation, the applicable marginal tax rate, and hence the value of the deduction, would be influenced by the amount of property income received.

The requirement that deductions or amortization charges be taken only against taxable earned income would disqualify housewives when they were not working outside the home.[11] This would not be as unfair as it may seem. Although a housewife's services have economic value and her contribution to the family's economic welfare is enhanced by her education, the value of her services does not enter into taxable income. Hence denial of a writeoff for educational costs that qualify the housewife to perform her services at home more effectively cannot be regarded as discriminatory in the same way as failure to take account of costs of earning a taxable income.

By analogy with physical assets, educational expenditures should be capitalized and written off against taxable income over the period in which they contribute to earnings, ordinarily the whole working life of the person. This approach, however, might be cumbersome for major expenditures and ridiculous for small items. A practical procedure would be to allow persons incurring large educational expenses to capitalize them and amortize them over a fixed period of say ten or twenty years, or the period ending at age sixty-five if that is shorter. Students could be permitted to begin amortization immediately or to postpone it until they are established in their occupations. Taxpayers incurring minor educational expenses might be given the option of capitalizing their outlays or deducting them currently.

Persons who become totally and permanently disabled and the estates of those who die before completing the amortization of their educational expenses might appropriately be allowed to deduct the unamortized balance in the last taxable year and be granted a carryback of net loss and refund of prior-year taxes if the deduction reduced the last-year's income below zero. Similar treatment might

[11] The attribution to a wife of part of the earnings of her husband under a state community property law should be disregarded in determining qualification for the deduction.

be urged for women who withdraw from the labor force after marriage, but this would be questionable since many of these women later resume outside employment.

Consequences of Revised Treatment

Estimated expenditures by college and university students for tuition and fees, books and supplies, and travel amounted to $1.6 billion in 1959-60, almost twice the estimated total in 1953-54 (Table 2). Comparable information is not available concerning trade schools, correspondence schools, and other institutions offering courses that would give rise to amortizable or deductible expenditures.

TABLE 2. Selected Expenditures of College and University Students, 1953-54 to 1959-60[a]

(In millions of dollars)

Item	Academic Years			
	1953–54	1955–56	1957–58	1959–60
Tuition and fees	508	667	873	1,075
Books and supplies	129	152	179	214
Travel[b]	190	219	260	313
Total	827	1,038	1,312	1,602

[a] Estimates for academic years 1953-54, 1955-56, and 1957-58 from Richard Goode, "Educational Expenditures and the Income Tax," in *Economics of Higher Education,* Selma J. Mushkin, ed. (U.S. Department of Health, Education, and Welfare, Office of Education, Bulletin 1962, No. 5; Brookings Institution Reprint No. 64, 1962), p. 294, with the figure for 1957-58 slightly revised; 1959-60 estimate made in the same way as the estimates for earlier years.

[b] Travel between home and a college or university located in another place; excludes local travel between college address and campus and "other" travel.

On the basis of assumptions that seem to me to be reasonable,[12] I estimate that, if the 1959-60 expenditures shown in Table 2 had been currently deductible or amortizable, the ultimate revenue loss would have been about $320 million. This loss would occur only over a period of ten or twenty years if the suggestions made above concerning amortization were adopted. After introduction of the

[12] That 90 percent of eligible expenditures would be deducted and that the average marginal tax rate of those claiming the deductions would be 22 percent; see my paper in *Economics of Higher Education,* pp. 293-95 for an estimate for an earlier year and lower tax rates.

plan, the annual revenue loss would increase year by year as successive groups began to claim deductions or amortization allowances for expenditures made in later years. If students' expenditures remained constant at the 1959-60 level, the annual revenue loss would stabilize at approximately $320 million after ten or twenty years. Educational expenditures, however, can be expected to increase rapidly with the growth of enrollment and with probable increases in tuition charges. On the basis of projected increases in enrollment and tuition charges, but assuming no change in prices of other items, amortizable or deductible expenditures made in 1969-70 may be placed at $3.1 billion or more.[13] The ultimate revenue loss with respect to that year might amount to $0.6 billion, spread over one or two decades. These estimates make no allowance for an increase in taxable income due to a stimulus to education provided by tax revision.

Regardless of its merits as a refinement of income measurement, adoption of a plan for amortization of educational expenditures would not be likely to have a great influence on the total investment in education and on the choice between occupations requiring different amounts of such investment. The role of economic calculations in educational and occupational choices is uncertain, and the tax benefits of an amortization plan would equal only a small proportion of the total personal costs of college and university education. Forgone earnings of college and university students, which are a part of personal costs but which would not be amortizable, are much larger in the aggregate than expenditures for items which might properly be subject to amortization (tuition and fees, books and supplies, and travel). In academic years 1955-56, 1957-58, and 1959-60, the amortizable items accounted for only about 15 to 17 percent of estimated total personal costs of college and university education, exclusive of any additional living expenses of students; the remaining 83 to 85 percent of personal costs consisted of forgone earnings.[14]

[13] For the derivation of the projection, see *ibid.,* p. 294.

[14] See estimates of expenditures for tuition and fees, books and supplies, and travel, Table 2. Theodore W. Schultz estimates forgone earnings of college and university students at $5,821 million in 1955-56 ("Capital Formation by Education," *Journal of Political Economy,* Vol. 68 [December 1960], p. 580). Applying Schultz's method, I estimate forgone earnings at $6,328 million in 1957-58 and $7,939 million in 1959-60. My estimates, however, rely on the Department of

On the assumption of a marginal tax rate of 20 to 25 percent, it appears that the tax saving attributable to amortization of educational expenditures would have equaled only about 3 to 4 percent of total personal costs of college and university education under conditions prevailing recently. This figure should be discounted because of the distribution of the tax saving over a period of years. An item as small as this can hardly be a strong influence on the amount of educational expenditures or on occupational choice.

The tax benefits from amortization would not represent a major fraction of personal costs of even the most expensive kinds of education. Although students' outlays for tuition and fees and other expenses at certain prestige colleges and at professional schools of private universities are much larger than average expenditures for all colleges and university students, forgone earnings are still the largest item of personal education costs.[15]

The most important incentive effects of the amortization plan might be a contribution toward overcoming reluctance to lend and to borrow for educational purposes. With better credit facilities and the amortization plan, much could be said for tuition charges high enough to cover the full marginal costs of instruction in vocational or professional courses, especially in fields such as medicine, where educational costs and earnings are much above the average.[16]

Objections Considered

Two kinds of objection can be raised against the amortization plan—one relating to its claim to be a refinement of the income measure and the other to its efficiency as an aid to education. The first, and more weighty, objection is that part of the educational expenses that would be deductible or amortizable are really consumption rather than costs of earning income. Although this is undoubtedly true, it is also true that part of the expenses are costs.

Labor figure for unemployment rather than on the series compiled by Clarence D. Long, which Schultz uses for 1955-56.

[15] See, for example, my estimates of the cost of medical education, in *Economics of Higher Education*, p. 298.

[16] Milton Friedman, "The Role of Government in Education," in *Economics and the Public Interest*, Robert A. Solo, ed. (New Brunswick, N.J.: Rutgers University Press, 1955), pp. 123-44; William Vickrey, "A Proposal for Student Loans," in *Economics of Higher Education*, pp. 268-80.

I know of no evidence that the consumption component is greater than the cost element, and I believe that it is good social policy to resolve doubts in favor of more liberal writeoffs.

A different kind of objection is that the amortization plan would offer less effective help to education than an immediate deduction for parents of students, as provided in many bills that have been introduced in Congress. However, a deduction for parents would be quite different in principle from the proposed deduction for students and should be evaluated by different standards. A deduction for parents could not be justified as a refinement in the measurement of the parents' earnings. The general rule is that costs, including investment outlays, are properly chargeable against the gross income that they generate, and neither the Internal Revenue Code nor popular opinion treats parents and their adult sons and daughters as a single economic unit.

A deduction for parents of college students would be subject to the objection that it would give the greatest amount of assistance to families with the largest incomes and no assistance to those with very small incomes; it would resemble a federal scholarship that increased as the parents' means increased. The tax value of deductions for students would also increase with the size of their income, but this is not a valid criticism of deductions for genuine costs of earning taxable income.

Proposals to allow parents to deduct tuition payments and other educational expenses call for a subsidy or special encouragement of a socially desirable form of expenditure and should meet the exacting standards that are properly applicable to such subsidies. In particular, the efficiency and equity of the deduction should be compared with that of additional government expenditures to aid education. Although this kind of comparison is not wholly extraneous to the evaluation of the proposal for amortization of educational expenses against students' income, it is less significant. Under the net income tax, there is a presumption in favor of the deduction of costs against the gross income to which they relate, but other deductions require special justification. Few would argue that depreciation allowances for each kind of physical capital should be allowed or denied on the basis of a judgment whether the government could do more to promote capital formation by denying the deduction and spending more for direct government investment or by allowing the deduction and relying on private investors.

Conclusions Regarding Educational Expenditures

Current and deferred deductions for students pursuing education that increases their earning capacity are consistent with income tax principles. A suitable plan would allow a refinement of the income definition, would improve equity, and would have incidental consequences of a desirable character. The particular scheme outlined here is intended only as a basis for discussion; further consideration might indicate that provisions different from those mentioned in the preceding pages should be adopted with respect to eligible expenditures and the amortization period. The essential point, in my opinion, is that the deductions should be limited to actual expenditures and should be available to students rather than parents. Although the adoption of the amortization plan would stimulate educational investment to some extent, this effect probably would not be great because forgone earnings, which would not be amortizable, are the major component of costs of education beyond high school. Nevertheless, the recognition for tax purposes that certain educational expenditures are investments would help establish an important principle that may be overlooked in personal and public decisions.

Depreciation of Earning Capacity?

From time to time, the comment is heard that the income tax, to be fair, should allow individuals to deduct from gross income a depreciation or depletion allowance to reflect the loss of their earning capacity with the passage of time. The argument is that an annual deduction for depreciation or depletion is as appropriate in the measurement of net income from personal effort as in the determination of net profits of business enterprise, since a man's productive life, like that of a machine or mineral deposit, is limited.

Although superficially plausible, this argument rests on a misunderstanding of the nature of depreciation allowances and, if literally followed, would lead to absurd conclusions. Depreciation allowances are intended to cover the cost of capital goods (usually measured on an historical basis but also measurable on the basis of estimated replacement cost). Depreciation is equal to the loss of earning capacity when the cost of a capital good equals the discounted present value of its expected future earnings, the normal situation in competitive equilibrium, but is greater or less than the loss of earning capacity when cost exceeds or falls short of the present value of expected future earnings. If an investor is fortunate enough to own a well-located building or an unusually productive piece of equipment, the depreciation allowances to which he is entitled may well be smaller than the loss of earning capacity during the year. The same is true of cost depletion for mineral deposits. On this basis, allowances would be designed to permit tax-free recovery of the cost of the deposit and working machinery, which would be substantially less than the earning capacity of the property in the case of a lucky discovery. The opportunity of obtaining percentage depletion allowances in excess of costs actually incurred in acquiring and developing mineral properties is widely regarded as an inequitable feature of the U. S. income tax.

In principle, net income from personal effort should be calculated with an allowance for the amortization of the costs of education or other investments in earning capacity, but no deduction should be made for the exhaustion of earning capacity due to innate ability, luck, or opportunities acquired without cost. To grant the latter deduction would be as inequitable as percentage depletion[17] and would be far more costly of revenue. Indeed, an exactly computed allowance would equal or exceed the full amount of earned income, for during the course of a year a person irretrievably loses whatever capacity he has to earn income during that year. Consider, as an illustration, the outlook on January 1 for an employee who faces compulsory retirement on December 31. He can look forward to one year's salary and to the disappearance over the twelve months of his expectation of receiving the salary; if he were allowed to treat the exhaustion of his earning capacity as a cost, the deduction would wipe out the salary—surely an absurd result.

[17] William Vickrey, *Agenda for Progressive Taxation* (New York: Ronald Press, 1947), pp. 50-51.

Travel and Entertainment Expenses

Travel and entertainment expenses, like educational expenditures, include both consumption and cost elements but have received far more liberal treatment under the income tax than educational expenditures. Deductions have been allowed for the costs of transportation, meals, and lodging while away from home on business trips, and business purposes have been broadly construed in deciding whether travel qualifies. Many kinds of expenditure for entertaining customers and clients, actual and prospective, have been ruled deductible, including expenses for meals, attendance at theaters and sporting events, club dues, the operation of hunting lodges and yachts. In the past, many gifts to business associates and customers were deductible, though not classified as taxable income of the recipients; however, deductions for gifts were limited by law in 1962.

Three kinds of tax avoidance have arisen: First, self-employed persons and officers of closely held corporations have deducted from taxable income outlays covering ordinary living expenses, vacations, and entertainment of personal friends. Second, employees have received nontaxable compensation in the form of travel and expense-account perquisites. Third, customers and clients and their employees have received nontaxable income in the form of entertainment and business gifts.

It is especially hard to determine whether travel and entertainment expenses are necessary business or professional costs and reasonable in amount. The question whether a particular trip or entertainment activity is required by business or professional considerations, though subject to some objective tests, is largely a matter of judgment. This is also true of the amount spent. Travel to conventions, entertainment for the purpose of creating goodwill, and other activities that are not intimately associated with ordinary business or professional transactions raise particularly close questions.

Most travel and entertainment expenses are for items that, except for a business or professional purpose, would be classified as personal consumption. Even when the activity serves a business or professional purpose, the self-employed person or employee may receive personal benefits. For persons subject to high tax rates, there is a great advantage in treating personal expenses as deductible costs and hence a temptation to decide close questions in their own favor. The difficulty of auditing a claimed deduction is accentuated by the subjectivity of the distinction between necessary costs and personal consumption. Whether a trip to a resort area or attendance at a musical comedy is a pleasure or a duty depends on individual taste and the novelty of the experience. Luncheons that appear lavish to some may be routine for others.

Successive Commissioners of Internal Revenue in the 1950's expressed concern about improper deductions for travel and entertainment, and special efforts were made to improve taxpayers' records and compliance and to examine these items. However, the administrative efforts were only partly successful, owing to the unique character of travel and entertainment expenses, and by 1961 the Treasury Department had concluded that administrative measures were inadequate to cope with the problem.[18]

In a message to Congress in 1961, the President characterized "widespread abuses" of expense accounts as "a matter of national concern, affecting not only our public revenues, our sense of fairness, and our respect for the tax system, but our moral and business practices as well."[19] Stating that tighter enforcement of existing law would not suffice, he called for legislation. The President's recommendations, as supplemented by the Secretary of the Treasury, included strict limits on the deductibility of entertainment expenses and business gifts, establishment of fixed maximums for deductions for meals and the cost of food and lodging while traveling, and requirements for additional records. The Treasury Department estimated that enactment of the recommendations would increase revenue by "at least $250 million per year."[20]

[18] U. S. Treasury Department, "Study on Entertainment Expenses," in *Revenue Act of 1962*, Hearings before the Senate Finance Committee, 87 Cong. 2 sess. (1962), Pt. 1, pp. 267-351, especially pp. 270-77. This study includes a review of administrative experience, an analysis of court decisions, and a compilation of comments in newspapers and magazines.

[19] *President's Tax Message Along with Principal Statement, Detailed Explanation, and Supporting Exhibits and Documents Submitted by Secretary of the Treasury*, May 3, 1961, House Ways and Means Committee, 87 Cong. 1 sess., H. Doc. 140 (1961), p. 10.

[20] *Ibid.*, pp. 10-11, 38-40.

Congress accepted the substance of the administration's recommendation on business gifts, by including in the Revenue Act of 1962 a provision barring deductions for gifts in excess of $25 a year to any one individual (or husband and wife), but did not go nearly as far as recommended with respect to other items.[21] While the act and regulations issued under it imposed some restrictions on the deduction of entertainment expenses and strengthened requirements for substantiation and recordkeeping, it is not clear that the previous situation was greatly changed.[22]

Administrative measures alone still seem inadequate to prevent improper deductions of travel and entertainment expenses. Additional legislation and regulations are needed, in my opinion. In view of the difficulty of making individual determinations, the most promising approach may be the denial of deductions for whole categories of entertainment expense and the establishment of maximum allowances for meals and lodging, as suggested by the Treasury Department in 1961. A narrower definition of business travel and more stringent provisions for allocating travel costs between business and personal purposes seem justifiable.

Admittedly, such rules would deny the deduction of some genuine costs of earning income and doubtless would seem harsh to many businessmen. However, the extent to which entertainment expenses are actually "ordinary and necessary" expenses for any one firm greatly depends on the practices of its competitors. If the disallowance of deductions curtailed business entertainment generally, the effect on sales might be small. Finally, it should be recognized that the deductibility issue relates to the definition of taxable income, not to the freedom to spend as one pleases, as some comments on past proposals seem to imply. The question is whether certain expenditures shall be met out of after-tax income or shall be deducted from gross income.

Conclusion

Although a net income tax should allow deductions for all costs of earning income, this principle is hard to apply because of the

[21] P.L. 88-272, sec. 4, amending Internal Revenue Code of 1954, sec. 274.
[22] See Jerome R. Hellerstein, *Taxes, Loopholes and Morals* (New York: McGraw-Hill, 1963), pp. 135-43.

difficulty of distinguishing between costs and personal consumption. Among doubtful items, a strong case can be made for more liberal deductions for educational expenditures that increase earning capacity. A general allowance for the depreciation or depletion of earning capacity, however, cannot be justified by analogy with the assessment of business income.

Proposed deductions for commuting expenses and additional household and personal expenses of working wives would be undesirable because the expenditures seem to be predominantly consumption or a reflection of personal preferences in regard to living arrangements. Nevertheless, a small special standard deduction for working wives or for all employed persons might be defensible in recognition of the existence of costs that cannot be accurately measured.

Present rules and procedures with respect to travel and entertainment expenses do not succeed in limiting deductions to necessary costs of earning income. Stricter standards are needed to check tax avoidance.

CHAPTER VI

Exclusions from Taxable Income

WHEN NET INCOME IS TAXED, there is a presumption that all of its components should be taken into account in assessing the tax. This is not to say that all net income should actually be taxed; personal exemptions and certain personal deductions are quite proper. Rather the presumption is that the assessment should begin with a comprehensive definition of income. In technical language, adjusted gross income should be an inclusive aggregate.

The primary justification for a broad definition is the opinion that taxpaying capacity can be better measured by total net income than by the sum of certain of its components. When important items are excluded, statutory tax rates must be higher than would otherwise be required to raise the same amount of revenue. Since the omitted items are not evenly distributed, some people gain while others lose. The effects on true tax rates are not widely appreciated and often are hard to ascertain. Moreover, efforts to obtain nontaxed income lead to changes in the use of resources that may impair economic efficiency.

The exclusion of a particular item from taxable income, nevertheless, is justifiable when it serves an important social or economic purpose that could not be so well served by other means. Exclusions are also appropriate when they obviate excessive costs of administration and compliance.

In this study, an "exclusion" is an item that appears to constitute income as defined by Haig, Simons, and other scholars but which is omitted from adjusted gross income (AGI) as defined in the Internal Revenue Code.[1] The Haig-Simons definition, it will be recalled, equates personal income with the algebraic sum of consumption and changes in net worth.

The exclusions discussed in this chapter are known to be large, although the size of some of them cannot be closely estimated. In 1960, items included in personal income, as estimated by the Office of Business Economics of the Department of Commerce, but not in AGI equaled a little less than one-fifth of AGI.[2] Reliable information is not available on items included in Haig-Simons income but not in personal income or AGI—gifts and inheritances, unrealized capital gains, and consumption treated as business costs.

Gifts and Inheritances

Receipts of gifts and inheritances fall within the Haig-Simons definition of income because they allow the recipients to consume more or to increase their net worth. These items are not included in taxable income in the United States, but special taxes are imposed on persons making certain gifts and on estates of deceased persons. Many states tax inheritances.

The Internal Revenue Code specifically excludes from AGI "the value of property acquired by gift, bequest, devise, or inheritance" (section 102) but does not define these terms. A rigorous definition of gift is hard to draw, since the essential distinction between gifts and other transfers turns on the intention of the

---

[1] Often the omitted items are referred to as tax-exempt income, but it seems preferable to reserve the term "exemption" for the personal exemptions. In deference to long-established usage, however, interest on state and local government securities will be called tax-exempt income.

[2] Estimated total AGI is $349.0 billion; items included in personal income but not in AGI total $70.1 billion (Table A-5); however, $3.7 billion of the latter sum (fiduciary income not distributed to individuals and property income of nonprofit organizations) is not properly includible in individual income.

parties. Generally, transfers made to discharge legal or moral obligations are not regarded as gifts; thus tips, bonuses, severance pay, and other voluntary payments by employers to employees are included in taxable compensation. But business gifts to customers and prospective customers are not regarded as income to the recipients, though their cost is deductible by the giver, subject to a limit of $25 per recipient per year. Doubtful items are classified as gifts or income payments on a case-by-case basis.

Here I wish to consider neither the treatment of business gifts nor the niceties of definition but the treatment of transfers between family members or friends which are generally acknowledged to be gifts.

Faithful to his general definition, Simons insisted that gifts, as well as bequests and inheritances, should be taxed as income to recipients. He also argued that, in general, gifts should be regarded as a form of consumption by donors and hence should not be deductible by them.[3] Only a few writers have followed Simons.[4]

Contrary to Simons' opinion, I believe that there are good reasons for continuing to exclude nonbusiness gifts from AGI. Transfers between living persons—which the word "gift" is intended to mean in the present context—may be regarded in many cases as a sharing of the giver's income rather than the creation of a new income. This characterization seems particularly appropriate for gifts to dependents or other close relatives, which must represent a large part of the total of such transfers. Many transfers of money and other property between close relatives seem essentially similar to benefits enjoyed from living in a common household, which is a clear case of income sharing.

Simons' contention that giving is a form of consumption is not persuasive. It seems more realistic to say that consumption is pooled for members of any one household and that gifts to persons who are not members of the household are voluntary transfers of consumption power. When A gives money to his married daughter,

[3] Henry C. Simons, *Personal Income Taxation* (Chicago: University of Chicago Press, 1938), pp. 125-47.

[4] Among them are Melvin I. White, in his article "Consistent Treatment of Items Excluded and Omitted from the Individual Income Tax Base," House Ways and Means Committee, *Tax Revision Compendium* (1959), Vol. 1, p. 321 and Earl R. Rolph and George F. Break, *Public Finance* (New York: Ronald Press, 1961), pp. 129-30.

who promptly spends it to meet the expenses of her separate household, is total consumption greater than if A had kept the money and spent it himself? Consumption is increased if A obtains a *quid pro quo,* but to ask whether he does is merely to repeat the question. If one concludes that most such cases represent sharing of income, there is still a choice between taxing the income to the donor or to the donee. Taxation to the donor seems preferable because, as Simons recognized, the alternative would undermine the progressivity of the income tax by allowing the rich to split income with relatives and others without transferring the corpus of their wealth.

Even if the principle of treating gifts as income to the recipient were conceded, the problem of administration would be difficult. It would be impracticable to include small items such as most Christmas and birthday presents and ordinary hospitality. Valuation of gifts often would be difficult. Many problems would arise because the recipient of a gift often does not control its form, value, or timing. Consider, for example, the embarrassment of the impecunious young couple who were offered a costly portrait of a rich uncle and who had to choose between rejecting it and paying income tax on its value.

Transfers at death and large, nonrecurrent gifts or systematic transfers made by living persons over a period of time may be distinguished from other gifts. The tax system of the United States, like most other systems, reflects the view that these transfers are best regarded as the division of an income source, rather than the sharing of income. Estate, gift, and inheritance taxes have been specially devised to tax such transfers and seem better suited to the purpose than the income tax.

Selected Government Transfer Payments

An important and rapidly growing group of nontaxable items consists of government transfer payments for public assistance, veterans' benefits, unemployment insurance, old-age retirement, disability, and survivors benefits. These items more than tripled from 1940 to 1950 and tripled again between 1950 and 1960 (Table 3).

TABLE 3. Selected Government Transfer Payments, 1940, 1950, and 1960[a]

(In millions of dollars)

Payment	1940	1950	1960
Public assistance[b]	1,035	2,395	3,804
Veterans' benefits[c]			
Non-service-connected disability or death	182	519	1,334
Service-connected disability or death	242	1,705	2,103
Unemployment insurance benefits[d]	535	1,468	3,025
Old-age retirement benefits[e]	100	828	8,790
Disability benefits[e][f]	31	77	715
Survivorship benefits[e][g]	7	321	2,517
Total	2,132	7,313	22,288

[a] U.S. Bureau of the Census, *Statistical Abstract of the United States, 1961*, p. 284; *ibid.*, 1963, pp. 286, 305.

[b] Old-age assistance, medical assistance to the aged (cash benefits only), aid to dependent children, aid to the blind, aid to the permanently and totally disabled, and general assistance.

[c] Retirement, disability, and monthly survivor benefits paid by the Veterans Administration. Excludes lump-sum survivor benefits and retirement and disability pay by Department of Defense. Allocated between non-service-connected disabilities and deaths and service-connected cases on basis of Veterans Administration budget expenditures in fiscal years 1940 and 1950 and annual rates of benefits being paid June 20, 1960. See *Veterans' Benefits in the United States*, Report of the President's Commission on Veterans' Pensions (1956), Vol. I, p. 108, and *Annual Report of the Administrator of Veterans Affairs*, 1960, p. 212.

[d] State unemployment compensation, railroad unemployment benefits, federal employee program, and veterans' programs.

[e] Payments under Old-Age, Survivors, and Disability Insurance and railroad retirement.

[f] Excludes temporary disability insurance under railroad retirement and state systems.

[g] Monthly benefits; excludes lump-sum payments.

Public Assistance, Veterans' Benefits, and Unemployment Insurance

Public assistance and veterans' benefits arising out of non-service-connected disability or death, which in 1960 made up 23 percent of the transfer payments listed in Table 3, are payable only to persons who demonstrate need by passing a means test. Public assistance for the aged, dependent children, the physically handicapped, and others is provided by state and local governments, with the aid of substantial federal grants, and standards differ among the states. In general, payments are intended to cover no more than the difference between the estimated cost of meeting a minimum budget and the resources available to the individual or family in the form of cash income, goods and services, and assets.[5]

[5] *Public Assistance*, Report of Advisory Council on Public Assistance, S. Doc. 93, 86 Cong. 2 sess. (1960), pp. 58-60.

For non-service-connected veterans' benefits, which are paid by the federal government, tests of need are prescribed by statute and differ according to the law in effect when the recipient qualifies. Under current legislation, the amount payable varies with income according to a sliding scale and also with assets.[6]

Veterans' benefits for service-connected disability or death and unemployment insurance are intended to compensate in part for loss of earnings, but payments are made without regard to the amount of income that beneficiaries may receive from property, their wealth, or the economic situation of other family members.[7] As an adjustment to presumed need, the veterans' benefits are varied with the degree of disability and the number of dependents. Under most state unemployment compensation plans, benefits depend only on the worker's previous wage, subject to a rather low maximum, but in twelve states dependency allowances are paid in addition to the basic benefit.[8]

There has been little public discussion of the merits of excluding from AGI public assistance, veterans' benefits, and unemployment insurance benefits. Perhaps most legislators and others who have considered the subject have felt that the tax immunity is obviously warranted because of the hardships suffered by the recipients and their need for aid. Scholars and official and unofficial groups who have examined the income-maintenance programs have not thought it necessary to defend the tax-free status of the transfer payments but have sometimes allowed for it in appraising their adequacy. Occasionally the assertion has been made that payments would have to be increased if they were subjected to income tax and that the main result would be merely to transfer money from one government account to another.

A few tax experts have argued that all transfer payments should be included in AGI.[9] They concede that the recipients may

[6] Veterans Administration, *Federal Benefits for Veterans and Dependents* (VA Fact Sheet IS-1, January 1962).

[7] An exception to the general rule is that surviving parents of veterans qualify only if their income does not exceed specified levels (*ibid.* p. 34).

[8] U.S. Department of Labor, Bureau of Employment Security, *Comparison of State Unemployment Insurance Laws as of January 1, 1962* (BES No. U-141, 1962), p. 18.

[9] For example, Joseph A. Pechman, "What Would a Comprehensive Individual Income Tax Yield?" in House Ways and Means Committee, *Tax Revision Compendium* (1959), Vol. 1, pp. 260-61; White, *ibid.*, pp. 319-20, 321, 326.

be needy by certain standards but contend that the personal exemptions set general standards for taxpaying ability under the income tax. Under present arrangements, many persons who receive the transfer payments, either throughout the year or for a shorter period, pay less tax than others with the same amount of income from wages or other taxable sources. This, the critics say, is inequitable. They suggest that, if the personal exemptions are considered too low, they should be increased for everyone. The critics argue, furthermore, that, whatever the level of the personal exemptions, exclusions are an inefficient means of helping the needy. The exclusions do not benefit those with the lowest incomes, who would not be liable for tax even if the transfer payments were counted as part of AGI, and are most advantageous to recipients who have enough income from other sources to use up their personal exemptions.

The great merit of this position is that it affords a general view of an area that is often seen only in detail and shows that provisions which may appear quite reasonable in themselves can result in inequities. Its major weakness is the questionable assumption that the personal exemptions under the income tax reflect a deliberate community decision concerning the socially acceptable minimum standard of living, and that the decision embodied in the tax law should override other standards. As shown in Chapter IX, the present income tax exemptions do not correspond closely with the judgments respecting minimum income requirements that are reflected in public assistance programs.

Although I recognize that inequities occur, I believe that the exclusion of all of the veterans' benefits and unemployment insurance benefits as well as public assistance payments is justified at least as long as personal exemptions for the income tax are held at low levels. My view is that, despite exceptions and some abuses, the government transfer payments generally meet needs that merit high priority.

Social Security and Railroad Retirement

Old-age retirement, disability, and survivors benefits are provided for workers and their dependents under Old-Age, Survivors, and Disability Insurance (OASDI) and the Railroad Retirement

System. In 1960, these systems covered 85 percent of all employed persons, including the self-employed; another 7 percent of workers were civilian government employees or members of the armed forces and generally were covered under separate retirement systems.[10] Benefits are financed by contributions of employees, employers, and the self-employed and by interest on accumulated trust funds.

All benefit payments under OASDI and railroad retirement are excluded from AGI. The exclusion of OASDI benefits was granted by administrative ruling in 1941[11] and has never been confirmed by statute, not even when the Internal Revenue Code was rewritten in 1954. Railroad retirement benefits are excluded by the Railroad Retirement Act.[12]

Both OASDI and railroad retirement benefits are paid to eligible persons without demonstration of individual need, and the system is certainly not confined to low income groups. Aside from government employees, the majority of those who are not covered are low-paid domestic and agricultural workers, unpaid family workers, and self-employed farmers. The broad coverage and contributions by workers sharply distinguish OASDI from old-age assistance and other income-maintenance programs.

OASDI and railroad retirement benefits are often spoken of as earned benefits and compared with private pensions and annuities. There are, however, important differences. Workers do not have property rights in social security benefits, and Congress may reduce or withdraw benefits at any time.[13] The benefit formulas give preferential treatment to workers who were already employed when the system was adopted or extended and to low-paid workers. Benefits are paid for dependents and survivors, although contribution rates and primary benefits do not vary with the number of

[10] U.S. Bureau of the Census, *Statistical Abstract of the United States, 1962*, p. 281.

[11] I.T. 3447, 1941-1 C.B. 191, as cited by Commerce Clearing House, *Federal Tax Guide*, 1962 (Chicago) para. 2838.

[12] 50 Stat. 316, 45 U.S.C. 228*l*.

[13] *Flemming* v. *Nestor*, 363 U.S. 603 (1960). This was a five-to-four decision of the Supreme Court; however, it appears that only two of the dissenters (Justices Black and Douglas) disagreed with the majority concerning the nature of the right to social security benefits.

dependents of the covered worker. Self-employed persons receive the same benefits as employed persons, although their contribution rate is in general only three-fourths of the combined rate paid by employees and employers. Finally, benefits are reduced or denied to persons over the retirement age, but under 72, who earn more than a certain amount.

The omission of social insurance benefits from taxable income cannot be justified on the same grounds as the exclusion of the transfer payments discussed in the preceding section. The existence of an inequity has been widely recognized. Congress attempted to mitigate the discrimination by introducing in 1954 a retirement income credit for persons receiving retirement income from sources other than OASDI and railroad retirement, but this is an unsatisfactory solution, and the ending of the exclusion of OASDI and railroad retirement benefits has been suggested.

It would be unfair to include all social insurance benefits in AGI because a substantial part of the benefits represents the return of the earlier contribution of the covered worker, which was included in his AGI when the contribution was made. This situation exists also under private pension plans, and an obvious possibility would be to treat OASDI and railroad retirement like the private plans. The rule for the private plans is that a retired person is allowed to recover his aggregate contributions free of tax over the period of his life expectancy and is required to include in AGI the remainder of benefits.

There would, however, be technical difficulties in applying to social insurance benefits the general rule for private pensions owing to the lack of vested property rights in social insurance benefits and the failure to follow actuarial principles. At the date of retirement, for example, it is not possible to determine the actuarial value of expected future social insurance benefits in the same way that the value of a private pension can be calculated because the social insurance beneficiary may be disqualified in the future if his earnings exceed the allowable minimum and because the amount of his benefits depends on the number of his dependents. It would be possible, though cumbersome, to require each retired person to amortize his individual contributions over his life expectancy.

A more serious objection is that the application of the rule for private pensions would achieve results that seem to conflict with the priorities that govern the benefit formulas. The proportion of benefits to be included in AGI would be highest for those who are most favored under the benefit formulas, that is, for those whose contributions pay for the smallest fraction of their benefits. Thus, the fraction of benefits included in AGI would be relatively large for low-paid workers and those with several dependents and relatively small for high-paid workers and those with no dependents. While these results are defensible from the standpoint of income theory, they are questionable from the viewpoint of probable need.

A more acceptable rule, which has been suggested, would be to require that recipients of pensions from OASDI or railroad retirement insurance include in AGI one-half of benefits. The fraction one-half is plausible because employee and employer contributions are equal, but this justification is superficial because of wide variations in the relation between benefits and contributions and because of interest accruals on the trust funds. The merit of a uniform fraction is its simplicity. Insured persons with high earnings would be treated less favorably for taxation, as well as for benefits, than lower-paid persons; however, under present OASDI benefit formulas and contribution rates scheduled to begin in 1969, a factor of one-half would not require even the most highly paid employees to include more in AGI than they would if social insurance old-age benefits were treated like a private pension but would require certain self-employed persons to do so.[14] The reason for the liberal results with a factor of one-half is the failure to allow for interest accruals. For many years to come, moreover, a factor of one-half would be liberal because retired people will not have been subject to current contribution rates throughout their working lives.

The discrimination in favor of social insurance beneficiaries is much less with respect to disability and survivorship benefits than with respect to old-age retirement benefits. Provisions governing

[14] For an extreme illustration, consider a man who earns $4,800 or more a year as a covered employee for 45 years, pays contributions at the rate now scheduled for 1969 and later years, and retires at age 65 without dependents. Under the private annuity rule, he would be allowed to exclude from AGI 44 percent of retirement benefits. If he had a wife or other dependent when he retired, the exclusion ratio would be lower. A self-employed man with the same earnings record, who retired without dependents at age 65, would have an exclusion ratio of 65 percent.

the taxation of disability and survivorship benefits under private plans are complex, but generally more lenient than those applicable to retirement annuities. Disability benefits in many cases may be excluded from AGI as workmen's compensation or health and accident insurance benefits or as sick pay. Life insurance proceeds, under either group term policies or individual policies, which are paid by reason of the death of the insured are excludable, and part of the death benefits paid under private pension and profit-sharing plans qualify for this exclusion. However, when a retired person dies after his pension has begun and payments are continued to his spouse or other survivor, the receipts are includible in AGI to the same extent that the annuity was during the lifetime of the retired worker.[15]

Unless the provisions governing benefits under private plans are changed, it would seem unfair to apply the one-half-inclusion rule to disability and survivorship benefits under the social insurance programs. Application of the rule only to old-age retirement benefits would have increased AGI by $4.4 billion in 1960; application to disability and survivorship benefits as well would have raised the figure to $6.0 billion. (See Table 3. The figures in the table do not include a comparatively small amount of lump-sum death benefits.)

An alternative approach that has been suggested is to allow employees and the self-employed to deduct from taxable income their social insurance contributions and to include all social insurance benefits in AGI when received. This seems inferior to the present rule and to the alternative of partial inclusion of benefits with no deduction of contributions. The deduction of social insurance contributions would be used as an argument for deductions for contributions under private plans and perhaps for other forms of saving. Since persons over 65 now enjoy extra personal exemptions and are likely to be subject to lower marginal tax rates after retirement than during their working years, the inclusion of all benefits in AGI would not make up for the deduction of contributions. Some beneficiaries, nevertheless, might find it inconvenient to be required to include the full amount received in AGI after retirement.

If a satisfactory method of taxing OASDI and railroad retire-

---

[15] Treasury Regulations, secs. 1.72-2, 1.402(a)-1.

ment benefits were adopted, elimination of the retirement income credit, which was adopted in 1954 to alleviate discrimination against recipients of taxable pensions, would be fully justified. The credit is a complex measure which has partly accomplished its purpose, but it does not touch the broader inequities in the treatment of retired persons compared with others.

Workmen's Compensation, Health Insurance, and Sick Pay

Also excluded from AGI are several kinds of payments received as compensation for loss of income because of sickness or injury. These items are (1) workmen's compensation benefits, which arise from work-related injuries; (2) amounts received by an individual under an accident or health insurance policy that he himself purchased; (3) amounts received by an employee under an accident or health insurance plan to the extent that the plan is supported by employee contributions; and (4) certain "sick pay" under employer-financed plans. Statistics on these items appear in Table 4.

Workmen's compensation payments are stipulated by law

TABLE 4. Selected Health and Welfare Benefits, 1950 and 1960

(In millions of dollars)

Benefit	1950	1960
Workmen's compensation[a]		
Disability	360	748
Survivor	55	105
Cash sickness benefits under group and public plans[b] [c]	294	817
Individual health insurance[b] [d]	153	386
Excludable sick pay[e]	—	675
Total[f]	862	2,731

[a] U.S. Bureau of the Census, *Statistical Abstract of the United States, 1963*, p. 305. Excludes medical and hospitalization payments.

[b] Benefits due to nonoccupational sickness and injury, as estimated by Alfred M. Skolnik, "Income-Loss Protection Against Short-Term Sickness, 1948-61," *Social Security Bulletin*, January 1963, pp. 12, 17.

[c] Employer plans, union-management trust funds, trade-union, and mutual benefit plans, state plans in four states, and railroad sickness benefits.

[d] Income-maintenance payments only; does not include reimbursement of medical expenses.

[e] U.S. Treasury Department, *Statistics of Income, Individual Income Tax Returns, 1960*, p. 4.

[f] There is an unknown amount of double-counting in the total since part of cash sickness benefits under group plans and public plans qualifies as excludable sick pay.

rather than the choice of the employer. Sick pay is much broader. It consists of amounts received from an employer as wages or payments in lieu of wages while absent from work because of any injury or illness. The part of sick pay that is excludable from AGI is determined by rather complex rules. If sick pay is more than 75 percent of regular wages, no exclusion is allowed for the first 30 days of absence from work; thereafter, sick pay up to $100 a week may be excluded. If, however, sick pay is less than 75 percent of regular wages, the employee may exclude up to $75 a week, from the first day of absence if he is hospitalized for at least 1 day, or after 7 days of absence if he is not hospitalized. After 30 days the ceiling rises to $100 a week. As noted above, the sick-pay exclusion applies to disability pensions as well as to payments received during short-term illness.

The present sick-pay provisions were enacted in 1964 as amendments of an exclusion originally adopted in 1954. Prior to the 1964 legislation, the exclusion applied to wage-continuation payments up to $100 a week in all cases of absence from work involving personal injury or hospitalization and in other cases after the first seven days. President Kennedy, terming the exclusion "clearly unjustifiable," recommended its withdrawal in his 1963 tax message.[16] Congress declined to repeal the exclusion but curtailed it.

Even in its more limited form, the sick-pay exclusion seems questionable. Generally, those who receive sick pay are better protected against economic loss due to temporary disability than those who are not covered by such plans. While the 1964 amendments greatly reduced the number of persons who will be able to escape tax on wage-continuation payments equal to the full amount of their regular wages, this will still be possible and will produce the anomalous result of allowing a person more take-home pay while he is absent from work than he receives when he is working. In evaluating the sick-pay exclusion, one should not lose sight of savings of work-related expenses realized by persons who are absent from work and the personal deduction for medical expenses.

[16] *President's 1963 Tax Message Along with Principal Statement, Technical Explanation, and Supporting Exhibits and Documents Submitted by Secretary of the Treasury,* House Ways and Means Committee, Committee Print, Feb. 6, 1963, p. 16.

Cash benefits under health insurance are excluded from AGI only when they are paid for by the beneficiaries. It would be unfair to include the benefits in AGI unless a deduction were allowed for premium payment. While that approach has a certain appeal,[17] it would have the questionable result of increasing insured persons' income tax liability in years in which they were sick or injured relative to tax in other years. The total tax base would be decreased, since aggregate insurance benefits fall short of premiums by a wide margin representing company expenses, taxes, and profits.[18]

Private and Government-Employee Retirement Plans

The treatment of private pension plans and plans for civilian government employees and career military personnel raises a question of income timing. The subject is considered here because it is related to the taxation of social insurance benefits and because timing of taxable income may be regarded as a matter of exclusion or inclusion in AGI in any one year.

Under most of the plans, employees are not taxable until they receive pensions or other benefits. Then they include in AGI all of the pension except the part that represents the return of any contribution that they have made toward the financing. Thus employer contributions and interest earned on pension reserves are taxable to beneficiaries when received as retirement income rather than when added to pension funds. Benefits from plans financed jointly by employers and employees are divided between the excludable contribution of the employee and the taxable remainder on the basis of actuarial calculations which allow recovery of the employee's contribution over the period of his life expectancy.[19]

[17] William Vickrey, *Agenda for Progressive Taxation* (New York: Ronald Press, 1947), p. 63.

[18] In the decade 1952-61, premiums on individual income-replacement insurance policies exceeded benefit payments by $3.3 billion or 110 percent (Alfred M. Skolnik, "Income-Loss Protection Against Short-Term Sickness," *Social Security Bulletin*, January 1963, p. 12).

[19] If the amount that the retired employee will receive during the first three years in which payments are made exceeds his total contribution, the life-expectancy rule does not apply; in that case, all receipts are excludable until the full amount of the employee's contribution is recovered, and thereafter all re-

TABLE 5. Public and Private Retirement Benefits and Contributions Under Private Plans, 1940, 1950, and 1960[a]

(In millions of dollars)

Item	1940	1950	1960
Benefits			
Private plans[b]	140	370	1,710
Federal government plans			
Civilian[c]	116	485	1,582
Military[d]	...	219	693
State and local government plans[c]	129	300	1,015
Total benefits	385	1,374	5,000
Contributions			
Private plans			
Employer	180	1,750	4,490
Employee	130	330	770

[a] Includes retirement, disability, and survivor benefit plans. All statistics except those for military retirement pay are from U.S. Bureau of the Census, *Statistical Abstract of the United States, 1963*, pp. 286, 295.

[b] Includes refunds to employees and their survivors and lump-sums under deferred profit-sharing plans.

[c] Excludes lump-sum payments.

[d] For fiscal years ended June 30; payments by Department of Defense in 1960 and by Army, Navy, Air Force, and Marine Corps in 1950; information not available for 1940; excludes pensions paid by Veterans Administration. Sources: 1950, *Retirement Policy for Federal Personnel*, Report of Committee on Retirement Policy for Federal Personnel, S. Doc. 89, 83 Cong. 2 sess. (1954), Pt. 2, pp. 66-67; 1960, *Budget of the United States Government for the Fiscal Year Ending June 30, 1962*, Appendix, p. 498.

If a pension or profit-sharing plan covers a large proportion of employees, is nondiscriminatory, and meets certain other requirements, it is a "qualified" plan, which is exempt from income tax on the return earned on its reserves. Employers may deduct from taxable income their contributions to qualified plans but can deduct contributions to other plans only if employees' benefit rights are nonforfeitable (fully "vested") at the time of the contribution. Since employees having vested rights under a nonqualified plan are currently taxable on their employer's contributions, nonqualified plans have tax disadvantages for either the employer or employees.

Benefit payments under the private plans and public-employee plans grew at the rapid rate of 13.8 percent a year over the decade 1950 to 1960 but were still much smaller than social insurance benefits in 1960 (Tables 3 and 5). Partly because the plans were

---

ceipts are includible in AGI. In 1960, one-third of all persons reporting income from pensions and annuities used the three-year rule (U.S. Treasury Department, *Statistics of Income, Individual Income Tax Returns, 1960*, p. 33).

expanding so rapidly, employer contributions to private pension funds were much greater than current benefits in both 1950 and 1960.

Those who question the present rule about the timing of income from pension and profit-sharing plans argue that the plans provide supplementary compensation for employees that should be reflected in AGI before the date of retirement. Everyone would agree that if an employer deposited part of an employee's salary to his credit in a savings account, where it remained at interest until the employee retired, this would not be a sufficient reason for omitting that part of the salary from current taxable income. The situation is not so simple when the deposits are placed with a trustee or insurance company pursuant to a formal retirement plan, but some of these plans are fundamentally similar to the savings-account scheme. In other plans, the similarity is less close.

Postponement of taxation is advantageous to employees in two ways. First, deferment allows a substantial interest advantage. To illustrate, suppose that $100 is deposited each year in a fund earning 4 percent, compounded annually. At the end of forty years, the amount accumulated will be $9,503. If this sum is then taxed at the rate of 25 percent, it will be reduced to $7,127. Alternatively, suppose that a 25 percent tax is deducted annually from the deposit and the interest earnings. Then the accumulated amount after forty years will total only $5,650, which is one-fifth less than the net amount available to the beneficiary when tax is deferred. Second, employees are likely to have smaller incomes after they retire than while they are working, and hence to be subject to a lower marginal tax rate, provided the schedule remains unchanged.

The tax advantages of private pension plans are widely appreciated, not only by high-paid executives but also by labor unions. Tax considerations may well have had something to do with the rapid growth of such plans. Self-employed persons long contended that they were being discriminated against, and in 1962 they finally persuaded Congress to extend to them some of the deferment privileges enjoyed by those who are covered by pension plans.

A possible alternative to the present rules would be to require that employees include in AGI employer contributions on their behalf and interest earned on pension reserves and to allow them to exclude pensions received. This seems fair and feasible where employees acquire vested rights to future benefits under fully funded plans but much less reasonable where rights are not vested, which is the more usual situation. Under a nonvested plan, an employee may receive no benefits if he leaves the firm before retirement. Although the expectation of benefits under a nonvested plan is worth something, it cannot be valued with the precision that is usually demanded for tax purposes.

A requirement that employees currently report employer contributions and interest accruals for pension plans providing vested rights, but not for other plans, might lead to arbitrary distinctions in marginal cases. It might also discourage the introduction of vesting provisions. This would be an undesirable side effect inasmuch as nonvested pension plans reduce labor mobility. An offsetting tax pressure in favor of vesting might be created by allowing employers to deduct their contributions to pension funds only when rights are vested in employees and by granting tax-exempt status only to pension trusts that provide for vesting. The adoption of such a rule would be opposed by many employers because vested plans are more expensive than nonvested plans and because employers often consider vesting disadvantageous for other reasons. It would be unfortunate if employers reacted by eliminating funding of retirement plans or by abolishing them.

Despite the shortcomings of the present method of taxing pensions, no clear lines of reform appear. On balance, the evils of tax postponement under the present system seem more tolerable than the likely results of an attempt to institute current taxation of employer contributions and accrued interest. A lesser revision that is feasible and desirable is the elimination of a provision offering preferential long-term capital gains tax rates to lump-sum withdrawals from retirement plans and profit-sharing plans. The legitimate concern about the tax consequences of bunching of income in a single year can be satisfied by a more equitable averaging method (see Chapter IX).

Self-Employed Individuals Tax Retirement Act

The approval of the Self-Employed Individuals Tax Retirement Act of 1962 (P.L. 87-792) came after legislation had been pending in Congress for ten years. The act extends to self-employed persons some of the tax-postponement privileges that had previously been available only to salary and wage earners. Self-employed persons are allowed to set up retirement plans and to deduct from current income a portion of their contributions to the plans. The deducted contributions and accumulated interest are includible in AGI when later received as distributions from the retirement plan.

Almost all self-employed business or professional individuals and partners are eligible, provided they perform personal services. Any full-time employees with three years or more of service must also be covered on a nondiscriminatory basis and in general contributions made on their behalf must be vested in them.

The limit on contributions of a self-employed person on his own behalf is $2,500 a year or 10 percent of earned income, whichever is less. Only one-half of the contribution can be deducted. Contributions must be set aside in a separate fund, which cannot be intermingled with other resources of the self-employed person; however, he may control the investment of the fund. Benefit payments may not begin before age 59½, except in cases of disability or death, or later than age 70½. Penalties are prescribed for premature distributions. A person is not required to retire in order to draw benefits. Benefits received in the form of annuities are subject to the general rules applicable to annuities or pensions, which in this case allow the beneficiary to recover tax-free the portion of his contributions which he did not previously deduct from taxable income and which require him to include in AGI benefits representing previously deducted contributions and earnings of the fund. When a distribution is made in a lump-sum in a single year, the income tax is limited to five times the increase in liability resulting from including one-fifth of the distribution in AGI in the year in which it occurs.

The 1962 act is much narrower than earlier proposals. These proposals had been criticized as a precedent for the questionable practice of excluding selected kinds of saving from taxable income. That efforts to obtain the legislation finally succeeded was due to an energetic campaign and to the recognition by officials and legislators that there was indefensible discrimination against self-employed persons. Moreover, the discrimination applied erratically. Business proprietors often qualified for pension plans by incorporating their businesses and putting themselves on salaries, but professional persons often were barred from this course of action because they could not incorporate under state laws. Many state laws were amended to allow professional persons to incorporate so that they could set up pension plans qualifying under the old law.

The 1962 act is a makeshift but defensible as a means of lessening discrimination. The legislation does not go nearly as far as its advocates wished, and requests for liberalization must be expected. The subject should be re-examined after there has been more experience with the act. In considering revisions, a cautious attitude is appropriate to avoid excessive favors to the self-employed. They enjoy advantages that may offset any remaining discrimination against them with respect to retirement income. In fact, many self-employed persons never retire; in these cases, the so-called retirement plans will be simply devices for postponing taxes. The same may be true of employer-financed pension and profit-sharing plans, since the law does not limit their benefits to persons who have actually retired. It appears, however, that in practice the benefits are usually paid after retirement.

Fringe Benefits

Many employees receive fringe benefits that are economically equivalent to supplementary compensation, such as life insurance coverage and hospitalization and medical insurance. They also may benefit from amenities such as airconditioning and recorded music, which are generally considered incidental conditions of employment, rather than compensation, even when designed to attract workers. Less easily classified are items such as discounts on merchandise, meals and living quarters provided free or at less than market prices, parking spaces, company recreational facilities, liberal travel and expense allowances, moving expenses, special clothing, and insurance against occupational hazards. Other items that are often called fringe benefits, such as paid vacation and holidays and bonuses, raise no special tax problem because for tax purposes they are treated as salaries and wages.

Employer contributions for life and accident insurance and hospitalization, surgical, and medical expense plans were approximately $3.3 billion in 1960.[20] Rough calculations suggest that in 1960 the value of employee discounts was of the order of $120 million and the value of meals furnished by employers in private industry about $490 million.[21]

The general rule now is that an employee receives income for tax purposes when his employer pays any of his "personal expenses." But there are major exceptions to this rule, and it seems likely that most fringe benefits are not included in AGI.[22] Specifically excluded from AGI are premiums paid by employers under group term life insurance policies for individual coverage up to $50,000, premiums for medical and hospitalization insurance, the value of meals and lodging furnished on the business premises for the convenience of the employer, and reimbursement of moving expenses. (Group term life insurance has no current cash surrender value; employees are taxable on employer payments of premiums of other life insurance when the proceeds of the policy are payable to the employee's estate or beneficiary.) Also excluded in practice are "courtesy" discounts when relatively small in amount and the value of most of the services under employee recreation and welfare plans.

The tax-free status of fringe benefits is an encouragement to this form of compensation. Employees and employers may be led to prefer a form of compensation and a consumption pattern different from those which they would choose if the income tax applied equally to all compensation. For example, an employee who is subject to a 20 percent marginal rate of income tax would rationally prefer tax-free insurance coverage worth only $81 to him to an

[20] Estimated at 57 percent of total contributions of $5,788 million (Alfred M. Skolnik, "Employee-Benefit Plans, 1954-60," *Social Security Bulletin*, April 1962, p. 9), which is Skolnik's estimate of the percentage of the cost of health and welfare plans, including sick leave, borne by employers in 1959 ("Trends in Employee-Benefit Plans, 1954-59: Part I," *Social Security Bulletin*, April 1961 [reprint, p. 8]).

[21] The estimates were derived by applying to estimated employer expenditures for insurance plans ($3.3 billion) the ratios of payroll costs for discounts and meals to payroll costs for the insurance plans as shown in Chamber of Commerce of the United States, *Fringe Benefits, 1961* (Washington, 1962), p. 9.

[22] For critical reviews and suggestions, see Joseph H. Guttentag, E. Deane Leonard, and William Y. Rodewald, "Federal Income Taxation of Fringe Benefits: A Specific Proposal," *National Tax Journal*, Vol. 6 (September 1953), pp. 250-72, and Hugh H. Macaulay, Jr., *Fringe Benefits and Their Federal Tax Treatment* (New York: Columbia University Press, 1959).

additional $100 of taxable salary. Economists classify such modifications of individual preferences as distortions which result in a loss of economic efficiency, unless the tax-induced change reflects an overriding social preference.

Support for the exclusion of employer contributions for group life insurance and for hospitalization and medical insurance can be mustered on the basis of the public interest in the promotion of family security and good health. But is it clear that the insurance schemes merit just the degree of encouragement that is provided by the exclusion? Protection can be provided by individual insurance as well as group insurance and by other means. The health insurance plans rarely cover the cost of ordinary preventive care, much less the cost of good nutrition and other items that contribute to health. The group plans often do not cover retired workers and, of course, do not extend to the self-employed.

In my judgment, the advantages of economic neutrality and tax equity are great enough to justify the termination of the exclusion of employer contributions for life insurance coverage and insurance against hospital and medical expenses. The best general rule, in my opinion, would be to include the contributions in current taxable salaries and wages but to continue to exclude benefit payments from employees' AGI. While compliance would be somewhat inconvenient for employers, they could allocate their contributions among employees on the basis of standard tables (similar to those provided by the Revenue Act of 1964 for life insurance policies of more than $50,000). When the amount allocable to an individual fell below a certain minimum, it might be appropriate to continue the exclusion.[23]

The inclusion in AGI of fringe benefits in the form of discounts on purchases and participation in welfare and recreation programs would involve acute difficulties of valuation and verification of compliance. Probably not much can be done to improve the present situation, in which the Internal Revenue Service has the right to assess tax when the amounts involved are important but does not attempt to take account of minor sums.

With respect to meals and lodging the convenience-of-the-employer and business-premises tests do not adequately distin-

[23] It appears that the amounts to be allocated to individual employees would be small in most cases but not trivial. For statistics, see Skolnik, *Social Security Bulletin*, April 1962, p. 11.

guish compensation from incidental conditions of employment.[24] Meals and lodging, like incidental conditions of employment, affect the attractiveness of a job; however, the meals and lodging seem to be a more direct substitute for ordinary compensation because they consist of goods and services that employees would often buy for themselves and because the consumption of individual employees can be measured, which is not generally true of incidental conditions of employment. Where the value of meals and lodging is great enough to be significant, it could appropriately be included in AGI, conservatively appraised to allow for the lack of free choice. Any extra costs due to a remote location or other unusual conditions would be omitted on the grounds that they are special costs of employment. It seems expedient to continue to overlook minor amounts of compensation in the form of subsidized meals in company cafeterias and dining rooms.

Work clothes provided by employers ordinarily involve elements of compensation—because they relieve employees of expenses even when the clothes are used only on the job—but also substitute for costs that would be deductible by the employees if incurred by them. The amounts of compensation appear to be small enough in most cases to justify overlooking them for income tax purposes.

Imputed Rent of Owner-Occupied Dwellings

A person who resides in his own house or apartment obtains an income in the form of consumer services. This imputed return is classified as personal income in national income and product accounts, and individuals often recognize that homeownership is an alternative to other income-yielding investments.[25]

Homeowners are often puzzled by economists' assertions that they derive an income from their houses; these owners look on their houses as a source of expense rather than income. They are

[24] When the statutory tests are met, the classification of meals as compensation, under an employment contract or a statute fixing the terms of employment, does not bar the exclusion of their value from the employee's gross income. See Treasury Regulations, sec. 1.119-1(a).

[25] For a more detailed treatment, see my paper "Imputed Rent of Owner-Occupied Dwellings Under the Income Tax," *Journal of Finance,* Vol. 15 (December 1960), pp. 504-30 (Brookings Institution Reprint No. 50, 1961).

right in insisting that homeownership entails expenses, but they neglect that part of their shelter costs are covered by the imputed return on their equity. A homeowner is an investor who takes his return in the form of services. If he wishes to do so, he can convert his imputed return to a cash return by moving and letting his house.

Imputed rent of owner-occupied dwellings is taxable in a number of countries, but is not included in AGI in the United States. The United Kingdom taxed imputed rent from the beginning of the income tax early in the nineteenth century but allowed the provision to become rather ineffective after World War II, owing to obsolete assessments, and dropped it in 1963.[26]

Under a net income tax, the item to be included in income would be imputed net rent, defined as gross rental value minus necessary expenses of ownership. The expenses consist of interest on mortgage debt, property taxes, depreciation, repairs and maintenance, and casualty insurance. Homeowners may now deduct interest and taxes, even though imputed rent is not included in AGI. The taxation of imputed net rent, therefore, would involve an addition to taxable income equal to gross rent minus expenses other than interest and taxes. This increase in the tax base would equal the sum of imputed net rent and the personal deductions now allowed for mortgage interest and property taxes on owner-occupied dwellings. Merely to increase the tax base by the amount of net rent would imply double deductions for interest and property taxes, one set in the form of the personal deductions now granted and a second set in the computation of net rent.

Estimates of imputed net rent, mortgage interest, and property taxes in selected years appear in Table 6. These items have been growing rapidly. In the 1950's, the annual rate of increase of the total was 9.7 percent, while the growth rate for total personal consumption was 5.3 percent.

[26] In April 1962, the then Chancellor of the Exchequer, Selwyn Lloyd, had announced the intention of making the change, mentioning the great increase in tax that would occur when pending revaluations of properties were completed and terming imputed rent "notional income." *The Economist* (London) characterized Mr. Lloyd's statement as "near double talk" (April 14, 1962, p. 168). In 1955, the Royal Commission on the Taxation of Profits and Income had supported the continued taxation of imputed rent. See its *Final Report,* Cmd. 9474 (London, 1955), pp. 249-51.

TABLE 6. Net Rent, Mortgage Interest, and Property Taxes on Owner-Occupied Dwellings, 1929, 1940, 1950, and 1960[a]

(In billions of dollars)

Item	1929	1940	1950	1960
Net rent	2.7	1.5	3.8	6.8
Mortgage interest	1.0	0.7	1.7	6.6
Property taxes	1.0	0.9	2.3	5.9
Total	4.7	3.1	7.8	19.3

Sources: Net rent and property taxes, estimates of Office of Business Economics, U.S. Department of Commerce, *National Income* (1954), pp. 214-15; *U.S. National Income and Output* (1958), p. 229; *Survey of Current Business,* July 1963, p. 39. Mortgage interest, estimates based on H. D. Osborne, "Rental Income and Outlay in the United States, 1929-52," *Survey of Current Business,* June 1953, p. 22; materials in Department of Commerce files; and my supplementary estimates.
a. Includes farm and nonfarm dwellings.

The omission of imputed net rent from AGI and the personal deductions for mortgage interest and property taxes discriminate in favor of homeowners compared with renters and with other investors. Homeowners obtain a tax-free return on their investment and at the same time are allowed to deduct important items of housing costs that tenants also pay as part of their contract rent but without obtaining a tax deduction.

The size of the discrimination is substantial. In recent years, net rent, mortgage interest, and property taxes have amounted to about two-thirds of the gross rental value of owner-occupied dwellings. Under the 1954-63 tax rates, the typical income tax payer who was a homeowner realized federal income tax savings which offset about 15 percent of his annual housing costs. Under the rates that will be effective in 1965, the saving will be about 12 percent. The saving rises with income and tax rates. At the $50,000 income level, it will equal almost one-third of housing costs in 1965.[27]

My estimates of the distribution of imputed net rent, mortgage interest, and property taxes among income classes in 1958 are

[27] The weighted average marginal rate under the 1954-63 schedule was approximately 23 percent on taxable income and is estimated at 18.5 percent under the 1965 schedule. For a married couple with $50,000 of AGI and the amount of personal deductions characteristic of that income level, the marginal rate will be about 48 percent under the 1965 schedule. The figures given in the text were obtained by multiplying 67 percent (the excluded and deducted portion of average shelter costs of owner-occupants) by the marginal tax rates.

TABLE 7. Net Rent, Mortgage Interest, and Property Taxes on Owner-Occupied Nonfarm Dwellings, by Income Classes, 1958[a]

	Percentage Distribution			Percent of Money Income[b]	
Family Money Income	Net Rent	Interest and Taxes	Net Rent, Interest, and Taxes	Net Rent	Interest and Taxes
Under $2,000	12	4	7	7	4
$2,000–$2,999	8	4	5	3	2
3,000– 3,999	9	5	7	3	3
4,000– 4,999	9	8	8	2	3
5,000– 5,999	11	14	13	2	4
6,000– 7,499	13	17	15	2	4
7,500– 9,999	16	24	21	2	4
10,000 and over	23	24	24	2	3
All classes	100	100	100	2	3

ª Derived from data from 1959 Survey of Consumer Finances and national income estimates. For details see Richard Goode, "Imputed Rent of Owner-Occupied Dwellings Under the Income Tax," *Journal of Finance*, Vol. 15 (December 1960), pp. 526-30 (Brookings Institution Reprint No. 50, 1961).
ᵇ Percent of money income of all nonfarm families in income class.

summarized in Table 7. Data are not available for later years. These estimates indicate that for families with money incomes above $2,000, imputed net rent plus mortgage interest and property taxes equaled about 5 to 6 percent of money income in each income class. If a breakdown were available above the $10,000 income level, perhaps the impression of rough proportionality would not be confirmed. The estimates for the lowest income class may be unrepresentative, because this class probably includes a high proportion of persons whose income is temporarily low and of retired persons who bought their houses when their money income was higher.[28]

If imputed net rent had been taxable in 1958, I estimate that the federal income tax liability of owner-occupants of nonfarm dwellings would have been increased by roughly $3.2 billion, including $1.2 billion of tax on imputed net rent proper and $2.0 billion of tax from eliminating the personal deductions for mort-

[28] Margaret G. Reid finds statistical evidence that housing expenditures rise about 1.5 to 2.0 times as fast as normal income, which she defines as income exclusive of positive or negative transitory items. See *Housing and Income* (Chicago: University of Chicago Press, 1962), p. 376 *et passim*.

gage interest and property taxes on the dwellings. The corresponding estimates for 1960 are about $3.8 billion, $1.2 billion, and
$2.6 billion.[29] With allowance for both the reduction in tax rates
provided by the Revenue Act of 1964 and the continued growth
of the exclusion and deductions, the effect on tax liability may be
about the same in the mid-1960's as in 1960. (Information is not
available on owner-occupied farm dwellings; however, these units
account for only about 5 percent of total imputed rent and inclusion of them would not appreciably raise the estimates.)

The information on imputed net rent in Table 7 suggests that
the ending of the exclusion and associated deductions would not
greatly alter the progressivity of the income tax. This finding is
at variance with the common opinion that the ratio of rental value
to income diminishes as income rises. As noted above, the findings
might be modified if the group with incomes above $10,000 could
be subdivided.

The tax saving due to the exclusion and deductions may be
viewed as a reduction in prices of housing services. The influence
on consumption of housing services depends on the elasticity of
demand with respect to price. The available evidence suggests that
price elasticity is on the order of -1,[30] which means that a small
reduction in price will be accompanied by an increase of consumption in the same proportion, leaving total expenditures for
housing services unchanged. If this is correct, the income tax advantages enjoyed by homeowners were responsible for additional
consumption of housing services of about $3.2 billion in 1958
and about $3.8 billion in 1960, or about 8½ to 9 percent of the
total housing consumption of homeowners and tenants.[31]

The above estimates relate to aggregates or averages. Pre-

[29] For the derivation of the 1958 estimates, see my paper in the *Journal of
Finance*, Vol. 15, pp. 527-30. The 1960 estimates were derived by applying the
1958 weighted average marginal rates for imputed net rent, for property taxes,
and for mortgage interest separately to the 1960 totals for these items, which
were obtained in the same manner as the 1958 totals. The estimates do not allow
for the use of the standard deduction by some homeowners; however, the standard deduction presumably would be reduced if itemized deductions were curtailed.

[30] Richard F. Muth, "The Demand for Non-Farm Housing," in *The Demand
for Durable Goods*, Arnold C. Harberger, ed. (Chicago: University of Chicago
Press, 1960), pp. 29-96; Reid, *Housing and Income*, p. 381.

[31] Derived from *Survey of Current Business*, July 1963, p. 20.

sumably the effect would be greater for higher-priced units of the kind which are likely to be occupied by persons who gain most from the exclusion and personal deductions.

Although its influence cannot be isolated, the favorable income tax treatment accorded to homeowners has probably been one of the factors responsible for the rapid increase in consumer expenditures for housing in the postwar period. In current prices, housing expenditures (space rental value of tenant-occupied and owner-occupied dwellings) were still a smaller fraction of total personal consumption in 1960 than in 1929 and prior years, but, in constant prices, housing expenditures represent a much larger share of total consumption than in 1929. Estimates of housing expenditures as percentages of total private consumption are shown in the accompanying table.[32] The constant price estimates are suspect,

Year	Current Prices	Constant (1954) Prices
1909	19.3%	. . .
1919	13.3	. . .
1929	14.4	10.0%
1950	10.9	11.4
1960	12.8	12.7

in view of the surprisingly small increase shown by the implicit price deflator for housing expenditures from 1929 to 1960.[33]

The income tax probably has more influence on the choice between homeowning and renting than on the total amount of housing services consumed. The price differential that will induce a shift from renting to owning is doubtless much smaller than that required to divert expenditure from other goods and services to

[32] The estimates for 1909 and 1919 are from J. Frederick Dewhurst and Associates, *America's Needs and Resources* (New York: Twentieth Century Fund, 1955), p. 206; the figures for later years are derived from estimates of the Office of Business Economics, U.S. Department of Commerce: *U.S. Income and Output* (1958) and *Survey of Current Business*, July 1963. The constant-price estimate given for 1929 (*U.S. Income and Output*, p. 5) is in 1957 prices.

[33] The increase in the OBE implicit price deflator from 1929 to 1960 is only about 25 percent for housing expenditures but is 177 percent for residential nonfarm construction (*U.S. Income and Output*, pp. 5, 220-21, 228, and *Survey of Current Business*, July 1963).

housing. There has been a sharp increase in homeownership in the postwar years. In 1960, 62 percent of all dwelling units were owner-occupied, compared with 44 percent in 1940.[34] Although the 1940 ratio may have been abnormally low owing to the great depression, a trend toward homeownership appears.

The preferential treatment of investment in owner-occupied dwellings greatly increases the attractiveness of homeownership relative to other investment. In 1958, the estimated net rate of return on owners' equity in nonfarm owner-occupied dwellings was only about 2.7 percent but, with allowance for the federal income tax saving attributable to the exclusion of imputed net rent from taxable income and the personal deductions for mortgage interest and property taxes, the rate of return was equivalent to a taxable yield of 4.1 percent. The average yield on common stocks was 4.0 percent in 1958.[35]

Nontax factors must have been important in the postwar growth of homeownership. Among these are the movement of population to the suburbs, the rise in real income, and the gains realized by debtors in a period of inflation.

There is no evidence that the present income tax treatment of owner-occupied houses was deliberately devised to promote housing and homeownership. The personal deductions for interest and tax payments are general allowances. Nor does the omission of imputed rent indicate special concern for housing, since other imputed income is also omitted.

In retrospect, however, the present treatment has been sup-

[34] U.S. Bureau of the Census, *Statistical Abstract of the United States, 1962*, p. 758.

[35] Based on: (1) estimates of net rent of owner-occupied dwellings by Office of Business Economics, U.S. Department of Commerce, *Survey of Current Business*, July 1962, p. 34 (assuming that nonfarm units accounted for 95 percent of the total); (2) my estimates of federal income tax saving; (3) estimates of owners' equity in owner-occupied units in one-to-four-family nonfarm houses (average of beginning and end of year) derived from Raymond W. Goldsmith and Robert E. Lipsey, *Studies in the National Balance Sheet of the United States* (Princeton, N.J.: Princeton University Press for National Bureau of Economic Research, 1963), Vol. I, pp. 261, 400; and (4) dividend yield of common stocks included in Standard & Poor's index (*Economic Report of the President, January 1964*, p 288). In calculating item 3, I allocated mortgages on owner-occupied nonfarm houses between owner-occupied units and rental units in these structures in proportion to the respective values of the two kinds of unit.

ported as a means of fostering homeownership and the civic virtues associated with it. While homeownership does seem to enjoy wide public esteem, the nature of the social advantages claimed for it is somewhat vague. A possible disadvantage is that home-ownership decreases mobility. Furthermore, if housing is like most other industries, landlords, being specialists, can provide services at lower cost than owner-occupants.

Like other special provisions, the treatment of imputed rent involves a conflict between the objective of encouraging a particular kind of behavior and the goal of equal taxation. And, as always, it is reasonable to ask whether the tax provision is more effective, relative to cost, than other governmental programs designed to accomplish the same social purpose. The present provisions afford assistance for housing and homeownership that varies directly with the family's income and marginal tax rate, whereas encouragement and assistance may be more needed in low-income and middle-income brackets than at the higher income levels. The loss of tax revenue due to the exclusion of imputed net rent and the personal deductions for mortgage interest and property taxes is large relative to the federal government's expenditures for housing and community development, including urban renewal, public housing, and the net cost of FHA mortgage insurance. For example, the revenue loss in the calendar year 1958 was approximately sixteen times the average annual federal expenditures for housing and community development in the fiscal years 1955 through 1959.[36] There seems to have been no systematic comparison of the merits of aiding housing and homeownership by the present tax provisions and by larger government expenditures.

When the federal, state, and local tax systems are considered simultaneously, it may seem that property tax payments outweigh the income tax advantages of housing. In 1960, for example, property taxes on owner-occupied dwellings amounted to $5.9 billion, compared with about $3.8 billion of federal income tax reduction attributable to the exclusion of imputed net rent and the associated personal deductions. Property taxes on owner-occupied dwellings would have amounted to only about $0.6 bil-

[36] *Budget of the United States Government for the Fiscal Year Ending June 30, 1964,* p. 427.

lion if they had been no higher in relation to gross rental value than the ratio of property taxes to gross national product originating in other industries.[37] The federal tax preference for owner-occupied dwellings can be defended on the ground that it merely offsets differential property taxation at the local level. A weakness of this argument is that it does not meet the point that the present treatment discriminates against renters compared with home-owners. Renters presumably have to bear much of the burden of the property tax on rental houses and apartments but obtain no federal income tax concession. The property tax, moreover, is partly a payment for services that specially benefit local residents and property owners; the criterion of neutrality derived by computing the ratio of tax to income originating is inappropriate.

The only method of eliminating the discrimination between homeowners and renters and of equalizing the return from owner-occupied dwellings and other investments would be to require that the net rental value of owner-occupied dwellings be included in adjusted gross income for tax purposes. Owing to the novelty of this solution in the United States and the undoubted difficulties of administration and compliance, the suggestion has been made that the discrimination between owners and tenants be attacked either by disallowing personal deductions for mortgage interest and property taxes or by allowing tenants to deduct rental payments. Inasmuch as the personal deductions for mortgage interest and property taxes on owner-occupied houses are considerably larger than the estimated net rent of these dwellings, the elimination of personal deductions associated with homeownership would accomplish a substantial part of the objective of taxation of imputed net rent. The disallowance, nevertheless, would be an incomplete solution. The elimination of the interest deduction, for

[37] In 1960, total property taxes other than those on owner-occupied dwellings were $10.5 billion, and GNP minus the $28.2 billion estimated rental value of owner-occupied farm and nonfarm dwellings was $474.4 billion. Applying the ratio 10.5/474.4 to the rental value of owner-occupied dwellings yields the figure of $0.6 billion. Estimates of GNP, rental value, and property tax accruals are from *Survey of Current Business,* July 1963. I assumed that the rental value of owner-occupied farmhouses equaled 74 percent of the rental value of all farm dwellings; according to Census data, 74 percent of the number of occupied farm housing units were owner-occupied in 1960 (*Statistical Abstract, 1962,* p. 758).

example, would have no effect on persons who own their dwellings free of mortgage debt and hence would do nothing to reduce the discrimination between this group and tenants. Among home-owners, denial of the interest deduction would remove a difference in the taxable income of those with and without mortgages which corresponds to a difference in economic income. From the stand-point of equity, the case for eliminating the property tax deduc-tion is stronger (see Chapter VII).

Under the Civil War income tax in the United States, tenants were allowed to deduct rental payments on their residences in computing taxable income. If this precedent were followed, the present discrimination against renters would be replaced by a dis-crimination in their favor, since the sum of the deductions and exclusion now allowed owner-occupants is less than gross rent. In the aggregate, rough equality could be achieved by allowing a deduction equal to about two-thirds of rental payments. The de-duction, however, would increase the favoritism for housing con-sumption over other goods and services and would further narrow the tax base.

The administrative problems in taxing imputed net rent, which would be substantial, would turn mainly on the establishment of rental value, by direct estimation or by taking a conventional per-centage of capital value or owner's equity. The valuation diffi-culties would not be novel, since appraisals are frequently made for mortgage loans and property tax assessments. However, higher standards of accuracy have customarily been demanded in the measurement of taxable income than in the establishment of values for the other purposes. Property tax assessments have been poor in many areas but fairly good in other places. Federal administra-tors could derive assistance from assessment records of govern-mental units with good administrations, whereas in other areas the availability of federal income tax valuation data might help improve local property tax assessments.

The gains in tax equity, economic efficiency, and federal revenue seem to be great enough to justify the effort that would be required to take account of imputed net rent in the assessment of the individual income tax. This tax reform merits serious consideration.

Life Insurance

Most life insurance policies combine pure insurance and saving features. The pure insurance is the protection against the risk of economic loss due to premature death. The savings take the form of reserves accumulated out of premium payments, which earn interest for the benefit of the insured. The pure insurance protection afforded by a policy at any time is the difference between the face amount and the reserve. Policies combine pure insurance and saving in varying proportions. A one-year term policy involves almost no saving; an endowment policy may be mainly a saving instrument.[38]

Both pure insurance proceeds and interest earned on savings accumulated under life insurance policies may be provisionally regarded as income in the broad sense. Yet, pure insurance proceeds are never included in AGI, and it appears that only a minor part of interest obtained by individuals through life insurance is included.

Under U.S. tax law, death benefits from life insurance policies are wholly excluded from the income of the insured person and of the beneficiary (but are included in the taxable estate of the deceased). No distinction is drawn between the components of death benefits, which comprise pure insurance proceeds, the return of the insured person's savings, and interest earned on the savings. When the proceeds of a life insurance contract are paid for reasons other than the death of the insured—on account of surrender or maturity —an attempt is made to take account of interest income for tax purposes. As shown below, however, the provision is defective and allows a large part of the interest to escape the individual income tax even in these cases.

The large size of life insurance benefits and of interest earnings on individual saving through life insurance makes the tax treatment of these items important. The subject, nevertheless, has received little attention.[39] In the following pages, pure insurance pro-

[38] Calculations are made for large classes of policyholders rather than for individual policies; and assumptions with respect to mortality, interest earnings, and expenses are not always realized.

[39] It is well analyzed by William Vickrey in "Insurance Under the Federal In-

ceeds and interest income will be separately treated, although the two elements are usually combined in an insurance policy.

Pure Insurance Proceeds

Pure life insurance proceeds are death benefits other than the return of the policyholder's accumulated savings and the distribution of interest income. These proceeds represent an increase in net worth of the beneficiary and are income according to the Haig-Simons definition. Life insurance is intended to replace part of the income that the insured person would have earned if he had continued at work, and the earned income would have been included in AGI.

An objection to including life insurance proceeds in taxable income is that they resemble bequests, which are not included. Actually, however, the close parallel is between a bequest and the return of the insured person's own contribution, not between a bequest and pure insurance proceeds. A bequest consists of property accumulated out of income by the deceased or an earlier owner; when originally received it was exposed to tax to the same degree as other income arising at that time from the same source. The pure insurance proceeds, on the other hand, are a new income item which partly replaces expected future earnings.

Nevertheless, there are good reasons for the continued exclusion of pure insurance proceeds from AGI. The death of the insured is often a time of economic loss for the family and therefore an inconvenient moment for paying an additional income tax. Application of graduated income tax rates to lump-sum insurance settlements would be harsh unless relief were granted, and the usual income-averaging plans might not be suitable for this purpose. There is, moreover, a social interest in encouraging individual efforts to provide for one's dependents. No close substitute exists for the pure insurance element of life insurance policies as a means for safeguarding dependents. In several countries, public approval of life insurance is expressed, not only by excluding pure

---

come Tax," *Yale Law Journal*, Vol. 52 (June 1943), pp. 554-85, and *Agenda for Progressive Taxation* (New York: Ronald Press, 1947), pp. 64-75. My own views are more fully stated in my paper, "Policyholders' Interest Income from Life Insurance Under the Income Tax," *Vanderbilt Law Review*, Vol. 16 (December 1962), pp. 33-55 (Brookings Institution Reprint No. 69, 1963).

insurance proceeds from taxable income, but also by allowing a deduction for a limited amount of insurance premiums.

Interest Income

Interest on personal savings built up through life insurance policies differs in an important respect from pure insurance proceeds. The interest income is related to the saving-investment features of insurance policies rather than their protective features.

The nature of personal saving through life insurance and the interest income from it can be clarified by an examination of different kinds of policy. An ordinary life policy, the most popular form of individual life insurance contract, calls for a constant annual premium and matures only at the death of the insured. In the earlier years of the contract, the annual premiums are much greater than the current cost of insurance, and savings are accumulated in a reserve fund, which is invested by the company and which earns interest. Limited-payment whole life policies also mature only at the death of the insured, but premium payments end after a stated number of years. Compared with an ordinary life policy, the limited-payment policies provide for heavier annual premiums, more rapid accumulation of savings, and greater interest earnings. A single-premium policy is the extreme form. Under this contract, the investment of the original premium yields an interest return which covers the cost of insurance and adds to the reserve. Endowment policies, in contrast to the whole life policies, mature either at the death of the insured or after a stated number of years, whichever is earlier.

Illustrative figures for the first twenty years for four insurance policies of $1,000 issued at age 45 are shown in Table 8. Although the policies have the same face value, the limited-payment and endowment policies provide less insurance protection (measured by the difference between the face amount and the reserve) on the average than the ordinary life policy. The premiums given in the table are net of the loading charges that are always added to cover company expenses. Because these charges vary among companies, they are omitted here for simplicity. The terminal reserve, which embodies the policyholder's accumulated savings at the end of the period, equals net premiums minus the cost of insurance plus interest earned.

TABLE 8. Illustrative Figures for First Twenty Years for Four Life Insurance Policies of $1,000 Issued at Age 45[a]

Item	Ordinary Life	20-Payment Life	Single-Premium Life	20-Year Endowment
1. Total net premiums	$600	$776	$551	$919
2. Total cost of insurance	271	207	122	154
3. Total interest earned	123	185	324	235
4. Terminal reserve	451	754	754	1,000

[a] Commissioners 1941 Standard Ordinary Mortality Table with interest at 2.5 percent. Line 4 = line 1 — line 2 + line 3, but figures may not check exactly because of rounding.

The question at issue is whether the interest earned on life insurance saving can be and should be included in individual income for tax purposes. Under present law, the interest is not taken into income as it accrues, and it is never included if the policy is paid because of the death of the insured. As the illustrative figures in Table 8 show, the interest element would constitute a large fraction of the sum received by the beneficiary if the insured died at the end of twenty years (but just before the maturity of the endowment policy).

If the insured survived, he could surrender the whole life policies for cash settlements approximately equal to the terminal reserves and could collect the face amount of the endowment policy. Under present law, he would then be required to report as income only the excess, if any, of the proceeds over the premiums paid. On the assumption that the proceeds would equal the terminal reserve, no income would have to be reported on the surrender of the ordinary life and twenty-payment life policies used for illustrative purposes in Table 8, and the amount to be reported for the other policies would be far less than the interest earned. In practice, the reportable income would be even smaller than the excess of the terminal reserves over the aggregate net premiums because the insured is allowed to deduct aggregate gross premiums, which exceed net premiums by the amount of the loading charge. The rule for determining income takes no account of the cost of insurance protection while the contract was in force. Interest earnings are included in AGI only to the extent that they exceed the cost of insurance and loading; in effect, personal insurance expenses are charged against interest income.

A different tax result would be obtained if the insured purchased insurance protection in the form of a series of one-year policies, which like the typical fire insurance or other casualty policy involve virtually no saving, and invested his savings in other assets. He would then be currently taxable on the interest earned on the savings. The contrast is most marked in the case of the single-premium policy but exists for the other policies as well. Channeling the saving through a life insurance company allows a large part of the return to escape individual income tax and postpones the taxation of the remainder.

Although the interest earned is not currently paid to the policyholder, it is used for his benefit. The policyholder, moreover, has access to his savings and accumulated interest. He can realize on the savings prior to the maturity of the policy by surrendering it for cash or by converting it to a paid-up policy or extended term insurance policy. He can also use the savings as collateral for a loan. Minimum surrender values, as provided by state laws, are somewhat less than policy reserves, but companies often offer more liberal surrender values.

The favored tax treatment enjoyed by life insurance policyholders is not offset by special federal taxation of the insurance companies. While opinions differ about the wisdom of the present provisions, it seems to be generally agreed that federal income taxes are lighter on life insurance companies than on other corporations. Those who consider the present taxation excessive do not deny this but maintain that there are valid reasons for lower income taxes on life insurance companies.[40]

The arguments that justify the exclusion of pure insurance proceeds from taxable income do not apply to interest on policy reserves. The interest income accrues as saving builds up, not just at the time of family misfortune, although the interest is often left with the company. Whereas no close substitutes for life insurance are available to an individual as a means of protecting his dependents against the risk of premature loss of his earning capacity, the saving provisions of insurance contracts are only one of a wide range of investment media. The benefit that a policyholder obtains from the preferential treatment of interest on life insurance reserves

[40] See the papers in House Ways and Means Committee, *Tax Revision Compendium* (1959), Vol. 3, pp. 1983-2066.

depends on the extent to which he uses insurance as an investment rather than on the amount of pure insurance coverage for his dependents.

The estimated net interest earnings on life insurance policy reserves amounted to approximately $2.0 billion in 1957, the latest year for which adequate data are available. This total is made up of approximately $1.9 billion of interest earned on the reserves of private companies and $0.1 billion of interest earnings on government life insurance reserves.[41] The net interest earned in more recent years may be somewhat greater; policy reserves and interest rates have been increasing, but federal income taxes paid by private life insurance companies have also increased.

The most careful estimates of the distribution of life insurance policy reserves according to the income of the policyholders are those of Goldsmith for 1949.[42] These estimates show that life insurance reserves were somewhat more concentrated in upper income classes than was money income but do not provide details for very high income classes. According to Goldsmith, those with incomes above $7,500, who received 20 percent of all money income in 1949, owned 25 percent of life insurance reserves in early 1950. Families headed by young persons, on the average, held much smaller claims against life insurance reserves than other families at the same income level.

After adjusting Goldsmith's estimates for the rise of income between 1949 and 1957, I roughly estimate that, if the interest income on life insurance policy reserves had been taxable to policyholders in the same way as other income, the federal income tax liability on it would have been some $0.3 billion to $0.4 billion in 1957.[43] The net addition to tax liabilities if the exclusion had been ended would have been smaller by the unknown (but probably minor) amount of interest income from life insurance reserves which is now taxable to individuals in connection with policies whose proceeds are paid for reasons other than death.

[41] For the derivation of these estimates see my paper in the *Vanderbilt Law Review*, Vol. 16, pp. 39-42.

[42] Raymond W. Goldsmith, Dorothy S. Brady, and Horst Mendershausen, *A Study of Saving in the United States* (Princeton, N.J.: Princeton University Press), Vol. III (1956), p. 126.

[43] Tax liability computed at the average marginal rate applicable to all income taxpayers; for details, see *Vanderbilt Law Review*, Vol. 16, pp. 43-44.

The preferential tax treatment of interest earned on policy reserves makes possible a larger net yield on saving through life insurance than could be obtained if this interest were taxed in the same way as other investment income. Savers who wish to avail themselves of the tax shelter, however, must incur costs for insurance protection and loading charges. This may not be a disadvantage for those who desire life insurance for its own sake, especially since saving and insurance can be combined in widely different proportions. It may, however, diminish the attractiveness of the tax shelter to wealthy persons, who have less need for life insurance protection than persons who depend mainly on earned income. Among investors, moreover, the management skill and guaranteed minimum return associated with a life insurance policy are more attractive to persons of moderate means than to those with large resources. For those in high tax brackets, municipal bonds offer tax exemption without the necessity of paying for life insurance company services. Up to 1957, the rate of net interest earned by life insurance companies was higher than the yield of high-grade tax-exempt securities, by a wide margin in the early postwar years. In 1957, the market yield of high-grade tax-exempt securities surpassed the average net return on life insurance company investments, and this may well have been true also in 1958-62.[44]

The favored tax treatment of the interest return on life insurance savings could be expected to have its greatest influence on the decisions of persons in the upper-middle income groups, particularly those who depend mainly on salaries or professional fees. A study by a Harvard Business School group, based on interviews in 1949 with a sample of active investors, confirmed the expectation regarding the appeal of life insurance to different income groups. In the $7,500 to $50,000 income classes, the percentage of respondents owning life insurance and annuities and the percentage of total wealth represented by the cash surrender value of these contracts were greater than in both lower and higher income classes. Only a very small percentage of the persons interviewed said that income tax considerations had led them to purchase more

[44] *Ibid.*, p. 40, and statistics on the average yield of high-grade municipal bonds included in Standard & Poor's index (*Economic Report of the President, January 1963*, p. 229).

insurance.[45] The Harvard study, indeed, found little sensitivity to earnings rates on individual investment in life insurance; but it is possible that persons who do not explicitly calculate the rate of return and the tax advantages may be influenced by premium rates and computations of the "net cost" of insurance policies as commonly presented by agents, and these reflect the opportunity of tax-free reinvestment and compounding of interest.

Aggregate statistics do not indicate whether the special tax status of life insurance has attracted savings to this medium. In the years 1946-60, when tax rates were high, the share of total net personal saving channeled through life insurance was considerably greater than in previous periods back to 1900, except for the 1930's. During the 1930's, saving through life insurance was relatively much higher than in other periods owing to a sharp fall in other forms of saving. Recently, however, the life insurance share of personal saving has fallen below its early postwar level.[46] The fraction of individual life insurance in the form of endowment and limited-payment policies has been declining in recent years. Whereas, in 1950, 40 percent of ordinary life insurance in force in the United States was in these two forms, in 1957, they represented only 30 percent of the total; only 11 percent of new purchases of ordinary life insurance in 1961 were endowment or limited-payment life policies.[47]

Equal treatment for savings through life insurance and fully taxable investment outlets would require that the accrued interest on life insurance policy reserves be allocated annually to policyholders and included in their AGI, even though the interest was

[45] J. Keith Butters, Lawrence E. Thompson, and Lynn L. Bollinger, *Effects of Taxation: Investments by Individuals* (Boston: Harvard University Graduate School of Business Administration, 1953), pp. 316-26. The statistics on holdings appear on p. 324.

[46] For the period 1900-45, based on estimates of Raymond W. Goldsmith (U. S. Bureau of the Census, *Historical Statistics of the United States, Colonial Times to 1957*, p. 156), with figures on saving through life insurance adjusted to exclude the increase in reserves of insured pension plans (see *Vanderbilt Law Review*, Vol. 16, p. 47); for 1946-60, based on flow of funds statistics from Board of Governors of the Federal Reserve System, *Flow of Funds Accounts, 1945-62*, 1963 Supplement, pp. 54-55. There are certain conceptual differences between the Goldsmith estimates and the flow of funds statistics.

[47] Institute of Life Insurance, *Life Insurance Fact Book, 1962* (New York), pp. 16, 21.

not currently received in cash. The procedures necessary to carry out this revision would be bothersome for the government, insurance companies, and policyholders.

The insurance companies do not routinely allocate interest earnings to individual policies; their calculations relate to large classes of policies and policyholders. The companies would have to be required to make individual allocations. For participating policies, which are eligible to share in surplus earnings through dividends and which account for two-thirds of total life insurance, the allocation could appropriately be made by applying the actual earned interest rate to the average policy reserve. The interest rate would be net of investment expenses and company taxes. Policy dividends would be treated as a reduction of premium and excluded from AGI, as they now are. For nonparticipating policies, the allocation would be made at the guaranteed rate provided in the policy.

An alternative procedure, which would be simpler but less satisfactory, would be to allocate to each policyholder an amount equal to the increase in the cash surrender value of his policy during the year minus the premium paid.[48] This procedure would apply to all policies the rule now followed when the proceeds are paid for reasons other than death, with the important modification that the income would be reportable annually. As explained above, the cost of current insurance protection would, in effect, be charged against interest earnings, with the result that the greater part of this income would continue to escape tax.

Allocation of interest to individual policies and company reporting to policyholders and the Internal Revenue Service would not assure that all of the income would appear on tax returns. The incomplete coverage of ordinary interest income suggests that special collection procedures might be needed. For participating policies, the companies might be required to withhold tax from policy dividends, but this procedure would be inapplicable to nonparticipating policies and unsuitable for participating policies when interest earnings exceeded policy dividends. "Withholding" by the companies might have to take the form of collection of an addition

[48] Suggested by Joseph A. Pechman in *Tax Revision Compendium*, Vol. 1, p. 263.

to the annual premium which would be remitted to the Internal Revenue Service and credited to the policyholder's liability.

Further study would be required to ascertain whether the inconvenience and expense for the insurance companies and the government would be as great as they appear at first sight. Attention should be given to the possibilities of using automatic data processing, which has already been installed by the large insurance companies and which is being adopted by the Internal Revenue Service. Consideration might also be given to an exemption from current reporting requirements for policies with small reserves, thus eliminating a large number of small items.

An alternative approach would be to defer reporting and taxation of interest income until it is realized through loan, surrender or maturity of the policy, or death of the insured.[49] This would allow tax deferral but would eliminate the permanent exclusion of a large part of interest on policy reserves. The approach would be subject to the same charge of harshness and inconvenience to taxpayers as mentioned in the comments on pure insurance proceeds. It might be acceptable, nevertheless, if applied only to new policies, inasmuch as the policyholders would have been placed on notice about their future liabilities.

In the light of the objections to the methods of taxing policyholders' interest income that have been considered above, it is not clear what, if any, revision of the law should be adopted. The proven adaptability of the income tax to complex situations, however, encourages the hope that a way of improving the present situation can be discovered. The effectiveness of any scheme for the taxation of policyholders' interest income would be enhanced if interest on state and local government securities were also taxed. Otherwise, savers could continue to avoid tax on interest income by switching from life insurance to tax-exempt bonds.

Interest on State and Local Securities

Of all the omissions from taxable income, the exclusion of interest on state and local government securities has attracted the

[49] Vickrey, *Agenda*, p. 73.

most attention.[50] It has been attacked by many writers on taxation and by several Secretaries of the Treasury but vigorously defended by state and local officials and by security dealers. The question whether the Constitution allows the federal government to tax this interest has been extensively debated but never resolved because the statutes have provided for the exclusion ever since 1913. Although the constitutional question will not be considered here, it can be said that authoritative opinion has tended toward the position that Congress could end the exclusion if it wished.

Statistics on interest payments by state and local governments and estimates of the amount received by individuals appear in Table 9. Like several other exclusions, tax-exempt interest has

TABLE 9. Interest Received by Individuals from State and Local Government Securities, Selected Years

(In millions of dollars)

Year	Total Interest Paid[a]	Amount Received by Individuals[b]
1942	706	277
1950	613	249
1955	1,059	399
1960	2,028	818

[a] From U.S. Bureau of the Census, *Statistical Abstract of the United States, 1962*, p. 421. Data relate to fiscal years ended in the calendar year shown, on June 30 for most state governments and school districts but on December 31 for the majority of other local governments.

[b] Estimated by multiplying total payments by the ratio of average estimated holdings of individuals on June 30 of the current year and the previous year to total amount of interest-bearing securities of state and local governments, territories, and possessions outstanding on these dates (*Annual Report of the Secretary of the Treasury, 1956*, p. 497; *ibid., 1961*, p. 625).

been growing rapidly. Between 1950 and 1960, the annual rate of increase in the amount received by individuals was 12.6 percent. The total, nevertheless, is still much smaller than that for several other exclusions which have received less attention.

The tax immunity of interest on state and local securities brings out in acute form the issues posed by other exclusions. Because state and local securities can be freely bought and sold with

[50] From the large literature, see Lucile Derrick, "Exemption of Security Interest from Income Taxes in the United States," *Journal of Business*, Vol. 19, No. 4, Pt. 2 (October 1946); the papers in *Tax Revision Compendium*, Vol. 1, pp. 679-791; George E. Lent, "The Origin and Survival of Tax-Exempt Securities," *National Tax Journal*, Vol. 12 (December 1959), pp. 301-16; David J. Ott and Allan H. Meltzer, *Federal Tax Treatment of State and Local Securities*, Studies of Government Finance (Washington: Brookings Institution, 1963).

little expense and little risk and without the necessity of buying consumer services at the same time, they are ideally suited for persons who wish to avoid high rates of income tax. One can obtain a tax-free return without the inconvenience and expenses associated with homeownership or life insurance. It is true that the market for state and local securities is less fluid than that for many other securities, but state-local bonds are more liquid than houses.

Current information is not available on the distribution of holdings of state and local government securities and of interest receipts from them among individuals classified by size of income. These securities are included in taxable estates, and data are available from federal estate tax returns. As expected, the data show a heavy concentration of holdings in large estates. On the basis of estate tax returns, Lampman estimates that in 1953 persons with wealth of $500,000 or more held almost 90 percent of all state and local securities that were then in the hands of individuals.[51]

In the absence of detailed information on the distribution of holdings by income classes, an accurate estimate of the amount of federal income tax being avoided by investors in state-local securities is not possible. Subject to a considerable margin of error, Robinson has placed the weighted average of the marginal federal income tax rates of individual holders at 60 percent in 1947-55.[52] With allowance for holdings by corporations and state and local governments themselves (through pension, amortization, and reserve funds), Ott and Meltzer estimate the over-all marginal rate in 1960 at 47 percent.[53] With 1965 tax rates and the 1960 distribution of holdings, the marginal rates may be placed at about 50 percent for individual holders and 41 percent for all holders.

Even if these estimates of the weighted marginal tax rates of present holders of tax-exempt securities are correct, they overstate to some extent the marginal rate of tax that would apply to interest on state-local securities if the tax immunity were ended. State-local

[51] Robert J. Lampman, *The Share of Top Wealth-Holders in National Wealth, 1922-1956* (Princeton, N.J.: Princeton University Press for National Bureau of Economic Research, 1962), p. 173.

[52] Roland I. Robinson, *Postwar Market for State and Local Government Securities* (Princeton, N.J.: Princeton University Press for National Bureau of Economic Research, 1960), pp. 191-92.

[53] *Tax Treatment of State and Local Securities,* p. 67.

securities would then be less attractive to high-income investors, who would seek other tax-sheltered investments, such as securities that are expected to yield capital gains rather than dividends and interest and mineral properties which are eligible for percentage depletion. Yields on state-local securities would rise and would become more attractive to investors subject to lower tax rates. Allowing for such shifts but assuming that the total quantity of financial and real investment would not be affected, the federal government's revenue gain from taxing (at 1965 income tax rates) interest on new issues of state-local securities may be estimated at roughly 36 percent to 38 percent of the interest payment.[54]

Many comments exaggerate the effect of the exclusion on the equity and progressivity of the income tax because they take no account of the compensating reduction in market yields of tax-exempt securities. If, for example, all holders of the securities were subject to a marginal tax rate of 50 percent and if yields on state-local securities were only half those on comparable taxable securities, the tax advantage would be fully discounted in the market. Although state and local governments would still gain from the tax immunity, high-income investors would be indifferent between state-local securities and other securities. In these circumstances, the effective rate of income tax would seem less progressive than it would without the exclusion, but the distribution of income would not be affected, and investors in state-local securities would receive no unfair advantage.

Questions of income distribution and equity arise because investors are subject to various tax rates and because the market does not fully discount the tax advantages of state and local securities for holders as a group. Even if yields on tax-exempt securities were half those on other securities, the holders of tax-exempts who were subject to marginal tax rates above 50 percent would gain an

[54] Derived by adjusting Ott and Meltzer's estimate of 41-43 percent, under 1960 rates (*ibid.*, p. 81), for the change in the weighted marginal rate of holders of tax-exempts from 1960 to 1965. The Ott-Meltzer estimate assumes the continuation of preferential treatment of capital gains and other tax shelters. If all tax shelters were simultaneously eliminated and the volume of investment remained unchanged, the present holders of tax-exempt securities would have no alternative but to invest in fully taxable assets, and the revenue gain could be calculated by reference to the marginal tax rates payable by them on ordinary income.

advantage. For example, a person subject to a marginal tax rate of 70 percent would be indifferent between a taxable security yielding 4.00 percent and a comparable tax-exempt security yielding 1.20 percent, whereas the market yield on the tax-exempt would be 2.00 percent.

There is reason to believe, moreover, that the yield differential is smaller than that which would be necessary to bring about an exact equivalence for the weighted average of all holders. The yield differential is almost certainly less than that required to compensate for the tax advantages enjoyed by individual holders as a group and probably less than the tax advantages of corporate and individual holders taken together. This is true because yields must be high enough to attract marginal investors, who are subject to tax rates lower than the weighted average for all holders, and to induce high-income buyers to acquire more of the securities than they would if the differential exactly equaled the tax advantage. Prudent investors will insist on a margin as insurance against a future reduction of tax rates. Ott and Meltzer estimate that in 1960 the yield on newly issued state and local government securities was about 24 percent to 35 percent less than it would have been if the interest had been subject to federal income tax.[55] Both higher and lower estimates of the spread have been made by others.

The exclusion of interest on state-local securities is economically objectionable because it diverts high-income investors from stocks and other risky private investments to government securities, and thus reduces risk-taking and innovation. This objection, however, seems to have been overrated in many past discussions. The state-local security holdings of top wealth-holders (those with gross estates of $60,000 or more) accounted for only 3.5 percent of their gross estates in 1953, according to Lampman's estimates.[56] Another objection to the exclusion is that choices between investment in the public sector and investment in the private sector are biased. But this criticism is hard to evaluate because it is uncer-

---

[55] They state the relation in a different form, saying that interest costs would have risen by 31 percent to 54 percent if tax exemption had been eliminated (*ibid.*, p. 60); 31/131 = 24 percent; 54/154 = 35 percent.

[56] Lampman, *Share of Top Wealth-Holders*, p. 170. At the end of 1960, state-local securities constituted about 3 percent of the total financial assets of all individuals and nonprofit organizations (*Flow of Funds Accounts, 1945-62*, p. 4).

tain whether the interest rate significantly affects the amount of borrowing and spending by state and local governments.[57]

The exclusion of interest on state-local securities has been defended as a necessary or desirable feature of federalism, regardless of whether required by the Constitution. The historic doctrine that each level of government should be completely immune from taxation by the other level, however, seemingly is being superseded by the opinion that a successful federal system requires only that each level be protected from discriminatory, and hence possibly destructive, impositions. Federal and state salaries have been taxable by both levels of government for the past twenty-five years with no apparent harm to the federal system. If the federal government were to tax interest on state-local securities, it is generally agreed that Congress should make clear that there would be no objection to nondiscriminatory state taxes on the interest on federal securities.

Viewed as a means of extending federal financial assistance to state and local governments, the exclusion is inefficient because the cost to the federal government considerably exceeds the saving to the borrowing governments. Furthermore, the allocation of benefits among state and local governments does not conform to any standard of need that would be likely to be chosen for a program of direct financial assistance.[58]

Although the tax immunity of interest on state and local government securities has resulted in inequities, it would be unfair simply to withdraw the exemption from outstanding issues. Investors have bought the securities at prices and yields reflecting the expectation of continued tax exemption and would suffer capital losses if the interest were made taxable. The usual suggestion is that the federal income tax should apply only to interest on future issues. While this approach would not immediately end the problem, it would stop the growth of tax-exempt interest. By suitable

[57] Abolition of the exemption might hamper borrowing in the short run because of statutory and constitutional limitations on interest rates, although in many jurisdictions the maximum rates are high relative to recent yields of taxable bonds. See Dick Netzer, "State-Local Response to Changing Credit Conditions: The Institutional Obstacles," *Journal of Finance,* Vol. 15 (May 1960), pp. 224-26. The ceiling rates presumably would be altered in time.

[58] See Ott and Meltzer, *Tax Treatment of State and Local Securities,* pp. 80-81, 107-12, 124-26; Robinson, *Postwar Market,* p. 197.

cash payments covering part of the interest on new issues of taxable securities, the federal government might be able to hasten the transition by encouraging state and local governments to refund outstanding issues.[59] Another approach would be to tax interest on outstanding as well as new issues but to offer holders of the old issues a tax credit intended to partly compensate them for the withdrawal of the exemption.[60] The design of an acceptable credit, however, would be complex and perhaps infeasible.

The ending of the tax immunity of future issues of state-local securities would be desirable from the standpoint of equity and economic efficiency and, in my judgment, would not pose a threat to a healthy federal system. This action might be coupled with a program of additional federal grants-in-aid to state-local governments or subsidies for state-local borrowing.

Excluded Dividends

Individual stockholders are allowed to exclude the first $100 of dividends received from domestic corporations; husbands and wives filing joint returns may exclude $200. Until 1964, the exclusion was equal to half these amounts. The exclusion and a 4 percent credit for dividends received were adopted in 1954 as a means of reducing the so-called double taxation of distributed corporate profits and encouraging corporations to finance themselves by stock issues rather than borrowing. The President recommended in 1961 and again in 1963 that both the exclusion and the credit be repealed on the grounds that they were inequitable and ineffective.[61] Congress agreed to drop the credit but doubled the exclusion.

Regardless of the merits of the controversy about the taxation

[59] Lawrence H. Seltzer, "Possibilities of Speeding the Elimination of Tax-Exempt Securities," *Proceedings of Thirty-fourth Annual Conference on Taxation*, National Tax Association (Washington, 1941), pp. 189-98.

[60] Lyle C. Fitch, *Taxing Municipal Bond Income* (Berkeley and Los Angeles: University of California Press, 1950).

[61] See *Internal Revenue Code of 1954*, Report of House Ways and Means Committee, H. Rept. 1337, 83 Cong. 2 sess. (1954), pp. 5-7; *President's 1963 Tax Message Along with Principal Statement, Technical Explanation, and Supporting Exhibits and Documents Submitted by Secretary of the Treasury*, House Ways and Means Committee, Committee Print, 88 Cong. 1 sess. (1963), pp. 16-17.

of distributed corporate profits, the dividend exclusion is an inequitable and ineffective means of reducing the differential tax on dividend income. While it is true, as pointed out by the congressional committees,[62] that the exclusion completely eliminates any double taxation on small amounts of dividends received by stockholders who are subject to individual income tax, this hardly justifies the provision. If double taxation of small amounts of dividends is objectionable, is it not also objectionable in respect of large amounts? More fundamentally, double taxation in the literal sense is not the real problem posed by the lack of integration of the corporate and individual income taxes. The problem is one of over-taxation or undertaxation of corporate profits compared with other income. The equalization of taxes cannot be accomplished by exclusion from the income of stockholders of part of dividends received, because the corporate and individual income tax rates differ in all brackets except one.

In 1960, the dividend exclusion reported on individual tax returns totaled $384 million, of which 41 percent was on returns with income above $10,000.[63]

Miscellaneous Items of Imputed Income

A few miscellaneous items of imputed income have nearly always been excluded from taxable income in all countries. Among these are the return from ownership of consumer durable equipment, part of the return on cash balances, and personal services performed for oneself. The value of farm-produced-and-consumed food and fuel is often omitted but is taxed in some countries, usually on the basis of an arbitrary valuation. No serious consideration seems to have been given to the possibility of taxing most of these items because legislators do not think of them as income. The virtual impossibility of assessing the items has convinced most of the specialists who have studied the subject that the exclusions must continue, even though certain inequities and economic distortions may result.

[62] *Revenue Act of 1963*, House Ways and Means Committee, H. Rept. 749, 88 Cong. 1 sess. (1963), pp. 32-33; *Revenue Act of 1964*, Senate Finance Committee, S. Rept. 830, 88 Cong. 2 sess. (1964), pp. 36-37.

[63] U. S. Treasury Department, *Statistics of Income, Individual Income Tax Returns, 1960*, p. 5.

I agree that the inclusion of these items in taxable income would be impracticable. The purpose of the following remarks is to consider whether the exclusions seriously impair the income tax.

Consumer Durable Equipment

Ownership of consumer durable equipment such as furniture, appliances, and automobiles is similar to homeownership. Much the same argument can be made for including the net service value of the durable equipment in AGI as for taking account of the net rent of owner-occupied dwellings. At the end of 1958, consumers' equities in durable equipment were about three-fifths as large as their equities in owner-occupied houses.[64] Presumably the net yield of the equities in durables was about the same fraction of that from houses. The opinion that consumer durables yield little net return because of their short average life is incorrect.[65] A short life means that depreciation is heavy relative to original cost, or service value, but does not imply that the net rate of return on the equity is small. With respect to business assets, it is well recognized that the gross yield of a short-lived item should exceed that of a long-lived one by a margin wide enough to cover the additional depreciation allowance on the less durable asset and to permit approximately equal net rates of return. The same principle seems applicable to consumer investments in equipment and houses.

Because the renting of consumer durables is less prevalent than the renting of dwellings, discrimination between renters and owners seems less acute for durables than for houses. In addition to renters, however, there are many consumers who buy services similar to those provided by consumer-owned durables. The patrons of commercial laundries and public transportation, for example, pay the whole cost of the services in cash, whereas owners of home laundry equipment and automobiles meet part of the cost of the

[64] The estimated equities of nonfarm households were about $142 billion in durable equipment and $237 billion to $244 billion in owner-occupied units of one-to-four family nonfarm houses. The estimates for owner-occupied houses were derived from Goldsmith and Lipsey, *Studies in the National Balance Sheet,* by the method described in footnote 35 in this chapter. Estimated equity in consumer durables is the total value of holdings (*ibid.,* Vol. II, p. 68) minus consumer installment debt in the form of automobile paper and other consumer-goods paper (*Statistical Abstract, 1963,* p. 467).

[65] I believe that Henry Simons' comments are incorrect or, at least, ambiguous (*Personal Income Taxation,* pp. 118-19).

services with the tax-free imputed net return on their investment in the equipment. The difference in tax treatment is similar to the difference between the taxation of tenants and homeowners.[66]

Experience with the general property tax indicates that tax officials could not discover and value household goods or impute net income to their owners. The omission of imputed income from consumer durables is a shortcoming of the income tax which must be accepted. The failure to take account of the yield of durables does not justify the continued exclusion of net rent of owner-occupied houses. Probably the ownership of durable equipment and houses is positively correlated. If so, the effects of omitting imputed returns on both kinds of investment are cumulative rather than offsetting.

Cash Balances

Large cash balances are convenient; they enable one to make advantageous purchases and, when held in checking accounts, to avoid bank service charges. The return on business balances is reflected in taxable business income, but this is not true of individual balances held for convenience in making consumption payments. Although direct evidence is not available on the point, it seems likely that the greater part of individual balances is intended to allow the holders to take advantage of investment opportunities or to avoid the necessity of borrowing and paying interest. If these purposes are actually realized, taxable income of the holders will be increased by virtue of larger investment income or smaller deductions for interest payments. Even if investments are not made, the sacrifice of interest on the cash balances may be regarded as a cost of seeking income. I conclude that the amount of income that ideally should be attributed to holders of cash balances is small and that the failure to take account of this item is not a significant defect of the income tax.

In the national income accounts, imputed interest income of persons amounted to $11.1 billion in 1960 (Appendix Table A-5). Of this, only about $2 billion, representing policyholders' interest

[66] C. Harry Kahn, *Personal Deductions in the Federal Income Tax* (Princeton, N.J.: Princeton University Press for National Bureau of Economic Research, 1960), pp. 118-19.

on life insurance reserves, seems to me a serious candidate for inclusion in AGI.

Farm-Produced-and-Consumed Food and Fuel

Another item that is omitted from gross income for tax purposes is the value of farm families' consumption of their own output. Although the imputed net income attributable to this consumption is less than the value of the products by an amount equal to the cost of supplies, depreciation, and other expenses properly assignable to the production of the home-consumed items, it seems likely that AGI is understated by the full value of the products. This will be true if, as seems to be the common practice, farmers deduct the full amount of their operating expenses and capital costs in arriving at AGI.

For the great majority of farmers, it does not seem to be practicable to ascertain the value of the home-consumed items or even to allocate costs between marketed and nonmarketed output. With the growth of specialized farming, the problem is becoming less important. According to estimates of the Department of Commerce, the value of farm-produced-and-consumed food and fuel has been declining in recent years, and in relation to the total value of farm output it has fallen sharply. Estimates spanning three decades are as follows:[67]

Year	Value	Percentage of Total Farm Output
1929	$1.7 billion	*12.5%*
1940	1.2	*11.8*
1950	2.2	*6.7*
1960	1.3	*3.3*

It should be feasible to assess home-produced-and-consumed items in cases where their value is large. As a minimum, a special effort could be made to disallow deductions for the cost of producing nonmarketed output in these cases, recognizing that for hobby farms the output may include recreational services as well as crops and livestock.[68]

[67] *National Income*, 1954 ed., pp. 214-15; *U.S. Income and Output* (1958), pp. 226-27, 229; *Survey of Current Business*, July 1963, pp. 38, 39.

[68] While the regulations disallow expenses incurred in a "sport, hobby or rec-

Personal Services

The consumption of one's own services is a form of income. Housekeeping, dressmaking, painting, carpentry, and gardening are examples of services that may be either done by family members or purchased. The performance of these chores, moreover, often competes for time with work for wages and salaries. Because it takes account of the salaries and wages, but not the value of services performed for oneself, the income tax results in inequities and penalizes specialization. If a homeowner takes time off from his regular job and repaints his house, his taxable income is reduced by much more than his real income. The most important case is that of housewives; the value of their services at home is excluded from taxable income, but any earnings that they obtain by taking a job away from home are taxable.

Any attempt to value the services performed within the household, however, would immediately come up against insurmountable obstacles of both a theoretical and practical nature. It would be impossible to distinguish activities that produce valuable services from relaxation or to separate the commercial from the noncommercial, the significant from the trivial. As Henry Simons points out, "if the value of goods and services produced within the household are [sic] to be accounted for, one must face, first of all, the necessity of stopping somewhere; and no convenient stopping-place is discernible. Shall one include the value of shaves? of instruction to children? of a mother's services as a nurse?"[69]

The exclusion of the value of services performed for oneself is less unfair than it may seem because to a great extent the performance of these services competes with leisure, which is another form of consumption, and hence a part of income, which escapes taxation. Between the suburbanite who spends weekends tending

---

reation" (Treasury Regulations, sec. 1.212.1(c)), the Internal Revenue Service has not been very successful in challenging taxpayers' claims that farms are profit-seeking enterprises, even though no profit is realized, and that operating losses are deductible from other income. A statutory disallowance of hobby losses applies only to the extreme case in which deductions exceed gross income by more than $50,000 in each of five successive years (Internal Revenue Code of 1954, sec. 270). See Harvard Law School, World Tax Series, *Taxation in the United States* (Chicago: Commerce Clearing House, 1963), pp. 482-84, 883-84.

[69] *Personal Income Taxation*, p. 110.

his garden and his neighbor who goes golfing, there is no tax inequity. There is an inequity, and possibly a perverse economic effect, in the treatment of these two compared with that of a third person who works overtime at his regular job on weekends.

General Remarks

The treatment of the miscellaneous items of imputed income is a matter of concern only when viewed in the light of the high standards of equity and neutrality that are properly demanded of the personal income tax. Under indirect taxes, such questions do not arise, not because they are resolved but simply because they are not considered. The personal expenditure tax, which aspires to the same degree of refinement as the income tax, would encounter most of the same problems as the income tax. I conclude that, though the income tax has unavoidable shortcomings in the treatment of imputed income, these weaknesses are not serious enough, or easily enough circumvented, to affect the ranking of the income tax and alternative taxes.

Recapitulation

Of the items discussed in this chapter, I consider it desirable and quite feasible to include in AGI the following: one-half of OASDI and railroad retirement old-age and disability benefits, the full amount of sick pay and interest on new issues of state and local government securities, and the part of dividends now excluded from AGI. Also justifiable and probably feasible is the inclusion of employer contributions to the cost of life, accident, health, and medical insurance for employees and imputed net rent of owner-occupied dwellings. In 1960, these items, including interest received by individuals on outstanding state-local securities as well as on new issues, totaled $16.8 billion. Part of social insurance survivorship benefits (total, $2.5 billion in 1960), but less than one-half, could also appropriately be included in AGI. Policyholders' interest income from life insurance reserves (about $2 billion in 1957) could justifiably be included in AGI, but it is not clear whether a fair and practicable plan for doing so can be devised. All of these items account for about two-fifths of the individual income items that are included in personal income as estimated by the Office of

Business Economics, Department of Commerce, but not in AGI (counting the full amount of social insurance retirement and disability benefits).

In principle, AGI should also include the value of farm-produced-and-consumed food and fuel, employee meals in private industry, and employee discounts (totaling about $1.9 billion in 1960), but I doubt that it would be worthwhile to attempt to assess these items except in the few cases in which amounts enjoyed by individuals are large. Although a good argument can be made for currently including in employees' AGI the amount of employers' contributions to private pension and deferred profit-sharing plans, I think it expedient to continue to reflect the value of these contributions mainly at the time when benefits are received rather than when contributions are made.

It would not be desirable, in my opinion, to include public assistance, veterans' benefits, unemployment insurance benefits, and individual health insurance benefits in AGI; these items amounted to $10.6 billion in 1960. Also, I think it undesirable or impracticable to attempt to include in AGI unrealized capital gains, gifts and inheritances, life insurance death benefits other than the part comprising interest on policyholders' savings, the service value of consumer durables, imputed interest on cash balances, and the value of personal services performed for oneself or family. The total of these items is not known.

CHAPTER VII

Personal Deductions

PERSONAL DEDUCTIONS are expenses that are subtracted from adjusted gross income (AGI) in arriving at taxable income. They cover living expenses and certain costs of obtaining income that do not qualify as business expenses, which are subtracted from gross receipts in computing AGI. The major items are interest paid, medical expenses, philanthropic contributions, and taxes paid. Minor items include uninsured casualty losses, child-care expenses, and miscellaneous deductions. Taxpayers may elect a limited standard deduction in lieu of itemized personal deductions.

Growth of Deductions and Their Distribution

The personal deductions have been growing rapidly, increasing from 9 percent to 15 percent of AGI between 1940 and 1960 (Table 10). From 1940 to 1950, the increase in relation to income seems to have been due to a new deduction for medical expenses and the introduction of the optional standard deduction; the other deductions grew much less than income. In the 1950's, however, the traditional itemized deductions for interest paid, contributions, and taxes grew more rapidly than income.

Because of the existence of the standard deduction, the deduction shown in Table 10 for a particular item is an incomplete re-

TABLE 10. Personal Deductions, Taxable Individual Returns, 1940, 1950, and 1960

Item	1940[a]	1950[a]	1960[b]
Percent of Adjusted Gross Income			
Interest paid	1.8	0.9	2.7
Medical expenses	—	0.8	1.5
Casualty losses	0.1	0.2	0.1
Contributions	2.2	1.3	2.2
Taxes paid	3.5	1.3	3.4
Other itemized deductions	1.4	1.2	1.2
Standard deduction	—	6.4	3.9
Total deductions	9.0	12.0	15.0
Percent of Deductions			
Interest paid	20.2	7.2	17.8
Medical expenses	—	6.6	10.0
Casualty losses	0.9	1.3	0.9
Contributions	24.6	11.1	14.4
Taxes paid	38.9	10.8	22.5
Other itemized deductions	15.4	10.1	8.3
Standard deduction	—	52.9	26.2
Total deductions	100.0	100.0	100.0

[a] From C. Harry Kahn, *Personal Deductions in the Federal Income Tax* (Princeton, N.J.: Princeton University Press for National Bureau of Economic Research, 1960), p. 36.
[b] Derived from U.S. Treasury Department, *Statistics of Income, Individual Income Tax Returns, 1960,* pp. 16, 55, 66.

port of taxpayers' outlays for it. Changes over time in the amount deducted are due to both the trend of outlays for the item and the extent to which taxpayers choose itemization rather than the standard deduction. Thus the decline in the ratio of itemized deductions to income between 1940 and 1950 was due at least in part to the introduction of the standard deduction, while the increase in the ratios for particular items from 1950 to 1960 was partly caused by the growing tendency to itemize deductions.

Prior to the Revenue Act of 1964, the personal deductions were greatest relative to income in the highest income classes and least in the lowest classes. The ratio at first rose with income but, over a wide intermediate range, tended to dip slightly. The 1960 profile, outlined in Table 11, was broadly similar to that for earlier years.[1] The 1964 act is expected to increase deductions by a sub-

[1] Figures for eleven years between 1918 and 1956 are given in C. Harry Kahn, *Personal Deductions in the Federal Income Tax* (Princeton, N.J.: Princeton Uni-

stantial fraction in the income classes below $3,000, owing mainly to the introduction of the minimum standard deduction, and to reduce deductions slightly in income classes above $5,000.[2] Under the 1964 act, a curve relating personal deductions to AGI probably will be generally U-shaped, with the upper ranges higher than the lower ranges.

TABLE 11. Personal Deductions by Adjusted Gross Income Classes, Taxable Individual Returns, 1960[a]

AGI Class ($000)	Percent of Total Deductions	Deductions as Percent of AGI
Under 2	2.0	12.2
2–3	3.8	13.5
3–5	16.1	14.6
5–10	48.5	15.6
10–25	20.5	14.4
25–50	4.6	13.8
50–100	2.3	15.1
100–500	1.7	20.0
500 and over	0.5	21.5
All classes	100.0	15.0

[a] Derived from U. S. Treasury Department, *Statistics of Income, Individual Income Tax Returns, 1960*, p. 66. Personal deductions = AGI—exemptions—taxable income.

Views on the Role of Deductions

The personal deductions have been increasingly called in question. When taxes were raised during World War II, suggestions

versity Press for National Bureau of Economic Research, 1960), p. 44. Throughout this chapter I have relied heavily on this excellent study.

[2] Estimates based on *Revenue Act of 1964*, Senate Finance Committee, S. Rept. 830, 88 Cong. 2 sess. (1964), p. 22, and 1960 Tax File. The 1960 Tax File consists of a random, stratified sample of 100,000 U. S. individual income tax returns for 1960. It is a sub-sample of the more than 400,000 returns included in the sample used by the Internal Revenue Service, U. S. Treasury Department, in the preparation of *Statistics of Income*. The tabulations and calculations from the tax file were prepared by George Sadowsky of Yale University, under the direction of Joseph A. Pechman, as a project of the Brookings Studies of Government Finance. A more complete description of the file is contained in a paper by Pechman presented at the Organization for Economic Cooperation and Development Conference on Government Finance and Economic Development, Athens, December 1963 (to be published in the proceedings of the conference).

were made for curtailing personal deductions. The adoption of the predecessor of the standard deduction in 1941 seems to have been motivated partly by doubts about the desirability of itemized deductions, the attitude being that the standard allowance wiped out certain unjustified differences in tax due to itemized deductions. More recently, many critics have come to regard the personal deductions as a cause of the erosion of the tax base and have suggested that they be restricted.

While a skeptical attitude toward personal deductions is justified, it should be recognized that properly limited deductions have advantages in adapting the income tax to individual circumstances and in advancing socially important objectives. The identification of such possibilities requires an examination of particular items. The experience of 1963-64, moreover, suggests that Congress may be more receptive to a critique of particular items than to a general attack on the deductions. Congress declined to accept an administration proposal for a blanket restriction on itemized deductions but in the Revenue Act of 1964 limited certain deductions while liberalizing others.

The original reasons for allowing some of the personal deductions are not clear; however, the deductions now seem to have four main purposes: (1) to allow the deduction of certain items that are costs of obtaining nonbusiness income or that are hard to distinguish from such costs; (2) to relieve hardships that would arise from strict application of a tax on economic income; (3) to encourage voluntary support of certain socially desirable activities; and (4) to promote intergovernmental comity in a federal system.[3] The allowance of costs of obtaining income appears to be the dominant reason for the deductions for interest paid, child-care expenses, and most of the miscellaneous minor deductions.[4] The

---

[3] Cf. Kahn, *Personal Deductions*, pp. 12-16.

[4] In 1960, the items classified as "other itemized deductions" in Table 10, accounting for 8.3 percent of total deductions, included 5.5 percentage points of items identifiable as costs of earning income (employee business expenses, entertainment expenses, educational expenses, and child-care expenses), 0.5 percentage points of alimony payments, and 2.3 percentage points of mixed items which included costs of obtaining investment income and interest and taxes paid by tenant-shareholders of cooperative housing corporations. Employee business expenses classified as personal deductions represent only items which could not be deducted in determining AGI and include unreimbursed expenses for special

deductions for medical expenses and casualty losses are intended to relieve hardships. That for philanthropic contributions is thought of primarily as an incentive to voluntary support of certain socially desirable institutions and their activities. The personal deduction for state and local taxes may be classified as a means of easing frictions in a federal system. The optional standard deduction is a surrogate for the itemized deductions, and in the lowest brackets is equivalent to a supplementary personal exemption.

Interest Paid

The deduction for interest paid, which goes back to 1913, has grown rapidly in the postwar period and among itemized deductions in 1960 was second only to taxes paid. The interest deduction is most important for the debt-laden middle classes. In 1960, the proportion of taxpayers with itemized deductions who claimed the interest deduction was greater in the middle brackets than at either lower or higher income levels (Appendix Table A-7). Interest payments also were a larger fraction of total itemized deductions in the middle brackets than in other brackets. The ratio of the deduction to AGI was highest in the $5,000 to $10,000 income class but varied somewhat erratically at other income levels (Appendix Table A-8).

A justification for the deduction of interest payments may begin with the proposition that the net return from assets can be determined only after subtracting interest paid on any indebtedness that allows the owner to hold the assets. This is generally recognized for business firms; there is an important sense in which the proposition also applies to people who are not in business. When the gross return on property is taken into account for tax purposes, failure to allow the deduction of interest on a debt incurred to carry it will result in an overstatement of net income. This is less obvious but may also be true when there is no formal link between the asset and the liability. For example, if a person owns securities

---

clothing and equipment, small tools and materials, union and professional-association dues, fees paid to employment agencies, and subscriptions to professional journals. See U. S. Treasury Department, *Statistics of Income, Individual Income Tax Returns, 1960*, pp. 16-17 (cited hereinafter as *Statistics of Income, 19. .*).

and owes a debt to a bank, the debt helps finance the security holdings even though the securities are not the collateral for the loan and the debt was not incurred for the explicit purpose of buying the securities. If the loan were called or fell due, the investor might well reconsider his portfolio. Also, he would have an incentive to dispose of securities and pay off the bank loan if the interest deduction were disallowed while the return on the securities remained taxable.

This justification does not apply, however, when the return on assets is excluded from gross income for tax purposes, as is true of owner-occupied dwellings, consumer durable equipment, and tax-exempt bonds (see Chapter VI). In these cases, the allowance of an interest deduction results in an understatement of income and a bias in favor of investment in the tax-sheltered kinds of property.

It is true that, regardless of the taxability of the yield of assets financed by the borrowing, the payment of interest is a negative item in economic income. As pointed out in the discussion of owner-occupied dwellings, a homeowner who has a mortgage has a smaller economic income, other things equal, than a person who owns his house free of debt. Similar statements can be made about owners of consumer durable equipment and tax-exempt securities. The allowance of an interest deduction differentiates between debtors and nondebtors and therefore may be defended as a means of recognizing real differences in income and taxpaying capacity, even when certain kinds of property income are excluded from AGI.[5]

The rebuttal to this argument is that the interest deduction not only recognizes real differences but creates differences in taxable income that do not correspond to any difference in economic income. To illustrate, consider three individuals, A, B, and C, each of whom receives a salary of $10,000 a year and no other income that is includible in AGI. Suppose that A and B own and occupy

[5] This seems to be the position of Melvin I. White; see "Deductions for Non-business Expenses and an Economic Concept of Net Income," in *Federal Tax Policy for Economic Growth and Stability,* Joint Committee on the Economic Report (84 Cong. 1 sess., 1955), pp. 357-60; and "Proper Income Tax Treatment of Deductions for Personal Expense," in *Tax Revision Compendium,* House Ways and Means Committee (1959), Vol. 1, pp. 365-66.

houses worth $20,000; A's house is subject to a $10,000 mortgage on which he pays interest of $600 a year, whereas B owns his house clear of debt. C is a tenant. Granted that A's interest deduction reflects a difference between his economic income and B's, it distorts the relation between A and C. While A's economic income is greater than C's by the amount of any imputed net return that A obtains on his equity in his house, the interest deduction makes A's taxable income $600 less than C's (other things equal).

No manipulation of the interest deduction can establish a relationship among the taxable incomes of A, B, and C corresponding to their economic incomes. The question is whether the relation between A and B or that between A and C is more important. Partly this depends on the number of people in the groups which A, B, and C represent; the amounts of interest payments are also relevant, although it is hard to say how they should be weighted.[6] A judgment that the inequity between A and C which is created by the interest deduction is more serious than the inequity between A and B which is prevented by the deduction might be defended on the grounds that, even without an interest deduction, A will be treated better than C so long as imputed rent is excluded from AGI. One might also argue that the difference between A and B may be ignored because the exclusion of imputed rent indicates a legislative decision to disregard this item in measuring taxable capacity.

The fundamental difficulty arises from the omission from AGI of the imputed return on owner-occupied houses and consumer durables. With the yield on these items excluded and all interest payments deductible, the taxable income of the owner is understated by the amount of the net yield plus interest paid on debt related to the property. Congress has recognized the inconsistency in the case of tax-exempt securities, and has attempted to deny the deduction of interest paid on debt incurred to finance holdings of these securities, but has not dealt with the general problem. If the gross yield of consumer capital were taken into account in computing taxable income, it would be quite proper to allow a deduction for interest payments—as a cost of obtaining income.

[6] For a suggestive but inconclusive treatment, see Shirley B. Johnson and Thomas Mayer, "An Extension of Sidgwick's Equity Principle," *Quarterly Journal of Economics*, Vol. 76 (August 1962), pp. 454-63.

The deduction of interest paid on a home mortgage may seem questionable, even if imputed rent were included in gross income, because the payment appears to be a consumption expenditure. This objection, however, is unwarranted. A homeowner acts in a dual capacity—as an investor and as a consumer. As an investor he is, in effect, a landlord; as a consumer, he is his own tenant. He takes the interest deduction in his capacity as a landlord, not as a tenant. That this is not a sophistry can be seen by noting that, if imputed rent were taxed, the houseowner's tax position would not be altered if he moved to another city, leased his house, and rented a similar one in the new location. Under present law, these transactions would increase his taxable income.

Although existing inequities cannot be completely eliminated so long as substantial amounts of monetary or imputed property income are excluded from AGI, an improvement could be made by allowing interest payments to be deducted only to the extent that they are costs of obtaining taxable income. One way of applying this principle would be to restrict the deduction to interest paid on debts contracted for business or professional purposes or for the carrying of taxable securities, denying the deduction for interest on consumer debt and for interest on home mortgages so long as imputed rent is not taxable. This is the rule in Canada.[7]

This procedure, however, is open to criticism on theoretical and practical grounds owing to the difficulty of pairing particular debts and assets. Since all of a person's debts and assets have to be consolidated in order to ascertain his financial position, any interest paid can be regarded as a cost of obtaining any property income received by the individual. This suggests that an appropriate procedure for tax purposes would be to pool all property income and interest payments and to allow the deduction of the latter from the former. Interest payments could be deductible up to the full amount of receipts of taxable income from property but not beyond, or could be allocated between taxable and nontaxable income according to a general rule.

Either the matching or the pooling procedure would eliminate the bulk of personal interest deductions (interest deductions claimed

[7] CCH Canadian, Ltd., *Canadian Master Tax Guide,* 18th ed. (Don Mills, Ont., 1963), para. 425.

against AGI as distinguished from interest payments taken into account in arriving at AGI). According to Treasury Department estimates, two-thirds of total personal interest deductions in 1960 were for interest paid on home mortgages.[8] No doubt a considerable fraction of other interest payments related to debt incurred to buy consumer durables.

TABLE 12. Itemized Personal Deductions for Interest Paid in Relation to Nonwage Income, by Adjusted Gross Income Classes, 1960[a]

AGI Class ($000)	Percent of Total Interest Deductions	Proportion of Interest Deductions	
		On Returns with No Nonwage Income[b]	"Excess" Deductions on Other Returns[c]
Under 2	0.9	0.27	0.19
2–3	1.9	0.48	0.12
3–5	11.8	0.56	0.17
5–10	53.6	0.60	0.21
10–25	23.2	0.32	0.28
25–50	4.7	0.03	0.12
50–100	2.0	—	0.09
100–500	1.5	—	0.04
500 and over	0.3	—	—
All classes	100.0	0.47	0.21

[a] Taxable and nontaxable returns with itemized deductions. Derived from 1960 Tax File; for identification of the file, see footnote 2, this chapter.
[b] Proportion of interest deductions in the AGI class claimed on returns reporting income only from salaries and wages.
[c] Computed as ratio of (1) excess of interest deductions on returns with nonwage income over nonwage income on these returns (negative nonwage income being treated as zero) to (2) total interest deductions in the AGI class.

Almost one-half of personal interest deductions in 1960 was on returns reporting income only from salaries and wages (Table 12) and hence could not have been a cost of obtaining taxable income. A large part of the remainder was claimed by persons whose interest deductions exceeded their taxable income from sources other than salaries and wages. If individuals had been allowed to deduct interest payments only up to the amount of their taxable income from property, seven-tenths or more of the deductions actually taken in 1960 would have been ruled out. In

[8] *President's 1963 Tax Message,* Hearings before the House Ways and Means Committee, 88 Cong. 1 sess. (1963), Pt. 2, p. 863.

the $5,000 to $10,000 income class, the fraction would have been eight-tenths or more. (These are minimum fractions because in Table 12 all income from unincorporated business enterprises, which includes a substantial amount of labor income, is treated as if it were property income.)

In my opinion, the interest deduction should be limited to payments related to the production of taxable income, as determined by a direct matching or the pooling arrangement described above. Students' payments of interest on debts contracted to finance education that increased their earning power should be classified as costs related to the production of their earned income and should be deductible against that income.

Casualty Losses

The Internal Revenue Code allows a deduction for "losses of property not connected with a trade or business, if such losses arise from fire, storm, shipwreck, or other casualty, or from theft." The amount deductible is the excess of the loss over $100 for any one occurrence.[9] Since the deduction cannot exceed the cost or other basis of the property, the disappearance of unrealized capital gains does not give rise to a deduction. Furthermore, in computing the deduction, the recognized loss is reduced by any insurance or other compensation received.

The limitation of the deduction to losses exceeding $100 was introduced in the Revenue Act of 1964. In adopting this clause, Congress made clear that it regarded the casualty-loss deduction as a hardship provision rather than a refinement of the income definition. The House Ways and Means Committee stated that its intention was "to allow the deduction only of those losses which may be considered extraordinary, nonrecurring losses, and which go beyond the average or usual losses incurred by most taxpayers in day-to-day living" and which are "sufficient in size to have a significant effect upon an individual's ability to pay Federal income taxes."[10]

[9] Internal Revenue Code of 1954, as amended, sec. 165(c)(3).
[10] Revenue Act of 1963, House Ways and Means Committe, H. Rept. 749, 88 Cong. 1 sess. (1963), p. 52. The same language appears in S. Rept. 830, p. 57. The President had recommended that nonbusiness casualty losses be allowed only

The case for the casualty-loss deduction as a means of relieving hardship is weak. For this purpose, a floor related to income, as for the medical-expense deduction, would be more appropriate than the present provision, since a $100 loss is not as great a hardship for a person with a high income as for one with a low income.

A more important objection is that persons who wish protection can insure themselves against most of the casualties. Since uninsured losses are deductible but insurance premiums are not, the income tax discriminates against those who carry insurance and favors those who do not.[11] Through the casualty-loss deduction, the government in effect acts as a coinsurer, with its participation varying according to the taxpayer's marginal rate.

The unneutrality extends also to measures to care for property. For example, a householder who does not take the trouble to protect his shrubbery from a quick freeze or sudden drought may experience a deductible casualty loss. Expenditures incurred to care for the shrubs, of course, would be nondeductible personal expenses. Nor would a deduction be allowed if a loss was suffered because of neglect extending over a long period of time.

While uninsured casualty losses would be appropriate deductions for a tax assessed on accrued income comprehensively defined, their allowance is questionable so long as important items of imputed income and accrued capital gains are not taken into account. In my judgment, the casualty-loss deduction should be confined to uninsured losses with respect to property yielding taxable income, and premiums paid on insurance against losses on such property should also be deductible. The reasoning is that the losses or insurance premiums are properly viewed as costs of obtaining the services of capital goods and should be charged against the yield of these goods. When the yield is taxable, the costs are properly deductible in computing taxable income; when the yield is not taxable, the deduction is inequitable for the same reason that a deduction for interest payments is inappropriate.

---

to the extent that they exceeded 4 percent of AGI (*President's 1963 Tax Message Along with Principal Statement, Technical Explanation, and Supporting Exhibits and Documents Submitted by Secretary of the Treasury*, House Ways and Means Committee, Committee Print, Feb. 6, 1963, pp. 15-16).

[11] William Vickrey, *Agenda for Progressive Taxation* (New York: Ronald Press, 1947), pp. 60-62.

Child-Care Expenses

The deduction of expenses for the care of young children and disabled dependents was adopted in 1954 and liberalized in 1964. It is available to women, widowers, and husbands whose wives are incapacitated or institutionalized, but only when care is provided for the dependent "for the purpose of enabling the taxpayer to be gainfully employed."[12] Inasmuch as one's spouse is never a dependent within the technical meaning of the Internal Revenue Code (but is a "taxpayer" regardless of whether he or she receives a separate income), the deduction does not cover expenses for the care for a disabled husband or wife. Often, however, these expenditures would qualify as medical expenses and would be deductible as such if within the limits prescribed for that item.

The deduction for the care of children and disabled dependents is limited to a maximum of $600 for the care of one person and $900 for the care of two or more. Generally, a married person may take the deduction only if he files a joint return with his spouse and the joint AGI is below $6,900.[13] However, the income limitation does not apply to single women, widowers, wives whose husbands are incapable of self-support, or husbands whose wives are institutionalized.

In 1960, when the maximum amount deductible was $600 and the income ceiling and other conditions were more restrictive, the child-care deduction equaled only about 0.03 percent of AGI, and was claimed on only 1.1 percent of all taxable returns with itemized deductions.[14] The 1964 amendments will allow a large percentage increase, but the deduction will remain a minor item.

The language of the statute makes clear that the primary purpose of the deduction is to cover certain costs of earning income. The Senate Finance Committee report on the bill which introduced the deduction refers to child-care expenses that "a widow or widower

[12] Internal Revenue Code of 1954, as amended, sec. 214.
[13] The requirement for joint returns is waived for wives who have been deserted by their husbands; for AGI's between $6,000 and $6,900, the deduction is reduced dollar for dollar by the excess of AGI over $6,000.
[14] *Statistics of Income, 1960,* pp. 16, 36, 55.

with small children must incur . . . in order to earn a livelihood" and holds that these expenses, "are comparable to an employee's business expenses." The committee also argued that "in many low-income families, the earnings of the mother are essential for the maintenance of minimum living standards, even where the father is also employed, and that in such situations the requirement for providing child care may be just as pressing as in the case of a widowed or divorced mother."[15] The comments about living standards, the income limitation for married women, and the strict limit on the total deduction suggest that a secondary purpose of Congress was the relief of hardship.

Expenditures for the care of children and disabled dependents, of course, are not the only kind of work-related expenses. They are, however, somewhat more easily identifiable than many other costs of earning income, and they may be especially burdensome to low-income families and the other classes of taxpayer who are eligible for the deduction. In my opinion, some further liberalization of the maximum amount deductible and of the income ceiling would be justifiable.[16]

Medical Expenses

The deduction for medical expenses was introduced in 1942. It applies to expenditures for medical and dental care, hospitalization, drugs and medicines, certain related goods and services, and health and accident insurance. The deduction is intended to cover only expenses that are extraordinarily large in relation to income.[17] It has always been restricted to expenses in excess of a certain minimum percentage of income and has also been subject to a dollar limit. The present limitation is 3 percent of AGI, but for drugs only amounts spent in excess of 1 percent of income may be

[15] *Internal Revenue Code of 1954*, Senate Finance Committe, S. Rept. 1622, 83 Cong. 2 sess. (1954), p. 36.

[16] See the recommendations of President Kennedy (*President's 1963 Tax Message*, p. 12) and of the President's Commission on the Status of Women (*American Women* [1963], pp. 20-22); also *Report of Committee on Social Insurance and Taxes to President's Commission on the Status of Women* (1963), pp. 59-63.

[17] According to the House Ways and Means Committee, "generally only what are considered abnormal medical expenses are deductible" (H. Rept. 749, p. 56).

included in the total. These limitations do not apply to persons over 65. The dollar ceilings range from $5,000 to $40,000.

The limitations do not seem highly restrictive. In 1960, for example, consumers' expenditures for medical care averaged 4.9 percent of personal income.[18] Fifty-nine percent of all taxpayers with itemized deductions were able to claim a deduction for medical expenses in 1960 (Appendix Table A-7).

With the liberalization of the deduction in 1951 and 1954 and the increased frequency of itemization, the medical-expense deduction has been increasing rapidly in amount and as a proportion of estimated total personal expenditures for medical care. The deductions on taxable returns equaled 14 percent of estimated total expenditures in 1942 and also in 1950 but by 1960 had risen to 23 percent.[19]

More than any other itemized deduction, that for medical expenses tends to decline as a fraction of income as income rises (Table A-8). This is true for all taxpayers with itemized deductions and also for those claiming the deduction for medical expenses. Medical deductions are also especially large on nontaxable returns; in 1960, they amounted to 14.5 percent of AGI on all nontaxable returns with itemized deductions.[20] Nevertheless, the bulk of the deduction is taken on middle-income returns, and a considerable proportion of high-income persons qualify (perhaps mainly because of the special provisions for those over 65).

The medical-expense deduction has been widely approved, even by some who are critical of other personal deductions. The attitude seems to be that a person has little control over the amount of his medical expenses and that these expenses are unforeseeable and sometimes catastrophically large. Above a certain normal level, medical expenses are regarded as a reduction of an individual's freely disposable income and hence a reduction in his ability to pay taxes relative to others with the same income.

[18] *Survey of Current Business,* July 1962, pp. 8, 14. The estimate of total expenditures is that of the Office of Business Economics, Department of Commerce. It includes some items that are not eligible for deduction but excludes other items that are eligible. See Kahn, *Personal Deductions,* pp. 136-37 (footnote).

[19] *Ibid.,* p. 127; U. S. Department of Commerce, Office of Business Economics, *U. S. Income and Output* (1958), p. 150; *Survey of Current Business,* July 1962, p. 14; *Statistics of Income, 1960,* p. 55.

[20] Excluding returns with no AGI.

This attitude reflects the high regard in which medical care is held and the faith that is placed in its efficacy. Given prevailing values, it is plausible. Yet, the attitude does understate the voluntary element in medical expenditures and the consumption component of these outlays. Surely, the difference between the cost of a private suite in a proprietary hospital and a bed in a voluntary hospital is to a large extent a living expense rather than a medical expense; nevertheless, the whole cost of both accommodations is deductible, subject to the dollar ceiling.

The difficulties of distinguishing between ordinary consumption and medical expenses are reflected in rulings and court decisions on particular cases. Perhaps the most troublesome items have been travel expenses and outlays for household equipment and other consumer durables that are allegedly required for health reasons. Distinctions sometimes seem rather arbitrary. Thus a deduction was allowed for the cost of an airconditioning device (which did not become a permanent fixture) required by an allergic patient, whereas the cost of an oil furnace purchased on the advice of a physician by one who was allergic to coal dust was not deductible. The cost of a clarinet was deductible when the taxpayer's son had a tooth defect that allegedly was helped by playing the instrument. Taxicab fares and other local transportation expenses in traveling to and from a doctor's or dentist's office or hospital are deductible, and taxicab fares to and from work were allowed as a medical-expense deduction by a physically disabled person whose employment was recommended by a physician as part of a therapy program but denied to a handicapped polio victim who apparently worked merely to support himself. In some cases, the costs of travel to sunnier climates have been ruled deductible and in other cases not deductible. The deductibility of living expenses while away from home for medical care or health reasons is unsettled. The cost of preparing salt-free food and of taxi rides to restaurants serving it—but not the cost of the food itself—has been held deductible by a taxpayer wintering in Florida on the advice of his physician.[21]

Despite the inclusion of medical insurance premiums in expenses for purposes of the deduction, those with insurance are less favorably treated than others. The expenditures of a person with

[21] Commerce Clearing House (Chicago), *Federal Tax Guide, 1963*, paras. 3783, 3785, *Federal Tax Guide Reports*, March 22, 1963, p. 4.

insurance against catastrophic medical expenses are more regular than those of an uninsured person and hence less likely to exceed the floor in any one year. If the floor were equal to the average annual ratio of medical expense to income, a representative taxpayer with insurance or a prepayment arrangement covering all medical bills would never be able to claim a deduction. Anyone who carries no insurance makes the government a coinsurer against extraordinary medical expenses. In this respect, the medical deduction resembles the casualty loss deduction but is less discriminatory. The discrimination is real enough, nevertheless, to raise the question whether it is good public policy to offer a tax preference to those who choose not to carry insurance.

The suggestion has been made that the deduction should be turned into a tax credit, that is, a direct offset against tax liability equal to a certain percentage of medical expenses. With a deduction the fraction of the cost of deductible expenses absorbed by the government depends on the taxpayer's marginal rate, which rises with income, whereas with a tax credit the percentage of the cost covered would be the same for all taxpayers whose liability was large enough to absorb the full credit. If the view is accepted, however, that extraordinary medical expenses are a prior claim on income, a deduction is more appropriate than a credit.

The priority accorded to medical expenses by public opinion and the widely recognized special governmental interest in their financing seem to justify the continuation of the deduction in substantially its present form. The restoration of the floor to the original level of 5 percent of income or a somewhat greater increase would be consistent with the purpose of limiting the deduction to extraordinary expenses. There would also be merit in defining extraordinary expenses by reference to average income over a period of several years rather than the income of the current year only; however, the added complexity probably would outweigh any gain in equity.

Philanthropic Contributions

A personal deduction for philanthropic contributions was proposed in 1913, when the first income tax bill after the Sixteenth Amendment was under consideration, but was rejected. The deduction was adopted in 1917 in response to the fear that high tax rates would cause contributions to decline.[22] The deduction is now allowed for contributions to religious, charitable, scientific, literary, and educational organizations and organizations for the prevention of cruelty to children and animals, provided their net earnings, if any, are not for the benefit of private shareholders or individuals and provided that "no substantial part" of their activities is for carrying on propaganda or otherwise attempting to influence legislation. Also eligible are contributions to the federal government, state and local governments, veterans' organizations, and nonprofit cemetery companies. The deduction has always been subject to a limit related to the taxpayer's income except for persons whose contributions and income taxes absorb more than nine-tenths of their income for several years.

In the 1920's and 1930's, deductions for philanthropic contributions amounted to a bit more than 2 percent of taxpayers' income in most years; in the late 1940's and the 1950's, the figure was usually a little higher than 4 percent for taxpayers with itemized deductions but tended to decline slightly toward the end of the period.[23] These statistics do not necessarily indicate a change in giving habits. As with other items, the introduction of the standard deduction causes a bias since heavy contributors will tend to itemize more frequently than others. Also, taxpayers may take more pains in fully reporting contributions when tax rates are high, and, indeed, they may overstate them.[24]

The deduction for philanthropic contributions is relatively more important in the top income brackets than any of the other personal deductions. A curve relating contributions to income of taxpayers with itemized deductions would be U-shaped, with higher ratios at the two extremes than in the middle brackets (Appendix Table A-8). In this respect it would be the opposite of the curve for the interest deduction.

The justification for deduction of philanthropic contributions is usually stated as the encouragement or reward of socially desirable activity, rather than the refinement of the income definition

---

[22] Kahn, *Personal Deductions*, pp. 6-7, 46-47.
[23] *Ibid.*, p. 49; *Statistics of Income, 1958*, p. 42; *ibid., 1960*, p. 55.
[24] See Kahn, *Personal Deductions*, pp. 67-69, for comments on the apparent overstatement.

or allowance for differences in taxable capacity. Occasionally, efforts have been made to justify the deduction on the grounds that contributions divest the taxpayer of income, but this reasoning has not been widely accepted in the United States. In the United Kingdom, on the other hand, contributors can obtain tax relief only because of the general doctrine allowing avoidance of tax on assigned income, and the conditions are much more restrictive than in the United States.[25]

Contributions finance educational, cultural, religious, and welfare activities which are highly important but which are not adequately provided by a market economy. The cost of many of these activities would be assumed by the state if they were not covered by contributions, and to the extent that the deduction stimulates their voluntary support it helps relieve pressure on the budget.

But many of the organizations and activities would not be supported by taxation or would be financed less liberally if they were no longer financed by contributions. This is the basis of a strong criticism of the deduction. The taxpayer, by making a deductible contribution, forces the government in effect to make a partially matching grant for a purpose of his own choosing and to an organization whose operations are not subject to government review or control. Sectarian, provincial, eccentric, or frivolous uses of money may be aided along with the most worthy. Public money would not be appropriated for the religious functions of churches, which are major recipients of deductible contributions, or for many other activities that benefit from the deduction.

This criticism can be met on its own terms by arguing that the lack of government control is a positive advantage. Granted a consensus on the general desirability of the purposes that are aided, the absence of detailed legislative specifications concerning eligibility for assistance allows divisive controversy about the relations of church and state to be avoided. Even a militant atheist can tolerate deductions for gifts to churches if he knows that he can deduct contributions to causes that he espouses.

With respect to educational, scientific, and cultural activities, voluntary support helps maintain diversity and independence. In

[25] Royal Commission on the Taxation of Profits and Income, *Final Report*, Cmd. 9474 (London, 1955), pp. 58-60.

my judgment, it is fortunate that Congress does not feel it necessary to scrutinize deductions for contributions as regularly and
carefully as it examines appropriations or to attach the same conditions to the two. The appropriations process is not well suited to
the nourishment of new or unpopular ideas or minority tastes; the
usual procedures for handling public funds would often be cumbersome or worse in this area.[26] Despite occasional agitation for
stricter limitations, Congress has placed only one political control
on the deductibility of contributions: it is denied for contributions
to organizations that are registered as communist-action organizations or that have been directed to register as such by the Subversive
Activities Control Board.[27] A considerable amount of waste and
personal gratification of donors to questionable philanthropies may
not be too high a price to pay for decentralized control and flexible
operations of the worthy organizations and activities.

A real issue remains concerning the effectiveness of the deduction as an incentive to giving. Even if the arguments in favor of
the deduction are conceded to be qualitatively valid, they would
not establish a case for its continuance if it could be shown that
the amount of giving stimulated by the deduction is very small
relative to the revenue loss. The loss of government revenue requires either that tax rates be raised or public expenditures be
curtailed.

The revenue cost of the deduction is substantial. According to
Kahn's estimates, it amounted to one-third or more of total contributions by living donors in 1954.[28] At 1965 tax rates, this figure
may be a little more than one-fourth.

There is little basis for judging how contributors are influenced
by the tax saving or how much weight they attach to the opportunity of turning over to the recipient organization an amount
exceeding their own sacrifice of disposable income. The introduction of the optional standard deduction in the early 1940's, which
removed the tax incentive for contributions by those whose total

[26] For a similar argument with respect to property tax exemptions, see the
comments by M. Slade Kendrick, "Property Tax Exemptions and Exemption
Policies," in *Proceedings of the Fifty-first Annual Conference on Taxation*, National Tax Association (Harrisburg, Pa., 1959), p. 88.

[27] Internal Security Act of 1950, sec. 11(a) (64 Stat. 996; 50 U.S.C. 790).

[28] *Personal Deductions*, p. 72.

personal deductions were less than the standard amount, provided an opportunity for observation. Kahn concludes that there is no evidence that this diminished the share of income devoted to philanthropy and suggests that contributors who are subject to marginal tax rates of no more than 20 percent to 30 percent may be little influenced by tax incentives.[29] Vickrey's judgment is, "On the whole, the evidence would seem to indicate that. . . , while the deductibility may increase the gross amount of contributions, it does so by less than the tax relief granted."[30]

Tax considerations probably are more important for persons subject to high rate brackets than for those in low and middle brackets. While contributions are larger relative to income at the high income levels, persons in lower tax rate brackets account for a large part of total contributions. In 1960, 58 percent of the total listed on taxable returns was reported by persons with income below $10,000, and those taking the standard deduction also made contributions, although probably less generously on the average than persons with itemized deductions. There seem to be significant qualitative differences, however, between contributions made by low income groups and middle income groups and those by large givers. Small givers appear to contribute mainly to churches, whereas large givers offer relatively more support for education, hospitals, and voluntary welfare agencies.[31]

A better balance between revenue cost and incentive effects might be struck by limiting the deduction for contributions to persons whose gifts exceed a certain percentage of income. Contributions, like medical expenses, would become a factor in determining income tax liability only when they rose above a routine level. The objective would be to focus the reward or incentive more sharply by withdrawing the deduction from persons whose contributions are small relative to income while continuing it for heavier contributions. Those whose gifts were close to the floor would find that an increase in contributions would qualify them

[29] *Ibid.*

[30] William S. Vickrey, "One Economist's View of Philanthropy," in *Philanthropy and Public Policy,* Frank G. Dickinson, ed. (New York: National Bureau of Economic Research, 1962), p. 54.

[31] F. Emerson Andrews, *Philanthropic Giving* (New York: Russell Sage Foundation, 1950), p. 56; Kahn, *Personal Deductions,* pp. 81-82.

for the deduction and thereby reduce the cost to them of the additional contributions.

Consideration might be given to a floor of about 3 percent of AGI. This figure is slightly lower than the average for middle-bracket taxpayers who itemized deductions in 1960 and is substantially below the averages for other brackets (Appendix Table A-8). The available information is insufficient for an accurate estimate of the proportion of deductions that would have been disallowed by a 3 percent floor. Among the deductions disallowed would be a large number of small items, which are almost impossible for the Internal Revenue Service to verify and which may not be accurately reported.

The rationale of the ceiling on deductions for contributions is not obvious. The limit is now 30 percent of AGI for contributions to churches, schools, hospitals, and most other organizations supported by the general public; it is 20 percent for contributions to scientific, literary, or educational organizations not so supported and to private foundations, fraternal societies, and war veterans posts. If contributions to the organizations to which the 30 percent limit applies exceed that figure in any one year, the excess may be carried forward for five years. When a person's income tax plus contributions to organizations subject to the general 30 percent limit (and to certain private foundations) exceeds 90 percent of taxable income for the current year and eight out of the past ten years, the ceiling does not apply.[32]

The ceiling may be intended to help check abuses in the form of contributions to organizations devoted primarily to the personal gratification or convenience of the donor rather than true philanthropy; however, it seems only a weak safeguard. A direct attack on abuses, with complete denial of improper deductions, would seem preferable. Another view might be that, beyond a certain point, the revenue needs of the government should have priority over the admittedly worthwhile activities supported by philanthropy. But the escape clause for those whose contributions plus taxes exceed 90 percent of their income is hard to reconcile with

[32] Internal Revenue Code of 1954, as amended, sec. 170. The general limitations were liberalized in 1964, but the 90 percent exception was somewhat restricted.

this attitude.[33] Although the ceiling provisions do not appear very restrictive in their present form, consideration might be given to lifting them, if the treatment of gifts of appreciated property were simultaneously revised as suggested below.

Gifts of property as well as money are deductible, but contributions of one's own services are not deductible. The latter provision is reasonable, although it may seem discriminatory at first sight. If one contributes $100 of his current earnings to charity, he will still be taxed on that sum unless a deduction is allowed. If he does unpaid work worth $100, no deduction is needed to remove the contribution from his taxable income.

Certain gifts of property are accorded especially favorable treatment. A person who gives securities, real estate, works of art, or other property is entitled to a deduction equal to the current market value. When the current value exceeds the original cost, he obtains a deduction with respect to gains that have never entered into taxable income. It is advantageous to give appreciated property direct instead of selling it and contributing the proceeds. If the property were sold, the realized capital gain would be included in income and offset by the deduction. But if the property is given direct, no gain is taken into account, and the deduction applies against other income.

A donor who gives appreciated property makes a smaller sacrifice, relative to what he could obtain from a sale, than one who makes another gift. If, for example, two art collectors who are both subject to a 60 percent marginal tax rate each give a museum a painting worth $10,000, the deduction will save each of them $6,000 of tax. Now if one collector bought his painting many years earlier for $1,000, he would have had to pay $2,250 of capital gains tax if he had sold it (25 percent of a $9,000 capital gain) and would have realized $7,750. Compared with selling, the net financial cost of the gift is $1,750 ($7,750 — $6,000). If the other collector bought his painting recently at a price equal to its current value, he could sell without paying a capital gains tax; the net financial cost of his contribution is $4,000 ($10,000 — $6,000), which is the same as the cost of a $10,000 cash contribution.

[33] These givers may be left with more disposable income than might be supposed; the 90 percent level may be reached by gifts of appreciated property (see below and, for illustrative data, President's 1963 Tax Message, pp. 236-39).

There seems to be no good reason for favoring those who contribute appreciated property compared with those who give other property or cash. The present provision, moreover, gives rise to difficulties in valuing gifts or art objects, books and manuscripts, and other items and apparently tempts some donors to place excessive values on their gifts, occasionally with the collusion of recipient institutions. The inequalities and administrative difficulties could be avoided by limiting deductions for gifts of property to an amount equal to the cost (or other basis). Another approach, which would be less simple but which would deal with the inequities and abuses and lessen the valuation problems, would be to treat a gift as a constructive realization of a capital gain for tax purposes (see Chapter VIII). Either of these reforms would reduce the special tax incentives for making gifts of appreciated property but would leave unimpaired the general incentives for contributions.

Taxes

The deduction for taxes paid covers state and local taxes on property, income, gasoline and other motor fuels and state and local general sales taxes. Other state and local taxes and federal taxes generally are deductible only if incurred in business or the production of income. Foreign taxes on real property and income are deductible, but other foreign taxes are not deductible unless connected with trade or business or the production of income. (Subject to certain conditions, taxpayers may credit foreign income taxes against their U. S. tax instead of deducting the foreign income taxes from gross income, and this option is ordinarily chosen.)

The personal deduction for taxes paid has been curtailed over the years. Originally, most taxes that were legally imposed on a person, including the federal income tax itself, were deductible. (The deduction of the income tax did not require the solution of simultaneous equations; payments were then made in the year after the accrual of liability, and a taxpayer on a cash basis deducted the amount paid during the year rather than the liability on the current year's income.) The deduction of the federal income tax was eliminated in 1917, and that of federal excise taxes was dropped in 1943. In 1964, the deduction was ended for state and local taxes on tobacco and alcoholic beverages, automobile and drivers' licenses, and other state-local selective excises except gasoline taxes. Death and gift taxes are also nondeductible; however, a special credit for state death taxes is allowed against the federal estate tax.

It appears that, of total state-local taxes, roughly four-tenths qualify as personal deductions, about five-tenths are deductible as business costs, and somewhat less than one-tenth are not deductible.[34] Not all of the taxes eligible can be expected to be claimed as personal deductions. In 1960, about three-fifths of the eligible total were taken as personal deductions on returns with itemized deductions.[35]

Almost everyone who itemizes deductions reports tax payments (Table A-7). In relation to AGI, deductions for taxes tend to decline gently as income rises (Table 13). Statistics on the composition of the deduction for taxes, available for the first time for 1960, reveal, as would be expected, that property taxes, sales taxes, and miscellaneous taxes decline in relation to income whereas state income taxes are progressive. The 1964 amendments eliminated the deductibility of about three-fifths of the "other" state-local taxes. State-local taxes that remain deductible, however, are increasing faster than income, and the ratio of deductions to AGI is not likely to fall.

An argument in favor of the personal deduction for taxes that formerly attracted popular support is that the failure to allow the deduction would result in a particularly objectionable form of double taxation, involving "a tax on a tax." Congress rejected this rationale when it ended the deductibility of federal taxes and certain state-local taxes.

[34] Estimates for 1960 state-local tax revenue but with 1964 provisions governing deductibility. Two sets of estimates were made. One was based on James A. Maxwell's estimates for 1957 in *Tax Credits and Intergovernmental Fiscal Relations* (Washington: Brookings Institution, 1962), pp. 107, 187-98; U.S. Bureau of the Census statistics of state-local tax revenues in fiscal year 1960, *Tax Revenue of State and Local Governments in Calendar 1962* (August 1963); and *Compendium of State Government Finances in 1962* (1963). The other set was based mainly on estimates of tax accruals for calendar year 1960 by the Office of Business Economics, U.S. Department of Commerce, *Survey of Current Business*, July 1963, pp. 23, 39.

[35] Includes taxable and nontaxable returns; estimate based on sources mentioned in the preceding footnote and *Statistics of Income, 1960*, p. 14.

The most widely accepted reason for deducting state and local taxes is to aid in fiscal coordination in a federal system. The common version of this argument is that a deduction is needed to prevent confiscation. The danger that marginal tax rates will exceed 100 percent is greatest with respect to income taxes, and many commentators have concluded that the deduction should be

TABLE 13. Personal Deduction for Taxes Paid, by Adjusted Gross Income Classes and Taxes, Taxable Individual Returns with Itemized Deductions, 1960[a]

AGI Class ($000)	Percent of AGI				
	All Taxes	Real Estate Taxes	Sales Taxes	State Income Taxes	Other Taxes
Under 2	6.5	2.1	1.5	0.3	2.6
2–3	6.0	2.1	1.3	0.3	2.2
3–5	5.8	2.1	1.2	0.4	2.0
5–10	5.8	2.4	1.2	0.6	1.6
10–25	5.6	2.3	1.0	1.2	1.1
25–50	5.5	1.7	0.6	2.5	0.7
50–100	5.4	1.3	0.4	3.0	0.7
100–500	5.7	1.1	0.2	3.6	0.8
500 and over	4.5	0.6	0.1	3.3	0.7
All classes	5.7	2.2	1.0	1.0	1.4

[a] Derived from U. S. Treasury Department, *Statistics of Income, Individual Income Tax Returns, 1960*, pp. 14, 55.

allowed only for state income taxes. Another view is that confiscation in the literal sense is merely an extreme example of injustices that may occur when two levels of government tax independently. The federal government, because of its greater financial strength and wider jurisdiction, is better able than the states to grant relief from burdens due to overlapping taxes.

By offering a deduction for state-local taxes, the federal government also aids the other governments. The state and local governments have more scope for taxation; their citizens are likely to resist tax increases less strongly, and governing bodies are likely to feel less worried about the risk of losing population and business to places with lower taxes. The state and local governments, therefore, may be enabled to finance more adequately the important public services that are their primary responsibility. Deductibility, however, should not be overrated. It stops far short of wiping out the differences between high and low taxes and between progressive and regressive taxes. When federal income tax rates are reduced, the significance of deductibility diminishes.

An objection that is sometimes made to deductibility of state income taxes is that it reduces the progressivity of the federal income tax. This is arithmetically correct, but it has little significance for tax policy. The objectives of progressive taxation—the allocation of governmental costs according to ability to pay and the reduction of inequality—are not compromised. The degree to which these objectives are attained can be better judged by reference to the combined total of federal, state, and local taxes than by concentrating on taxes at one level of government. The federal government is in a better position than the states to take account of all taxes and to adjust its demands to help achieve a desired distribution.

In my judgment, the best balance between considerations of equity and intergovernmental fiscal coordination would be struck by continuing the personal deduction for state and local income taxes and broad sales and use taxes while eliminating it for property taxes and gasoline taxes. Taxes other than income taxes and general sales and use taxes would be deductible only as costs of obtaining taxable income. By allowing both income taxes and sales taxes to be deducted, the federal government would avoid exerting pressure on states to choose one or the other revenue source. Payments of income tax and sales taxes depend less on individual tastes and living arrangements than other tax payments and are less often used to finance services that especially benefit those who pay the taxes. The amount of income tax paid is easily ascertained; and, with the development by the Internal Revenue Service of tables showing standard amounts of deductions for sales tax in the various states, reporting and auditing of this item have been simplified.

The elimination of the personal deduction for gasoline taxes is justified because most of the proceeds of these taxes are used for the special benefit of those who pay them. Acting as a subsidy for commuting and other travel by automobile, this deduction makes its own small contribution to congestion and smog.[36]

The property tax is a doubtful item. Although it has special-benefit aspects, the tax is a major source of general revenue for local governments and may be sensitive to political pressures and competition between competing jurisdictions. Since the deduction is available only to homeowners, however, it gravely discriminates against renters, who bear a large part of the property tax on their dwellings. This inequity, in my opinion, outweighs the advantages of property-tax deductibility as a coordination measure. Others may think differently.[37] If imputed rent of owner-occupied dwellings were included in gross income, property taxes as well as other costs of ownership should be deductible.

Standard Deduction or Floor for Deductions

There are two possible methods of limiting the use of itemized personal deductions which are superficially quite different but actually rather similar. One is an optional standard deduction, which allows a person to deduct a certain percentage of his income or a fixed sum in lieu of itemized deductions. This method has been used in the United States for more than two decades. The other method is a provision, considered but not accepted in 1963-64, that would allow itemized deductions only to the extent that the total reported by a taxpayer exceeded a certain percentage of his AGI.[38] The latter idea is somewhat misleadingly called a "floor" for deductions, and I shall follow that usage.

The basic similarity between the optional standard deduction and a floor for itemized deductions is that both would lessen the extent to which income tax liability depends on expenditures for

[36] In the bill which became the Revenue Act of 1964, the House of Representatives included a provision eliminating the personal deduction for gasoline taxes as well as automobile and drivers' licenses; the Senate restored the deduction for all of these automotive taxes; the final version of the bill continued the deduction for gasoline taxes but eliminated it for the license fees.

[37] Maxwell believes that the rationale for deductibility of property taxes, income taxes, and sales taxes is "much superior" to that for deductibility of excises that are levied on a benefit basis or that serve sumptuary purposes (*Tax Credits*, pp. 97-100).

[38] *President's 1963 Tax Message*, pp. 14-15, 42-44, 98-99.

deductible items. Both measures are based on the belief that small expenditures for deductible items should not influence tax liability, either because the deductions are really unjustifiable but politically entrenched or because the deductions are best regarded as a form of special relief or incentive for people who incur unusually large expenditures for deductible items. A particular reason for disregarding small itemized deductions may be the belief that these are inaccurately reported and often are a means of petty cheating.

A difference between the standard deduction and the floor is that the former may require higher marginal tax rates than the latter in order to raise the same amount of revenue. Part of the difference in rates may be only nominal. For example, a rate of 15 percent on AGI minus a 10 percent standard deduction is really the same as a rate of 13.5 percent with no deductions. But once the standard deduction was exceeded the marginal rate under the former would be higher than that under the latter. In practice, furthermore, the floor is more likely to affect high-income persons than is the standard deduction.

On equity grounds, it is hard to put forward a positive case for either a standard deduction or a general floor. Neither device can distinguish between desirable and undesirable deductions. An express disallowance is necessary in order to eliminate unjustifiable items. There seems to be no good reason for making the deductibility of interest on a mortgage on an owner-occupied house, for example, turn on its ratio to the taxpayer's income. A homeowner with an unusually expensive house, a heavy mortgage, and a high interest rate seems no more deserving of relief than an average homeowner; both have voluntarily chosen their consumption patterns and financial arrangements. On the other hand, smallness is not a good reason for denying a deduction for interest paid on a debt relating to the production of taxable income. As argued above, separate floors can be rationalized for medical expenses (because the deduction is a form of government insurance against unusually heavy expenses) and for contributions (as a means of sharpening the incentive effects of the deduction). These considerations do not support a general floor.

The standard deduction, nevertheless, is well established and does simplify tax compliance and auditing. Simplification was the principal objective when the standard deduction was introduced in rudimentary form in 1941 and further developed in 1944. In 1964, the introduction of the minimum standard deduction was equivalent to a selective increase in personal exemptions (see Chapter IX).

The standard deduction, which may be taken in lieu of all itemized personal deductions, is equal to the greater of (1) 10 percent of AGI or (2) $200 plus $100 for each exemption shown on the return. Thus the minimum standard deduction is $300 for a single person or $400 for a married couple, plus $100 for each dependent.[39] The standard deduction is subject to a limit of $1,000 ($500 for married persons who file separate returns).

The standard deduction no doubt greatly facilitated the extension of the income tax during World War II to millions of persons who had not previously filed returns. While the number of taxable individual returns increased tenfold from 1939 to 1944, the number of returns with itemized personal deductions only doubled.[40] In 1944, more than four-fifths of all taxpayers elected the standard deduction, and this ratio was approximately maintained in the early postwar years. By 1960, however, the proportion using the standard deduction had fallen to 54 percent (Table 14). The standard deduction represented more than half of the amount of all personal deductions in 1950 but only a little more than one-fourth of the total in 1960 (Table 10).

The decline in the frequency of use of the optional standard deduction is attributable primarily to the growth of expenditures for deductible items and secondarily to the growth of income, which made the dollar limits more restrictive. If the proportion of taxpayers in each income class using the standard deduction had remained constant, the percentage of all taxpayers taking the standard deduction would have declined from 81 in 1949 to 71 in 1960 (instead of to 54 percent in 1960).[41] The adoption of the minimum

[39] Note that wives are not technically classified as dependents of their husbands for tax purposes even when they have no separate income.

[40] Number of taxable returns from U.S. Bureau of the Census, *Historical Statistics of the United States, Colonial Times to 1957*, pp. 714-15; number of taxable returns with standard deduction, Kahn, *Personal Deductions,* p. 163.

[41] Derived from Kahn, *Personal Deductions,* p. 163, and *Statistics of Income, 1960,* p. 65.

TABLE 14. Optional Standard Deduction by Adjusted Gross Income Classes, Taxable Individual Returns, 1960[a]

AGI Class ($000)	Percent of Returns Taking Standard Deduction	Standard Deduction as Percent of Total Deductions	Percent Distribution of Standard Deduction
Under 2	87.7	70.9	5.4
2–3	74.7	55.0	8.1
3–5	61.4	41.7	25.6
5–10	41.8	26.3	48.6
10–25	29.3	15.2	11.9
25–50	8.8	1.9	0.3
50–100	3.0	0.4	—
100–500	—	—	—
500 and over	—	—	—
All classes	53.8	26.2	100.0

[a] Derived from U. S. Treasury Department, *Statistics of Income, Individual Income Tax Returns, 1960*, pp. 55, 65.

standard deduction will increase the proportion of taxpayers choosing the standard deduction in the lowest income classes but will have little effect in income classes above $5,000. The restrictions on itemized deductions for casualty losses and the denial of deductions for certain taxes, which were included in the 1964 tax revision, will also cause some taxpayers to switch to the standard deduction. It seems unlikely, nevertheless, that the standard deduction will be restored to its original popularity.

Conclusion

On the basis of the review of individual items, it seems that a substantial curtailment of personal deductions would be justifiable but that a large part of the deductions should be continued. The major restrictions that seem appropriate are (1) the limitation of the deductions for interest and casualty losses to items associated with the production of taxable income; and (2) the restriction of the deduction for taxes to income taxes and broad sales taxes and to liabilities relating to the production of taxable income. If these principles had been in effect in 1960, they would have eliminated almost $11 billion of deductions on taxable returns or about one-third of all itemized deductions on these returns.[42]

Consideration should also be given to: (3) raising the floor for the medical-expense deduction; and (4) the introduction of a floor for the deduction for contributions. Owing to lack of data, I have not attempted to estimate the amount of deductions for these items that would be disallowed by the new provisions.

Any significant curtailment of the itemized deductions would make appropriate a cut in the optional standard deduction, which amounted to $11.7 billion on taxable returns in 1960. The revisions would allow a reduction in tax rates without loss of revenue and would bring about a reapportionment of taxes among individuals.

[42] The estimate reflects the assumption that the following would have been eliminated: three-fourths of personal deductions for interest paid, all personal deductions for real estate taxes, and the part of personal deductions for miscellaneous taxes and casualty losses that was not eliminated by the Revenue Act of 1964. The 1964 act eliminated about three-fifths of the deductions for miscellaneous taxes and three-fourths of those for casualty losses, or about 5 percent of all itemized deductions allowed in 1960. Data on deductions in 1960 are from *Statistics of Income, 1960*, pp. 14, 16, and 55.

CHAPTER VIII

Capital Gains and Losses

THE TAX TREATMENT of capital gains and losses has undergone several sweeping revisions since 1913. The present provisions have been vehemently attacked as too lenient and as too strict, a fact that unfortunately does not imply that they are close to the golden mean.

Present Treatment

Capital gains and losses are those realized on the sale or exchange of "capital assets," which, according to the Internal Revenue Code, comprise all property except stock in trade or other items held primarily for sale to customers in the ordinary course of trade, depreciable property and land used in business, copyrights, and certain other enumerated items. Gains realized on capital assets held six months or less are taxed as ordinary income, whereas gains on assets held longer than six months, so-called long-term gains, are subject to only one-half the regular tax rates with a maximum rate of 25 percent. Capital losses may be offset against capital gains in full and against other income to the extent of $1,000 in any one year. Any loss not offset in the year in which it occurs may be carried forward for an unlimited number of years.

184

Capital gains and losses are taken into account only when they are realized by a sale or exchange. Gifts are not considered realizations, and the recipient takes over the basis of the donor for the computation of capital gains. (The "basis" of a capital asset is usually, but not always, the cost; it is subtracted from the amount realized from a sale or exchange to compute the gain or loss.) The rule for gifts means that when the recipient sells the asset his taxable gain is the difference between the cost or other basis of the previous owner and the selling price, not the difference between the value at the time of the gift and the selling price. For computing a capital loss, the recipient's basis is the value at the time of transfer or the donor's basis, whichever is lower. For property passing at death by bequest or inheritance, no gain is considered to be realized by the decedent or the estate, and the heir takes as his basis the value at the date of death (or, in some cases, one year later). Thus, any unrealized gain or loss that had accrued between the time of acquisition by the decedent and his death is never brought to account under the income tax.

Special treatment is accorded capital gains on sales of personal residences. Generally, recognition and taxation of the gain are deferred if another residence of equal or greater value is bought within one year before or after the sale. If the cost of the new house or apartment is less than the sales proceeds from the old, tax is currently payable on a fraction of the gain equal to the ratio of the value of the new residence to the value of the old. The basis of the new residence is reduced by the amount of unrecognized gain on the sale of the old house. Hence, if the homeowner sells and does not replace within the time limit he is taxable on the cumulative amount of deferred gains on past residences as well as any gain on the most recent one. A person who is 65 or older may exclude from adjusted gross income (AGI) any capital gain attributable to the first $20,000 of the sales price of his personal residence. When the price exceeds $20,000, the gain is apportioned.[1]

A few other special provisions should be noted. Although depreciable property used in business is not classified as a capital

[1] This exclusion, which was adopted in 1964, is available only once and is subject to certain other conditions; when property is owned jointly by a husband and wife, only one of them is required to be over 65. See Internal Revenue Code of 1954, as amended, sec. 121.

asset, gains from its sale may be taxed as capital gains,[2] whereas losses are treated as ordinary losses and are deductible from income without regard to the limitation that applies to capital losses. The same is true of livestock held for breeding, dairy, or draft purposes and unharvested crops. Certain kinds of income that do not arise from the transfer of capital assets are taxed at the capital gains rates. These pseudo capital gains include: income from cutting or disposal of timber, coal royalties, iron ore royalties, certain lump-sum distributions from retirement plans, certain lump-sum employment-termination payments, and gains associated with qualified employee stock-option plans. Proceeds of the sale of patents are classified as long-term capital gains regardless of the form in which payment is received, whereas capital gains treatment is expressly denied for the sale of copyrights, literary, musical, and artistic compositions.

The origins and apparent purposes of the special provisions will not be reviewed in detail here. The provisions with respect to the lump-sum payments may have been intended as a crude substitute for averaging income that accrues over several years and that might be subject to unfairly high rates if taxed at ordinary graduated rates in one year; however, the special provisions were not repealed when a general averaging plan was adopted in 1964. Capital gains treatment for income from cutting timber and coal and iron ore royalties might be rationalized on the grounds that this treatment could be gained by sale of the standing timber or deposit and that in the absence of the special provision uneconomic sales would be stimulated. This argument, however, would be equally applicable to other mineral deposits and perhaps also to buildings and other long-lived properties and would not support special treatment for coal, iron ore, and timber. The special treatment of depreciable property does not seem to conform to any clear principle; it may be characterized as an incentive scheme or

[2] Gains on sales of depreciable personal property are classified as ordinary income to the extent to which depreciation has been allowed since January 1, 1962, while any remaining gain is treated as a capital gain (Internal Revenue Code of 1954, as amended, sec. 1245 [added in 1962]). Gains on depreciable real property are treated as ordinary income only to the extent that depreciation allowances in excess of straight-line depreciation have been taken since January 1, 1964, and the amount to be included in ordinary income is reduced according to the length of time the property is held (*ibid.*, sec. 1250 [added in 1964]).

as special-interest legislation, depending on one's point of view. The distinction between patents and copyrights may reflect the relative standing of technicians and artists and writers in American society.[3]

The following discussion concerns the general provisions for capital gains and losses of individuals, but toward the end of the chapter further comments will be made about the special provisions.

Capital Gains and the Income Definition

The definition of income that was endorsed in Chapter II makes no distinction for tax purposes between capital appreciation and other sources of power to consume. Adherents to a broad definition have conceded that it may be necessary to confine the income tax to realized gains and have recognized that, under a graduated tax, this may give rise to inequities unless relief is granted with respect to gains on assets held for more than one year. Others, who do not accept the Haig-Simons definition, have vigorously contended that capital gains and losses are basically different from ordinary income and losses and that they cannot fairly be subjected to the general income tax even if allowance is made for spreading them over the period during which they accrued or otherwise tempering the graduated rates. The question of tax justice will be examined in the next few pages; then attention will be turned to economic and administrative problems.

Nature of Capital Gains

One line of thinking, more common in Great Britain than in the United States, is that capital gains are not income—or at least are not income of the kind that the income tax is intended to reach —because of their casual and nonrecurrent nature. According to this approach, which has had a profound influence on the British

[3] There were, however, special circumstances leading up to the statutory formalization of the different treatments of patents and copyrights and literary, musical, and artistic creations. See Peter Miller, "Capital Gains Taxation of the Fruits of Personal Effort: Before and Under the 1954 Code," *Yale Law Journal,* Vol. 64 (November 1954), pp. 8-13; and Dan Throop Smith, *Federal Tax Reform: The Issues and a Program* (New York: McGraw-Hill, 1961), p. 139.

tax, income must come from a continuing source, as a fruit from a tree. This attitude seems to have originated in a predominantly agricultural economy in which landed property was the chief form of wealth and in which entailed estates were an important means of preserving family riches and power. Life-tenants and trustees had disposal over the annual harvest but were not allowed to sell the land.[4] In principle, capital gains were not taxable under the British law, and capital losses were not deductible, until 1962, when "speculative," short-term gains were made taxable at regular rates.[5] Long before that time, however, many items that would be classified as capital gains in the United States were brought under the regular income tax in Great Britain.

Early departures in the British tax from the requirement of strict annuality in relation to a continuing source turned on the apparent intention of the taxpayer. A royal commission recommended in 1920 that the income tax be applied to gains from all transactions entered into with a view to profit, but not to ordinary changes in investments unless trading was a regular source of profit.[6] Although this recommendation was not enacted in legislation, it influenced administrative interpretations, and the courts upheld the taxation of profit from isolated or occasional profit-making transactions.[7] Canada has followed British precedents but in the postwar period has tended to expand the tax base by narrowing the scope of tax-free capital gains.[8]

The emphasis on the investor's intentions is also reflected in

[4] For an especially interesting discussion, see Lawrence H. Seltzer, *The Nature and Tax Treatment of Capital Gains and Losses* (New York: National Bureau of Economic Research, 1951), pp. 25-108.

[5] The British income tax (standard rate and surtax) will apply to gains resulting from the sale of securities, land, buildings, commodities, and interests in such assets but not to gains from movable tangible property, a house owned and occupied by the seller, or fixed assets of a business. Gains will be taxed only on assets held six months or less except for gains on land, which will be taxed if realized within three years after purchase. House of Commons, Parliamentary Debates, *Weekly Hansard,* No. 555, April 1962, cols. 978-83.

[6] *Report of the Royal Commission on the Income Tax,* Cmd. 615 (London, 1920), para. 90-91, as quoted in *Final Report* of the Royal Commission on the Taxation of Profits and Income, Cmd. 9474 (London, 1955), pp. 27-28.

[7] Cmd. 9474, p. 28. See also A. R. Ilersic, *The Taxation of Capital Gains* (London: Staples Press, 1962), pp. 26-39, 94-109.

[8] Irving J. Goffman, "The Tax Treatment of Capital Gains in Canada," *National Tax Journal,* Vol. 14 (December 1961), pp. 356-61.

certain theoretical writing. Hicks, for example, develops a concept of windfall gains and losses that seems to bear a family resemblance to the distinction applied by the Inland Revenue Commissioners.[9] Hicks would exclude windfalls from economic income.

American thinking on the nature of income has differed from British. Probably because of different economic and social conditions, the annuality requirement never became firmly established in the United States. The American custom has been to refer to a man's wealth as a capital sum whereas in Britain the evaluation is ordinarily made in terms of annual income. Furthermore, in the American environment, actual and prospective appreciation in the selling value of land, structures, and securities has always attracted much attention.

The origin of the British tax in a schedular system (a group of separate taxes on income from different sources), in contrast with the unitary approach in the U. S. tax, may also have influenced attitudes toward capital gains.[10] For whatever reasons, it has been widely agreed in the United States that capital gains should be taxed, but the method of doing so has been in dispute. In the years 1913 through 1921, including a period of high wartime tax rates, capital gains were taxed as ordinary income; the treatment of capital losses varied from no provision for their deduction (1913-16), to offsetting against capital gains (1916-18), to full offsetting against ordinary income (1918-23). Since 1921, capital gains have always been taxed, but important categories of gain have been subject to lower rates than ordinary income. And, since 1923, there have always been limitations on the deductibility of capital losses against ordinary income.[11]

In a modern economy, it is impossible to draw a clear distinction between capital gains and other income from property. There is no fundamental difference between the yield of a bond or note that is originally issued at a discount—for example, a U. S. treasury

[9] J. R. Hicks, *Value and Capital*, 2d ed. (Oxford: Clarendon Press, 1946), pp. 179-80.

[10] This point is developed by Raymond L. Richman in his unpublished doctoral dissertation, "A Contrast of American and British Income Taxation" (University of Chicago, 1956).

[11] See Anita Wells, "Legislative History of Treatment of Capital Gains under the Federal Income Tax, 1913-1948," *National Tax Journal*, Vol. 2 (March 1949), pp. 12-32.

bill or savings bond—and a coupon bond. The difference is at most a matter of the timing of the yield. If the discount appears in the market after a security has been issued, it is an integral part of the yield for a prospective buyer and is equivalent to an additional final coupon. Investors in stocks and real estate act as if the prospect of selling the property for more than their purchase price is as important as dividends or rent in their decisions. Investment companies are ready to assume responsibility for the selection of securities that promise to rise in value and to distribute realized gains to individual investors in the convenient form of capital gains dividends (which are taxed to shareholders as long-term capital gains). The list of instances in which capital appreciation is a form of investment yield could easily be extended. Other kinds of income, including certain labor income, can be converted into capital gains and often have been so transformed in order to obtain a tax advantage. The U. S. law explicitly denies capital gains treatment to original-issue discount on bonds,[12] but market discount is eligible for the preferential tax rate as are other types of capital gain that are economically indistinguishable from fully taxed income.

The expected or unexpected character of the receipt does not afford a basis for a useful distinction. A large part of capital gains consists of the capitalization of reinvested corporate profits and other investment returns that are deliberately sought. Other capital gains are windfalls or casual income, but it is hard to see that this provides any guidance for tax policy. There is no way of discovering whether a particular gain is a windfall, and windfalls may take the form of dividends as well as capital appreciation. Nor is it clear that true windfalls, if identifiable, should be taxed more lightly than other income; heavier taxation seems at least as appropriate. Predictability and regularity of recurrence are not criteria of taxability in the American system, and—to American writers—they have no intuitive appeal as possible standards.

This line of reasoning indicates that investment and so-called speculation cannot be clearly separated. Virtually all investors are speculators in the sense that they risk their wealth in the light of

---

[12] Internal Revenue Code of 1954, as amended, sec. 1232. There was doubt about the exact status of original-issue discount before 1954.

their expectations of future prices and yields. Speculative gains and losses are commonly associated with changes in asset prices but these reflect changes in yields; speculative gains and losses can be experienced without a sale.

Double Taxation?

Since capital values reflect expected earnings, an increase in the market value of an asset indicates that its yield is expected to rise in the future (assuming a constant rate of discount or capitalization). To illustrate, suppose that an investor owns 100 shares of stock on which current and expected annual dividends are $1 per share and the market value $16 per share. Suddenly the expected annual dividends increase to $2 per share and the market price of a share rises to $32. The investor has an accrued capital gain of $1,600, and if the expectation concerning yields proves correct he will receive $100 more dividends each year for as long as he continues to hold the shares. Would it be unjust double taxation to tax both the accrued capital gain and the additional dividends? Will the answer be different if capital gains are taxed only at the time of realization?

Even though the appreciation of the shares is due solely to the expectation of increased dividends, the capital gain and the receipt of the additional dividends, in my view, may justifiably be regarded as separate taxable events. The appreciation represents an immediate increase of consumption power, due either to the retention of past corporate profits or improved earnings prospects, and the receipt of the dividends represents a further gain of consumption power.[13] There is no injustice in taxing both accretions to consumption power; failure to tax the capital gain will mean the omission of part of the investor's income. The reasoning in this case is analogous to that applicable with respect to the so-called double taxation of saving (Chapter II). Fundamentally, the question whether capital gains are taxed as accrued or only at realization is irrelevant

---

[13] When an appreciation is due merely to the expectation of a nonrecurrent dividend or other distribution, the market value of the shares will decline after the distribution. In this case, accrued net capital gains over the whole period will be zero.

to the double-taxation point. However, when gains are taxed only at realization, even the appearance of double taxation is dispelled because it is then clear that the appreciation of the value of the asset and the additional earnings are separable.

The argument that preferential treatment of capital gains is justifiable as a means of abating the so-called double taxation of corporate profits is also unpersuasive. Although corporate shares are an important source of capital gains, they are not the only source. Among stocks, the greatest capital gains tend to be realized on issues of corporations which retain the largest fraction of their profits and whose earnings hence are least exposed to any double taxation resulting from the application of the corporation income tax and the individual income tax on dividend income.

Price-Level Changes

Several writers who agree that certain capital gains are equivalent to ordinary investment income argue that a large proportion of nominal gains are spurious, being attributable to changes in interest rates or the price level. The point about changes in interest rates was examined in Chapter II, where it was concluded that a rise in market value due solely to a decline in the relevant rate of interest represents a real gain to the investor and that no injustice is done in taxing him on it. The question of price-level changes was left for consideration here.

Appreciation in the price of an asset that reflects only a general rise in prices is a fictitious gain because it gives the investor no increased command over consumer goods. Fictitious gains of this kind could be removed from the tax base by deflating the values of capital assets by a suitable price index and recognizing gain or loss only to the extent of changes in deflated values. The appropriate price index would be one of consumer goods or of all commodities, rather than an index of the price of capital assets, because deflation by the latter index would eliminate genuine gains associated with increases in earnings and relative prices of capital assets. In a period of declining consumer prices, the application of the deflator would convert some nominal losses into real gains, just as some nominal gains would be turned into real losses when the price index was rising.

Capital gains and losses are not the only income items affected by changes in the price level. An increase in wages, for example, that only matches the rise in consumer prices is just as fictitious as a capital gain due solely to a general price change. There is, to be sure, a difference in the degree to which people are affected. To illustrate, suppose that the consumer price index, annual wages, dividends, and the average market price of common stocks all rise by 20 percent. Both wage earners and shareholders have a nominal increase in current income receipts but no increase in real income; the shareholders also have an accrued nominal capital gain. So long as the shareholders refrain from realizing their nominal capital gain, their taxable income will be overstated no more than that of the wage earners. If, however, the shareholders sell some of their stock, their taxable income will be further increased.

Application of a price deflator to capital gains and losses but not to other items affecting income tax liabilities would produce results that seem more unjust than the consequences of failure to allow for price level changes. In a period of rising prices, holders of corporate stock, real estate, and other equities would pay less income taxes than they do under the present system whereas liabilities of others would not be affected (or would be increased somewhat to make good the revenue lost from the tax on capital gains). Since holders of equities, who would obtain tax relief, gain relative to persons with fixed incomes during an inflation, the unfairness of inflation would be accentuated. In a period of falling prices, the deflation of capital gains and losses would accentuate the problems of equity investors, who are often debtors, but would not reflect the real gains enjoyed by recipients of fixed incomes.

Discrimination could be minimized by applying a price deflator to all incomes, but this does not seem feasible. Furthermore, it would conflict with the principles of compensatory fiscal policy. An automatic increase in tax liabilities, such as occurs at present in a period of rising prices, is desirable because it limits the inflation. If the income tax were assessed on deflated income, its stabilizing power would be lessened.

Implications for Equity, Progressivity, and Administration

In the period 1949-60, net capital gains reported on individual income tax returns ranged between 1.7 percent and 3.9 percent of reported adjusted gross income.[14] The total income tax yield would have been increased by some 5 to 10 percent if capital gains had been taxed in full at ordinary rates and the volume of realized net gains had not been affected.[15]

The treatment of capital gains is far more significant for the income tax than these statistics may suggest. The progressivity and equity of the tax are greatly affected because of the concentration of gains in the hands of high income groups and because of variations in the amounts of gains realized by persons in the same income class. The close relation of capital gains to the ownership of corporate stock and other business assets gives them strategic economic importance.[16]

Information on the distribution of net capital gains in 1949 and 1959, the postwar years of minimum and maximum net gains, is summarized in Table 15. The table shows that in both years capital gains were an important income source in high brackets but a minor income source in middle and low brackets. About half of all reported net gains appeared on the 1 percent of returns with the highest adjusted gross incomes, those above approximately $15,000 in 1949 and approximately $25,000 in 1959. Since these returns reported about one-tenth of all gross income, capital gains are much more concentrated than total income.

Owing to the distribution of capital gains, the preferential tax

[14] Taxable and nontaxable returns. Derived from *Federal Revenue System: Facts and Problems, 1961*, Joint Economic Committee, Committee Print, 87 Cong. 1 sess. (1961), p. 235, and U. S. Treasury Department, *Statistics of Income, Individual Income Tax Returns*, annual volumes (cited hereinafter as *Statistics of Income, 19 . .).

[15] My estimates are based on estimates by Wilfred Lewis, Jr. in his study, *Federal Fiscal Policy in the Postwar Recessions*, Studies of Government Finance (Washington: Brookings Institution, 1962), p. 284, and data from *Statistics of Income*. They range between 5½ percent in 1957 and 10 percent in 1955. For an estimate of tax yield under a proration plan, see below.

[16] For information on the sources of capital gains, see *Statistics of Income, 1959, Supplemental Report, Sales of Capital Assets Reported on Individual Income Tax Returns*, p. 10.

TABLE 15. Net Capital Gains as Percent of Gross Income and Their Distribution by Adjusted Gross Income Classes, 1949 and 1959[a]

AGI Class ($000)	Net Capital Gains as Percent of Gross Income		Cumulative Percent of Net Capital Gains	
	1949	1959	1949	1959
Under 5	0.6	1.8	22.4	13.6
5–10	1.7	1.2	40.9	26.8
10–15	3.3	3.1	49.0	36.6
15–20	3.8	6.4	54.1	43.2
20–25	4.0	8.5	57.7	48.1
25–50	5.2	11.5	68.2	62.4
50–100	8.5	18.6	77.6	75.2
100–150	12.9	31.3	82.2	81.6
150–200	16.6	39.7	85.1	84.7
200–500	23.7	49.9	91.7	92.2
500–1,000	31.0	62.8	94.9	95.8
1,000 and over	44.9	59.5	100.0	100.0
All classes[b]	1.8	4.0	...	...

[a] Taxable and nontaxable individual returns. Net capital gains are the full amount of gains minus capital losses, without regard to the statutory limitations on the amount of gains and losses taken into account for tax purposes. Gross income is adjusted gross income plus the part of net capital gains not included in AGI. Derived from U.S. Treasury Department, *Statistics of Income, 1949*, Pt. 1, pp. 13, 22, 75-76, 154-57, and *Statistics of Income, Individual Income Tax Returns, 1959*, pp. 24, 65.
[b] Includes returns with no AGI.

rates for them have little effect on average effective tax rates in lower brackets but substantially reduce average effective rates at the top, thereby lessening progressivity. Statistics relating to the influence on effective rates are given later in this chapter (Table 16) and in Chapter IX (Chart 3) and Appendix A (Table A-10). Of course, particular individuals are affected more or less than the average for their income class depending on the composition of their income.

Low rates on capital gains are favorable to investors; however, since 1929, the low rates have been accompanied by an unfavorable provision consisting of limitations on the deductibility of capital losses from ordinary income. The intention apparently is to prevent investors from timing their gains and losses so that the losses are offset against ordinary income which is subject to higher tax rates than capital gains. Successful use of this technique would mean that the net tax attributable to the cumulative amount of net capital gains (gains minus losses) over a period of years would be even lower than the nominal rate on capital gains. The limitations, however, may work hardships on those whose gains and losses occur irregularly. These investors may be taxed on gains in certain years without ever being able to deduct fully losses incurred in other years. (Skillful investors with diversified portfolios can avoid this by careful timing of gains and losses.) A limitation on deductibility of losses is not a suitable averaging device to correct for possible anomalies under graduated rates; the purpose of averaging would be to allow more liberal treatment than would be accorded by full deductibility in a single year.

To the extent that losses are experienced by persons who never realize equivalent gains, the favorable taxation of gains can hardly be regarded as an offset to the restrictions on loss deductibility. In the absence of continuous records of the investment experience of a representative sample of identical persons, it is not clear to what extent gains and losses are realized by different persons. Within any one year, it is usual for certain individuals to have losses far in excess of their gains.[17]

Even if capital gains were taxed as heavily as ordinary income, Congress might hesitate to allow full deduction of capital losses because of fear of manipulations. Full deductibility would surely encourage the realization of accrued losses. Persons with diversified portfolios might be able to schedule transactions so as to minimize their exposure to higher-bracket tax rates. But, if capital losses are indeed negative income items, the chief objection to this practice would be that such persons would have especially good opportunities for averaging taxable income—not a grave inequity if all capital gains, including those accrued at death, were included in gross income. Full deductibility would offer an additional incentive to claim artificial losses, but the problem of auditing such claims would not be wholly new and does not seem likely to be very difficult.

A consequence of the present tax treatment of capital gains that is not widely appreciated is that it inhibits other tax reforms.

---

[17] Seltzer (*Capital Gains and Losses,* pp. 181-97) stresses that favorable tax treatment of capital gains does not necessarily justify the limitation of capital-loss deductions because gains and losses may be experienced by different persons.

An illustration is percentage depletion. Supporters of percentage depletion argue that little would be accomplished by restricting depletion allowances to the recovery of actual costs because this would merely encourage owners of mineral deposits to sell in order to take advantage of the capital gains tax rate. Percentage depletion allowances may amount to as much as 50 percent of net income from the mineral property (computed without allowance for depletion), and in extreme cases, where costs depletion would be negligible, income tax liability is virtually halved. Under present capital gains provisions, if percentage depletion were eliminated, the owner of the deposit could sell at a price reflecting the present value of expected future net production[18] and be taxed at a rate not higher than one-half that applicable to ordinary income. The new owner could claim cost depletion on the basis of his purchase price. Given accurate foresight and a fairly active market for mineral properties, present owners could escape much of the possible effect of elimination of percentage depletion unless capital gains provisions were simultaneously tightened.[19]

Another objection to the present provisions is that they allow conversion of ordinary income into capital gains in order to take advantage of the lower rate. Income from personal effort, profits from the active conduct of a business enterprise, and returns from passive investments can all be turned into capital gains in certain circumstances, but in general the ease with which the conversion can be made varies in inverse order to this listing. The history of the income tax discloses many ingenious schemes, which led to preventive legislation, which in turn prompted new efforts to qualify for long-term capital gains treatment.[20] Several of the more transparent schemes are no longer allowed, but it will never be possible to preclude all conversions. The fundamental method, which is per-

[18] That is, the discounted value of output less production costs other than depletion and less income tax.

[19] So long as new owners were allowed to take cost depletion on the basis of their purchase price, the elimination of percentage depletion would not depress the value of a mineral property to prospective buyers since cost depletion would ordinarily be more advantageous to them in any case. See Stephen L. McDonald, *Federal Tax Treatment of Income from Oil and Gas,* Studies of Government Finance (Washington: Brookings Institution, 1963), pp. 92-100.

[20] Seltzer, *Capital Gains and Losses,* pp. 211-53.

fectly legal, is to reinvest profits in a corporate business and later sell the shares at a price that reflects the earning power of accumulated profits or, better still, pass on the shares to one's heirs. This technique is suitable mainly for closely held corporations, but it can also be adapted to publicly held companies. For the latter it is facilitated by the periodic issuance of small nontaxable stock dividends, a growing practice.

An aspect of the capital gains problem that has received far less attention than it deserves is the complexities of law, administration, and compliance that are attributable to the preferential treatment of long-term capital gains. When the tax rates applicable to one form of income differ widely from those on other income, taxpayers must be expected to make great efforts to bring their income receipts within the preferred area while tax administrators try to protect the revenues by resisting these efforts.

One expert has summarized his views as follows:

The income tax provisions of the 1954 Internal Revenue Code [most of which are still in effect] represent probably the most complex revenue law ever enacted in the fiscal history of any country. The subject singly responsible for the largest amount of complexity is the treatment of capital gains and losses. And the factor in that treatment which is accountable for the resulting complexity is the definition of capital gain and of capital loss.[21]

He saw no escape from difficulties "formidable almost beyond belief" so long as there is a large difference between tax rates on capital gains and ordinary income, the refined and intricate definitions of the present code are followed, and Congress continues to grant relief from ordinary income tax rates by bestowing capital gains status on certain kinds of income.[22] The exclusion of capital gains from taxable income would not obliterate definitional problems, but would intensify them because it would increase the difference between the tax on capital gains and other income.

[21] Stanley S. Surrey, "Definitional Problems in Capital Gains Taxation," in *Tax Revision Compendium,* House Ways and Means Committee (1959), Vol. 2, p. 1203; for an earlier version of this paper, see *Harvard Law Review,* Vol. 69 (April 1956), pp. 985-1019.
[22] *Tax Revision Compendium,* Vol. 2, pp. 1228-29.

A New Method of Taxing
Capital Gains and Losses

The arguments so far examined point to the conclusion that capital gains should be taxed like other income, except for a provision to alleviate the effect of the application in one year of graduated tax rates to gains that have accrued over several years. Equity also seems to call for full deductibility of capital losses from taxable income, again with a provision for correcting the effect of bunching.[23]

Even the case for relief from discrimination due to bunching of realized gains and losses is weaker than is sometimes implied. The discrimination is partly or wholly offset by the advantages of postponing tax until the gain is realized. Tax postponement allows the investor to earn a return on the amount that will later be paid in tax. Bunching, moreover, increases the tax only when the investor is raised into a higher tax bracket than he would occupy if the gains were distributed over the years during which they accrued. Movements between brackets may not occur when the gain is small relative to taxable income. If gains on different assets are realized in more or less equal amounts each year no discrimination occurs even if gains are bunched on each asset and are large relative to total income.

Some form of spreading of gains and losses, nevertheless, would be desirable to avoid harsh treatment of recipients of large and irregular capital gains or losses. The objective would be to approximate the tax result that would have occurred if the gain or loss had been realized in equal installments over the period during which the investor held the asset. Since it would be impracticable to reopen past-year returns, the adjustment would have to be made on the

[23] The bunching under consideration occurs because losses are taken into account only when realized; its alleviation is in principle distinguishable from general averaging of income for tax purposes (see Chapter IX). Capital gains and losses would be irregularly distributed among years even if taken into account as accrued; indeed the year-to-year fluctuations might be accentuated. The term "allocation" or "proration" will be used to refer specifically to the correction of bunching due to adherence to the realization requirement, whereas "averaging" will be reserved for the broader problem of smoothing out all kinds of irregularities in taxable income.

basis of the tax return of the year in which realization takes place (as in the limited general averaging plan adopted in 1964; see Chapter IX). Basically, the method would be to allocate or prorate the gain or loss and to determine the tax rate applicable to the whole gain or loss by regarding the pro rata amount as a marginal addition to, or deduction from, current-year income.[24]

Where only a few transactions were involved, it might be feasible to prorate gains or losses separately for each transaction by dividing by the number of years the asset was held; but this would not be practicable for large portfolios. It would be much simpler and almost equally effective to prorate by dividing the aggregate net long-term gain or loss by an arbitrary factor of say 3 or 5. To illustrate, suppose that the proration factor is 5 and consider the case of a married couple with taxable income from ordinary sources of $20,000 and a long-term capital gain of $20,000. The pro rata capital gain would be $4,000, and the marginal tax rate on an increment of income of this size would be 32 percent (under the schedule for 1965 and later years). Applying this marginal rate to the whole gain would yield a $6,400 tax on the gain; the total tax liability would be $10,780 ($4,380 of tax on $20,000 of ordinary income plus $6,400 of tax on the $20,000 long-term capital gain). If capital gains were taxed at ordinary rates without proration, the couple's total tax would be $12,140; under present law it is $7,880.

A more complete and formal statement of the proposal illustrated above is as follows: A taxpayer would first determine his net long-term capital gain or loss by combining gains and losses realized on assets held longer than 12 months. If he had a net long-term gain he would proceed as follows: (1) prorate the net capital gain by dividing it by 5, 3, or some other arbitrary figure; (2) compute a tentative tax at regular rates on his ordinary income plus the pro rata net capital gain; (3) compute tax on his ordinary income; (4) compute the tax on his net capital gain by (a) subtracting the tax on ordinary income, as computed in step 3, from the tentative tax computed in step 2 and (b) multiplying by the proration factor; and (5) determine final tax liability as the sum of the tax on or-

[24] For an early discussion of the idea, see U. S. Treasury Department, Tax Advisory Staff, *Federal Income Tax Treatment of Capital Gains and Losses* (1951), pp. 89-90.

dinary income, as computed in step 3, and the tax on the net capital gain, as computed in step 4. If a net capital loss was realized, the procedure would be analogous but would be directed toward determination of the tax reduction (or negative tax) attributable to the loss. Loss carrybacks and carryforwards would be granted when the pro rata loss exceeded ordinary income. Even when this did not occur, the tax reduction due to a capital loss could exceed the tax on ordinary income; in these cases, the excess could be set off against tax of prior or future years.

Proration would minimize the tax consequences of bunching by, in effect, widening the tax brackets for long-term capital gains or losses by a multiple equal to the proration factor. A proration factor of 5, for example. would be equivalent to setting up brackets for capital gains or losses 5 times as wide as the brackets for ordinary income. For persons realizing gains in roughly equal amounts each year, the tax on capital gains would continue to be less progressive than that on ordinary income. For those with widely fluctuating gains or losses, the timing of realization would affect tax liability because of variations in marginal tax rates due to fluctuations in ordinary income and changes in statutory tax rates. This kind of variation, though not peculiar to capital gains or losses, is especially important for them owing to the irregularity of accrual of gains and losses and the great flexibility that investors have in timing their realization. It could not be avoided, however, without a complex plan of cumulative income averaging.

Table 16 gives estimates of the tax on net capital gains in 1960 under the provisions then in effect and with full taxation at regular rates under a proration plan with a divisor of 5. The actual tax on capital gains was about half the amount that would have been payable under the proration plan. (With a proration factor of 3, the tax on capital gains would have been about 8 percent larger than that with a factor of 5; with a proration factor of 10, about 8 percent smaller.) In making the estimates, net capital gains were treated as marginal increments to income.[25]

[25] The estimated tax on net capital gains is the algebraic sum of the tax on gains and the negative tax, or tax reduction, attributable to net capital losses. The proration computations were made by electronic computer separately for each return in the 1960 Tax File (see footnote 2, Chapter VII) that reported capital gain or loss, and the aggregates were estimated by applying sample

TABLE 16. Total Income Tax and Estimated Tax on Net Capital Gains by Adjusted Gross Income Classes, Taxable Individual Returns, 1960ᵃ

(Money amounts in millions of dollars)

AGI Class ($000)	Total Tax	Estimated Tax on Capital Gains		Additional Tax on Capital Gains under Proration Plan	
		Actual	Under Proration Plan	Amount	Percent of Actual Total Tax
Under 5	$ 6,332	$ 34	$ 19	$ −15	−0.2
5–10	15,404	111	167	56	0.4
10–15	6,140	94	135	41	0.7
15–20	2,355	87	131	44	1.9
20–25	1,452	63	86	23	1.6
25–50	3,676	251	374	123	3.3
50–100	2,198	283	516	233	10.6
100 and over	2,123	696	1,900	1,204	56.7
All classes	$39,680	$1,620	$3,326	$1,706	4.3

ᵃ Derived from 1960 Tax File, a sample of individual income tax returns (see footnote 2, Chapter VII) and U. S. Treasury Department, *Statistics of Income, Individual Income Tax Returns, 1960*, p. 76. Total tax is actual tax after credits, including actual tax on net capital gains; it differs slightly from the amounts shown in *Statistics of Income* owing to sampling errors. The proration plan provides for ordinary 1960 tax rates with a proration factor of 5; for explanation see text. The estimates reflect the deduction of net capital losses; under the proration plan an allowance is made for full current deductibility of capital losses, but net losses in excess of the statutory limitation that was applicable in 1960 were not prorated.

For taxpayers with incomes below $5,000, the estimated aggregate tax is slightly smaller under the proration plan than under the 1960 law. In this income group, the limitation on the deductibility of losses increased tax liability more than the preferential treatment of gains reduced it. Of course, the persons who suffered from the limitation on loss deductibility were not the same ones who benefited from the capital gains provisions. Table 16 also shows that, if the tax under the proration plan is taken as the norm, the capital gains provisions had only a trivial influence on aggregate tax liability of persons with AGI below $15,000 but a

weights. Since the Tax File tapes showed the amount of net capital losses that was currently deductible, rather than total net losses before the statutory limitation, I estimated the effect of full deductibility of capital losses on the basis of *Statistics of Income* data, by applying marginal tax rates to reported losses. The result is an estimate reflecting full deductibility of losses, but with proration only of the part of losses that was currently deductible in 1960. The aggregate net tax under the proration plan is overstated but not greatly.

major influence on aggregate liability of those with AGI above $100,000.

In 1960, the adoption of full taxation of capital gains, under the proration plan, would have allowed statutory tax rates to be cut by 4 percent on the average without loss of revenue. If the rate cut had been evenly distributed over all brackets, the revision would have considerably increased the progressivity of the income tax. On the other hand, if the rate cut had been devised so as to maintain over-all progressivity unchanged, deep reductions in top bracket rates would have been possible. Under the latter approach, the average statutory rates applicable to persons with AGI above $100,000 could have been slashed by 36 percent (57/157). No doubt, some compromise between the two extremes would be accepted if the revision were enacted. Even with compensatory rate adjustments, taxpayers who received more than the average amounts of capital gains would find their liabilities increased, while those with less than average amounts of capital gains would have the opposite experience.

Admittedly, a proration plan like that described above would be complex. Although the computations would be similar to those required for the general averaging plan introduced in 1964 and for the proration schemes that had previously applied to certain kinds of income, the capital gains plan would affect far more taxpayers. In 1960, capital gains or losses were reported on about one-twelfth of all individual returns, taxable and nontaxable. However, the tax liabilities of many of those with gains or losses would not be affected by proration, because the amounts would be too small to cause the taxpayer's income to pass across the boundaries of a tax rate bracket. In 1960, 26 percent of the persons with gains or losses reported amounts of less than $200 and another 22 percent reported more than $200 but less than $1,000.[26] For these persons, the tax payable under the proration plan would not differ greatly in absolute amount from that payable if gains were made fully taxable and losses fully deductible without proration (though in some cases proration would effect a large percentage change in

[26] *Statistics of Income, 1960,* pp. 36-37, 59. The figures given in the text were obtained by doubling the amounts included in AGI, on the assumption that all net gains and losses were long term, which is not true but which yields figures that are accurate enough for present purposes.

tax). Moreover, for many persons with gains or losses greater than $1,000, proration would have little or no significance. It should be possible to devise a return form that would allow these taxpayers to omit the proration computations.

The effect of proration cannot be approximated by exclusion from taxable income of a fraction of realized gains or losses, as under present law or the more elaborate system in use in 1934-37 which scaled down the proportion of gain or loss taken into account for tax purposes according to the length of time the asset was held. Exclusion of a certain fraction of gains from taxable income gives a tax benefit that varies directly with the investor's marginal tax rate, whereas the benefit of proration depends on the width of the ordinary tax bracket and the difference in tax rates between brackets. To take an extreme example, partial exclusion would be most beneficial to those whose gains would fall entirely in the top rate bracket, whereas proration would not affect the liabilities of these persons.

A provision for constructive realization of capital gain or loss when assets are transferred by gift or at the death of the owner would be a desirable feature of any revision that increased tax rates on realized gains. Otherwise, the tax incentive for postponing the realization of gains would be unduly increased. (See the discussion of "locking-in" below.)

Effects on Investment

However strong the case in equity for taxing capital gains at the same rates as other income, this will not be acceptable if there is reason to believe that the economic consequences would be highly detrimental. It has been argued that preferential taxation of capital gains is a necessary means of shielding investment from the effects of high tax rates, that the lure of lightly taxed capital gains is needed to entice investors into risky ventures.

Since the favorable treatment of capital gains applies to only one form of investment return, it does not offer general tax relief for investment. Indeed, on the assumption that total revenue is to be maintained, it requires taxes to be higher on other income, including investment income. As shown above, a small general reduction in income tax rates or a substantial reduction in top-bracket rates would be possible without sacrifice of revenue or over-all progressivity if the differential in favor of capital gains were eliminated. Or consideration might be given to a more selective measure such as the further liberalization of depreciation allowances or loss offsets. On the other hand, the preferential taxation of capital gains may be supported on the grounds that the kinds of investment that benefit are especially likely to be discouraged by the income tax or have special social importance.

The preferential tax rate on capital gains offers an inducement to seek out investments that promise a return in the form of capital appreciation in preference to those that offer dividends, interest, rent, or other annual yield. A Harvard Business School study, based on extensive interviews in 1949 with a sample of 746 investors, confirmed that those with large incomes were greatly attracted by the differentially low tax rate on capital gains. According to the authors, "inherently venturesome" or "appreciation minded" investors had been induced "to shift funds out of relatively conservative investments, offering little or no opportunity for capital appreciation, and into more venturesome types of investments such as relatively speculative marketable common stocks, closely held companies, new ventures, real estate, and oil properties."[27] Although the study concluded that, for equity-type investors as a whole, the net influence of taxation was to induce a shift to less risky investments, the authors thought that the flow of funds to certain investments offering unusually large capital gains potentialities, such as new ventures, might actually be increased.[28]

The limitation on the deductibility of capital losses must partly offset the attractions of the low tax rate on capital gains. The limitation, however, applies mainly to the deduction of capital losses from ordinary income; capital losses may be deducted in full from capital gains in the current year and within an unlimited carryover period. For investors with diversified portfolios, the restriction on loss deductibility may not seem severe. Among the investors inter-

[27] J. Keith Butters, Lawrence E. Thompson, and Lynn L. Bollinger, *Effects of Taxation, Investments by Individuals* (Boston: Harvard University Graduate School of Business Administration, 1953), pp. 41-42.
[28] *Ibid.*, pp. 50-51.

viewed by the Harvard Business School group, a large proportion of whom were high-income persons, many more were attracted by the favorable tax rate differential than were repelled by the restrictions on loss deductibility.[29]

Although investments promising capital gains usually may be more risky than others, they are not always so. As already mentioned, a high-grade bond selling at a discount is virtually certain to produce a capital gain if held to maturity, but there is no economic difference between this security and another of the same quality and maturity that is selling at par because its coupon rate equals the market rate.

On the whole, it seems likely that the tax differential in favor of capital gains causes individual investors to allocate a larger fraction of their resources to risky items than they would if capital gains and losses were taxed as ordinary income and losses. The differential almost certainly encourages the retention of corporate profits and thus favors investment that can be financed from this source.

Although risk-taking is commonly regarded as wholesome, it may waste capital when carried too far. A prudent policy, therefore, might aim at neutrality toward risk assumption rather than its stimulation or discouragement. According to this standard, a tax preference for capital gains could be supported to the extent that it counterbalanced discrimination against risk-taking due to other provisions but would be undesirable if it did more. The standard is not very helpful because its application would require more precise knowledge about investors' reactions to taxation than is now available. A further difficulty is the lack of selectivity in capital gains tax treatment, which extends to gains from land speculation and other activities that contribute little to innovation and growth as well as to gains from highly productive investments.

The consequences of a tax incentive for retaining corporate profits, instead of paying dividends, are debatable. Many economists argue that capital will be most efficiently allocated if profits are distributed and individual shareholders are allowed to decide whether they should be reinvested where earned or placed else-

[29] *Ibid.*, p. 42. The capital loss provisions in 1949 were similar to the current ones but the carryforward of losses was limited to five years.

where. This attitude seems to be based on general confidence in the market mechanism rather than a systematic comparison of the investment decisions of shareholders and the executives of profitable corporations. The dividend-payout ratio, moreover, may affect shareholders' consumption and thus the total amount of resources available to corporations as well as the allocation of capital among firms.

The conclusion with respect to investment allocation must remain somewhat indefinite. On balance, the allocative effects of a tax differential in favor of capital gains may be economically desirable, but they are not unambiguously so. The capital gains potential of financial and real investments is not a reliable indicator of their social contribution, and there is much waste motion in turning investment income into capital gains.

"Locking-in"

A persistent criticism of the capital gains tax—which would become more powerful if the tax rate were raised—is that it "locks-in" investors, making them reluctant to change their portfolios because by doing so they incur a tax liability that can be postponed or avoided by not selling. Locking-in is said to accentuate fluctuations in security prices. At a time of rising security prices, when many investors have substantial unrealized gains, the discouragement of sales is alleged to cause the market to go still higher, ultimately provoking a greater corrective decline than otherwise would be necessary. The decline, in turn, may be accentuated if investors sell in order to take tax-deductible losses. Locking-in is also said to impair the efficiency of the capital market as a means of allocating resources. According to this view, efficiency is reduced because the capital gains tax discourages venturesome investors from selling appreciated shares and moving into unseasoned issues.[30]

---

[30] For effective presentations, see Harold M. Somers, "An Economic Analysis of the Capital Gains Tax," *National Tax Journal*, Vol. 1 (September 1948), pp. 226-32, "Reconsideration of the Capital Gains Tax," *National Tax Journal*, Vol. 13 (December 1960), pp. 292-99, and "Capital Gains Tax: Significance of Changes in Holding Period and Long Term Rate," *Vanderbilt Law Review*, Vol. 16 (June 1963), pp. 509-33.

Why Locking-in Occurs

Although its extent may be often exaggerated,[31] some locking-in will occur so long as the income tax applies to capital gains only as realized. If the tax were assessed on accrued gains without waiting for realization, locking-in would disappear. Postponement of sale of appreciated assets is now encouraged, not only by the privilege of postponing tax, but by the opportunity of escaping tax on assets held until death.[32]

The reason why locking-in occurs may be brought out by a simple illustration. Suppose that an investor owns stock bought more than six months ago at a price of $50 and now selling for $100. If he sells, he will pay (under rates scheduled to go into effect in 1965) a tax of $3.50 to $12.50 per share, depending on his marginal rate bracket. (Only half of net long-term gains is taken into account for tax purposes, and marginal rates on that half range from 14 percent in the first bracket to a maximum of 50 percent.) It will be advantageous to sell in order to switch investments only if the asset that can be bought with the remaining $96.50 to $87.50 promises a greater amount of return, in the form of appreciation and dividends or other yield, than can be obtained from $100 worth of the old shares. For this to be true, the expected rate of return on the new asset, allowing for any brokerage fees or other expenses of selling and buying, must be from 3.6 percent to 14.3 percent better than that on the old asset

[31] For skeptical treatments of locking-in, see Walter W. Heller, "Investors' Decisions, Equity, and the Capital Gains Tax," in *Federal Tax Policy for Economic Growth and Stability*, Joint Committee on the Economic Report, Committee Print, 84 Cong. 1 sess. (1955), pp. 381-94; Raymond L. Richman, "Reconsideration of the Capital Gains Tax—A Comment," *National Tax Journal*, Vol. 14 (December 1961), pp. 402-04, and "Incentive Effects of Alternative Tax Treatments of Capital Gains," in *Proceedings of Fifty-third National Tax Conference*, National Tax Association (Harrisburg, Pa., 1961), pp. 597-603.

[32] Especially enlightening analyses of the considerations that are relevant for investors can be found in Charles C. Holt and John P. Shelton, "The Implications of the Capital Gains Tax for Investment Decisions," *Journal of Finance*, Vol. 16 (December 1961), pp. 559-65, and "The Lock-in Effect of the Capital Gains Tax," *National Tax Journal*, Vol. 15 (December 1962), pp. 337-52; Beryl W. Sprinkel and B. Kenneth West, "Effects of Capital Gains Taxes on Investment Decisions," *Journal of Business*, Vol. 35 (April 1962), pp. 122-34. I have drawn heavily on these papers.

in this case.[33] Similar reasoning can be applied to a sale made in the expectation of a price decline and subsequent repurchase of the same asset. If the investor expects the value of an asset that he holds to decline by more than the amount of any tax liability that he avoids by not selling (plus selling expenses), he should certainly sell, because in this case a movement into cash will be advantageous. A smaller decline will justify a sale if there is an alternative investment with a positive yield.

TABLE 17. Annual Rate of Return on New Investment Required to Make a Switch Advantageous, Selected Tax Rates and Gains on Old Asset

(As multiple of rate of return on old investment)

Marginal Tax Rate on Capital Gains (Percent)	Gain on Old Asset as Fraction of Its Market Value[a]				
	1/10	3/10	5/10	7/10	9/10
10	1.010	1.031	1.053	1.075	1.099
25	1.026	1.081	1.143	1.212	1.290
35	1.036	1.117	1.212	1.324	1.460
50	1.053	1.176	1.333	1.538	1.818
60	1.064	1.220	1.429	1.724	2.174
70	1.075	1.266	1.538	1.961	2.703

[a] When the gain on the old asset is the indicated fraction of its market value, the ratio of the rate of return on the new asset to that on the old must exceed the figure given below. In the terminology of footnote 33, the ratio is $\dfrac{M}{M - t_c (M - C)}$.

The relationship that must be expected to exist between the rate of return on a new investment and an old one in order to justify a switch is shown for a wide range of situations in Table 17. The additional rate of return that must be expected on the new asset increases with the size of the unrealized gain on the old asset in relation to its market value and the investor's marginal tax rate.

[33] More generally, an investment switch will be advantageous if: $r_2 [M - t_c (M - C)] > r_1 M$, where C is the cost or other basis of the old asset; M is its current market value; r_1 and r_2 are, respectively, the expected after-tax return on the old asset and the new asset, discounted for futurity and risk; and t_c is the marginal tax rate on capital gains. For refined analysis, it is desirable to break down r_1 and r_2 into their components: $d (1 - t) + g (1 - t_c)$, where d is the dividend yield before tax, t is the marginal tax rate on dividends, and g is the expected rate of appreciation.

Under present law the maximum marginal rate of tax on long-term capital gains is 25 percent (with inconsequential exceptions); the higher rates are included to indicate the situation that would exist if capital gains were fully taxed. The table shows, for example, that an investor subject to a 25 percent marginal tax rate who holds an asset which carries an unrealized gain equal to 3/10 of its current value (3/7 of its original cost) can gain by switching to a new asset that offers a rate of return more than 1.081 times that on the old asset; if the old asset yields 3.000 percent, the new one must yield more than 3.243 percent. With a marginal tax rate of 60 percent and conditions otherwise the same, the break-even point for the new investment is a yield of 3.660 percent.

Over most of the range covered by the table, the additional yield required under present law to justify an investment switch does not seem to be great in comparison to the short-run fluctuations that occur in the prices of stocks or the differences in dividend yields of stocks. Under full taxation of capital gains, however, the barriers to investment switches look more formidable toward the upper end of the rate scale.

Escape of Capital Gains Tax at Death

The possibility, which exists under present law, of escaping capital gains tax on assets held until death is an additional cause of locking-in. Certain switches that will increase the earning power of an investor's portfolio will nevertheless reduce the size of his estate. For example, a switch that is fully justified by rate-of-return calculations will reduce an investor's estate if it involves the payment of a substantial capital gains tax and the investor dies shortly thereafter. If the deceased had held the old asset until his death, the switch could have been made by his executors or heirs without incurring a capital gains tax liability. It is difficult to decide what allowance to make for the possibility of escaping tax at death, not only because the date of death of any individual investor is unforeseeable, but also because the attitudes of investors toward the size of their estate and their heirs surely vary widely.

Holt and Shelton have made an illuminating analysis of the possibility of escaping capital gains tax at death.[34] They assume

[34] In *Journal of Finance*, Vol. 16, pp. 571-75, and, more elaborately, in *National Tax Journal*, Vol. 15, pp. 340-50.

that an investor wishes to maximize his income and the value of his estate and that he will not consider an investment switch warranted unless he expects it to increase his income and also to leave his estate unimpaired (that is, to allow recovery of any capital gains tax that would have been avoided if the switch had not been made). This implies that the investor has a strong interest in the size of his estate, in fact, that he will not deliberately sacrifice any part of his estate for additional income during his lifetime. On the basis of mortality tables, one can calculate the probability that

TABLE 18. Expected Capital Gains Tax Saving Because of Death, Investors at Selected Ages and with Selected Holding Periods[a]

(In percent per year of potential liability on an immediate sale)

Investor's Age	Extended Holding Period[b]		
	5 Years	10 Years	Life
30	0.197	0.228	2.41
40	0.396	0.500	3.09
50	0.956	1.24	4.20
60	2.46	3.12	6.21
70	6.03	7.30	9.99
80	13.51	15.41	17.14

[a] Abstracted from Charles C. Holt and John P. Shelton, "The Implications of the Capital Gains Tax for Investment Decisions," *Journal of Finance*, Vol. 16 (December 1961), p. 574.
[b] Period over which the investor expects to continue to hold the asset if he does not sell immediately.

capital gains tax will be avoided by reason of the investor's death during the period over which he would otherwise hold an asset. From such calculations it is possible to estimate the additional annual return required on a new investment to offset the actuarial value of the opportunity of tax avoidance at death.[35]

Table 18, abstracted from a paper by Holt and Shelton, shows the actuarial value of tax avoidance at death under present law, for investors at different ages and for different holding periods, as

[35] An investor who follows the Holt-Shelton rule will consider an investment switch advantageous if
$$r_2 [M - t_c (M - C)] > r_1 M + p [t_c (M - C)],$$
where p is the weighted annual probability that the investor will die during the period he expects to continue holding the asset if he does not switch immediately and the other symbols have the same meaning as in footnote 33 above.

an annual percentage of the tax that would be paid on an immediate sale. These figures, of course, rise with the investor's age and the length of time that he would hold the old asset if he did not switch. To illustrate the use of Table 18, consider again a stockholder whose shares have doubled in value and who is subject to a 25 percent tax on capital gains. If he sells $1,000 worth of shares he must pay a capital gains tax of $125, which his estate would escape if he held the shares until death. For an investor aged 60, the table shows that the expected annual value of the tax saving at death is 6.21 percent of $125 or $7.76 if he assumes that the alternative to an immediate sale is to hold the shares the rest of his life. On the basis of his life expectancy, he can recoup the capital gains tax by earning an additional $7.76 a year, which equals 0.89 percent of the $875 that he will have left to invest in a new asset. If the old shares yield 3.00 percent, he must find a new issue that he expects to yield 4.31 percent in order to maintain both his income and the probable value of his estate.[36] Of course, it will be hard for the investor to predict whether he will hold the old shares for the rest of his life, but even if he does not deliberately decide to do so there is a calculable probability that he will die before he gets around to selling. Past experience, for example, may suggest that he would be likely to hold the shares for another 5 years; in that case, the table shows that the expected value of tax avoidance by death during the extended holding period is 2.46 percent of $125 or $3.08 a year (0.35 percent of the value of the new investment).

These calculations may exaggerate the importance of the opportunity of escaping capital gains tax at death because they imply that people are more interested in their estates and their heirs than they in fact are. Furthermore, it would be an exceptional investor —or investment adviser—who would make formal calculations along these lines. The actuarial approach, nevertheless, has the merit of posing the alternatives open to investors and of thus providing a common basis for discussion.

[36] Table 17 shows that the new shares must offer a rate of return of 1.14 times 3.00 percent or 3.42 percent in order to maintain income; adding 0.89 percentage points to cover the amortization of the capital gains tax brings this to 4.31 percent.

Extent and Consequences of Locking-in

Given preferential tax rates on long-term capital gains, the great uncertainty and differences of opinion that always prevail with respect to future investment yields, and the wide short-run fluctuations that often occur in stock prices, Sprinkel and West seem justified in concluding that "investors frequently overestimate the extent of the 'lock-in' effect."[37] How much behavior has been influenced by this misapprehension is unknown. Replies to direct questions on the subject are likely to be self-serving and therefore of little value unless the questions are adroitly posed. In 1949, a poor year in the stock market, the Harvard Business School survey found that only 6 percent of the investors who were interviewed alleged that the timing of their investment transactions was affected by the capital gains tax, except for the postponement of profit-taking for six months in order to qualify for the preferential rate on long-term gains.[38] In 1960, after a decade of generally rising stock prices, a survey of investor attitudes conducted for the New York Stock Exchange indicated that the tax had great influence and that a reduction of its rates would unlock large amounts of securities.[39]

If locking-in were a dominant influence, the volume of transactions should tend to decline as asset prices rise and larger paper profits accrue. No such tendency is evident in the stock market in the postwar period. There seems to have been little correlation in this period between the volume of stock-market trading and the level of share prices or changes in prices. In the years 1926-40, a fairly close positive correlation appears to have existed between the level of stock prices and the volume of trading.[40] These data

[37] In *Journal of Business*, Vol. 35, p. 133.

[38] Butters, Thompson, and Bollinger, *Investments by Individuals*, p. 339.

[39] New York Stock Exchange, *On the Effects of Reducing the Capital Gains Tax Rate* (1961), summary of a survey by Louis Harris and Associates, Inc.

[40] These generalizations are based on an examination of the following statistics: (1) Standard & Poor's composite and combined stock price indexes; (2) ratio of value of shares traded on the New York Stock Exchange to value of shares listed on the exchange; and (3) ratio of number of shares traded on the New York Stock Exchange to number of shares listed on the exchange—annually 1926-40, 1946-60, and monthly 1946-60. Ordinary times-series charts and scatter diagrams were prepared for the series and for the changes in the annual values of the series, but coefficients of correlation were not computed.

neither support nor refute the charge that locking-in has been important.

Locking-in would be increased if tax rates on capital gains were raised. Increased locking-in due to the enhanced value of tax avoidance on appreciated assets held until death could be avoided by adoption of a provision for constructive realization of gains on property held at death. Such a provision would be desirable under present capital gains tax rates and with higher rates would become more important for reasons of equity and economic policy.[41] Constructive realization, however, would not alleviate locking-in due to income considerations.

The social consequences of locking-in, as well as its extent, may be debated. Locking-in does not necessarily have any direct influence on the total volume of financial or real investment. If present holdings of appreciated securities were unlocked, funds would be transferred from the purchasers to the present holders, leaving the buyers less liquid and the sellers more liquid. In the simplest case, the sellers would use their receipts for the same purposes that the buyers would have, and the only result would be a reshuffling of the ownership of outstanding securities and new issues. Precisely this outcome does not seem likely, however, because seasoned securities and new issues are not perfect substitutes. Nevertheless, the principal effects of locking-in must be sought in the composition of portfolios and the allocation of real investment rather than in the amount of resources devoted to investment over a period of time.

Unlocking of holdings of appreciated securities at a time when the stock market was rising would moderate the rise only if those who sold took part of the proceeds out of the market; to the extent that they merely switched holdings of stock, supply and demand would increase equally and prices would not be affected. Probably

[41] In 1963, the President recommended a tax on gains accrued at the time of death or gift, as part of a program for reducing tax rates on ordinary income and capital gains. Several exceptions and relief provisions were coupled with the recommendation. See *President's 1963 Tax Message Along with Principal Statement, Technical Explanation, Supporting Exhibits and Documents Submitted by Secretary of the Treasury,* House Ways and Means Committee, Committee Print (Feb. 6, 1963), pp. 20, 49-51, 122-34. The recommendation was not accepted by Congress.

there would be some movement out of stocks into bonds and cash on the part of investors who felt that the general level of stock prices was too high, and hence some moderating influence, but the net outward movement would surely be much smaller than the total value of sales attributable to unlocking.

Although most commentators take it for granted that locking-in impairs the efficiency of real capital allocation, there have been skeptics. Keynes, for one, thought that excessive trading in the securities markets tended to destabilize real investment and suggested that there might be grounds for making "the purchase of an investment permanent and indissoluble, like marriage, except by reason of death or other grave cause."[42] He discarded this expedient—on the grounds that the liquidity, or the illusion of liquidity, offered by the stock market calmed the nerves of investors and made them more willing to run risks—but he did not seem at all disturbed by the impediments to trading in London in the form of high brokerage charges and transfer tax. Indeed, Keynes recommended that the United States consider a transfer tax as a means of mitigating "the predominance of speculation over enterprise."[43]

Since World War II, speculation does not appear to have affected real investment as badly as did the excesses of the 1920's and the subsequent crash, and Keynes' judgment on the stock market seems harsh today. Even if its social contribution is smaller than the financial press likes to believe, active trading does facilitate transactions that are convenient for individuals and, on the whole, useful for the community. Locking-in does not seem to be a great economic problem, but surely there is a legitimate presumption that it is an undesirable side effect of the taxation of realized capital gains.

"Roll-over" Proposals

A proposal for avoiding locking-in while raising taxes on capital gains is the so-called "roll-over" plan. This plan would defer tax

[42] J. M. Keynes, *The General Theory of Employment, Interest and Money* (New York: Harcourt, Brace, 1936), p. 160.

[43] *Ibid.*, pp. 159-60. In this context, Keynes defined speculation as "the activity of forecasting the psychology of the market" and enterprise as "the activity of forecasting the prospective yield of assets over their whole life" (p. 158).

on realized gains that were reinvested but collect tax when gains were withdrawn for consumption or at the time of death of the investor. The proposal calls for an extension of the present treatment of gains on the sale of a personal residence.

A specific roll-over proposal includes the following provisions.[44] The taxpayer would determine his realized net gain or loss each year without regard to the length of time he had held the assets disposed of during the year. Any net loss would be recognized immediately, and provisions for the deduction of capital losses against ordinary income would be liberalized. Tax on net gain would be deferred to the extent that it was reinvested in any capital asset, and the basis of the new asset would be reduced by the amount of untaxed gain on old assets. The adjustment of basis would be confined to assets acquired in the current year and would be apportioned among all such assets. If purchases were smaller than sales, it would be presumed that part of the gain had been withdrawn, and realized gain would be taxed dollar for dollar up to the amount of the excess of sales over purchases (with perhaps a short grace period to allow for spillovers between years). No pairing of specific sales and purchases or detailed tracing of unrecognized gain would be required; all sales and purchases of any one year would be pooled. An essential part of the proposal would be that transfer of assets at death be considered a realization and tax assessed at that time on previously unrecognized gains. The rate of tax applied to recognized gains might be the full rate for ordinary income, the full rate with provision for averaging or spreading gains over a period of years, or a preferential rate.

This plan appears to entail considerable, but not insuperable, problems of compliance or administration. Investors would be called on for more information and computations than are now required; initially this would not be likely to arouse hostility since it would be part of a relief measure, but the requirements might seem more vexatious as the relief began to be taken for granted with the passage of time. The Internal Revenue Service would have more difficulty than it now does in verifying the taxpayer's representations concerning the basis of assets because of the adjust-

[44] Reuben Clark, "The Paradox of Capital Gains: Taxable Income That Ought Not To Be Currently Taxed," in *Tax Revision Compendium*, House Ways and Means Committee (1959), Vol. 2, pp. 1243-56.

ments which would often introduce a big difference between the basis and purchase price. The basis of a listed security can now be verified from readily available publications, if its purchase date is known. Under roll-over, both the government and the taxpayer would need a set of accounts showing the details of investment transactions for each year of the taxpayer's investment career.

The main objection to roll-over is that it would offer inequitable advantages to persons who realize capital gains. To bring out this, consider the unrealistic case of a person who receives all his income in the form of capital gains and reinvests all his savings in capital assets. During his lifetime, he would in effect be subject to a spendings tax rather than an income tax, since he would be taxed only on gains withdrawn for consumption. On the other hand, a person who received only ordinary income would be taxed on both his consumption and his saving. The arguments that can be advanced in favor of an expenditure tax do not support roll-over because it provides tax deferral for reinvested capital gains but not for other saving.

Full taxation of capital gains with roll-over would allow investors maximum opportunities for timing gains so that they would be assessed at relatively low rates. Thus gains might be withdrawn in years in which tax rates were temporarily reduced or in which the investor's other income was low or negative. Most persons are subject to lower marginal tax rates after retirement, and deferral of gains until that time would be especially beneficial to them.

It is uncertain whether taxation of capital gains at regular rates, together with roll-over, would impose heavier taxes on investors as a group than the present system does. If investors were subject to constant marginal tax rates, the value of additional tax deferral probably would be less than the increased tax that would ultimately be assessed on capital gains. The value of tax deferral to investors would be the amount that could be earned on the deferred tax, and the additional earnings would themselves be subject to tax. Hence, the value of deferral can be computed by ascertaining the present value of the future tax discounted for the years of postponement at a rate of compound interest equal to the after-tax rate of return on an addition to the investor's portfolio. At a 3 percent discount rate, the deferral period would have to be about 23 years in order to cut in half the present value of the deferred tax; at a 4 percent rate, about 18 years; and at 6 percent, about 12 years. Under present law, the tax on long-term gains is never more than half that on ordinary income, and for high-income persons it is less. Although there seems to be no sound basis for estimating the average period of deferral and the appropriate discount rate, it is plausible to suppose that on the average deferral per se would be worth less than 50 percent of the amount ultimately paid. But this might easily be outweighed by increased freedom of investors in having gains taxed in years when low rates apply.

The outlines of a dilemma thus emerge. Roll-over seems unfair because it would broaden tax deferral opportunities for recipients of capital gains. But, even without roll-over, investors can defer tax on capital gains by postponing realization. For this privilege they pay a price in the form of forgone freedom to switch investments, and the community may suffer a loss in efficiency of allocation of real capital owing to diminished fluidity of financial capital markets. Any social cost of this nature would be increased if higher tax rates were levied on all realized capital gains. The question for policy makers is whether the economic disadvantages of lessened capital mobility would outweigh the inequities of roll-over. In my judgment, roll-over is unjustifiable so long as capital gains enjoy a substantial degree of rate preference but would be acceptable if its adoption were necessary to clear the way for full taxation of capital gains under a proration plan.

Improvements Without Fundamental Revision

Worthwhile improvements in the taxation of capital gains and losses could be effected by measures less sweeping than those discussed so far in this chapter. If for any reason a fundamental revision is not acceptable, consideration should be given to the following actions:

1.   Extension of the holding period for long-term gains and losses from six months to twelve months. A holding period shorter than one year is not needed in order to avoid bunching. The length of the holding period is not a satisfactory basis for

distinguishing between speculation and ordinary investment; however, a twelve-month period seems slightly better in this respect than a six-month period inasmuch as investors who buy securities for income will usually plan to hold them for at least a year, if for no other reason, because profits and dividends are ordinarily related to annual accounting periods. A one-year holding period would cause a six-month delay of some sales of appreciated assets, but it is not evident that there would be a serious loss of market fluidity.

2. Elimination of the special ceiling rate (alternative tax) for long-term gains. This would make the tax on long-term capital gains uniformly half that on ordinary income, eliminating the additional preference now enjoyed by those whose marginal tax rates on ordinary income exceed 50 percent. This revision would be justified if, as I think, the hardship due to bunching of gains and the incentive to seek capital gains turn mainly on the relative differential between tax rates on capital gains and rates on ordinary income.

3. Withdrawal of long-term capital gains treatment from the special items such as coal and iron ore royalties, income from timber cutting, executive compensation under stock-option plans, and lump-sum receipts from retirement plans and employment termination arrangements. In general, these items seem to be similar to other income that is subject to ordinary rates, and it is not clear why capital gains treatment should be considered the best means of offering their recipients any tax relief that may be warranted. General income averaging or special proration seems to be a more equitable way of avoiding hardship in the taxation of lump-sum payments and other irregular receipts. Present provisions that treat as ordinary income part of the gains on sales of depreciable property could justifiably be broadened to classify as ordinary income all such gains up to the full amount of depreciation deductions already taken, on the grounds that the gains are evidence that depreciation allowances have exceeded the exhaustion of useful life.

4. Elimination of the deferral of recognition and taxation of capital gains on owner-occupied dwellings and of the partial

exclusion of such gains by persons over 65 years old. The current taxation of all realized gains on dwellings would no doubt retard mobility to some degree, but little attention has been given to the question whether the economic effects would be objectionable enough to justify the special treatment. The present provision seems to have been supported mainly on grounds of equity, and by dubious logic. There is little merit in the common assertion that the sale of a dwelling in connection with a move from one neighborhood to another or from one city to another is an involuntary conversion or is not a true realization if another dwelling "must be bought." Except for condemnation proceedings, people must be presumed to decide whether to move and to buy a new house by balancing advantages and disadvantages—deliberately or impulsively, according to temperament. Decisions to sell and to replace houses seem to be essentially similar to other decisions to switch investments, even though noneconomic considerations play a bigger role in the former. The special exclusion for the elderly which was added in 1964 is a highly discriminatory form of tax relief.

5. Adoption of the principle of constructive realization of gain or loss when capital assets are transferred by gift or at death. Existing provisions with respect to gifts allow appreciated assets to be transferred from owners in high tax brackets to persons in lower tax brackets without incurring an income tax liability and permit indefinite deferral of capital gains tax. Transfers at death wipe out potential capital gains tax liability. The present provisions involve an arbitrary distinction between gratuitous transfers and other transfers, and they contribute to locking-in. Assessment of both capital gains tax and gift tax or estate tax at the time of gratuitous transfer would not be unfair double taxation. The fact that income tax was assessed in prior years on current income is not considered a reason for exempting the savings built up out of that income from gift tax or estate tax. The transfer of assets would be the occasion for the assessment of both income tax and estate or gift tax only if the holder had previously enjoyed income tax deferral, compared with a person who had taken his investment return in currently taxable form. The simultaneous assessment could more accurately be viewed as evidence of a prior tax advantage than as a

hardship. The combined application of income tax and gift or estate tax would not be confiscatory since the income tax liability would be deductible from the value of the gift or estate subject to taxation.

Conclusion

Capital gains fall within a broad definition of income and are not clearly distinguishable from other kinds of income as regards contribution to taxpaying capacity or economic function. While special treatment of capital gains and losses is warranted because they often accrue over many years and are realized at irregular intervals, the present provisions go far beyond those required to avoid discrimination against capital gains. Realized capital gains, in fact, are taxed at much lower rates than other income. Taxpayers' attempts to convert ordinary income into capital gains and the government's efforts to prevent this are responsible for many complexities.

Realized net capital gains, though small relative to total income, are heavily concentrated in the hands of high-income investors. At very high income levels, the present capital gains provisions are the most important single factor accounting for the difference between nominal and effective tax rates and thus holding actual progressivity below apparent progressivity.

The present tax provisions offer investors an inducement to seek capital appreciation in preference to other returns. The investments that are fostered include risky commitments associated with innovations but also certain routine investments and various speculative activities. The preferential tax rates for long-term capital gains are less likely to inhibit changes of investment than would higher tax rates; however, prolonged holding of appreciated assets is encouraged by the opportunity of escaping income tax on accrued gains on property transferred by bequest.

Considering both equity and economic effects, I believe that the best solution would be to tax capital gains fully and to allow capital losses to be fully deducted, under a proration plan, relying on reasonable rates and other provisions to avoid harmful economic consequences. If agreement cannot be reached on a fundamental reform it would still be possible to make worthwhile improvements in the taxation of capital gains.

CHAPTER IX

Rates and Personal
Exemptions

AN OPINION THAT GAINED ACCEPTANCE in the 1950's was that income tax rates were too high in the United States whereas the tax base was too narrowly defined. This view influenced the discussions leading up to the Revenue Act of 1964. As finally passed, this act included both rate reductions and revisions recouping part of the revenue loss; however, the main feature of the legislation was tax reduction, rather than reform.

Different combinations of tax rates and personal exemptions and income definitions that yield the same revenue are not equivalent in other respects. They result in different distributions of tax among income classes and among persons in the same income class. They may also produce different relations between average effective tax rates and marginal rates. An increase in personal exemptions, for example, will reduce the effective tax rate for all taxpayers but for many persons, who remain in the same rate bracket, it will have no influence on the marginal tax rate payable on the last dollar of income.

This chapter examines several questions relating to the personal exemptions and tax rates. Topics covered include the adequacy of the exemptions, the yield of various parts of the tax rate schedule, the significance of income splitting between husbands and wives, splitting of income among family members by trusts and similar devices, averaging of fluctuating incomes, and arguments for taxing earned income at lower rates than property income.

Personal Exemptions

Personal exemptions under the federal income tax were fixed at $600 each for the taxpayer, spouse, and each dependent in 1948 and have remained unchanged since then. In addition a special exemption of $600 is allowed for a taxpayer or spouse who is 65 or older or who is blind. The exemptions are additive: a person who is both blind and over 65 is entitled to three exemptions. The minimum standard deduction, adopted in 1964, may be regarded as a supplement to the personal exemption at low income levels.[1]

The regular personal exemptions removed from the tax base about $101 billion, or 29 percent of total adjusted gross income (AGI), in 1960.[2] This includes estimated exemptions of persons not covered on tax returns. In addition, there were 6.8 million exemp-

---

[1] In writing this section, I found particularly helpful a manuscript by Lawrence H. Seltzer, *The Personal Exemptions in the Federal Income Tax* (draft, January 1962, of study to be published by the National Bureau of Economic Research) and a manuscript by Harold M. Groves that has since been published under the title *Federal Tax Treatment of the Family*, Studies of Government Finance (Washington: Brookings Institution, 1963). The Groves paper served as background for an experts' conference at Brookings in April 1963, which provided a stimulating discussion of personal exemptions, income splitting, and related topics.

[2] Estimated total AGI, $349 billion (*Survey of Current Business*, May 1963, p. 3). The total of $101 billion of income removed from the tax base consists of: (1) exemptions on taxable returns, $79.2 billion; (2) AGI less personal deductions on nontaxable returns, $14.5 billion; (3) estimated AGI of persons not covered by tax returns, $6.9 billion. Items 1 and 2 are from U. S. Treasury Department, *Statistics of Income, Individual Income Tax Returns, 1960* (cited hereinafter as *Statistics of Income, 19..*), pp. 36, 55, 66, 72. Item 3 was estimated on the assumption that average income of the 13.8 million persons who were not covered by tax returns equaled that of persons represented on nontaxable returns (about $500). The amount of unreported AGI is estimated at $33.5 billion rather than $6.9 billion (Appendix Table A-6); however, the larger figure reflects underreporting by persons who filed returns and also may be affected by errors of estimation.

tions for age and blindness, amounting to $2 billion for those filing taxable returns and $2 billion for nontaxable returns.

Over the past half century, personal exemptions have been reduced sharply in dollar amounts, in purchasing power, and in relation to average income (Table 19). Exemptions for children and other dependents have been increased relative to those for taxpayers. The reduction in the level of exemptions and the transformation of the income tax into a mass tax dates from World War II.

Since its adoption in 1948, the $600 per capita exemption has declined substantially in purchasing power and in relation to average income. By 1960, the exemption was smaller in these terms than it had been when taxes were heaviest during World War II.

Functions and Adequacy

Personal exemptions have four major functions: (1) keeping the total number of returns within manageable proportions and

TABLE 19. Personal Exemptions in Current and Constant Prices and as Multiples of Per Capita Personal Income, Selected Years, 1913-60[a]

Exemption	1913	1917	1929	1939	1944	1948	1960
Current prices							
Single person	$3,000	$1,000	$1,500	$1,000	$ 500	$ 600	$ 600
Married couple	4,000	2,000	3,500	2,500	1,000	1,200	1,200
Each dependent	—	200	400	400	500	600	600
Family of four	4,000	2,400	4,300	3,300	2,000	2,400	2,400
Constant (1960) prices[b]							
Single person	8,982	2,309	2,591	2,128	842	738	600
Married couple	11,976	4,619	6,045	5,319	1,684	1,476	1,200
Each dependent	—	462	691	851	842	738	600
Family of four	11,976	5,543	7,427	7,021	3,367	2,952	2,400
Multiple of per capita personal income[c]							
Single person	8.80	1.69	2.13	1.80	0.42	0.42	0.27
Married couple	11.73	3.38	4.98	4.50	0.84	0.84	0.54
Each dependent	—	0.34	0.57	0.72	0.42	0.42	0.27
Family of four	11.73	4.05	6.12	5.94	1.68	1.69	1.08

[a] In 1913-32, the exemptions were for normal tax only; in 1944, for surtax only.

[b] Current-price figures deflated by the consumer price index (base shifted to 1960 = 100), from U.S. Bureau of the Census, *Historical Statistics of the United States, Colonial Times to 1957,* pp. 125-26; *Economic Report of the President,* January 1962, p. 258.

[c] Exemptions in current prices divided by per capita personal income, derived from *Historical Statistics,* pp. 7, 139; U.S. Department of Commerce, Office of Business Economics, *U.S. Income and Output,* 1958; and *Survey of Current Business,* August 1961, p. 13. The personal income figure for 1913 is an average for 1912-16 and for 1917 an average of 1917-21; for 1960, includes Alaska and Hawaii.

particularly holding down the number with tax liability less than the cost of collection; (2) freeing from tax the income needed to maintain a minimum standard of living; (3) helping achieve a smooth graduation of effective tax rates at the lower end of the scale; and (4) differentiation of tax liability according to family size.

Although administrative considerations may have dictated exemption levels in the United States in the past and still may be decisive in less developed countries, they are unimportant in the determination of personal exemptions in the United States today. Experience with the income tax, the introduction of withholding, the growth of nonfarm employment, the spread of literacy, and the introduction of automatic data processing systems have lessened the administrative advantages of high exemptions. Indeed, for income that can be brought under withholding—salaries and wages, dividends, and interest—the simplest procedure would be to eliminate the exemptions. Their reduction to a low level would be less convenient but still possible.

The justification for freeing the income for a minimum standard of living from direct taxation is that families below that level would feel excessive hardship in paying taxes or would suffer an impairment of health and working efficiency. Ideas about the minimum standard change over time and presumably are related to average levels attained. This is the reason for comparing income tax exemptions with average personal income. This comparison, of course, does not imply that everyone below the average income should be free of personal income tax, but the figures on average income provide a rough indication of the probable trend of the socially acceptable minimum.

Many commentators reject the idea that people below a socially acceptable minimum standard of living should be exempt from income tax. They argue that government is a necessity and that everyone should pay his share of the cost just as he must pay for food and shelter. This argument, however, is not controlling. Although governmental costs are unavoidable for the community as a whole, their allocation among citizens is a matter of choice. Families with resources that are considered inadequate receive public assistance in paying for nongovernmental necessities, and there is a stronger case for relieving them from part of the cost of government. Furthermore, those who pay no income tax make a contribution to government in the form of indirect tax payments.

As a means of freeing from tax the income needed for a minimum standard of living, the personal exemptions are supplemented by the standard deduction. From 1948 through 1963, the tax-free minimum was $667 per person, consisting of $67 of standard deduction for an AGI of $667 and $600 of personal exemption. With the adoption of the minimum standard deduction in 1964, the tax-free minimum (personal exemption plus standard deduction) was increased to $900 for single persons, $1,600 for married couples, and $700 for each dependent.[3] For taxpayers with personal deductions greater than the minimum standard deduction, the tax-free minimum of AGI is greater.

Perhaps the most objective evidence on the socially acceptable minimum standard of living consists of the amounts allowed under public assistance programs. The Social Security Administration collected information on the amounts determined by the states as the cost, in January 1961, of meeting the "basic needs" of families applying for assistance under federally aided programs for old-age assistance and aid to dependent children. Applicants are considered needy if their income and other resources are less than the cost of the basic budget, and the budget determines the amount of assistance for basic needs. While many states do not provide enough assistance to cover the full basic budget, additional assistance may be given in other cases for special needs such as medical care and special diets. The median amounts of the basic budgets, at annual rates, are summarized in Table 20.[4]

The tax-free minimum exceeds the basic budget for each of the cases shown in the table, but the margin is narrow for the mother with one child. The excess for the single woman and the aged

[3] Until 1964, the standard deduction was 10 percent of AGI, subject to a limit of $1,000 ($500 for married persons filing separate returns). The Revenue Act of 1964 provided a minimum standard deduction of $200 plus $100 for each personal exemption. Because of the dollar limit on the standard deduction, the tax-free minimum will revert to $667 per person after eight exemptions have been used.

[4] A similar survey for July 1958 is reported in *Public Assistance*, Report of Advisory Council on Public Assistance, S. Doc. 93, 86 Cong. 2 sess. (January 1960), pp. 75-87.

couple is due to the special additional exemptions allowed people over 65. The basic budgets do not cover medical expenses (though most of them include an allowance for medicine-chest supplies) and do not reflect the extra costs associated with working outside the home, including social security taxes, transportation, additional food and clothing, and other work-related expenses. Minimum budgets for self-supporting families must be considerably larger than the basic public-assistance budgets.

TABLE 20. State Public Assistance Budgets for "Basic Needs" of Persons Who Are Not Employed Compared with Minimum Amounts Free of Federal Income Tax

Family	Public Assistance Budget, 1961[a]	Tax-Free Minimum[b]
Single woman		
Under 65	...	$ 900
Over 65	$1,180	1,600
Couple		
Under 65	...	1,600
Over 65	1,722	3,000
Mother (35) and boy (5)	1,442	1,600
Mother (35), boy (14), girl (9), and girl (4)	2,293	3,000
Incapacitated father (40), mother (35), boy (11), and girl (5)	2,286	3,000

[a] Annual amounts, derived by multiplying by 12 monthly amounts for January 1961. Medians for 50 states, the District of Columbia, Guam, Puerto Rico, and Virgin Islands. All families assumed to live in rented quarters. No adjustment for possible seasonality was made in deriving annual amounts from monthly amounts. Derived from U. S. Department of Health, Education, and Welfare, Social Security Administration, "Monthly Cost Standards for Basic Needs Used by States for Specified Types of Old-Age Assistance Cases and Families Receiving Aid to Families with Dependent Children, January 1961" (December 1962).
[b] Personal exemption plus minimum standard deduction under Revenue Act of 1964.

According to estimates prepared in 1963 by the Community Council of Greater New York for the information of voluntary and public health and welfare agencies, work-related expenses in New York City then ranged between $450 and $650 per employed person per year, depending on age and sex.[5] These figures do not include social security taxes, amounting to 3⅝ percent of the first $4,800 of annual wages in employment covered by federal old-age and survivors and disability insurance. The estimates are for families maintaining an "adequate but modest level of living."

[5] Community Council of Greater New York, *Annual Price Survey and Family Budget Costs, October 1963* (New York, 1964), p. 17.

The function of the personal exemptions and minimum standard deduction as an instrument of progressivity is less obvious than their role in freeing from tax those below a minimum income level, but it affects far more people. This is true because the great majority of exemptions are claimed by persons who are subject to income tax.

In 1960, 60 percent of all taxable returns fell within the first bracket[6] and hence were not subject to rate graduation; effective rates payable by persons filing these returns nevertheless ranged from almost 0 to 14 percent because the personal exemptions and standard deduction diminished relative to AGI as AGI increased. Since the old first bracket has been divided into four narrower brackets by the Revenue Act of 1964, the proportion of taxpayers falling wholly within the first bracket and therefore not exposed to rate graduation has been substantially reduced.[7]

Under the 1965 schedule, effective rates for married couples who have no dependents and who take the standard deductions will range from 0 to 3.3 percent (of AGI) in the first bracket. Progressivity at lower income levels, however, will still be due mainly to the effect of the personal exemptions and minimum standard deductions rather than rate graduation. For example, only about one-sixth of the difference between the income tax payable by a married couple with two dependents and an AGI of $4,000 and the tax of a four-person family with an income of $8,000 will be attributable to rate graduation.[8] Though progressivity of effective rates could be achieved without personal exemptions, a large number of narrow rate brackets would be needed, even if no provision were made for differentiation of tax by family size, and discontinuities of marginal rates would occur much more often than under the present system.

Throughout the income scale, the personal exemptions cause

[6] *Statistics of Income, 1960,* pp. 63-64.

[7] Estimated at 12 percent at the 1960 income level on the basis of data from the 1960 Tax File (see footnote 2, Chapter VII).

[8] Computed at 1965 rates, assuming use of the standard deduction. The actual tax will be $140 for the family with $4,000 of AGI and $772 for the family with $8,000, a difference of $632. With the actual exemptions and minimum standard deduction but with a flat tax rate of 14 percent (the first-bracket rate), the amounts payable by the two families would be $140 and $672, respectively, a difference of $532.

the income tax to vary with the number in the family. In the bottom bracket, the addition of one dependent reduces a married couple's tax by $98 (1965 rates, with minimum standard deduction). This sum rises with income and the marginal tax rate. It is about $150 for a married couple with a $20,000 income, and it reaches a maximum of $420 in the highest bracket.

Those who view the personal exemptions primarily as a means of protecting a minimum standard of living often argue that exemptions are not needed in middle and upper income classes, since, in these classes, an income tax without exemptions would not infringe on the socially acceptable minimum. The suggestion has been made that the exemptions be gradually withdrawn as income increases. This arrangement, called a vanishing exemption, has been used by several countries in the British Commonwealth. An example is the following: exemption for a family of four, $2,400 minus one-fourth of the amount by which net income exceeds $2,400. Under this schedule, the exemption would fall to zero—vanish—at an income of $12,000. At that income the same tax would be paid by all taxpayers with no more than four exemptions.

The minimum standard deductions adopted in the United States in 1964 are similar to the addition of vanishing exemptions to the $600 per capita continuing exemptions; the amount of income that one can have before becoming subject to the income tax is raised, but the amount freed from tax by the provision diminishes as income increases.[9] An important difference between the minimum standard deduction and an ordinary vanishing exemption is that the former does not benefit a person whose itemized personal deductions exceed the standard deduction.

Another view is that some differentiation of tax according to family size is justified above the socially acceptable minimum but that it is unfair to grant a tax reduction for an additional dependent that increases with the taxpayer's income and marginal tax

[9] The minimum standard deduction raises the tax-free minimum AGI by $233 for single persons (from $667 to $900), $267 for married couples (from $1,333 to $1,600), and $33 for each dependent (from $667 to $700). The additions to the tax-free minimum, however, are reduced by 10 percent of the amount by which AGI exceeds $667 per capita and, in any case, disappear completely at an AGI of $10,000. The addition to the tax-free minimum is also reduced dollar for dollar by the amount by which itemizable deductions exceed 10 percent of AGI.

rate, as is true with continuing exemptions, such as those traditionally granted in the United States and many other countries. This approach leads to the proposal that a fixed credit be substituted for the personal exemptions. Thus, for example, tentative tax might be computed on net income without allowance for personal exemptions and a credit of $100 deducted for each family member. Tax credits are used in lieu of personal exemptions in several state income taxes.

A quite different attitude is taken by critics who argue that uniform exemptions produce too small a difference between tax liabilities of large and small families in upper and middle income classes. They point out that the differences in amounts of taxes paid in these brackets by, say, childless couples and families with three or four children are small relative to the cost of rearing children. They suggest that personal exemptions be stated as a percentage of income, within limits, rather than as a fixed dollar amount.[10]

The choice between vanishing exemptions and increasing exemptions turns on the emphasis placed on the objective of varying the income tax with family size in middle income classes and high income classes. Both forms of exemption can protect a minimum standard of living and facilitate progressivity at lower income levels, but the vanishing exemption deliberately omits differentiation by family size in upper income classes. While it seems clear that the principle of ability to pay requires differentiation of tax liability by family size at income levels close to the socially acceptable minimum, it is not obvious how far up the income scale this differentiation should be carried. In my opinion, the ability-to-pay principle does not require differentiation by family size at high income levels and vanishing exemptions are justifiable. (See also the comments in the later section on income splitting.) Although the case for continuing exemptions seems weaker in logic than that for either vanishing or increasing exemptions, the difference between continuing exemptions and vanishing exemptions may not be very important so long as exemptions are small.

Regardless of the exact system employed, equal per capita exemptions, such as adopted in the United States in 1944, are questionable in the light of information on living costs. The addition of

[10] For a careful comparison of the different kinds of exemption and in-lieu credits, see Michael E. Levy, *Income Tax Exemptions* (Amsterdam: North-Holland Publishing Co., 1960).

the minimum standard deduction in 1964 improved the relation between single people and married couples, but the tax-free minimum remains less adequate for single persons than for married couples and dependent children.

Further evidence on relative needs is provided by Bureau of Labor Statistics (BLS) studies of consumption patterns. Estimates of the amounts of income required to provide approximately equal welfare for families of different sizes are compared with the tax-free minimums in Table 21. The BLS estimates are based on ex-

TABLE 21. "Equivalent" Incomes for City Families of Different Sizes Compared with Personal Exemptions and Tax-Free Minimums Under Federal Income Tax

(Relatives, four-person family, 100)

Family	"Equivalent" Income[a]	Personal Exemption	Tax-Free Minimum[b]
One person	50	25	30
Husband and wife	66	50	53
Husband, wife, 1 child	87	75	77
Husband, wife, 2 children	100	100	100
Husband, wife, 3 children	120	125	123
Husband, wife, 4 or more children	137	150	147

[a] Defined as "percentages of the income of the base family required to provide the same level of living for city families of different size, age, and composition." The base family consists of husband, wife, one child aged 6-16, and one younger child. The relatives shown are for families whose oldest child is aged 6 to 16. Family heads in all cases are aged 35 to 55. Source: "Estimating Equivalent Incomes or Budget Costs by Family Type," *Monthly Labor Review*, November 1960, p. 1198.

[b] Personal exemption plus minimum standard deduction.

tensive field surveys conducted in 1950. Incomes are considered "equivalent" at the level at which the percentage spent for food was equal to that for a four-person family selected as the reference standard. The studies confirm the impression that single persons need substantially more than half as much income as childless couples in order to enjoy the same level of living and that less is needed to support children than adults. Statistics not shown in the table indicate a considerable range for children depending on their age.[11]

[11] For other estimates, based on welfare budgets, see Martin David, "Welfare, Income, and Budget Needs," *Review of Economics and Statistics*, Vol. 41 (November 1959), pp. 393-99; James N. Morgan, Martin H. David, Wilbur J. Cohen, and Harvey E. Brazer, *Income and Welfare in the United States* (New York: McGraw-Hill, 1962), pp. 188-89; and Community Council of Greater New York, *Annual Price Survey, October 1963*, pp. 16-18.

Possible Revisions

Although the introduction of the minimum standard deduction in 1964 lessened the urgency of a revision of regular personal exemptions, the legislation does not embody a well-considered solution of exemption problems. The combination of per capita exemptions and the minimum standard deduction is clumsy. It is hard to justify additional vanishing exemptions only for those who choose not to itemize personal deductions; the minimum standard deduction, like the regular standard deduction, is the child of expediency rather than principle (see Chapter VII). For middle income classes, the $600 per capita exemptions are obsolete and otherwise questionable.

For the long run, a restructuring of the personal exemptions seems desirable in order to take account of the increase in prices since 1948 and to bring the exemptions more closely into line with amounts required to provide equivalent budgets for different-sized families. From 1948 to 1963, the consumer price index increased a little more than one-fourth. If this factor is applied to the personal exemption for a married couple, the adjusted figure is $1,500 to $1,600, or approximately the tax-free minimum for a couple under the 1964 act. The relationship shown in Tables 20 and 21 would indicate an exemption for single persons equal to about two-thirds to three-fourths of that for couples, or about $1,000 to $1,200. The budget data suggest that for dependent children an exemption equal to about one-third of that for married couples would be reasonable. If this relationship were accepted, approximately $500 would be the appropriate exemption for dependents. Higher figures would be required for taxpayers and dependents if account were taken of the growth of average income since 1948 as well as the increase in prices.

Although a reduction in the exemption for dependent children combined with an increase for single persons and no change for married couples would constitute a major departure from the per capita system and may seem politically infeasible, it would leave the exemption for dependents much higher relative to that for couples than it was prior to World War II (Table 19). When the per capita system was adopted in 1944, it represented a sharp change from practice up to that time. The legislation was heavily influenced by a great premium on simplicity, at a time when millions of new taxpayers had just been brought under the income tax and people were restive because of rationing and other wartime controls. Actually, the gain in simplicity appears to be minor. The adoption of the minimum standard deduction was a minor break with the per capita principle and may indicate willingness to reconsider the subject after two decades.

Introduction of continuing exemptions of $1,000 for single persons, $1,500 for married couples, and $500 for dependents would reduce revenue by roughly $3.0 billion.[12] The sum would be considerably smaller if the allowances were converted into vanishing exemptions.

Exemptions for Age and Blindness

Taxpayers and their spouses who are over 65 or blind receive a special exemption of $600 and an additional minimum standard deduction of $100. For example, if a husband and wife are both over 65, their AGI must exceed $3,000 before they are taxable. This is the same figure as for a younger couple with two dependent children. Furthermore, many elderly people receive income that is now excluded from AGI. In 1960, two-thirds of all persons over 65 received tax-free old-age, survivors, and disability benefits, and 14 percent received tax-free railroad retirement benefits or veterans' compensation and pensions.[13]

The special exemptions can fairly be characterized as makeshift welfare legislation. It is true that the average income of the aged, and probably also of the blind, is low, but their income tax would be correspondingly low without special treatment. Presumably the special exemptions are based on the idea that the aged and the blind have special living expenses. As regards the aged, this is questionable. Budget studies by the Bureau of Labor Statistics indicate that, for single people, much less income is required to maintain a given standard of living by persons over 65 than by younger people; for

[12] Estimate based on 1960 income and 1965 tax rates, assuming simultaneous repeal of minimum standard deduction.

[13] U. S. Bureau of the Census, *Statistical Abstract of the United States, 1961*, p. 266. Some of these persons may have received benefits under more than one program.

families headed by persons over 65, equivalent incomes are less than for families with younger heads, but the difference is smaller than for single people.[14] The elderly spend much more for medical care than younger people do;[15] however, these expenditures are deductible for tax purposes, on more favorable terms for the elderly than for others. Information on the budgets of the blind is not readily available. Although they likely incur some special expenses, it is not evident that these expenses are greater than those of other physically handicapped persons who receive no special tax concession.

The special exemptions are not related to need but are indiscriminately allowed to all. They are of no benefit for the most needy. Though clumsy and inequitable, the special exemptions for the elderly and the blind are not quantitatively important. In 1960, they accounted for 4 percent of exemptions on all returns, taxable and nontaxable.[16] Repeal of the special exemptions, in my opinion, would be justified but is not a high priority item.

Rates

Individual income tax rates were substantially reduced in all brackets by the Revenue Act of 1964. The rates that had been in effect from 1954 through 1963 were widely regarded as excessive. While it is true that these rates were high compared with prewar or early postwar rates (Appendix Table A-9) and rates in many other countries, effective rates were lower and less progressive than the nominal rates that received much attention.

Rates Prior to 1964

Many comments on tax rates neglected the influence of exclusions, personal deductions, and the preferential rates for long-term capital gains. The effect of income splitting between husbands and wives was commonly overlooked. Sometimes, even the personal exemptions were neglected.

[14] *Monthly Labor Review,* November 1960, p. 1198.
[15] Herman M. Somers and Anne R. Somers, *Doctors, Patients, and Health Insurance* (Washington: Brookings Institution, 1961), pp. 214, 426-51.
[16] *Statistics of Income, 1960,* p. 72.

The influence on true effective tax rates of the numerous exclusions from AGI cannot be exactly delineated owing to lack of reliable statistics on several items. It is possible, however, to show the effects of the personal exemptions and deductions, the special provisions for realized capital gains, and income splitting. This is done in Chart 3 and Appendix Table A-10. In the chart, the highest curve, labeled "nominal rates," traces the effective rates that would have obtained had the statutory rates for single persons applied to total income. (Total income consists of AGI plus the excluded portion of realized capital gains and excluded dividends and sick pay; it does not take account of excluded items that are omitted from tax returns.) The successively lower curves show the influence on the nominal rates of personal exemptions, personal deductions, the special treatment of capital gains, and income splitting for husbands and wives (together with the special rates for heads of households) and, finally, the actual effective rates with respect to total income.[17]

For 1960, the difference between the nominal and actual effective rates for all taxable returns can be accounted for as follows:

Nominal tax 28.1%
Deduct: Allowance for
    Personal exemptions 7.5%
    Personal deductions 4.6
    Capital gains provisions 1.2
    Income splitting 1.6
    Other provisions 0.1
Equals: Actual tax 13.1%

The influence of the various provisions, and of all the provisions collectively, differs greatly among income classes, as can be seen from Chart 3 and Appendix Table A-10. For low incomes, the personal exemptions are the main factor abating the potential tax; over a wide middle range, the personal deductions and income

[17] The influence assigned to the separate provisions depends partly on the order in which they are considered. For example, if income splitting had been introduced before the other provisions, the personal exemptions and deductions would have had less influence on the nominal rates. The actual effective rates would not have been changed.

CHART 3. Influence of Various Provisions on Effective Rates, Taxable Returns, 1960

Effective Rate (Percent)

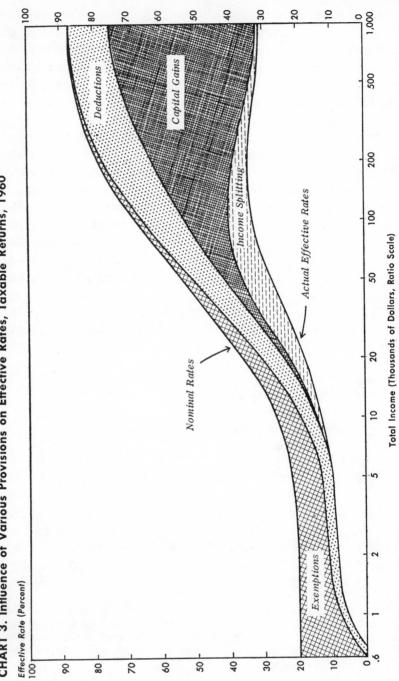

Total Income (Thousands of Dollars, Ratio Scale)

Source: Appendix Table A-10.

splitting are relatively most important; and, at the highest income levels, the influence of the capital gains provisions is notable. A striking point is that the effective tax rate on total income did not exceed 33.3 percent in any income class and did not increase in income classes above $100,000 in 1960; this appears to have been true also in earlier years, although computations cannot be made as precisely as for 1960.

The combination of steeply graduated rates on ordinary taxable income and the several provisions that remove income from the tax base or abate the rates means that the marginal tax rates, which are applicable to a small increment of income, are much higher than the average effective rates. This relation is depicted for 1960 in Chart 4 and Appendix Table A-11. The rates shown here are based on AGI rather than total income and hence are higher than those in Chart 3. (Since the major item that is included in total income but not in AGI is part of realized capital gains, the difference between the average rate curve in Chart 4 and the actual effective rate curve in Chart 3 is due mainly to the special treatment of capital gains.) The marginal rates shown in Chart 4 and Table A-11 were obtained by recomputing the liability on each return included in the 1960 Tax File (using an electronic computer) and are more accurately measured than in previous estimates based on grouped data.[18]

The computed marginal rates, although higher than average rates, are not as high as might be supposed merely by inspection of the statutory rate schedule. In 1960, the marginal rate exceeded 50 percent only in AGI classes above $50,000, although the statutory rates reached 50 percent at a taxable income of $16,000 for single persons and $32,000 for married couples. The highest marginal rate computed for any of the several AGI classes is 69 percent, whereas the maximum statutory rate was 91 percent. Computed marginal rates declined above $500,000 of AGI.

Computations such as those underlying Chart 4, which relate to aggregates or averages for broad income classes, do not reveal the range of effective rates paid by people in the same income

[18] The marginal rate for each AGI class is the ratio of additional tax to additional AGI when each taxpayer in the class is assigned $1 of additional ordinary AGI and his tax is recomputed, assuming a 10-cent increase in the standard deduction where appropriate but no increase in itemized deductions.

CHART 4. Average and Marginal Tax Rates, Taxable Returns, 1960

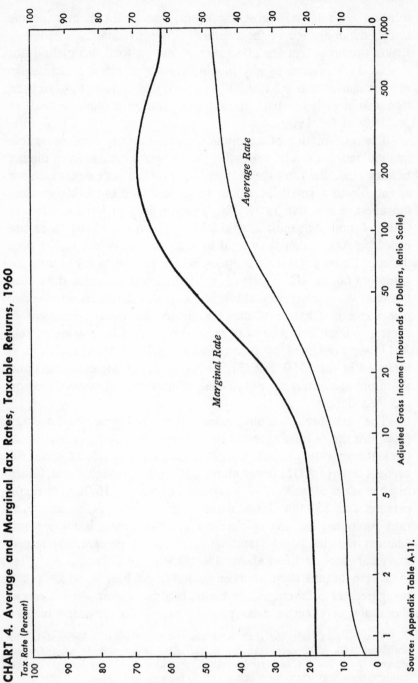

Source: Appendix Table A-11.

classes. Many pay rates well above or below the mean for their income class. A considerable number are exposed to very high statutory rates at the margin. Data for 1961, which lend themselves more readily to the calculation than do the 1960 statistics, indicate that almost 21,000 returns—about 0.04 percent of all taxable returns—were subject to marginal tax rates (on ordinary income) above 69 percent,[19] which is the highest marginal rate shown in Chart 4. These taxpayers must have differed from others in their income classes by having below-average ratios of capital gains to AGI and of personal deductions to AGI.

The estimates discussed above reveal that, prior to the Revenue Act of 1964, it would have been possible to cut statutory income tax rates drastically without loss of revenue, if offsetting structural revisions had been adopted. For example, under 1960 conditions, nominal rates could have been cut by 36 percent on the average, without revenue loss, if the personal exemptions had been continued at $600 per capita but all personal deductions, special capital gains provisions, and income splitting had been eliminated.

If this rate reduction had been spread proportionately over all brackets, the statutory rates could have been reduced from a range of 20 percent to 91 percent to a range of approximately 13 percent to 58 percent. This particular revision would have substantially increased the over-all progressivity of the income tax, since the provisions that would have been eliminated benefit high-income taxpayers relatively more than low-income taxpayers. A program that would have preserved revenue yield without changing actual progressivity would have allowed much deeper cuts in high bracket rates. Many intermediate distributions would have been possible.

Despite many endorsements of the idea of combining base broadening and rate reduction, programs as drastic as those outlined above drew little support in the discussions leading up to the Revenue Act of 1964. While I agree that such programs would go too far in certain respects, the computations omit other possibilities that I consider worthy of serious attention, particularly the taxation of excluded items of income that are not reported on tax returns.

Without structural revisions, it would not have been possible to narrow the differences between effective tax rates payable by

[19] *Statistics of Income, 1961,* pp. 3, 172.

persons with the same amount of income, but top bracket rates could have been reduced with only minor revenue loss. Owing to the special provisions and the large aggregate amount of income received by those in the lower income classes, only a minor part of the total yield comes from the high bracket rates. From 1954 to 1961, the average effective rate on taxable income was remarkably stable at approximately 23 percent. This indicates that a flat-rate tax equal to the first-bracket rate of 20 percent would have yielded about seven-eighths of the revenue actually obtained from the graduated rates. The proportion of the total revenue contributed by those subject only to the first-bracket rate was of course considerably smaller.

In 1961, all bracket rates above 50 percent could have been cut to 50 percent at a revenue cost of only 1.4 percent of the total yield of the individual income tax. Only 0.43 percent of taxpayers would have been affected, and their liabilities would have been reduced by only about one-tenth.[20] Estimates for 1955-60 are similar.

While the smallness of the yield from the top brackets has long been stressed by advocates of rate reduction, Congress and the executive branch, under both major parties, were unwilling to slash top rates before a general reduction became possible. All rates had been sharply increased during World War II and the Korean War, in an effort to allocate the tax burden justly, and it would have been considered unfair to cut top rates without reducing other rates. The function of the top rates is primarily to establish a proper relation between taxes on large and small incomes; their revenue significance is to be found mainly in their influence on lower bracket rates.

The smallness of the yield of the top-bracket rates is not a reliable indication of their importance. High rates accentuate the inequities due to unjustifiable special provisions, and they stimulate efforts to take advantage of special provisions that entail waste and distortions. It is also possible that the yield is small partly because the high rates deter people from earning large incomes.

[20] Estimates based on *Statistics of Income, 1961*, pp. 3, 172. Estimates of the yield of different parts of the rate schedule are facilitated by new tables included for the first time in the 1961 volume, pp. 146-73.

Revenue Act of 1964

The Revenue Act of 1964 provided substantial reductions in individual income tax rates over a two-year period and introduced the minimum standard deduction, which, as explained above, is similar to an additional personal exemption. The act somewhat restricted itemized personal deductions and included certain other structural revisions, which together recouped about 5 percent of the revenue lost through the rate reductions and the minimum standard deduction.[21]

In 1965, when the act is fully effective, individual income tax rates in most brackets will be about one-sixth to one-fifth lower than the old rates, analyzed above; however, the cuts will be somewhat greater in the lowest and highest brackets (Appendix Table A-9). The old first bracket has been split into four brackets of $500 each for single persons or $1,000 each for married couples filing joint returns, with rates ranging from 14 percent to 17 percent. The highest rate will be 70 percent, applicable to taxable incomes above $100,000 for single persons or $200,000 for married couples. The average rate reduction is estimated at one-fifth.[22]

While statistical data are not yet available for a full analysis of the new rates and other provisions, it seems clear that the relation between nominal and actual rates and between marginal and effective rates will be generally similar to that prevailing under the old law. To be sure, the reduction in statutory rates has diminished the influence of personal exemptions, personal deductions, and income splitting; nevertheless, a wide gap between nominal and actual rates remains.

Income Splitting

Husbands and wives filing joint returns use a rate schedule with brackets twice as wide as those in the schedule for single persons

[21] Estimate for calendar year 1965 liabilities, based on *Revenue Act of 1964*, Senate Finance Committee, S. Rept. 830, 88 Cong. 2 sess. (1964), pp. 14-17. The estimated gain in revenue due to unlocking of capital gains owing to general rate reduction is omitted.

[22] *Ibid.*, pp. 22, 25.

and married persons who file separate returns; therefore, the married couples who file joint returns are subject to lower marginal tax rates than single people. The arrangement is called income splitting because the law says that the tax on joint returns "shall be twice the tax which would be imposed if the taxable income were cut in half." The separate schedules were devised by the Treasury Department to simplify the tax return. Single persons who qualify as "heads of households" use a third rate schedule which provides approximately one-half the benefits of income splitting.[23]

Income splitting was adopted in 1948 to meet two kinds of inequity due to opportunities that some married persons had to divide their income for tax purposes. One inequity arose from the advantages enjoyed by residents of community property states, whose earned income and property income were considered as belonging equally to husbands and wives. The courts had upheld the right of married couples in these states to file separate federal income tax returns. Originally there were eight community property states, which had inherited the arrangement from the civil law of Spain and France, but community property laws were being adopted in other states with the frank purpose of obtaining income tax advantages. The second inequity was due to opportunities of dividing property income between husbands and wives in common law states by transfers of the property. Earned income could not be so divided.[24]

The 1948 legislation dealt effectively with these inequities, by extending to all married persons the benefits formerly enjoyed by residents of community property states, but at the same time it brought about a major income tax reduction and reallocation. Income splitting had no value or little value for the great majority of couples whose income fell entirely in the first one or two brackets and also had relatively little value for the few with extremely high incomes. In a wide intermediate range, the progressivity of the income tax was sharply reduced, and large differences were intro-

[23] A head of household is a single man or woman who maintains a household for a dependent. A widow or widower with dependents, who has not remarried, may use the rates applicable to joint returns for the first two years after the spouse's death.

[24] For a brief review of the background of the 1948 legislation, see Groves, *Federal Tax Treatment of the Family*, pp. 57-65.

duced between amounts of tax paid by married and single persons with the same income.

With the division of the old first bracket by the Revenue Act of 1964, the benefits of income splitting were extended to lower incomes. Relative to tax, the difference between the liabilities of a single person and a married couple is greatest at a taxable income of $24,000 (under the 1965 rates; this was also the point of maxi-

TABLE 22. Comparison of Income Tax of Single Persons and Married Couples, at 1965 Rates

Taxable Income	Tax Liability		Difference	
	Single Person	Couple	Amount	Percent of Single Person's Tax
$ 500	$ 70	$ 70	—	—
1,000	145	140	$ 5	3.4
2,000	310	290	20	6.5
5,000	910	810	100	11.0
10,000	2,190	1,820	370	16.9
15,000	3,940	3,010	930	23.6
20,000	6,070	4,380	1,690	27.8
24,000	8,030	5,660	2,370	29.5
30,000	11,150	7,880	3,270	29.3
50,000	22,590	17,060	5,530	24.5
100,000	55,490	45,180	10,310	18.6
200,000	125,490	110,980	14,510	11.6
400,000	265,490	250,980	14,510	5.5
1,000,000	685,490	670,980	14,510	2.1

mum percentage difference under the 1954-63 rates). At this level a married couple's tax is 29.5 percent less than that of a single person (Table 22). In absolute amount, the difference rises to a maximum at a taxable income of $200,000. The reduction of tax rates in 1964 cut the absolute size of the effect of income splitting, except at low income levels. These comparisons, based on taxable income, do not reflect the small difference in tax due to the larger personal exemption of the couple.

The consequences of income splitting for the allocation of taxes between income groups and married and single persons seem to have been little appreciated in 1948 and have not been extensively discussed since then. Most of those who were aware of the effects apparently believed that inequities then in existence could be ended only by compulsory joint returns, which had been repeatedly rejected by Congress, or by income splitting. In fact, however, discrimination between married couples could have been eliminated in a third way, which would not have involved a major redistribution of taxes.

The third method would have been to enact a new rate schedule for husbands and wives who filed separate returns that contained brackets only half as wide as those in the schedule applicable to other returns. This would have been as effective in ending inequities in the taxation of married people as was income splitting, which doubled the brackets for joint returns, since the tax advantage of separate returns would have been ended. Married persons would usually have an incentive to file a joint return when the incomes of the spouses were unequal and at least one of them had income extending beyond the first bracket for separate returns. In practice, husbands and wives would nearly always file joint returns and be taxed as a unit, although they would have the option of separate returns.[25]

Although this may sound paradoxical, income splitting, like the other arrangement described above, provides for taxing a married couple as a unit. This is justifiable on the assumption, which seems realistic in American society, that husbands and wives ordinarily pool their income and exercise joint control over it. Furthermore, income splitting could be extended to children, as in France, thereby taxing the family as a unit.

Acceptance of the principle of taxing husbands and wives or whole families as units does not resolve the question of the appropriate relation between the tax liability of married people and single people. That relation is determined by the personal exemptions and rate schedules. The present arrangements, in effect, involve three rate schedules—one for single persons, a second for married couples filing joint returns, and a third for single persons who are heads of households. Since the exemption for couples is

---

[25] Joseph A. Pechman, "Income Splitting," in *Tax Revision Compendium*, House Ways and Means Committee (1959), Vol. I, pp. 473-86. A U. S. Treasury Department study issued in 1947 discussed the possibility of a dual rate schedule but assumed that the same schedule would apply to single persons and to married persons filing separate returns. *The Tax Treatment of Family Income* (June 1947, mimeo.), pp. 11-12.

twice that for single persons and couples' rate brackets are twice as wide as those of single persons, a husband and wife pay the same tax as two single persons each of whom has half as much income as the couple (neglecting the minimum standard deduction). Generally, the tax of a single person who qualifies as the head of a household lies about halfway between the amounts payable by single persons and married couples with the same taxable income.

An alternative approach would be to differentiate only on the basis of personal exemptions, applying the same rates to taxable income of married people filing joint returns and all single people. This was done for the majority up to 1948, but, as explained above, some married couples were able to avoid the full impact of the graduated rates. Another possibility would be to continue three separate rate schedules but to reduce the differences between the rates payable by married couples, single persons, and heads of households.

The relationship between the taxes of single people and married people should be re-examined because the present situation seems to be an incidental result of the 1948 legislation rather than a reflection of a consensus. Although unanimity on tax rates is not to be expected, the subject needs to be aired by informed discussion.

My opinion is that the income tax on single people is now unduly heavy relative to that on married people. I think that the same rate schedule should be applied to the taxable income of single persons and married persons who file joint returns and that husbands and wives who choose to file separate returns should be required to use a rate schedule with brackets half as wide as those in the schedule for joint returns. This arrangement would reduce the tax of single people relative to that of married people. For the majority, the change in the amount of tax would be small, but for a few it would be substantial.[26]

[26] With 1965 rates and the 1961 distribution of returns, the difference between the tax payable under the schedules for single persons and for married persons filing joint returns is less than $70 in the income range including 87 percent of all single taxpayers and 60 percent of all married taxpayers filing joint returns; the difference is less than $250 for 99 percent of all single taxpayers and 79 percent of all married taxpayers filing joint returns. These percentages were derived from *Statistics of Income, 1961*, p. 172; the percentages for single persons include married persons who filed separate returns; heads of households, who account for less than 3 percent of all taxable returns, are not included.

My reason for favoring a realignment of taxes is the belief that a married couple with a given income enjoys more consumption opportunities and can exercise more economic power than two single persons with the same aggregate income. At low and lower-middle income levels, this generalization is supported by the BLS budget studies cited above in the discussion of exemptions and by other studies. The advantage of married couples is attributable to economies of scale in consumption and the imputed value of housewives' services at home. In upper-middle income groups, living standards depend to a great extent on customs and conventions that take the married couple as the norm. Veblen long ago recognized that, in these circles, a wife did not reduce a husband's welfare but enhanced his status by carrying out vicarious consumption. At the highest income levels, the economic and political power conveyed by income is the primary consideration in rate graduation, and there seems to be no reason to suppose that the power of a couple with a given large income is less than that of a single person with the same income.

The opposing view, which is favorable to the present arrangement, is that income can be meaningfully defined only on a per capita basis.[27] Those who take this view hold that any economies in consumption enjoyed by married couples are attributable to genuine efficiencies and should not be penalized by taxation. Some of them concede, however, that at very high income levels the per capita concept is inappropriate.

If taxes on single persons and married couples were equalized within the framework of constant total revenue, liabilities of single people would be reduced while liabilities of married people were increased by a compensating amount. The rate reduction for the single people would be much greater than the rate increase for the married people because the taxable income of the former is much larger than that of the latter (more than 3½ times as large in 1961).[28] On the more realistic assumption that equalization would be carried out at a time of revenue reduction, it would take the form of a disproportionate tax cut for single persons.

[27] Vigorously supported by several participants in the experts' conference on the taxation of the family convened at the Brookings Institution in April 1963; see Groves, *Federal Tax Treatment of the Family*, pp. 94-97.

[28] *Statistics of Income, 1961*, pp. 172-73.

The revision, therefore, may be regarded primarily as tax relief for single persons rather than as a means of increasing taxes of married persons. Nevertheless, it is true that, under a unified rate schedule, marriage would often increase the combined tax payable by a man and a woman. The increase could be substantial if each had a large separate income before and after marriage. This possibility has led some critics to brand the proposal as a tax penalty on marriage that would encourage living in sin. Whether this is a real danger is problematical. In the United Kingdom, where joint returns are required and income splitting is not allowed, a royal commission concluded in 1954 that "very little weight" should be given to the argument that taxation discouraged marriage. The commission was "skeptical of the suggestion that men and women are in fact dissuaded from marriage by any nice calculation of the financial odds . . . ," recording its view that "the reasons that impel men and women to prefer marriage to more casual associations are many and powerful. . . ."[29]

Division of Income with Other Family Members

Income taxes may be reduced by dividing income with children or other family members. This cannot be accomplished merely by assigning the income itself, even if the assignment is a legally enforceable contract. Income-producing property must be transferred.[30] This provision, although a safeguard against tax avoidance, means that property owners have opportunities for tax minimization that are not open to those who receive mainly earned income.

Intra-family gifts will reduce the total taxes paid by the family if, as is usually the case, the recipient has a smaller income than the donor and falls in a lower tax bracket. Minor children are tax-

[29] Royal Commission on the Taxation of Profits and Income, *Second Report*, Cmd. 9105 (London, 1954), p. 36.

[30] However, the transferer need not always divest himself permanently of the property. He can escape tax on the income from property placed in trust which will revert to him after ten years or more or at the death of the beneficiary. For a summary of the complex provisions of law relating to the subject treated in this section, with brief comments on the adequacy of the provisions, see Harvard Law School, World Tax Series, *Taxation in the United States* (Chicago: Commerce Clearing House, 1963), pp. 347-50, 434-41, 905-44.

able on the income from the property given to them. (The minor children are each entitled to the usual $600 exemption, and the parents may also claim a $600 exemption for them if they provide more than half the children's support; however, if a child is over 19 and is not a student, he qualifies as a dependent only if his gross income is less than $600.) Under a uniform law for gifts to minors, which has been adopted by many states, splitting of property income with children is facilitated. A parent may serve as custodian and manage the property but may not use the income for his own benefit. He may use the income to support the child, but if he does he remains taxable on it to the extent that this use discharges his legal obligation to provide support.

Trusts are an especially convenient vehicle for gifts because they obviate the necessity of turning over immediate control to the beneficiary and allow flexibility in the final disposition of the property. A trust is an arrangement under which a trustee (often a bank or trust company) holds legal title to property for the benefit of designated persons. Trusts may be created by gifts during the life of the grantor or by will.

A special income tax advantage of a trust is obtainable when income is accumulated rather than distributed to the beneficiaries. The trust is a legal entity and is separately taxable on its retained income (at the rate schedule for single individuals) but is not taxed on income distributable to beneficiaries. The beneficiaries are taxable only on the distributable income. Furthermore, more than one trust may be created for the same beneficiary, with each a separate taxable entity. Through multiple trusts, the top rate on accumulated earnings may be held to the first-bracket level, regardless of the income of the beneficiary. If the income is retained by the trust longer than five years, it is not taxable to the beneficiary when received. Earlier distributions are generally taxable to beneficiaries, but there are exceptions to this rule.[31]

Trusts are adaptable to the avoidance of estate taxes as well as income taxes. Despite their tax advantages, these entities do not

---

[31] In extreme cases, multiple trusts for identical beneficiaries may be treated as single taxable units under existing law, but the limits of this possibility have not been clearly established. See *Boyce* v. *United States,* 190 F. Supp. 950 (1961), affirmed *per curiam,* 296 F. 2d 731 (5th Circuit, 1961), and *Taxation in the United States,* pp. 930-31.

appear to have grown disproportionately. Over the period 1937 to 1958, the investment income of fiduciaries (trusts and estates) increased no more rapidly than that of persons, and there was no clear trend toward retention of a larger proportion of income by fiduciaries (Table 23). Less reliable balance sheet data indicate that

TABLE 23. Growth of Investment Income of Persons and Fiduciaries and Fraction of Net Income Distributed by Fiduciaries,[a] 1937-58

Year	Investment Income (Relatives, 1937–39 = 100)			Fraction of Net Income Distributed[b]	
	Persons[c]	Fiduciaries[d]	Taxable Fiduciaries[d]	Fiduciaries	Taxable Fiduciaries
1937	107	66	102	0.50	0.39
1938	93	109	89	0.82	0.46
1939	100	126	110	0.82	0.50
1946	155	...	184	...	0.40
1950	230	...	231	...	0.46
1954	266	274	164	0.72	0.44
1956	304	304	198	0.71	0.44
1958	335	327	196	0.71	0.41

[a] Fiduciaries include estates and trusts. Taxable fiduciaries are those that do not distribute all of their net income.
[b] Distributions to beneficiaries plus charitable contributions. Derived from U.S. Treasury Department, *Statistics of Income*, annual volumes.
[c] Monetary investment income only. Underlying statistics derived from personal income series of the Office of Business Economics, U.S. Department of Commerce, by summing rental income, dividends, and interest and subtracting imputed net rent of owner-occupied dwellings and imputed interest. Sources: *National Income, 1954*, pp. 212-15; *U.S. Income and Output* (1958), pp. 144-45, 229; *Survey of Current Business*, July 1962, pp. 8, 33-34.
[d] Net income minus net capital gains and net gains from sale of property other than capital assets. Derived from *Statistics of Income*.

the assets of personal trusts grew somewhat faster than the assets of nonfarm households in the period 1912-45 but more slowly than household assets in the years 1945-58.[32]

For the income tax, the most equitable principle and the one that would be most conducive to the effectiveness of the tax in re-

[32] Raymond W. Goldsmith, Dorothy S. Brady, and Horst Mendershausen, *A Study of Saving in the United States* (Princeton, N. J.: Princeton University Press, 1956), Vol. III, pp. 44-45, 54-55; Raymond W. Goldsmith, Robert E. Lipsey, and Morris Mendelson, *Studies in the National Balance Sheet of the United States* (Princeton, N. J.: Princeton University Press for National Bureau of Economic Research, 1963), Vol. II, pp. 118-21. The generalizations hold regardless of whether the comparisons are made between total assets or intangible assets only.

ducing the concentration of income and economic power would be to make the taxable unit identical with the economic family or consumer unit. Income would be aggregated for tax purposes to the extent that its control and use are pooled within the family. Ordinarily this would call for combining the income of minor children with that of the parents. In some cases, aggregation of income of older children and other family members would also be indicated.

It does not seem feasible, however, to work out an acceptable set of rules for aggregation of all family income. Property arrangements and family practices differ so greatly that attempts to carry out aggregation would be likely to be meddlesome and arbitrary. This would be true even if aggregation were limited to parents and minor children. Parents sometimes lack effective control over the income of their minor children and in other cases have control over the income and property of adult children and other dependents.[33]

Although income splitting through gifts of property cannot be stopped, efforts should be continued to assure that it entails a genuine transfer of ownership of the income-producing property. The attractiveness of gifts can be reduced, moreover, by reform of the transfer taxes, a complex subject that cannot be reviewed here.

The income tax advantages of accumulating income in trusts should be ended if feasible or, at least, should be confined as narrowly as may be possible without undue interference with property arrangements designed for purposes other than tax avoidance. One attack might be to further narrow opportunities for creators of *inter vivos* trusts to divest themselves of liability for tax on the income of the trust property in cases where the income does not become currently taxable to a beneficiary or where the property may revert to the grantor.[34] A second possibility would be to continue to tax trusts as separate entities on their undistributed income but to determine the applicable tax rates by reference to the income

[33] Prior to 1944, parents were taxable on the earned income of their minor children—but not the property income of the children—unless they could prove that, under state law, the earnings belonged to the child (U. S. Treasury Department, Bureau of Internal Revenue, *Supplement to Regulations 111, Income Tax* [1946], sec. 29.51-3).

[34] Compare Dan Throop Smith, *Federal Tax Reform: The Issues and a Program* (New York: McGraw-Hill, 1961), pp. 283-98.

of the beneficiaries or creators.[35] A less ambitious move would be to minimize the advantages of multiple trusts by requiring the aggregation of the undistributed income of all trusts with substantially the same beneficiaries.[36]

Restriction of the tax advantages now available through trusts would not prevent the proper use of these instruments for other purposes. Any lessening of the use of trusts, owing to the decrease in their tax advantages, would have the incidental economic result of freeing capital from the conservative control often exercised by trustees.

Averaging of Fluctuating Incomes

Under progressive rates, the total tax payable on a given aggregate income over a period of years may be greater if the income is received in unequal installments than if it is obtained in equal annual installments. This is often considered inequitable and a discouragement to activities that are especially likely to result in fluctuating incomes. The subject has received much attention, and several plans have been proposed for averaging income for tax purposes.

An averaging scheme applicable to persons experiencing wide fluctuations of income was included in the Revenue Act of 1964. Under this scheme, "averageable income" is defined as the amount of "adjusted taxable income" in excess of 133⅓ percent of the average of the four preceding years (the base period). In computing base-period income, years of net business losses do not give rise to negative income but are entered as zeros. If averageable

---

[35] Henry A. Fenn, "The Present Method of Taxing Trust Income: A Criticism and Proposed Revision," *Yale Law Journal*, Vol. 51 (May 1942), pp. 1143-59.

[36] A proposal for aggregation, subject to certain exceptions, was made in 1957 by a special advisory group of the Subcommittee on Internal Revenue Taxation of the House Ways and Means Committee, and legislation was proposed in 1960 (H.R. 9662, 86 Cong. 2 sess.) but was not passed by Congress. See *General Revenue Revision*, Hearings before the House Ways and Means Committee, 85 Cong. 2 sess. (1958), Pt. 3, pp. 2691-2805; *Trust and Partnership Income Tax Revision Act of 1960*, House Ways and Means Committee, H. Rept. 1231, 86 Cong. 2 sess. (1960); and *Trust and Partnership Income Tax Revision Act of 1960*, Senate Finance Committee, S. Rept. 1616, 86 Cong. 2 sess. (1960).

income exceeds $3,000, the tax on it is computed by: (1) calculating a tentative tax on a sum equal to 1⅓ times base-period income plus ⅕ of averageable income; (2) subtracting the tax on 1⅓ times base-period income; and (3) multiplying the remainder by 5. The final tax is the sum of (a) the tentative tax on an amount equal to 1⅓ times base-period income plus (b) the tax on averageable income. The base period is a moving one, with the earliest year dropped and one year added annually.

Averaging does not apply to capital gains, income attributable to the receipt of gifts and inheritances, and net wagering gains, since these items are excluded from adjusted taxable income. An attempt is also made to exclude persons who were students during part of the base period or who were not members of the labor force during both the current year and the four-year base period. The new averaging plan replaces special averaging provisions previously in effect for selected kinds of income.[37]

The approach followed in the 1964 legislation is to abate the tax payable by a person realizing a sharp increase in income, either temporarily or as the result of a movement from a lower to a higher income level. Beneficiaries may include professional persons, writers, and businessmen who realize in one year rewards for work extending over several years. Anyone who greatly betters his income by changing his job or business activity may gain a little delay in the application of the full graduated rates. Tax relief could be obtained every year, if one's income grew fast enough; however, the required growth rate is too high to be reached by many.[38]

Persons experiencing a decline in income will not obtain any immediate tax relief under the 1964 averaging plan. To be sure, these persons' current-year tax falls along with their income, but if averaging were currently available they might be entitled to a greater tax reduction or to the refund of prior-year taxes. Any averaging relief that may be obtained as the result of a temporary fall

---

[37] The averaging provisions are in Internal Revenue Code of 1954, as amended, secs. 1301-05. See also *Revenue Act of 1963*, House Ways and Means Committee, H. Rept. 749, 88 Cong. 1 sess. (1963), pp. 109-15; S. Rept. 830, pp. 139-45.

[38] A steady growth of 12.6 percent or more per annum would satisfy the requirement that each year's income exceed average income of the preceding four years by one-third.

in income will come when income recovers. Unless the misfortune is both severe and prolonged but followed by prosperity, averaging will not apply. For example, a person who suffers one year of catastrophic unemployment or poor business which brings his normally stable income down to zero in that year will not be able to apply the 1964 averaging scheme when his income returns to normal.[39]

The timing of relief under the 1964 legislation conflicts with the principle of taxing people most heavily "when their ship is in," which seems in accord with ability to pay and convenience.[40] The plan, on the other hand, avoids giving tax refunds to persons who fully or partly retire, which would seem undesirable.

The new averaging scheme will do little or nothing to relieve those whose income fluctuates just above and below the tax-free minimum. Such fluctuations result in wastage of personal exemptions (and minimum standard deductions) and can have considerable influence on the effective tax rate. A man who would pay no income tax if his exemptions could be fully offset against his income over a period of years will be subject to tax in years in which his earnings temporarily rise above the exemption level. Most of those in this situation will be barred from averaging by the $3,000 limitation and by the complexity of the scheme.[41] The $3,000 limitation was included in the 1964 legislation on the grounds that little benefit would be obtained from averaging when fluctuations were smaller.[42] This would not be true if wastage of personal exemptions were taken into account. The limitation does have the merit of helping keep the number of cases within manageable pro-

[39] This is because of the limitation of averaging to income which exceeds that of the base period by more than one-third. To illustrate, suppose that a man's normal income is $20,000 a year but that it drops to zero in one year and then returns to $20,000 the next year. The average income of the base period will be $(3 \times \$20{,}000) \div 4 = \$15{,}000$. Averageable income in year 5 will be $\$20{,}000 - (4/3 \times \$15{,}000) = 0$.

[40] As suggested by Harold M. Groves.

[41] Under the rate schedule for 1965 and later years, the minimum tax value of the personal exemptions and minimum standard deduction is $230 for a married couple, $450 for a family of four, and $696 for a family of six.

[42] *President's 1963 Tax Message, Along with Principal Statement, Technical Explanation, and Supporting Exhibits and Documents Submitted by Secretary of the Treasury,* House Ways and Means Committee, Committee Print, Feb. 6, 1963, p. 84; H. Rept. 749, p. 111; S. Rept. 830, p. 141.

portions. While this is only prudent, at least until the Internal Revenue Service gains experience with averaging, the denial of benefits to an especially needy group raises doubts about the plan.

Two of the important kinds of income fluctuation are not brought under the new averaging plan but will still be dealt with by separate provisions. One of these is business net losses, which will continue to be offset against income by means of carrybacks and carryforwards. The other is capital gains and losses (Chapter VIII).

Although the extent to which the new averaging provisions will be used cannot be accurately predicted, it seems likely that they will apply in only a limited number of cases, owing to the restrictive conditions already mentioned. Even where applicable, the averaging plan will usually not produce dramatic results. This is partly due to the form of the plan, but it also reflects the insensitivity of the average effective tax rate over a period of years to rather wide fluctuations of income. Except at the bottom, the tax brackets are wide, especially for married couples filing joint returns, and the difference in rates between adjacent brackets usually is small.

The 1964 provisions constitute only a limited averaging plan. Experience with them and more analysis of income fluctuations (by use of an identical sample of persons over a period of years or simulation) may offer a better basis for deciding whether further steps should be taken toward comprehensive averaging or whether the 1964 plan should be rescinded.

At present, an attitude of mild skepticism concerning the desirability of extensive averaging seems justified. While no one can deny that strict annual accounting may result in inequities under a progressive income tax, not all kinds of income irregularity appear equally deserving of tax relief. The case for relief is strongest with respect to compensation received in one year for activities extending over several years and for cyclical fluctuations; it is weak with respect to windfalls, movements from one normal income level to another, and sustained upward or downward trends in income. There is little information on income fluctuations and the actual severity of discrimination against irregular incomes. Many taxpayers have opportunities for smoothing out irregularities in taxable income by planning the timing of receipts, business expenditures, and personal deductions and by the adoption of plans for spreading income over long periods. From the economic standpoint, the most significant advantage of averaging may be attained by carrybacks and carryforwards of business losses and capital losses, which do not require full averaging. Finally, averaging plans are unavoidably complex.[43]

Earned Income

There has long been a body of opinion holding that income from personal effort, commonly called earned income, should be taxed more lightly than property income. This can be accomplished by allowing part of earned income to be deducted or excluded from taxable income or by applying a separate rate schedule to earned income. Both techniques have been called earned income credits. In the United States, an earned income credit, in the form of a deduction, was allowed in 1924-31 and 1934-43,[44] and in the United Kingdom, a credit is still allowed. Schedular income taxes often differentiate in favor of earned income.

One source of support for preferential taxation of earned income is closely allied to the belief that wealth, as well as income, should be taxed (Chapter II). A reduced rate for earned income, or an additional tax on property income, is regarded as a means of reaching the taxpaying capacity associated with wealth. This arrangement, however, is a poor substitute for a personal wealth tax since property income bears no uniform relation to wealth. Taxation of property income is not a satisfactory means of reaching holdings of idle or underemployed wealth.

A related consideration adduced in favor of an earned income credit is the "precarious" and terminable nature of income from personal effort, which depends on the health and working capacity

[43] Many tax specialists take a more favorable view of averaging. See, for example, Henry C. Simons, *Personal Income Taxation* (Chicago: University of Chicago Press, 1938), pp. 153-54; Harold M. Groves, *Postwar Taxation and Economic Progress*, Committee for Economic Development Research Study (New York: McGraw-Hill, 1946), pp. 223-36; William Vickrey, *Agenda for Progressive Taxation* (New York: Ronald Press, 1947), pp. 172-95; and the papers in *Tax Revision Compendium*, Vol. I, pp. 579-677.

[44] Certain minimum amounts of income ($3,000 in 1934-43) were treated as earned income, regardless of source, and above certain levels ($14,000 in 1934-43) all income was treated as unearned.

of the individual. This attitude is embodied in Samuelson's re-
mark, "A so-called 'personal income tax' that treats the perpetual
earnings of securities the same as the earnings of a doctor or actor
in the prime of life chooses to ignore a substantive difference."[45]
Granted that differences exist between such incomes, it is not true
that property incomes are always more secure and longer-lived than
earned incomes. Since each category includes a wide range of items,
differentiation between property income and earned income would
not distinguish generally between precarious and secure incomes
or between terminable and perpetual ones. An annual tax on income will apply only as long as income is received, whether the
source be property or personal effort; it is not clear that differentiation of tax on the income when received is appropriate merely because of the uncertain flow or limited duration of the stream. I
have already argued in Chapter V that an amortization allowance
should be granted for the disappearance of personal earning capacity with the passage of time only to the extent that the capacity
is attributable to past investment in education.

An additional argument for favoring earned income is that
those who receive this income must incur real costs in the form of
personal effort, sacrifice of leisure, and restricted choice of place
of residence. Investors, to be sure, often spend time and effort in
selecting and supervising their portfolios; however, they can hire
someone else to do this for them, if they choose, and can deduct
the fee from their taxable income. The fatal weakness of the real-
costs argument is that the amount of earned income bears no ascer-
tainable relation to presumed psychic costs. These costs depend on
the nature of the employment, the hours of work, place of employment, and personal tastes. The best-paying jobs usually have the
greatest prestige and often seem the most interesting. Who can say
how these attractions should be balanced against the long working
hours and tensions of many executives and professional men?

A weighty practical objection to an earned-income credit is the
difficulty of defining earned income of self-employed persons and

[45] Paul A. Samuelson, "The Evaluation of 'Social Income': Capital Formation
and Wealth," in The Theory of Capital, Proceedings of a Conference Held by
the International Economic Association, F. A. Lutz and D. C. Hague, eds. (New
York: St. Martin's Press, 1961), p. 39n. See also Royal Commission on the Taxation
of Profits and Income, Second Report, Cmd. 9105 (London, 1954), pp. 66-69.

stockholders of closely held corporations who are active in management. In most cases, income from sole proprietorships and partnerships is a mixture of return from capital and reward for personal effort. In closely held corporations, the distinction between salaries and wages and profits is often tenuous. The Self-Employed Individuals Retirement Act of 1962 includes arbitrary allocation rules for identifying earned income where both personal services and capital are material income-producing factors.[46] Such rules are acceptable when the amount of tax at stake is fairly small, as it is under that act, and as it would be in connection with the proposed plan for amortization of certain educational expenditures, but they would become questionable if they were the basis of large differences in tax liability.

An earned income credit of substantial size, applicable over a wide range of income sizes, would not be a desirable addition to the U. S. income tax, in my opinion. However, I think that it would be appropriate to grant a small allowance for certain monetary costs of earning income that it would be impracticable to make specifically deductible and for the opportunities of doing household chores that are given up when one takes an outside job. One possibility would be a small deduction from earned income of all employed persons. Since the costs under consideration are particularly noticeable in the case of housewives, consideration might be given to a special credit or allowance when both husband and wife report earned income on a joint return. Precedents for this approach can be found in the United Kingdom and Sweden. The British tax provides, in addition to a general earned income allowance, a preferential tax rate on the first £140 of a wife's earned income; a figure for the United States bearing the same relation to 1960 per capita income would be $810.[47] The Swedish tax allows a married woman a special deduction which frees from tax the first SKr 300 of earned income; for women with children at home, the

[46] Internal Revenue Code of 1954, as amended, sec. 401(c)(2)(B). See also Chapter VI.

[47] On the British tax, see Harvard Law School, World Tax Series, *Taxation in the United Kingdom* (Boston: Little, Brown, 1957), pp. 366-67, and 1961 cumulative supplement. U.K. and U. S. per capita GNP at market prices derived from Organization for Economic Cooperation and Development (OECD), *General Statistics,* November 1962.

deduction increases by 20 percent of earned income up to a maximum of SKr 2,000. In relation to per capita income, a comparable deduction in the United States would range from $99 to $659.[48]

Conclusion

The introduction of the minimum standard deduction in 1964, which was equivalent to a limited increase in personal exemptions and a minor departure from the uniform per capita system adopted during World War II, is encouraging evidence of willingness to reconsider the tax-free minimum. Relative to socially acceptable minimum consumption, as indicated by public assistance standards and other estimates and by family budget data, the combined exemptions and minimum standard deduction are least adequate for single persons and are more liberal for dependent children than for taxpayers. The special exemptions for age and blindness are welfare measures of doubtful efficiency and fairness.

Owing to exclusions from the tax base, personal deductions, capital gains provisions, and income splitting, actual effective tax rates are lower and less progressive than would be inferred from the statutory rate schedule. If the gap between nominal and effective tax rates were equally wide everywhere and this were generally known, the result might be a harmless illusion. In fact, the operation of the provisions that mitigate the nominal rates is neither uniform nor generally appreciated. These conditions invite inequities, public confusion, and the risk of economic damage due to marginal tax rates higher than would otherwise be required.

While income splitting for husbands and wives eliminates inequities that used to occur in the taxation of married people, it makes the income tax much heavier and more progressive for single people than for married couples. This difference could be lessened or eliminated by adjusting rates and brackets, without reviving the old inequities or compelling husbands and wives to file joint returns. Tax avoidance by dividing income with children or

[48] The special deduction is described in Harvard Law School, World Tax Series, *Taxation in Sweden* (Boston: Little, Brown, 1959), p. 195; however, the amounts allowed have been increased to the figures given in the text. Swedish per capita GNP at market prices is derived from OECD, *General Statistics*, November 1962.

other family members cannot be prevented but could be somewhat restricted.

Proposals for averaging of fluctuating incomes for tax purposes may have received more attention from experts than is warranted. Experience with the limited averaging plan adopted in the United States in 1964 and further study may help determine whether the plan should be modified, extended, or dropped.

The arguments that have been advanced for a substantial earned income credit or preferential rates for income from personal effort seem to me unconvincing. A better case can be made for a small concession to all employed persons or to employed wives in recognition of certain nondeductible costs of working and forgone opportunities of doing household and personal tasks.

CHAPTER X

Effects on Distribution of Income and Wealth

A BASIC SOURCE OF SUPPORT for a progressive income tax is the expectation that it will reduce economic inequality or check the growth of inequality. The influence of the income tax on the size distribution of income and wealth, therefore, is an important part of the evaluation of American experience with the tax.

There are varying beliefs concerning the actual influence of the income tax in the United States. A common opinion is that steeply progressive income tax rates have greatly narrowed economic inequality over the past thirty years. Although this view has been taken more often by journalists than by scholars, it has had adherents among well-informed economists. Schumpeter, for example, in discussing redistributive taxation in 1947, wrote, "To an extent which is not generally appreciated, the New Deal was able to expropriate the upper income brackets even before the war" and added that "irrespective of the war, a tremendous transfer of wealth has actually been effected, a transfer that quantitatively is comparable with that effected by Lenin."[1] Among specialists in income

[1] Joseph A. Schumpeter, *Capitalism, Socialism and Democracy*, 3d ed. (New York: Harper & Row, 1962), p. 381. The passage cited was introduced in the second edition, originally published in 1947.

distribution, on the other hand, the tendency has been to regard the income tax as a relatively unimportant influence on distribution. For example, Kravis refers to statistical support for the "impression that an increase in the progressivity of the tax structure has played little if any part in making the income distribution more equal" after 1929.[2]

In view of these differences of opinion and the unavoidable complexity of the subject, readers will not be surprised by a warning that the facts concerning the influence of the income tax on the distribution of income and wealth, as on many other questions relating to the tax, are far from clear and that skeptics question the statistics that are available. The purpose of this chapter is to bring together some of the relevant information and to attempt to interpret it. Emphasis is placed on the shares of groups with high incomes or large estates since this is the area in which the direct impact of a progressive income tax can be most clearly observed.

The first step is to consider the simplest aspect of the influence of the income tax on economic inequality, that is, its impact on a given distribution of income before taxes. For this purpose, the before-tax and after-tax distributions of 1960 are compared with each other and with the after-tax distribution that would have obtained in that year with different income tax structures.

The second and more difficult step is to consider whether the income tax has caused an alteration of the before-tax distribution of income that either reinforces or counteracts the equalizing effects of progressive rates.

Third, limitations of the available statistics are examined with a view to ascertaining whether they understate or overstate changes in the concentration of income and the possible influence of the income tax.

Fourth, the distribution of wealth is briefly surveyed because it may be affected by the income tax through changes in saving and accumulation and by division of property for the purpose of avoiding top income tax rates. Also, data on wealth holdings are helpful as a check on the completeness and reliability of the income statistics.

Finally, some concluding remarks are offered concerning the

[2] Irving B. Kravis, *The Structure of Income* (Philadelphia: University of Pennsylvania, 1962), p. 220.

objective of greater economic equality and the contribution that the income tax and other measures can reasonably be expected to make to its attainment.

In order to isolate the influence of the income tax, government expenditures will be taken as given, and it will be assumed that the same public expenditures would be financed by other taxes if the income tax were not levied. Thus, the discussion abstracts from the possibility that the direct distributional effects of the income tax are offset by government expenditures that are made possible or induced by the levy of the tax. Although this simplifying assumption does not seem so unrealistic as to be seriously misleading, it cannot be denied that a radical change in the tax system would be likely to have some influence on public expenditures. For example, the substitution of regressive taxes for the income tax might stimulate additional welfare expenditures which would mitigate the distributional effects of the change. If more reliance were placed on indirect taxes, it is possible—but in my judgment unlikely—that political opposition to government spending would diminish, and the budget would grow more rapidly.

Impact on a Given Before-Tax Distribution of Income

Ideally, the influence of the income tax on income concentration should be measured by reference to statistics based on a comprehensive definition of accrued or realized income such as that described in Chapter II. Unfortunately, such data are not available. The best statistics covering a period of years on a comparable basis are those of the Office of Business Economics (OBE) of the Department of Commerce. These statistics relate to the size distribution of "family personal income," which is the portion of total personal income received by consumer units consisting of families and unattached individuals. Income received by members of the armed forces living on posts, persons in institutions, and nonprofit organizations is excluded. The series includes important items of imputed income such as the rental value of owner-occupied dwellings and the value of farm-produced-and-consumed food and fuel.[3]

[3] See U. S. Department of Commerce, Office of Business Economics, *Income Distribution in the United States*, Supplement to *Survey of Current Business*

For present purposes, an important shortcoming is the omission of net capital gains and the income tax on them. Other statistical limitations are discussed below.

The OBE estimates of the 1960 distribution of family personal income before and after federal individual income tax are summarized in Table 24. The statistics show that the tax does reduce

TABLE 24. Distribution of Family Personal Income Among Consumer Units and Effective Rates of Federal Individual Income Tax, 1960[a]

Before-Tax Income	Percent Distribution of Income		Lower Limit, Before-Tax Income	Mean Amount of Income		Effective Tax Rate (Percent)
	Before Tax	After Tax		Before Tax	After Tax	
Top 1 percent	7.6	6.3	$30,130	$51,969	$38,491	25.9
Next 4 percent'	12.0	11.4	16,240	20,422	17,516	14.2
Remainder of top quintile	25.8	26.0	9,270	11,728	10,629	9.4
4th quintile	22.7	23.1	6,530	7,731	7,075	8.5
3d quintile	16.4	16.8	4,660	5,574	5,159	7.4
2d quintile	10.9	11.5	2,770	3,725	3,515	5.8
Lowest quintile	4.6	4.9	...	1,562	1,507	3.5
All units	100.0	100.0	...	$ 6,819	$ 6,132	10.1

[a] Derived from U. S. Department of Commerce, Office of Business Economics, *Survey of Current Business,* April 1964, pp. 5-9. Units are ranked by family personal income before tax. Income after tax is family personal income net of federal individual income tax liability other than tax liability on net capital gains. The effective tax rate is the amount of federal individual income tax liability, other than liability on net capital gains, as a percentage of family personal income. Figures for the top 1 percent and next 4 percent are based on my interpolations.

income concentration; however, the reaction of those who examine such estimates for the first time is often surprise that the effect is not greater. The percentage share of the top 1 percent of consumer units in after-tax income in 1960 is about one-sixth smaller than their share in before-tax income (6.3 percent compared with 7.6 percent). For the next 4 percent, comprising families and unattached individuals with before-tax incomes of about $16,000 to $30,000, the after-tax percentage share is only one-twentieth less

(1953). The Survey of Consumer Finance data used in Chapter IV and Appendix C relate to money income only and therefore are not directly comparable with the OBE estimates.

than the before-tax share.[4] The remaining members of the highest fifth and all lower groups have greater percentage shares in after-tax income than in before-tax income, but the differences are small.

There are three factors that may contribute to readers' surprise about the estimates. First, the income tax is less progressive than commonly believed. The tax extends far down the scale. While effective rates rise with income, the slope of the rate curve is less steep than might be expected.

Second, it may not be generally appreciated that the degree to which percentage shares in disposable income are equalized depends on differences between effective tax rates on high, middle, and low incomes, rather than the average height of the rates. A proportional tax, no matter how high, would not bring about any redistribution of income—provided the before-tax distribution remained constant, as is assumed in this part of the analysis. With progressive rates, groups whose effective tax rates are above the average for the whole population will have smaller percentage shares in after-tax income than in before-tax income, while the reverse will be true for groups whose effective rates are below the average.[5] This explains why, of the groups shown in Table 24, only the top 1 percent and the next 4 percent of units have smaller shares in after-tax income than in before-tax income. Furthermore, there is little difference between the before-tax and after-tax shares of the middle groups because their effective tax rates are not far from the average effective rate.

Third, some readers may think of equalization in terms of the absolute differences between high, middle, and low incomes rather than relative differences or income shares. As can be seen from Table 24, the federal income tax in 1960 sharply reduced the difference between the average income of the top 1 percent of consumer units and of all units, from about $45,000 before tax to about $32,000 after tax. While such figures are of interest, they

---

[4] The breakdown between the top 1 percent and the next 4 percent is based on my interpolations from OBE estimates. The interpolations are linear in the logarithms of (a) cumulated numbers of units; (b) cumulated amounts of before-tax income and after-tax income; and (c) class limits.

[5] The ratio of a group's after-tax share to its before-tax share is $(1 - r)/(1 - R)$, where r is the effective tax rate of the group and R is the effective tax rate for the whole population. This can be readily seen by noting that the group's before-tax share is y/Y, where y is the amount of its before-tax income and Y is total before-tax income, and that the group's after-tax share is $[(1 - r)y]/[(1 - R)Y]$.

do not distinguish between the weight of taxation and its redistributive effect. Estimates of percentage shares isolate the redistributive effect. These estimates can be readily compared over periods of change in income levels and tax rates and between countries. Finally, and more fundamentally, inequality is a relative concept and hence better measured by income shares or differences in relative size of income than by absolute income differences.

The effects of applying different income tax structures to the 1960 distribution of income are illustrated in Table 25. The whole population is divided into only two groups, the 5 percent of consumer units with the highest incomes and the remaining 95 percent of units. While this procedure sacrifices some information, particularly with respect to the very top of the income pyramid, it greatly simplifies the estimates and thereby minimizes errors and the need for arbitrary assumptions.

The table refers to "tax structures" rather than tax rates, because an effort has been made to take account of personal exemptions, deductions, and other relevant provisions as well as statutory rate schedules. This is done, however, in only a rough way. The figures for the 1935-36 structure, for example, show the effect of applying in 1960 an income tax with the relative yield and progressivity of the 1935-36 tax (yield being measured as a fraction of family personal income and progressivity by the division of liability between the top 5 percent and lower 95 percent of consumer units). The other figures are similar.[6]

As pointed out above, income shares are affected by differences of tax rates between income classes. These differences reflect both the progressivity of the tax, as measured by the ratio of high-bracket rates to low-bracket rates, and its relative yield, as measured by the ratio of total tax to total income.[7] The two elements can be

[6] Lines 5 and 8 are estimates of the actual distribution of tax liabilities between the two income groups in 1929 and 1935-36, and the items for all consumer units in lines 6 and 9 are estimates of actual average effective rates based on OBE and Treasury data. The effective rates for the top 5 percent and lower 95 percent, however, are derived figures which are not necessarily equal to actual effective rates in the earlier years.

[7] My definition of progression is similar to that which has been called "average rate progression." Other definitions have been proposed, including one that measures progression by the degree of equalization of disposable income. According to the latter definition, progressivity and relative yield are not separable. See Richard A. Musgrave and Tun Thin, "Income Tax Progression, 1929-48," *Journal of Political Economy*, Vol. 56 (December 1948), pp. 498-514.

TABLE 25. Effects of Applying Different Income Tax Structures to 1960 Income Distribution, Top 5 Percent and Lower 95 Percent of Consumer Units[a]

(In percent)

Tax Structure and Item	Consumer Units (Ranked by Income Before Tax)		
	All	Top 5 Percent	Lower 95 Percent
A. 1960 actual			
1. Before-tax income	100.0	19.6	80.4
2. Income tax	100.0	36.1	63.9
3. Effective tax rate	10.1	18.6	8.0
4. After-tax income	100.0	17.7	82.2
B. 1929 income tax structure			
5. Income tax	100.0	100.0	—
6. Effective tax rate	0.7	3.6	—
7. After-tax income	100.0	19.0	81.0
C. 1935–36 income tax structure			
8. Income tax	100.0	96.3	3.7
9. Effective tax rate	1.4	7.0	0.1
10. After-tax income	100.0	18.5	81.5
D. 1960 income tax yield, maximum progressivity			
11. Income tax	100.0	100.0	—
12. Effective tax rate	10.1	51.4	—
13. After-tax income	100.0	10.6	89.4
E. 1965 income tax structure			
14. Income tax	100.0	37.9	62.1
15. Effective tax rate	8.1	15.6	6.2
16. After-tax income	100.0	18.0	82.0

[a] Before-tax income is family personal income; income tax is federal individual income tax liability, excluding tax liability on net capital gains; effective tax rate is that liability as a percentage of family personal income; after-tax income is family personal income minus federal individual income tax liability. Lines 1 to 4 derived from U. S. Department of Commerce, Office of Business Economics, *Survey of Current Business*, April 1964, pp. 5-9. Lines 5 to 16 are my estimates.

seen by comparing the 1960 distribution with the estimates based on the 1929 tax structure. The 1929 tax structure was more progressive than that of 1960; in fact, the whole federal income tax was borne by the top 5 percent in 1929. But the relative yield of the 1929 income tax was so low that the absolute difference between the effective rate payable by the top 5 percent and the zero rate of the remaining units was much smaller than the difference between the 1960 rates of the two groups. Hence the 1929 tax would have only a small influence on income distribution.

Between 1929 and 1935-36, total income tax liability doubled in relation to income, and nearly all of the increase fell on high incomes. According to the rough test being employed here, the 1935-36 tax would do more than half as much equalizing as the 1960 tax.[8] (In 1960, the after-tax share of the top 5 percent was 1.9 percentage points smaller than their before-tax share; with the 1935-36 tax, the difference would be 1.1 percentage points.) When the 1935-36 and 1960 tax structures are compared, equalizing power is found to grow less rapidly than yield; this reflects the reduction of personal exemptions and the sharp increase in low-bracket rates.

Section D of Table 25 shows the maximum equalization that could have been accomplished in 1960 merely by changing the allocation of income tax liabilities. It is assumed that the total income tax yield would have been maintained at the actual 1960 level but that the whole tax would have been assessed against the top 5 percent of income recipients. The figures are included only to mark off an extreme, without any suggestion that it would have been desirable or feasible to have adopted such a tax structure. Even with maximum progressivity, the average disposable income of the top 5 percent of consumer units would still have been more than twice as great as the average for all other units (indicated by the estimate that 5 percent of the units would have received 10.6 percent of total after-tax income).

Table 25 also gives rough estimates of the impact of the income tax rates and other tax provisions that are scheduled to be in effect in 1965, according to the Revenue Act of 1964. The estimates given in Section E are intended to show the effect that the 1965 provisions would have had if they had been in force in 1960.[9]

[8] A more refined measure can be derived from Gini concentration ratios. A comparison of Gini coefficients is affected by changes throughout the income distribution but gives ambiguous answers when the Lorenz curves of before-tax and after-tax incomes cross. For a treatment using both the Gini coefficient and the share technique, see Selma F. Goldsmith, George Jaszi, Hyman Kaitz, and Maurice Liebenberg, "Size Distribution of Income Since the Mid-Thirties," *Review of Economics and Statistics*, Vol. 36 (February 1954), pp. 1-32.

[9] Based on the OBE distributions for 1960 and estimates of tax liability under the 1964 act given in *Revenue Act of 1964*, Senate Finance Committee, S. Rept. 830, 88 Cong. 2 sess. (1964), p. 28 *et passim*.

While the estimates are only rough approximations, they should give fairly accurate indications of orders of magnitude.

The 1965 income tax structure will be somewhat less equalizing than the previous structure, as indicated by the small increase in the fraction of after-tax income left in the hands of the highest 5 percent of income recipients (18.0 percent compared with 17.7 percent). In this respect, the influence of the over-all tax reduction outweighs the fact that the cut in effective rates was proportionately somewhat greater for the lower 95 percent than for the top 5 percent.[10] In order to maintain the equalizing power of the income tax while reducing yields, it would have been necessary to allocate a larger part of the tax reduction to low brackets.

These comments relate to the effect of applying different tax structures to a given before-tax distribution. A large tax cut, such as that made by the Revenue Act of 1964, could stimulate economic activity and reduce unemployment to such a degree that gains in before-tax income realized by lower income groups would more than offset the apparent loss in equalizing power. However, there seems to be little basis for predicting such an outcome. The available statistics reveal no obvious effect on size distribution of fluctuations in the level of income and unemployment rates of the magnitude that have occurred since the end of World War II.

There are some data suggesting that, if judged solely by impact on the top 5 percent of income-receiving units, the federal income tax in the United States may have been less equalizing in the period 1948-52 than the income taxes of the United Kingdom, the Netherlands, Denmark, and Sweden.[11] The statistics, however, vary so greatly in concepts and coverage that a comparison cannot be confidently made.

[10] According to the estimates in Table 25, the substitution of the 1965 tax structure for the actual tax structure in 1960 would have increased the disposable income of the top 5 percent of consumer units by 3.7 percent (from 81.4 percent to 84.4 percent of the group's before-tax income) while increasing the disposable income of the lower 95 percent by 2.0 percent (from 92.0 percent to 93.8 percent of before-tax income).

[11] United Nations, *Economic Survey of Europe in 1956* (Geneva, 1957), Chapter IX; for further comparisons, see L. Needleman, "The Burden of Taxation: An International Comparison," *National Institute Economic Review* (London), March 1961, pp. 55-61.

Changes in Before-Tax Distribution of Income

Statistics of the kind examined in the preceding pages will understate or overstate the equalizing power of the income tax if its existence causes the before-tax distribution to be less concentrated or more concentrated than it otherwise would be. The income tax may lessen the inequality of before-tax income by reducing the saving, wealth accumulation, and property income of high-income families; by inducing high-income investors to shift toward assets with lower actual or nominal rates of yield; by encouraging the splitting of property and income among family members who are in separate income units or its dispersal through philanthropic contributions; and by deterring highly remunerated personal effort. On the other hand, inequality of before-tax income can be increased if the income tax causes compensating rises in profit rates, executive salaries and bonuses, and professional fees. The existence of the tax may stimulate the use of forms of compensation that do not enter into the income statistics and may thus impair their reliability as indicators of inequality. Of course, the income tax is only one of many factors affecting the before-tax distribution of income.

Historical Information

Information on income distribution is scanty for the period prior to the introduction of the mass income tax and the development of large-scale field surveys of consumer budgets. Expert opinion, based on conjecture and scattered evidence, holds that a period of growing concentration of income in the United States ended about 1890 and was followed by a phase of diminishing inequality lasting until about 1920.[12]

For the period 1919 to 1938, Kuznets detected no increasing or decreasing trend in the income shares of the top 1 percent and top 5 percent of the population, but he found a sharp decline in the percentage of income received by these groups between 1938 and 1944.[13] His estimates, based on data from tax returns covering

[12] Kravis, *Structure of Income,* pp. 208-15.
[13] Simon Kuznets, *Shares of Upper Income Groups in Income and Savings* (New York: National Bureau of Economic Research, 1953), p. xxxvii *et passim.*

only a small fraction of the population, do not provide a breakdown for the lower range of incomes.

Estimates on the OBE basis begin with 1929. They show a considerable decrease in income concentration from 1929 to 1935-36, an even greater decrease between 1935-36 and 1944, and little change after 1944 (Table 26).[14] The percentage share of the top 5 percent of consumer units was reduced by almost one-third between 1929 and 1944, while the share of the next 15 percent increased slightly and the shares of lower income groups increased more.

TABLE 26. Distribution of Family Personal Income Before Tax Among Consumer Units, Selected Periods, 1929-60[a]

(In percent)

Before-Tax Income	1929	1935–36	1944	1950–59[b]	1960
Top 5 percent	30.0	26.5	20.7	20.4	19.6
Next 15 percent	24.4	25.2	25.1	24.9	25.8
4th quintile	19.3	20.9	22.2	22.4	22.7
3d quintile	13.8	14.1	16.2	16.4	16.4
2d quintile	12.5	9.2	10.9	11.2	10.9
Lowest quintile		4.1	4.9	4.8	4.6

[a] Derived from U. S. Bureau of the Census, *Historical Statistics of the United States, Colonial Times to 1957,* p. 166; and U. S. Department of Commerce, Office of Business Economics, *Survey of Current Business,* April 1964, p. 8.
[b] Averages (arithmetic means) of annual percentages.

The year-to-year record of the share of the top 5 percent of consumer units since 1929 is depicted in Chart 5.[15] The chart reveals

Kuznets' estimates relate to income per person rather than income per recipient or per consumer unit.

[14] The estimates for 1944 and later years are official OBE estimates; those for 1929 and 1935-36 are based on other studies adjusted for comparability. For the earlier years, see Goldsmith, Jaszi, Kaitz, and Liebenberg, *Review of Economics and Statistics,* Vol. 36, pp. 1-32; Selma F. Goldsmith, "The Relation of Census Income Distribution Statistics to Other Income Data," in *Studies in Income and Wealth,* Vol. 23, Conference on Research in Income and Wealth (Princeton, N. J.: Princeton University Press for National Bureau of Economic Research, 1958), pp. 65-107; and U. S. Bureau of the Census, *Historical Statistics of the United States, Colonial Times to 1957,* p. 166.

[15] The broken line connecting points for the earlier years indicates that estimates are not available for the intervening years. The estimates include Alaska and Hawaii for 1960-62.

CHART 5. Percentage of Total Family Personal Income (Before Taxes) Received by Top 5 Percent of Consumer Units, 1929-62

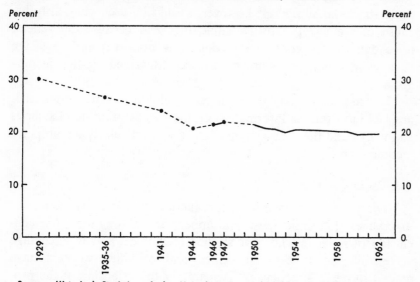

Source: *Historical Statistics of the United States, Colonial Times to 1957; Survey of Current Business,* April 1964.

no large fluctuations after 1944 but suggests a slight downward drift of the share of the top 5 percent after 1950.

The use of 1929 as the beginning date for the historical record based on OBE estimates may somewhat exaggerate the decrease in inequality. Kuznets' estimates for 1929 show that the income share of the top group in that year, though not unprecedentedly large, was greater than the average for the preceding decade.[16]

Movements in the absolute size of income do not parallel changes in percentage shares. Between 1929 and 1944, when the percentage share of the top 5 percent of units was falling sharply, the average before-tax income of these families and individuals declined only slightly, measured in dollars of constant purchasing power. Between 1944 and 1960, the average income before taxes of the highest 5 percent increased about 11 percent in constant dol-

[16] His "basic variant" estimates place the before-tax share of the top 5 percent of the population at 26.1 percent in 1929 and at 24.6 percent in 1919-28 (arithmetic mean of annual percentages); see *Shares of Upper Income Groups,* p. 599.

lars.[17] The explanation of the diverse movements of percentage shares and dollar amounts is that total income grew faster than the population. These figures, however, should be used cautiously because of the usual statistical difficulties and because the general price deflator for consumer income may not adequately measure changes in prices of goods and services consumed by high income groups.

In order to explain the changes in global income shares, it is desirable to examine information on the size distribution of salaries and wages and the composition of income, particularly the property income share.

Salaries and Wages

There seems to have been a reduction of inequality of salaries and wages at both the lower and upper parts of the range. The conclusion of scholars who have studied the subject is that percentage wage differentials between skilled and unskilled workers have tended to decline secularly.[18] Apparently the extension of the progressive income tax to the majority of regularly employed people has not caused wage adjustments counteracting the forces making for a narrowing of skill differentials.

There is some evidence that over the past three decades the compensation of top business executives has increased less than that of the majority of workers and that differences between pay of the top executives have narrowed. A study by Burgess finds that the average total before-tax compensation of the 75 men comprising the 3 top executives of each of the 25 largest manufacturing corporations increased by 61 percent from 1929 to 1958, while their estimated

[17] Derived from *Survey of Current Business*, April 1964, pp. 5, 8, 11, and Table 26.

[18] Melvin W. Reder, "The Theory of Occupational Wage Differentials," *American Economic Review*, Vol. 45 (December 1955), pp. 833-52, and "Wage Differentials: Theory and Measurement," in *Aspects of Labor Economics*, Conference of Universities-National Bureau Committee for Economic Research (Princeton, N. J.: Princeton University Press for National Bureau of Economic Research, 1962), pp. 257-311; Paul G. Keat, "Long-Run Changes in Occupational Wage Structure, 1900-1956," *Journal of Political Economy*, Vol. 68 (December 1960), pp. 584-600; and other studies cited by Reder and Keat. In the period 1950-61, the unskilled lost part of their previous gain in relative position; see Herman P. Miller, *Rich Man, Poor Man* (New York: Crowell, 1964), pp. 44-51.

after-tax compensation increased by only about 1 percent.[19] During the same period, the average compensation of full-time employees in manufacturing increased by 246 percent before tax and by an estimated 191 percent after federal income tax.[20] Burgess' figures for executives include, in addition to salaries and wages, allowances for the discounted value of pensions and deferred compensation but do not include the value of life insurance coverage and liberal expense accounts. Stock option gains are measured as the difference between the option price and the market price when the option is exercised. (Average compensation of the top executives was substantially greater in 1955-56 than in 1958 because of larger stock option gains in the earlier years.) The estimates for the average employee include the value of employer contributions to social insurance and private pension, health, and welfare plans.

Among the top executives, Burgess' figures show the differential between the highest executive in each company and the second-ranking man narrowing considerably from 1929 to 1948 and widening a little between 1948 and 1958. Taking the pay of the second-ranking executives as 100, the average before-tax compensation of the top and third-ranking executives was as follows:[21]

	1929	1937	1948	1958
Top	182	150	137	145
Third	77	82	79	103

If Burgess' figures are representative, highly paid executives partly avoided the income tax by obtaining a greater part of their

[19] Leonard Randolph Burgess, *Top Executive Pay Package* (New York: Graduate School of Business, Columbia University and Free Press of Glencoe, 1963), pp. 114-16 *et passim*. The firms studied were the 25 largest in each year, rather than an identical group.

[20] Average annual compensation per full-time equivalent employee, including supplements to salaries and wages (employer contributions for social insurance, private pension, health and welfare plans) as estimated by U. S. Department of Commerce, Office of Business Economics, *National Income* (1954), pp. 178, 196, 200, and *Survey of Current Business*, July 1962, pp. 28-29. After-tax compensation is my estimate based on computed federal income tax liability for a married couple with two dependents and the standard deduction (or tax table).

[21] Derived from Burgess, *Top Executive Pay Package*, pp. 174-77. Some of the figures are approximations read from Burgess' charts. The average pay of the third-ranking executives exceeds that of the second-ranking in 1958 because some companies paid their third-ranking men more than other companies paid their second-ranking executives.

compensation in the form of stock options and deferred compensation and pensions but did not secure as large percentage increases in before-tax or after-tax pay as did the average employee in manufacturing. Furthermore, the second- and third-ranking executives narrowed the gap between themselves and their seniors. The figures, of course, do not rule out the possibility that the range of compensation would have narrowed even more under a different tax system, but they offer no support for such an assertion. Taken at face value, they indicate that changes in before-tax compensation and in the income tax both contributed to the reduction of inequality.

Property Income

A substantial part of the decline in the income share of the top income groups after 1929 seems to have been due to property income's falling more rapidly than other income in the early 1930's and growing less rapidly than other income thereafter. The following figures show the actual percentage-point decline in the total income share of the top 5 percent of consumer units and the decline that would have occurred owing to the decrease in the relative size of the property income component, even if the group had received the same fraction of property income as in 1929:

	1929 to		
	1935-36	1944	1960
Total decrease	3.5	9.3	10.4
Attributable to relative decrease in property income[22]	1.8	5.9	4.5

A considerable part of the relative decline in the property income component of total personal income can be traced to developments that appear to be unrelated to the income tax, but part of the

[22] Calculated on the assumption that the top 5 percent of consumer units received the same percentage of dividends, personal interest income, and rental income of persons in the later years as in 1929. Data on the total amount of these items are OBE estimates (*Economic Report of the President, January 1963*, p. 189). The 1929 share of the top 5 percent in each of the three items of property income is assumed to equal the percentage share of the 5 percent of the population with the highest incomes, as estimated by Kuznets (*Shares of Upper Income Groups*, p. 649). The OBE estimates of total income shares relate to consumer units whereas Kuznets' estimates relate to persons, hence the composition of the top 5 percent differs somewhat between the two sets of estimates.

remaining decline may have been caused by the tax. One factor that depends on total tax yields but that cannot be directly attributed to individual income tax is the behavior of government expenditures. From 1929 to 1960, the proportion of national income produced that originated in the government sector increased by 6.9 percentage points and the proportion of family personal income that consisted of government net transfer payments increased by 3.8 percentage points.[23] According to official estimates, none of the government items is classified as property income.

Another factor, in which the income tax may be involved, is the decrease in the property income component of income produced in the private sector. This decrease reflects a declining capital-output ratio and a declining average rate of return on private capital. From 1929 to 1957, the capital-output ratio fell from 4.3 to 3.8, while the computed average rate of return on private capital declined from 6.2 percent to 5.4 percent.[24] A decline in the capital-output ratio can be expected if, as is often alleged, the income tax retards saving and investment, and employment of labor is not equally depressed. Although this may have occurred, it is hard to reconcile with a stable or declining before-tax rate of return on capital. Maintenance of employment in the face of a retardation of investment would imply a capital shortage in the private sector and would lead one to expect a tendency toward rising rates of return.

[23] OBE estimates, from *National Income* (1954), pp. 176, 212; and *Survey of Current Business,* April 1963 and July 1963. Government net transfer payments consist of payments for social security benefits, veterans' benefits, public assistance, and other transfers, minus personal contributions for social insurance.

[24] The capital-output ratio is the ratio of the value of private capital to private product, both expressed in current prices. Private capital is national wealth, excluding military assets, minus the value of public civilian structures, public land, consumer durables, and monetary metals, as estimated by Raymond W. Goldsmith (*The National Wealth of the United States in the Postwar Period* [Princeton, N. J.: Princeton University Press for National Bureau of Economic Research, 1962], pp. 117-18). Private product is national income minus income originating in government and government enterprises (U. S. Department of Commerce, Office of Business Economics, *U. S. Income and Output* [1958], pp. 130, 126, and *Survey of Current Business,* July 1962, pp. 6, 11). The average rate of return on private capital is the ratio of the sum of rental income of persons, corporate profits before tax plus inventory valuation adjustment, and net interest (national income components, *ibid.*) to the value of private capital; it is understated because the numerator does not include the portion of proprietors' income consisting of the return on capital.

The possible magnitude of the influence of the income tax on saving, wealth accumulation, and property income of upper income groups and lower income groups can be tested by some illustrative figures based on the record of the 1950's. Suppose that, in the decade 1950-59, the federal income tax had been proportional rather than progressive and that the same amount of revenue had been raised from it. Suppose further that the marginal propensity to save of the top 5 percent of income recipients was 50 percent and that of the lower 95 percent zero. On the assumption that the average yield on savings is 5 percent, the top income group would have had $31.1 billion more wealth and $1.6 billion more before-tax income in 1960 than it actually had, while the wealth and income of the lower group would have been unaffected. On this set of assumptions, the before-tax share of total income received by the highest 5 percent in 1960 would have been 20.0 percent rather than 19.6 percent.[25] If a lower saving propensity had been assumed for the top income group, the redistribution would have been smaller.

Without denying that changes in the distribution of wealth and income of the magnitude shown in the illustrative computations are socially significant, one may conclude that income taxation at the rates prevailing in the 1950's will not exert an impressive influence on the concentration of before-tax income, via effects on wealth accumulation, unless continued for a long time. This is true even if rates of return on wealth are somewhat higher than the 5 percent assumed in the illustration.

A substantial part of the decline in the income share of top income recipients after 1929 can be attributed to the behavior of dividends relative to other income. (According to my estimates, dividends received by the top 5 percent equaled 5.6 percent of total family personal income in 1929 but only 1.8 percent in 1960.[26])

[25] These computations allow for annual compounding at 5 percent and a 10 percent proportional income tax during the accumulation period (1950-59). They are based on the extreme assumption that all individuals or families who were in the top 5 percent of the income distribution at any time in the years 1950-59 were still there in 1960 or had passed on their additional saving intact to heirs who were in the top group.

[26] Based on OBE estimates of total dividends and family personal income; Kuznets' estimates of the share of the top 5 percent of the population in 1929 (*Shares of Upper Income Groups*, p. 660); and my estimates of the share of the top 5 percent in 1960, derived from *Statistics of Income*.

The individual income tax may be partly responsible for the decline in the relative importance of dividend income if, as has been suggested, corporations have held down their distributions in order to shield stockholders from the individual tax.[27] This factor, however, can explain only a small fraction of the total decline in the income share of the top 5 percent of individuals and families. The increase in the corporation income tax from 1929 to 1960 seems to have been more influential in this respect.[28]

The income tax no doubt causes some decline in the before-tax income share of high-income investors by inducing them to try to avoid taxation by seeking out tax-sheltered assets such as state and local government securities, owner-occupied residences, and property promising capital gains rather than current yield. These assets usually have a lower gross yield than fully taxable substitutes, though they may be attractive to high-income persons when their tax advantages are taken into account (see the discussion of tax-exempt securities in Chapter VI).

The influence of this factor cannot be precisely measured because to do so would require knowledge about how people would act if the tax system were quite different. There are, however, reasons for doubting its importance. High-income persons probably obtain higher average yields on their financial assets than middle-income persons do. The high-income persons generally hold a greater proportion of their assets in the form of corporate stock while the middle income groups hold relatively more cash and savings deposits. In a study of financial asset holdings of Wisconsin individuals in 1949, Atkinson found a pronounced tendency for average rates of yield to rise with size of income, owing mainly to differences in portfolio composition. However, average yields obtained on bonds declined as the investors' incomes rose, and this

---

[27] John A. Brittain, "The Tax Structure and Corporate Dividend Policy," *American Economic Review*, Vol. 54, Papers and Proceedings (May 1964), pp. 272-87 (Brookings Institution Reprint No. 78, 1964).

[28] My computations indicate that, if corporations had distributed the same proportion of their cash flow (after-tax profits plus capital consumption allowances) in 1960 as in 1929, the before-tax income share of the top 5 percent would have been increased by 0.8 percentage point. If corporate tax rates had been the same in 1960 as in 1929, and the dividend-payout ratio had been at its actual 1960 level, the income share of the top 5 percent would have been increased by 1.1 percentage points.

was also true of traded stocks up to a high income level.[29] Tax-return data for the United States for 1959 indicate that high-income investors realized a much greater proportion of their total return from corporate stock in the form of long-term capital gains than middle-income and low-income investors did,[30] but this difference probably was due at least partly to more active trading by the high-income investors rather than to lower dividend yields.[31] Information is not available on rates of return on real estate and interests in unincorporated business enterprises.

The most conspicuous item on which low yields are accepted in order to avoid taxation is fully tax-exempt securities. The estimated yield differential on these securities in 1960, however, amounted to a sum equal to only about 0.1 percent of total family personal income,[32] a small part of the income of the high income groups.

Evaluation

The timing of the changes in the distribution of before-tax income casts doubt on the importance of the income tax as a cause. While it is true that the tax was increased sharply between 1929 and 1944, when the substantial reduction in concentration of before-tax income occurred, the usual analysis would stress delayed or cumulative effects on income distribution rather than immediate effects. Changes in compensation arrangements and investment patterns would be likely to take place slowly, and effects operating through wealth accumulation would be spread over a long period. It appears that other factors associated with the collapse of the boom in 1929, the great depression, and World War II were the major forces accounting for the reduction in income concentration

[29] Thomas R. Atkinson, *The Pattern of Financial Asset Ownership* (Princeton, N. J.: Princeton University Press for National Bureau of Economic Research, 1956), pp. 79, 131, 141, 143.

[30] U. S. Treasury Department, *Statistics of Income, Individual Income Tax Returns, 1959* (cited hereinafter as *Statistics of Income, 19 . .*), p. 4, and *Statistics of Income, 1959, Supplementary Report, Sales of Capital Assets*, p. 11.

[31] For 1959-60 survey data on trading activity by investors in different income groups, see George Katona and John B. Lansing, "The Wealth of the Wealthy," *Review of Economics and Statistics*, Vol. 46 (February 1964), p. 10.

[32] Estimated on the basis of statistics cited in Chapter VI, placing the yield differential at the upper limit of the range estimated by Ott and Meltzer (pp. 140-44).

between 1929 and 1944. The relative stability of income shares in the postwar period, despite continued high income tax rates, does not support the hypothesis that the tax had important cumulative effects on the distribution of before-tax income; however, it is possible that long-run cumulative effects were operating but were offset by other forces.

In the light of admittedly incomplete and unsatisfactory evidence, it may be concluded that the individual income tax probably contributed to the reduction in the before-tax share of income received by top income groups between 1929 and the end of World War II and to the prevention of a reversal of this change after the war. Among the consequences of the income tax that may have worked in this direction are a reduction in the amount of wealth accumulated by high-income people, increased attractiveness of tax-sheltered investments yielding comparatively low rates of return before tax, lower corporate dividend-payout ratios, and willingness of business executives to accept deferred compensation and other perquisites in lieu of part of current salaries. Although the influence of these factors cannot be reliably measured, there is no evidence that it was great in the aggregate.

Without an allowance for its influence on before-tax income, the individual income tax can be credited with only about one-tenth of the decline in the share of disposable family personal income of the top 5 percent of consumer units between 1929 and 1960.[33] While the net contribution of the tax probably was greater than this, it still seems to have been only a minor factor in the reduction in inequality of measured disposable income.

Limitations of Statistics

With minor exceptions, the statistics discussed in this chapter omit capital gains and the income tax attributable to them. While this omission may be appropriate for size distributions tied to the

[33] The share of the top 5 percent in after-tax income dropped from about 29.5 percent in 1929 (my estimate) to 17.7 percent in 1960 (OBE estimate) or by 11.8 percentage points. Since the share of the top 5 percent in before-tax income was 30.0 percent in 1929 and 19.6 percent in 1960, the drop in their disposable income in the absence of the individual income tax would have been 10.4 percentage points, which is about nine-tenths of 11.8 percentage points.

national income aggregates, which properly exclude capital gains, it impairs the usefulness of the statistics as a basis for the appraisal of tax policy.

Since the ownership of price-sensitive assets is concentrated in the hands of high income groups, the share of these groups in total income including capital gains is greater than their share in income exclusive of net capital gains in years in which positive gains occur. It does not follow, however, that the income series which omits capital gains overstates the decline in the income share of the top group over time. Whether this is true depends to a great extent on the particular years compared.

Inasmuch as realized capital gains were unusually large relative to other income in 1929, an income series that included these gains would generally show a greater decline in the share of the top group after 1929 than is indicated by the OBE statistics which exclude capital gains. (1959 is an exception; realized capital gains were even greater relative to other income in that year than in 1929.) However, comparisons between the late 1930's and recent years would show a smaller decline in the share of the top group if realized capital gains were included. Unfortunately, it is not feasible to make comprehensive adjustments in the statistics to reflect capital gains. Some information on the subject is given in Appendix D.

The statistics have other shortcomings which are briefly discussed in Appendix D. The various factors cannot be quantified; if they could be, the statistics could be corrected. On the whole it seems likely that the usual statistics overstate the reduction in income inequality since 1929; however, I do not think that the statistical deficiencies are great enough to cast serious doubt on the statement that a genuine reduction in income concentration has occurred.

Distribution of Wealth

Statistics on wealth, like those on income, show less concentration in recent years than in the 1920's. Lampman's study,[34] based on estate tax data, finds that the share of top wealth-holders in total

[34] Robert J. Lampman, *The Share of Top Wealth-Holders in National Wealth, 1922-1956* (Princeton, N. J.: Princeton University Press for National Bureau of Economic Research, 1962).

personal wealth fell sharply from 1929 to 1949. Thereafter, their share increased, but tentative estimates for 1961 indicate that only about half of the previous decline had been recovered up to that time. Lampman's estimates are summarized in Table 27.

Lampman infers that the most important proximate cause of the change in the position of the richest group was that its share of personal saving was well below its share of personal wealth, par-

TABLE 27. Share of Personal Wealth Held by Top Wealth-Holders, Selected Years, 1922-61[a]

(In percent of total personal equity or net worth)

Year	Top 1 Percent of Adults	Top 0.5 Percent of All Persons	Top 2 Percent of Families[b]
1922	31.6	29.8	33.0
1929	36.3	32.4	...
1933	28.3	25.2	...
1939	30.6	28.0	...
1945	23.3	20.9	...
1949	20.8	19.3	...
1953	24.2	22.7	28.5
1956	26.0	25.0	...
1961	28.0[c]	...	...

[a] Share of total equity (net worth); basic variant, which does not include interests in personal trust funds, annuities, and private and governmental pensions, but which does include estimated equity in life insurance. For 1922-56, from Robert J. Lampman, *The Share of Top Wealth-Holders in National Wealth, 1922-1956* (Princeton, N. J.: Princeton University Press for National Bureau of Economic Research, 1962), p. 24.
[b] Families defined as all adults less married females.
[c] *Business Week*, Jan. 27, 1962, p. 31; estimate attributed to Lampman.

ticularly between 1939 and 1949. While the income tax probably was partly responsible, the hypothetical figures mentioned above suggest that its influence can easily be exaggerated. A factor in the decline of wealth concentration is the increased importance of consumer durables and pension and retirement funds, which are more widely held than are securities and equities in unincorporated businesses.[35] Investment in durables and pension funds may have been encouraged by the favorable income tax treatment of the returns,

[35] Cf. Raymond W. Goldsmith, *A Study of Saving in the United States* (Princeton, N. J.: Princeton University Press, 1955), Vol. I, p. 161.

but other social and economic forces probably were more important.

A second cause of decreased concentration of wealth, at least in the statistical sense, is changes in property-transfer practices, which placed a larger fraction of wealth in the hands of women and young persons after 1922. Lampman attributes to these changes the fact that the share of the top 1 percent of adults fell more than the share of the top 2 percent of families from 1922 to 1953 (Table 27).[36] Income tax considerations, as well as the desire to minimize estate taxes, may have encouraged the splitting up of fortunes. Income tax incentives for splitting with wives disappeared after the universalization of splitting privileges between spouses in 1948 but continued with respect to splits with children and other relatives.

Two other factors that Lampman identifies as contributing to the fall in the share of wealth held by the top group—changes in relative prices of assets and demographic changes—seem not to be directly related to the income tax. Although the share of the richest group was influenced by cyclical swings in the composition of estates, Lampman finds "remarkably little noncyclical change [in estate composition] over the decades."[37] It is interesting that the most significant cyclical shift was the reduction in the top group's concentration on price-sensitive assets, such as corporate stocks and real estate, in the boom period 1922-29, which held down the growth of its share of total wealth.[38] These were years of low income tax rates, and it seems unlikely that the tax was responsible for the shift.

How can the estimates showing a partial reversal, after 1949, of the previous decline in wealth concentration (Table 27) be reconciled with the income statistics, which show no tendency for the share of the top income group to increase during the 1950's? Although there is no formal inconsistency, trends toward increasing or decreasing concentration might be expected to be parallel with respect to wealth and income. An important part of the reconciliation may be found in the way capital gains influence the two sets of statistics. Capital gains, regardless of whether realized or not,

[36] *Share of Top Wealth-Holders*, pp. 237-43.
[37] *Ibid.*, p. 21.
[38] *Ibid.*, pp. 208-09, 244.

are reflected in the wealth statistics but are not included in the OBE income statistics, even if realized. A comparison of Lampman's current-price and constant-price estimates of the wealth share of the top 1 percent in 1949 and 1953 indicates that capital appreciation was largely responsible for the increase in concentration over that four-year period. In constant dollars, the increase in the share of the richest group was less than one-third as large as the increase in current dollars which is shown in Table 27.[39] Lampman does not give constant-price estimates for years after 1953.

The data contradict the popular belief that the high income tax rates of the postwar period have prevented the creation of new private fortunes. According to Lampman's estimates, the number of millionaires, that is, persons with gross estates of $1 million and over, increased from 13,297 in 1944 to 27,502 in 1953. Even with allowance for the fall in the purchasing power of the dollar, the number of millionaires grew by one-third.[40] During this period, the population grew by only 15 percent and per capita personal income in constant prices by about 4½ percent.[41]

Concluding Remarks

This extended review of the statistics neither corroborates the opinion that the income tax is a Draconian measure for redistribution nor justifies writing off its equalizing effects as inconsequential. Although the difference between the before-tax and after-tax distributions of income in recent years is not striking, neither is it trivial.

There is no evidence that the redistributive impact of the income tax has been offset by changes in before-tax income shares.

[39] In constant (1922) dollars, the share of personal wealth held by the top 1 percent of adults increased from 21.2 percent in 1949 to 22.3 percent in 1953, while in current dollars the increase was from 20.8 percent to 24.2 percent (*ibid.*, pp. 227, 24).

[40] *Ibid.*, p. 276. Lampman estimates that in 1953 there were 17,611 persons with estates equivalent to one million or more 1944 dollars. The deflator here is the consumer price index, whereas the constant-price estimates mentioned in the preceding paragraph were derived by applying asset price indexes to the principal components of wealth.

[41] Derived from *Economic Report of the President, January 1962*, pp. 214, 226, 227; personal income converted to constant prices by application of the implicit price deflator for the personal consumption component of GNP.

Income before tax has become less unequal, and there is reason for believing that the tax has contributed to a minor extent to this change. Part of the apparent decline in the before-tax share of the highest income classes after 1929 probably is spurious, reflecting efforts to avoid taxes and other factors that changed measured personal income more than true income; however, it seems unlikely that the major part of the apparent change can be explained in this way. It appears, therefore, that although the individual income tax has contributed significantly to lessened inequality of disposable income over the past three decades, it has been considerably less important in this respect than other governmental actions and developments in the private economy.

If Congress were determined to bring about a drastic reduction in economic inequality, it could do much more by means of the income tax. But extreme equalization has not been accepted even as an ultimate goal. The primary popular and legislative support of progressive taxation seems to derive from ideas about ability to pay or sacrifice rather than an intention to equalize incomes (Chapter II). Among those who explicitly advocate taxation to reduce inequality, most would concede that substantial differences in income are justifiable on the basis of needs as indicated by family size, age, and other personal circumstances and on the basis of contribution to production and the public good.[42] Another source of differences between after-tax earned incomes that seem fully justifiable on egalitarian premises is the amount of time invested in preparing for occupations. A person in a profession requiring many years of education should have a higher annual income than a clerk, if for no other reason, because his earnings begin later and are received over a shorter period of time. Relatively noncontroversial differences of these kinds can account for a considerable amount of inequality.

Progressive taxation, moreover, is not the only means of reducing economic inequality. The wider dissemination of education,

[42] On the implications of such factors, see George Garvy, "Comment," in *Studies in Income and Wealth,* Conference on Research in Income and Wealth, Vol. 13 (New York: National Bureau of Economic Research, 1951), pp. 217-18. Garvy remarks that the standard of full equalization and departures from it, as measured by the Lorenz curve (and Gini coefficient), have "a mathematical rather than economic meaning."

improved programs for health and medical care, and the breaking down of racial discrimination are desirable in themselves and may make a lasting contribution to the reduction of economic inequality by raising the incomes of the poor.[43] Transfer payments, though directed to the satisfaction of particular social needs, also have a significant influence on the distribution of personal income. Further improvements in these programs can be expected to reduce inequality unless the expenditures are financed by regressive taxes.

Progressive taxation and government expenditures cannot deal with all kinds of inequality since differences in measured wealth and income are not the only sources of privilege and power. Extreme efforts to reduce economic inequality would be subject to the risk that they would merely transfer to government and corporate bureaucrats powers that were formerly exercised by property owners.

The best approach to income distribution—both as a subject of analysis and a field of social action—is to adopt what Dahl and Lindblom call an "incremental attitude."[44] This attitude directs attention toward small changes rather than drastic redistributions. It supports the belief that inequality can be moderately reduced or increased by changes in the effective progressivity of the income tax, without radically altering the economic and political system.

[43] For effective statements of this view, see two papers by Allan G. B. Fisher: " 'Full Employment' and Income Inequality," *Economic Journal*, Vol. 56 (March 1946), pp. 18-26; and "Alternative Techniques for Promoting Equality in a Capitalist Society," *American Economic Review*, Vol. 40, Papers and Proceedings (May 1950), pp. 356-68.

[44] Robert A. Dahl and Charles E. Lindblom, *Politics, Economics, and Welfare* (New York: Harper, 1953), p. 148.

CHAPTER XI

Countercyclical Effects

ONE OF THE STANDARDS by which a national government tax is now judged is its effectiveness in moderating instability of economic activity. A tax can act as a stabilizer if accrued liabilities or payments move in the same direction as general business activity and thereby curtail private demand more during periods of business expansion and prosperity than during recessions. Provided the changes in revenues do not induce offsetting changes in government expenditures, variations in the government's budget surplus or deficit will partly or wholly compensate for fluctuations in private investment and consumption.

The acceptance of a compensatory fiscal policy means that annual balancing of the government's budget should no longer be regarded as a criterion of financial responsibility. Cyclical instability of revenue, once considered a defect, is now widely regarded as a desirable characteristic of a national government tax system. It still may be troublesome to state and local governments because of limitations on their jurisdiction and monetary and fiscal powers.

Variations of tax liabilities that occur automatically in response to cyclical fluctuations, without change in statutory tax rates, are called "built-in flexibility." Countercyclical effects may also be obtained by changes in statutory tax rates and other provisions

286

which by advance agreement are put into operation when economic indexes behave in a certain way—"formula flexibility"—or by ad hoc changes—"discretionary flexibility."

Taxes differ both in flexibility of yield and in the economic effects of variations in yield. This chapter compares the individual income tax with other major taxes in these respects. Toward the end of the chapter some remarks are made about the relation between countercyclical policy and longer-run problems of economic growth and government finance.

Built-in Flexibility and Elasticity
of Individual Income Tax

The built-in flexibility of a tax is measured by the ratio of change in tax liability (or tax collections) to change in aggregate income.[1] Income may be represented by statistics of gross national product (GNP), personal income, personal income originating in current production (personal income less transfer payments), or another broad aggregate. The change in tax liability reflects the change in the tax base and the marginal tax rate. Built-in flexibility, therefore, depends on the amplitude of fluctuations in the tax base relative to fluctuations in aggregate income and on the marginal tax rate.

Relation of Built-in Flexibility to Elasticity

Built-in flexibility differs from income elasticity of yield, with which it is sometimes confused. Elasticity is the ratio of the percentage change in tax yield to the percentage change in income.[2]

---

[1] In the analysis of built-in flexibility, I was aided greatly by the study *Federal Fiscal Policy in the Postwar Recessions,* Studies of Government Finance (Washington: Brookings Institution, 1962), by Wilfred Lewis, Jr., and by discussions with Lewis.

[2] Built-in flexibility equals $\Delta T/\Delta Y$, whereas income elasticity of yield equals $\Delta T/T \cdot Y/\Delta Y$, where T is tax liability and Y is income. See Joseph A. Pechman, "Yield of the Individual Income Tax During a Recession," *National Tax Journal,* Vol. 7 (March 1954), p. 2, and in *Policies to Combat Depression,* Conference of Universities-National Bureau Committee for Economic Research (Princeton, N. J.: Princeton University Press for National Bureau of Economic Research, 1956), p. 124.

An elasticity measure can be converted into a built-in flexibility measure by multiplying by a factor relating the tax yield to aggregate income: $\Delta T/T \cdot Y/\Delta Y \cdot T/Y = \Delta T/\Delta Y$.

A tax with a yield that is small relative to income and the change in income can have high elasticity but cannot have great built-in flexibility. Two taxes with the same built-in flexibility can have radically different elasticities. The difference between the two concepts may be illustrated by comparing the behavior of three hypothetical taxes—T_1, T_2, and T_3—in two time periods, on the assumption that income increases from 100 in period I to 110 in period II:

	T_1	T_2	T_3
Yield, period I	20	1	10
Yield, period II	21	1.20	11
Built-in flexibility	0.10	0.02	0.10
Elasticity	0.50	2	1

Built-in flexibility is more directly relevant to economic stabilization than elasticity is. Variations in tax liabilities act as stabilizers only to the extent that they offset the effects on income and output that would otherwise be associated with autonomous fluctuations in demand. The larger these offsets are, the smaller will be the change in aggregate income resulting from any primary change in demand. Although the size of the offsets attributable to different taxes should not be assumed to be proportional to their built-in flexibility, it is much more closely related to built-in flexibility than to elasticity.[3]

Elasticity measures, nevertheless, are useful in analyzing the effect on automatic stabilizers of substituting one tax for another or of revising tax rates. If a tax has high elasticity, but its built-in flexibility is small simply because its rates are low, its built-in flexibility might be increased by raising the rates. In the foregoing illustration, if the rate of T_3 could be doubled without affecting its elasticity, its yield in period I would equal that of T_1 and its built-in flexibility would then be twice that of T_1. In the following discussion, emphasis will be placed on built-in flexibility, but reference will be made also to elasticity, especially in the comparison of the individual income tax with other taxes.

[3] E. Cary Brown, "The Static Theory of Automatic Fiscal Stabilization," *Journal of Political Economy,* Vol. 43 (October 1955), pp. 427-30. According to Brown, and the approach adopted in the text, a tax is an automatic stabilizer if the absolute size of the change in income, in response to a fluctuation in autonomous demand, is smaller when the tax is in existence than it would be in the absence of the tax. Other definitions have been proposed.

Sources of Built-in Flexibility

The characteristics of the individual income tax that lead one to expect the tax to have great built-in flexibility are the broad base, the responsiveness of the base to changes in economic activity, and the rather high marginal rate. Rate graduation, although often mentioned in this connection, is not an essential condition for built-in flexibility. Given the tax base, built-in flexibility depends on the average marginal tax rate and is not directly affected by the relation between the average marginal rate and the average effective rate.[4] A flat-rate tax or, indeed, a regressive tax, can have an important degree of built-in flexibility. Built-in flexibility, moreover, does not require that the tax base fluctuate proportionately more than aggregate income; the essential condition is that the base vary in the same direction as income.

Estimates of Built-in Flexibility

The built-in flexibility of the income tax can be measured by reference to several different income concepts, for different time periods, and for different yield concepts. Factors affecting built-in flexibility and estimates of built-in flexibility are described below.

STRUCTURAL ESTIMATES. The statistical data on which estimates of built-in flexibility can be based are summarized in ratio form in Table 28. Using these data, I estimate that the built-in flexibility of the individual income tax at constant 1954-60 statutory rates was 8.7 percent of GNP in the period 1949-60. This means that, with the statutory rate schedule (and exemptions) held constant, changes in income tax liabilities equaled 8.7 percent of changes in GNP.

The estimate of built-in flexibility is based on statistical estimates of the relation between taxable income and GNP and between tax liability and taxable income. The estimates indicate that,

---

[4] As used here, the average marginal rate is the ratio of the change in tax to the change in the base, and the average effective rate is the ratio of the total tax to the total base. Sometimes the marginal and average rates are calculated with respect to aggregates broader than the tax base. For example, calculations for the income tax might relate tax liability or payments to GNP or personal income rather than taxable income; in Chapter IX marginal rates by income classes are computed with respect to adjusted gross income.

on the average, (1) the change in taxable income from one year to the next equaled 38 percent of the change in GNP and (2) the change in tax liability at constant statutory rates (the marginal tax rate) was 23 percent of the change in taxable income.[5] Built-in flexibility is the product of these two ratios: $0.38 \times 0.23 = 0.087$.

TABLE 28. Gross National Product, Personal Income, Taxable Income, and Individual Income Tax Liabilities at Constant Statutory Rates, 1949-60[a]

Year	GNP (billions)	PI/GNP	TI/PI	TI/GNP	T/TI	T/GNP
1949	$258.05	.807	.344	.278	.238	.066
1950	284.60	.803	.369	.296	.245	.073
1951	328.98	.789	.387	.302	.239	.072
1952	347.00	.787	.393	.310	.233	.072
1953	365.39	.789	.401	.316	.228	.072
1954	363.11	.798	.398	.317	.231	.073
1955	397.47	.780	.412	.322	.232	.074
1956	419.18	.794	.425	.337	.231	.078
1957	442.77	.794	.425	.337	.230	.078
1958	444.55	.810	.414	.336	.230	.077
1959	482.70	.795	.433	.345	.232	.080
1960	502.60	.798	.427	.341	.230	.079

Sources: Ratios computed from U. S. Department of Commerce, Office of Business Economics, estimates of GNP and personal income (*Survey of Current Business*, July 1963, p. 12); Leo Cohen's estimates of taxable income and tax liabilities at 1954 statutory rates, 1949-53 ("A More Recent Measure of the Built-in Flexibility of the Individual Income Tax," *National Tax Journal*, Vol. 13 [June 1960], p. 123); and data on taxable income and tax liabilities, 1954-60, from U. S. Treasury Department, *Statistics of Income, Individual Income Tax Returns*, annual volumes.

a Symbols: GNP, gross national product; PI, personal income; TI, taxable income; T, federal individual income tax liabilities at 1954-60 statutory rates.

Ratios involving TI or T for 1949-53 may not be exactly comparable with those for later years owing to inaccuracies in the adjustment of the underlying statistics for changes made by the Internal Revenue Code of 1954 and other legislation.

In deriving the relationship between taxable income and GNP, the intermediate relations between personal income and GNP and taxable income and personal income were omitted because it seemed possible to simplify the calculations in this way without serious loss of explanatory value. Over the years 1949-60, which were a period of generally rising income, the ratio of taxable income to GNP (*TI*/GNP) tended to increase. The year-to-year

[5] Derived from linear regressions of first differences. See Appendix E.

change in this ratio, which is estimated at 38.0 percent of the change in GNP, is higher than the ratio of taxable income to GNP observed in any year of the period.

The rise in the ratio of taxable income to GNP over the period 1949-60 is due mainly to the fact that, with growing income and constant personal exemptions, a larger fraction of aggregate income enters the tax base. While the ratio of personal income to GNP (PI/GNP) rose in the recession years 1954 and 1958, other developments prevented the ratio of taxable income to personal income (TI/PI) from rising.[6]

The behavior of the effective tax rate on taxable income (T/TI) at constant statutory rates is somewhat peculiar. The effective rate appears to have been slightly higher in the earlier years than in later years; however, the apparent decline may be due to minor inaccuracies in estimating the liability that would have resulted from application of the 1954-60 rate schedule to the income of the earlier years. From 1954 to 1960, there seems to be no systematic relation between effective rates and movements of GNP; the average effective rate and average marginal rate (both computed with respect to taxable income) appear to have been approximately constant at about 23 percent.

The stability of the average effective rate on taxable income (T/TI) in the face of rising income is surprising but presumably was due to offsetting changes in the amounts of taxable income falling in different rate brackets. When incomes are rising, many persons move into higher rate brackets, but others remain in the same bracket and still others are drawn into the income tax system for the first time and are subject only to the beginning rate. Rate graduation does not assure that marginal rates computed from a time series of taxable income will exceed average rates on taxable income.

If my estimates are correct in showing an average marginal tax rate no higher than the average effective rate (with a constant statutory rate schedule), it follows that rate graduation did not contribute to built-in flexibility in the period under study. A flat-rate tax of 23 percent on all taxable income would have produced virtually the same degree of built-in flexibility as was experienced in

---

[6] On the relationship between personal income and GNP, see Appendix E.

the years 1954-60. The increase in the ratio T/GNP as GNP rose was attributable to the personal exemptions.

Further study is needed to ascertain whether the simple statistical techniques used here have adequately measured built-in flexibility over the period 1949-60 and whether the estimate of 8.7 percent is applicable to a wider range of fluctuation and higher levels of GNP than were experienced in that period. Some alternative measures are described in Appendix E.[7]

It would have been preferable to base the structural estimates of built-in flexibility on quarterly data since, for countercyclical purposes, short-run responses are important. This was not possible, however, because of lack of quarterly statistics on taxable income, difficulties in estimating tax liabilities on a quarterly basis, and complications with respect to adjustment for seasonal variations in tax collections.[8] The quarterly data are discussed below and in Appendix E.

HISTORICAL ESTIMATES. A number of estimates of the built-in flexibility of the federal individual income tax for selected periods between 1949 and 1960 appear in Appendix Tables E-1 and E-2. The periods examined are the expansions of 1949-53 and 1954-57; the recessions of 1953-54 and 1957-58; and 1958-60, which was predominantly an expansion period but which cannot be unambiguously classified since a recession began about mid-1960. Except for 1958-60, both annual and quarterly estimates are given in the appendix tables. The annual estimates show, not only built-in flexibility of tax liability with respect to GNP, but the intermediate relations between changes in taxable income and GNP and tax liabilities and taxable income which "explain" built-in flexibility. In the quarterly estimates, the intermediate relations cannot be shown because of lack of a quarterly series on taxable income.

The estimates may be called "historical estimates" to distinguish them from the structural estimates discussed above. The historical estimates differ from the structural estimates in derivation and significance. The historical estimates were derived only from

[7] For more elaborate formulations, see a study published in late 1963, after I had substantially completed this chapter: Albert Ando and E. Cary Brown, "Lags in Fiscal Policy," in *Stabilization Policies,* Research Studies for the Commission on Money and Credit (Englewood Cliffs, N. J.: Prentice-Hall, 1963), pp. 97-163.

[8] Lewis, *Federal Fiscal Policy,* pp. 280-88.

the initial and terminal statistics for the subperiods, whereas the structural estimates were obtained by mathematical procedures that took account of all the annual figures. The historical estimates, hence, are more likely to be influenced by conditions peculiar to the initial and terminal years or quarters of the subperiods examined. More important, the historical estimates reflect both the structural characteristics of the tax system and the influence of trends in population, GNP, personal deductions, and other factors affecting income tax liabilities. In the structural estimates, an effort was made to minimize the influence of trends (by basing the estimates on first differences rather than the original data). The structural estimates, therefore, can be more readily used to predict built-in flexibility in recessions and expansions of different magnitude and duration.

The historical estimates, nevertheless, are of interest. Most of the estimates place built-in flexibility of the federal income tax at constant (1954-60) statutory rates within the range of 8 to 10 percent with respect to GNP, regardless of whether based on annual or quarterly data and regardless of whether the tax attributable to net capital gains is included or excluded. However, built-in flexibility cannot be satisfactorily measured from annual data for the brief and rather mild recessions of 1953-54 and 1957-58.

Elasticity

The structural estimate of the built-in flexibility of the federal individual income tax at constant (1954-60) statutory rates and the ratio of tax liability to GNP given in Table 28 indicate that the elasticity of income tax liability with respect to short-run changes in GNP was approximately 1.1 at 1960 income levels.[9] This means that a 1 percent change in GNP would be accompanied by approximately a 1.1 percent change in individual income tax liabilities. Over a wide range of fluctuation or growth carrying GNP far above or below the 1960 level, this relationship might not hold.

My estimate of short-run elasticity would have been higher had it been related to variations in personal income, as certain earlier

[9] Obtained by dividing the estimate of built-in flexibility by the 1960 ratio of income tax liability to GNP: $0.087/0.079 = 1.1$. Given the estimate of built-in flexibility, the estimate of elasticity would be slightly higher for earlier years, when the ratio of tax liability to GNP was lower.

estimates were, rather than to GNP. In the long run, elasticity with respect to personal income and elasticity with respect to GNP will be about the same unless the ratio of personal income to GNP tends to increase or decrease over time. In the short run, however, elasticity is lower with respect to GNP because the year-to-year fluctuations of GNP tend to be proportionately greater than the fluctuations in personal income. (For further comments and references to earlier estimates, see Appendix E.)

Effects of Changes in Tax Law

Built-in flexibility of the individual income tax was reduced by the tax cut enacted in 1964. The Revenue Act of 1964, when fully effective (in 1965), is expected to lower individual income tax liabilities by one-fifth.[10] If the act had not altered the relationship between taxable income and GNP or between average and marginal tax rates, built-in flexibility would be proportionately reduced, from 8.7 percent to approximately 7 percent. The actual reduction in built-in flexibility may be less than this because of the introduction of the minimum standard deduction, which is equivalent to a supplementary vanishing personal exemption, and the splitting of the old first rate bracket into four narrower brackets. These changes may somewhat increase elasticity, though the net effect of the act is to reduce built-in flexibility.[11]

Comparison with Other Taxes

The only other tax now imposed by the federal government that has built-in flexibility rivaling that of the individual income tax is the corporation income tax. Other broad-based taxes that

---

[10] Estimate obtained by applying rates and other provisions that will be effective in 1965 to income levels assumed for calendar year 1963; see *Revenue Act of 1964,* Senate Finance Committee, S. Rept. 830, 88 Cong. 2 sess. (1964), pp. 12-24.

[11] For general discussions of the effects of statutory changes, see E. Cary Brown and Richard J. Kruizenga, "Income Sensitivity of a Simple Personal Income Tax," *Review of Economics and Statistics,* Vol. 41 (August 1959), pp. 266-69; and E. Cary Brown, "The Personal Income Tax as an Automatic Stabilizer," in *Tax Revision Compendium,* House Ways and Means Committee (1959), Vol. 3, pp. 2357-62.

might be substituted for a substantial part of the individual income tax probably would have lower elasticity and less built-in flexibility.

Corporation Income Tax

A comparison of the corporation income tax with the individual income tax is complicated by the variability of the relation between corporate profits and GNP. Profits tend to absorb a larger fraction of the change in GNP in a mild recession than in an expansion. Moreover, taxable corporate profits seem to have declined in relation to GNP, at comparable levels of prosperity, over the postwar period (partly because of liberalized depreciation methods adopted in 1954 and 1962). In view of these difficulties, I have not attempted to develop structural estimates of the built-in flexibility of the corporate tax but have contented myself with historical estimates.

The historical estimates of the built-in flexibility and elasticity of the corporate tax, together with information on the cyclical behavior of corporate profits and the computed marginal tax rate, are given in Appendix Table E-3. These estimates are based on seasonally adjusted quarterly statistics from the national income accounts prepared by the OBE, with recessions and expansions dated from peak and trough quarters of GNP.

The built-in flexibility of the corporate tax has been highly variable. In the recessions of 1953-54 and 1957-58, corporate tax liabilities at annual rates fell by more than 30 percent of the decline in GNP (at annual rates), and in the 1960-61 recession the built-in flexibility of the tax approached 90 percent. In the expansions of 1954-57 and 1958-60, built-in flexibility was at the much lower levels of 4.6 percent and 8.4 percent, respectively. In the early quarters of business recovery, built-in flexibility was considerably greater than in the expansion periods as a whole but still far less than in the recessions. Over the period for which estimates are available for both taxes, the built-in flexibility of the corporate tax greatly exceeded that of the individual income tax in recessions but was less than that of the individual income tax in expansions. Since the yield of the corporate tax is much smaller than that of the individual tax, the built-in flexibility of the corporate tax can surpass that of the individual tax only when its yield elasticity is much greater than that of the individual tax.

Other Broad-Based Taxes

Since consumption is more stable than income, the short-run elasticity of yield of a personal tax on consumption expenditures would be lower than that of the individual income tax, given comparable personal exemptions and rate graduation. This means that the substitution of an expenditure tax for the income tax would reduce the built-in flexibility of the revenue system. I have not attempted to quantify the difference between the two taxes in this respect.

A uniform indirect tax on all consumption expenditures would have lower elasticity and smaller built-in flexibility than a direct tax on consumption expenditures because of the lack of personal exemptions in the former. In practice, however, indirect taxes do not cover all consumption items. Even a broad-based retail sales tax would omit many services and goods that are included in consumption in the social accounts. Whether the yield of such a tax would be more or less elastic than that of a hypothetical tax on all consumption expenditures is not clear. It seems safe to suppose, nevertheless, that the short-run yield elasticity of a retail sales tax would be considerably less than that of the individual income tax and that the substitution of a sales tax for the income tax would appreciably reduce built-in flexibility.[12]

A wealth tax would be likely to have the minimum short-run elasticity. Personal wealth includes a large amount of fixed claims, which maintain a fairly stable value, except in deep depressions. The values of personal equities in dwellings, corporate stock, and unincorporated businesses are more variable. The value of corporate stock, in particular, is known to be highly variable; however, movements of stock prices do not coincide closely with general business cycles. Information on short-run changes in the values of personal equities in dwellings and unincorporated businesses is not reliable enough to indicate their sensitivity to the business cycle. In practice, wealth tax assessments probably would be more stable than "true" market values and hence would lag behind changes in market values, except for marketable securities upon which current quotations could easily be obtained.

[12] See Appendix E.

Economic Significance of Built-in Flexibility

Measurement of built-in flexibility is only the first step in the appraisal of the efficiency of taxes as automatic stabilizers. If the variations in tax liabilities reduce fluctuations in private consumption and investment, built-in flexibility will act as an economic stabilizer, provided the government does not alter its own expenditures because of revenue fluctuations. Other things equal, the greater the response of private expenditures to variations in tax liabilities, the greater the stabilizing force of a tax with a given built-in flexibility.

Built-in flexibility cannot prevent fluctuations and cannot itself reverse movements that are already under way. It can moderate the fluctuations by limiting the secondary or cumulative effects of a primary change in aggregate demand. This may advance the date at which other forces operate to turn a business contraction into an expansion.

The principal stabilizing effect of built-in flexibility is usually attributed to its influence on consumption. Built-in flexibility of direct taxes reduces the changes in disposable personal income that would otherwise be associated with any initial fluctuation in GNP. Inasmuch as disposable income seems to be the main determinant of consumption, it follows that built-in flexibility of direct tax yield will help stabilize this important segment of aggregate outlay. It is not easy, however, to go beyond these broad generalizations and to estimate the effects of particular taxes over short periods of time.

In the period 1948-62, the ratio of change in personal consumption from one year to the next to the change in disposable personal income—the marginal propensity to consume—was approximately 81 percent. (This is a short-run marginal propensity to consume and is lower than the estimated long-run marginal propensity; see Appendix E.) Combination of this figure with the structural estimate of built-in flexibility of the federal individual income tax of 8.7 percent suggests that at 1954-60 statutory rates the tax lessened fluctuations of consumption by amounts equal to about 7 percent of changes in GNP. Built-in flexibility also reduces the fluctuations in total GNP associated with any autonomous change in demand.[13]

The foregoing is a highly simplified explanation of consumption behavior. The statistical relation between changes in aggregate disposable income and consumption takes no account of many other factors that may influence consumption, including the composition of income, wealth, liquidity, and previous and expected future levels of income and consumption. Since these other factors are affected only indirectly, if at all, by fluctuations in current income tax liabilities or payments at constant statutory rates, their recognition tends to detract from the stabilizing value attributed to built-in flexibility of the personal income tax. Nevertheless, the simple consumption function which incorporates only changes in current disposable income seems to account for a large fraction of changes in consumption, and it provides a rough but useful measure of the influence of built-in flexibility of the income tax as a stabilizer of consumption.[14]

The effect on consumption of the built-in flexibility of the corporation income tax is the indirect result of its influence on dividend distributions and disposable income of stockholders. (There may also be some relation through influences on stock prices and capital gains, but its nature is obscure.) Although a change in the statutory rate of the corporate tax would doubtless affect dividend payments, it is not clear how the changes in corporate tax liabilities that accompany cyclical fluctuations of profits influence the amount and timing of distributions. In many corporations, management seems reluctant to alter dividend payments abruptly in response to an increase or decrease in profits after taxes. Statistical studies by Lintner and Brittain covering long spans of years indicate that dividend payments may change by only about 15 percent to 20 percent of the year-to-year change in profits after taxes or cash flow, although in the long run corporations seem to aim at distributing greater frac-

[13] The cumulative change in total GNP associated with an autonomous change in demand is measured by the consumption multiplier. For illustrative computations, see Appendix E.

[14] The marginal propensity to consume can also be estimated from family budget data, such as used in Chapter IV and Appendix C, but this approach is less suitable for present purposes than the time-series method. The budget data indicate a lower marginal propensity to consume and a smaller stabilizing influence due to built-in flexibility.

tions of earnings or cash flow.[15] Disposable income of stockholders does not change by the full amount of dividend payments since part of the dividends received by stockholders (apparently about one-fourth in 1960) is absorbed by the individual income tax.[16]

The cushioning effect of corporate saving and the individual income tax reduce the influence on disposable income of the built-in flexibility of the corporate tax to a small fraction of the automatic change in corporate tax liabilities. If, for example, dividend distributions change from one period to the next by 15 percent of the change in profits after tax or in cash flow and the marginal rate of individual income tax of stockholders is 25 percent, the change in disposable income of stockholders is about 11 percent of the change in corporate profits tax liabilities ($0.15 \times 0.75 = 0.11$). For use in conjunction with the measures of built-in flexibility shown in Appendix Table E-3, even the figure of 11 percent may overstate the effect on disposable income of individuals since built-in flexibility is measured from quarterly statistics whereas Lintner's and Brittain's relations were derived from annual data.[17]

The built-in flexibility of sales taxes and excises operates differently from that of the individual income tax and the part of the corporate tax that is reflected in dividend payments. The existence of the indirect taxes lessens the impact on business receipts of changes in final demand but does not directly affect disposable income of consumers. To illustrate, suppose that consumer expenditures for a commodity that is subject to a 20 percent ad valorem

[15] John Lintner, "Distribution of Incomes of Corporations among Dividends, Retained Earnings, and Taxes," *American Economic Review,* Vol. 46, Papers and Proceedings (May 1956), pp. 97-113; John A. Brittain, "The Tax Structure and Corporate Dividend Policy," *American Economic Review,* Vol. 54, Papers and Proceedings (May 1964), pp. 272-87 (Brookings Institution Reprint No. 78, 1964).

[16] The weighted marginal individual income tax rate on dividends included in AGI on taxable returns was 41 percent in 1960 (derived from marginal rates computed from 1960 Tax File [footnote 2, Chapter VII] and *Statistics of Income 1960,* p. 5). These dividends were 63 percent of total dividends (OBE estimate, *Survey of Current Business,* July 1963, p. 36). Thus the weighted marginal rate on total dividends was $0.41 \times 0.63 = 0.26$.

[17] An estimate by Fromm, applying Lintner's formula to quarterly data, indicates that in the period 1953-60 dividend distributions changed by only 5 percent of the change in profits after taxes. See Gary Fromm, "Inventories, Business Cycles, and Economic Stabilization," in *Inventory Fluctuations and Economic Stabilization,* Joint Economic Committee, Committee Print, 87 Cong. 2 sess. (1962), Pt. IV, p. 86.

tax decline from 100 to 70. Tax payments will fall by 6 and sellers' receipts net of tax by 24. Business firms are likely to cut their production and inventories less than they would if they had suffered a decline of 30 in receipts, as they would have in the absence of the excise tax; if so, the built-in flexibility of the excise tax will help maintain employment and consumer income. The fall in excise tax payments does not warrant a price cut since tax rates (taxes per dollar of sales) remain unchanged.[18]

The built-in flexibility of the corporation income tax operates mainly through its influence on internal funds of business firms if it is true, as it seems to be, that only a small part of automatic changes in corporate tax liabilities is reflected in dividend distributions in the short run. Although profits after taxes decline less than profits before taxes, any profits realized from current operations or new investment will be subject to the corporation income tax. For large firms, which account for most of the production of the corporate sector, the marginal tax rate is constant over the relevant range. Hence, the incentive effects of the corporate tax should be essentially the same during a recession as in a prosperous period.

A large volume of internal funds is favorable to current operations and to new investment since many firms lack ready access to external capital and managers often seem to be more willing to invest internal funds than to seek outside capital. Built-in flexibility of the corporate tax and of indirect taxes, therefore, should have some stabilizing influence because it reduces fluctuations in internal funds. Whether this influence is important is not clear. Internal funds (retained profits plus depreciation and depletion accruals) of corporations are usually larger relative to the increase in plant and equipment, inventories, and receivables in recession years than in other years, but internal funds were insufficient to cover the non-financial investment of corporations in the 1957-58 and 1960-61 recessions.[19] Substantial amounts of external finance have been

[18] Lewis classifies excises as "indirect stabilizers" and cautions against "the temptation . . . to apply ordinary incidence theory—according to which excise taxes are for the most part paid by consumers—in assessing their effects as built-in stabilizers" (*Federal Fiscal Policy*, p. 66).

[19] *Variability of Private Investment in Plant and Equipment*, Joint Economic Committee, Committee Print, 87 Cong. 1 sess. (1962), Pt. I, "Investment and Its

obtained by corporations at cyclical peaks. Although the statistics are inconclusive, it seems unlikely that built-in flexibility of the corporate tax and indirect taxes has much power as a stabilizer of investment. This does not imply that investment is unresponsive to permanent changes in tax rates.[20]

Policies that stabilize consumption and investment are mutually reinforcing. If consumption demand is cushioned by built-in flexibility, manufacturers and distributors are likely to vary their inventories less than they would if consumption fluctuated more widely over the business cycle, and plant and equipment outlays may be similarly affected. Reduction of investment outlays, in turn, helps stabilize disposable income and consumption. A full quantitative analysis of built-in flexibility would have to try to incorporate these interrelations in an econometric model.[21]

Formula and Discretionary Flexibility

Formula and discretionary flexibility depend on changes in statutory tax rates for countercyclical purposes. Rates would be temporarily cut in recessions and temporarily raised in periods of inflation due to excessive demand. Although advocated by many economists beginning in the late 1930's, the idea of varying tax rates for stabilization purposes won acceptance only slowly. In 1961, the Commission on Money and Credit recommended that the President be given limited power to vary income tax rates.[22]

Financing" (material prepared by U. S. Department of Commerce), p. 43. The data are for years ended June 30 and exclude banks and insurance companies.

[20] For a fuller statement of reasons for skepticism concerning the countercyclical effectiveness of the corporate tax, see my paper "The Corporate Income Tax in a Depression," in *Policies to Combat Depression* (Princeton, N. J.: Princeton University Press for National Bureau of Economic Research, 1956), pp. 149-70.

[21] For examples, see James S. Duesenberry, Otto Eckstein, and Gary Fromm, "A Simulation of the United States Economy in Recession," *Econometrica,* Vol. 28 (October 1960), pp. 749-809; and Fromm, in *Inventory Fluctuations and Economic Stabilization,* pp. 50-133. On feedback effects, see Paul E. Smith, "A Note on the Built-in Flexibility of the Individual Income Tax," *Econometrica,* Vol. 31 (October 1963), pp. 704-11.

[22] *Money and Credit, Their Influence on Jobs, Prices, and Growth,* Report of the Commission on Money and Credit (Englewood Cliffs, N. J.: Prentice-Hall, 1961), pp. 129-37.

President Kennedy made a similar proposal in his three annual messages at the beginning of 1962.[23]

All proposals to vary tax rates through legislation or Presidential proclamation raise large political and administrative issues and the question whether the need for countercyclical action can be accurately appraised. I do not wish to examine these issues but to consider the narrower subject of the relative suitability of the individual income tax and other taxes as instruments of formula flexibility or discretionary flexibility.

Advantages of the individual income tax in this respect include its wide coverage, large yield, and the prompt collection of a substantial part of the tax. Withholding on salaries and wages accounts for almost three-fourths of gross collections.[24] Withheld tax is deducted in each payroll period and remitted monthly by large employers and quarterly by small firms. When a special effort is made, a new withholding rate can be put into effect quickly. In 1964 and 1950, only seven days were required and, in 1951, only eleven days. The tax bills, of course, had been under consideration for some time before they were finally enacted by Congress and signed by the President.

For non-withheld tax, the adjustment would be slower. This part of the tax is payable in quarterly installments on the basis of annual estimates of current-year liabilities. For taxpayers who report on a calendar-year basis, as most individuals do, the estimate and first installment are due April 15, and the subsequent installments are payable June 15, September 15, and January 15. The fourth installment is usually substantially larger than the first three; the final payment is not made until the definitive return is filed in April. There would be no easy way of making sure that any change in tax rates adopted during the year would be reflected in the non-

[23] The President recommended the legislation in his State of the Union Message of January 11, 1962, and his Budget Message of January 18, 1962. He amplified the proposal in the *Economic Report of the President, January 1962*, pp. 18-19.

[24] Estimated at 72 to 74 percent in the fiscal years 1961 and 1963. Refunds were estimated at about 10 percent of gross collections in these years. See *The Budget of the United States Government for the Fiscal Year Ending June 30, 1963*, p. 49.

withheld part of the tax before the fourth installment and perhaps not before the final return was filed. Probably the best solution would be to issue instructions to taxpayers, along with the statements that are now sent out, telling them to increase or decrease their installment payments by amounts representing an approximation of the change, deferring exact adjustment until the final return. Compliance with such instructions might be poor, especially when rates were increased, and application of penalties for noncompliance would be difficult because, under present law, taxpayers have great freedom in revising their estimates of current-year liability.[25] A certain inequity in the treatment of wage and salary earners and other taxpayers would occur, but it might not be considered any more serious than the present differences between the treatment of these groups.

A detail worth mentioning is how intrayear changes in tax rates would affect full-year liabilities. Suppose, for example, income tax rates were cut by 5 percentage points in all brackets effective July 1. Should an effort be made to distinguish between income accruing in the first half of the year and that accruing in the second half and to apply different rates to the income of the two periods, or should income for the whole year be aggregated and the rates reduced by 2.5 percentage points in each bracket? The second procedure was followed in the Revenue Acts of 1950 and 1951. It seems much simpler and fairer considering the arbitrary nature of allocation of many kinds of income to periods of less than one year.

Countercyclical changes in tax rates would be temporary in nature, and this characteristic complicates the appraisal of their economic effects. It seems plausible that a change in individual income tax liabilities will affect consumption expenditures less within a period of six months to a year if the change is expected to terminate at the end of the period than if the new rates are expected to continue indefinitely. This deduction, however, is not clearly supported by statistical evidence. One large item of nonrecurrent receipts that has been examined carefully is the special dividends paid to veterans on government life insurance policies in 1950.

---

[25] As a minimum, it would be necessary to eliminate the option of basing current payments of estimated tax on the liability of the previous year.

Bodkin concluded that recipients spent as large a proportion of the dividends as they did of their regular income.[26] Although it is fairly clear that a temporary reduction in individual income tax rates will stimulate consumption and that a temporary tax increase will retard it, the extent and timing of the reaction are uncertain, particularly in recession or boom periods, when countercyclical tax changes might be instituted.

Changes in corporate tax rates will not be reflected in revenue collections as promptly as will changes in individual income tax rates. They will, however, affect tax accruals immediately and will begin to influence business decisions at the time of accrual. A temporary change in tax rates will alter the profitability of production and investment on which the returns are expected in the near future but will not directly affect profit estimates for periods after the expiration of the temporary rates. In this respect, temporary changes of rates have somewhat greater stabilizing value than variations of tax liability due to built-in flexibility of the corporate tax. The difference may not be significant for changes expected to be in effect for brief periods but may become more important as the length of the period is extended. An offsetting consideration is that changes in corporate tax rates may be disturbing to business management because they increase uncertainty. The Commission on Money and Credit opposed countercyclical changes in these tax rates for this reason.[27]

Changes in rates of excises and sales taxes will show up in tax collections with only a short lag and will likely affect prices with little delay. Real consumption and consumer outlays will respond in accordance with the price elasticity of demand for the taxed items. Changes in indirect tax rates differ sharply in this respect from automatic fluctuations in indirect tax yield at constant rates. Changes in rates of taxes that apply before the retail stage will create windfall gains or losses with respect to inventories and goods in process unless special provisions are adopted to prevent windfalls. A more serious objection to countercyclical variations of in-

[26] Ronald Bodkin, "Windfall Income and Consumption," *American Economic Review*, Vol. 49 (September 1959), pp. 602-14. For different appraisals, see Ando and Brown in *Stabilization Policies*, pp. 132-35, and other references cited there.

[27] *Money and Credit*, p. 134.

direct tax rates is that the announcement or expectation of an increase or decrease of rates will stimulate anticipatory buying or encourage postponement of expenditures. This may destroy much of the stabilizing potential of rate changes. The problem would be more serious for legislative changes than for formula-dictated changes or changes made at the discretion of the President, owing to the time lag and publicity involved in congressional action. However, speculation about possible rate changes would no doubt occur also under a formula plan or a plan giving discretion to the President.

Longer-Run Implications of Revenue Flexibility

Built-in flexibility and temporary variations in tax rates can make their greatest contribution in an economy that tends to operate at a high and satisfactory level without a persistent tendency toward stagnation or inflation. Built-in flexibility is particularly desirable if fluctuations are brief and mild and if movements above and below an acceptable growth trend are equally likely. These are the conditions in which moderation of the business cycle is a prime objective of policy.

If, however, the economy suffers from a slow growth rate and a chronic tendency toward unemployment, built-in flexibility becomes, in the words of the Council of Economic Advisers in January 1963, "an ambiguous blessing." In these circumstances, the Council held: "The protection it gives against cumulative downward movements of output and employment is all the more welcome. But its symmetrical 'protection' against upward movements becomes an obstacle on the path to full employment, throttling expansion well before full employment is reached."[28]

The ideal solution would be to restore vigor to the economy without weakening cyclical stabilizers. A permanent tax cut was proposed in 1963 as a means of lessening the "persistent drag on purchasing power" due to high rates. While the purpose was not primarily to reduce built-in flexibility, the Council recognized that some reduction was unavoidable. In fact, the tax cut that was fi-

[28] Annual Report of the Council of Economic Advisers, printed with *Economic Report of the President, January 1963*, p. 68.

nally adopted in early 1964 may have reduced built-in flexibility of the individual income tax almost as much as it reduced the average yield.[29]

Over a long sweep of years the elasticity of yield of the individual income tax at constant statutory rates may be somewhat higher than its short-run elasticity. At 1954-60 statutory rates, long-run elasticity might be 1.2 or more with respect to GNP, as contrasted with the estimate of 1.1 for short-run elasticity given earlier.[30] Elasticity may have been slightly increased by the Revenue Act of 1964.

Revenue from the individual income tax, therefore, can be expected to grow considerably faster than GNP, unless statutory rates are periodically reduced. The yields of most broad sales taxes or production taxes, on the other hand, will grow little, if any, faster than GNP, and specific excises on items such as alcoholic beverages and tobacco and many import duties may have much lower elasticities. Since government expenditures tend to grow faster than total output and since increases of tax rates are likely to arouse controversy, the comparatively high-yield elasticity of the income tax is convenient. While the Ways and Means Committee of the U. S. Congress may not have taken a technical view of elasticity in 1913, the committee did recommend the income tax as an elastic revenue source, and this feature of the tax has been attractive in many other countries. On the other hand, a person who wishes to hold back the expansion of government activities may regard the high elasticity as objectionable.

Conclusion

The individual income tax seems to have greater counter-cyclical effects than other major taxes. Since the elasticity of yield

[29] If the tax cut had not affected the elasticity of income tax yield, it would have reduced average yield and built-in flexibility in the same proportions. Although evidence on the point is inadequate, it appears that elasticity may have been increased to a minor extent; if so, built-in flexibility was reduced less than average yield. "Average yield" in this context refers to yield over a full business cycle.

[30] An elasticity of 1.2 is obtained at 1960 income levels if the estimate of built-in flexibility is raised from 8.7 percent to 9.4 percent by taking account of trend factors which were minimized in the structural estimates derived from regressions of first differences of income. See Appendix E.

of the individual income tax is greater than that of a broad sales tax, partial substitution of that tax for the income tax would somewhat reduce the built-in flexibility of the revenue system. Substitution between the corporation income tax and the individual income tax probably would have the opposite effect, particularly in mild recessions; however, the irregularity of the estimates for the corporate tax casts doubt on this generalization. Automatic variations of individual income tax liabilities impinge more clearly and directly on consumption than do variations of the other taxes. Although this characteristic suggests that the individual income tax is a more powerful stabilizer, it offsets only a small part of the fluctuations in disposable personal income that would otherwise occur. When the economy tends to fall short of capacity operation even at cyclical peaks, built-in flexibility will have the disadvantage of making it still harder to reach full employment.

The individual income tax is more easily adaptable to formula or discretionary changes in tax rates for countercyclical purposes than the corporate income tax or sales or excise taxes. The direction of response to such changes can be confidently predicted, but the extent of response and hence the appropriate amount of change at any time are unclear in the present state of knowledge.

CHAPTER XII

Future of the Income Tax

FIFTY YEARS LATER, the judgment, stated by the Ways and Means Committee in 1913, that an individual income tax is the fairest of all taxes still commands assent. No other tax accords as well with ability to pay or serves better to moderate economic inequality.

A well-designed income tax also has economic advantages. For the broad range of activities that call for neither special promotion nor restraint, the income tax, although not completely neutral, is more impartial than other widely used taxes. Where special encouragement or discouragement is desired, preferential or penalty income tax provisions are convenient and sometimes effective. The built-in flexibility of individual income tax yield helps reduce cyclical fluctuations in employment and production. These characteristics, together with a large and elastic yield potential, have won for the individual income tax a prominent place in the revenue systems of the United States and many other countries.

While proposals to repeal the income tax are occasionally heard, they now seem outside the range of realistic alternatives. The significant questions are how big a role the income tax should play and what modifications in it are desirable.

No one contends that the U. S. income tax is a model tax, attaining, in the highest degree possible, equity and economic effi-

308

ciency. Opinions differ greatly, however, on the seriousness of its defects and the feasibility of remedying them.

Remediable Defects

Many of the present defects of the income tax are due to unjustifiable exclusions and deductions from taxable income, rather than to inherent characteristics of income taxation. The clearest objection to these provisions is their inconsistency with the high standards of equity and reasonable progressivity that are rightly applied to the income tax. But such provisions also have economic disadvantages. Their existence causes rates on fully taxable income to be higher than would otherwise be required and induces behavior that would not occur under a more uniform tax. Economic efficiency is likely to be impaired and the growth of national product retarded. More subtly and perhaps more seriously, the tax-induced changes in production may lessen the satisfactions obtained from measured income and output.

The origin of some of the exclusions and deductions is obscure; they were adopted without wide public discussion or appreciation of their consequences. Others were enacted after successful campaigns by interested groups. Some exclusions and deductions were intended to serve widely approved purposes but were adopted without enough consideration of their efficiency and likely side effects. Regardless of origin, special provisions are difficult to eliminate because of inertia and because beneficiaries are often alert in their defense whereas most other citizens have given little thought to the advantages of uniform taxation.[1]

One reaction to the deficiencies of the income tax is to recommend that their importance be lessened by reducing income tax rates and relying more on other taxes. Direct taxes on personal

[1] On the origins and persistence of provisions resulting in unequal taxation, see the papers by Stanley S. Surrey, Geoffrey J. Lanning, Walter J. Blum, and Herbert Stein in *Tax Revision Compendium,* House Ways and Means Committee (1959), Vol. 1, pp. 1-60, 77-86, 107-18; also Stanley S. Surrey, "The Congress and the Tax Lobbyist—How Special Tax Provisions Get Enacted," *Harvard Law Review,* Vol. 70 (May 1957), pp. 1145-82; and William L. Cary, "Pressure Groups and the Revenue Code: A Requiem in Honor of the Departing Uniformity of the Tax Laws," *Harvard Law Review,* Vol. 68 (March 1955), pp. 745-80.

consumption and wealth have been advocated partly as a means of circumventing the special provisions that have grown up in the income tax over the years. However, the introduction of the new taxes would be more difficult, technically and politically, than the revision of the income tax. Excises and sales taxes could be expanded more easily, but this would not minimize nonfunctional inequalities of taxation. The burden of the indirect taxes always varies greatly with personal tastes and needs. Where income tax administration and compliance are as complete as in the United States, the substitution of indirect taxes for part of the income tax would aggravate inequalities in taxation of people with similar means.

The Issue of Progressivity

Greater reliance on indirect taxation has been recommended by persons who believe that the income tax lends itself too readily to excessive rate graduation. They favor not only overt substitution of federal excises or sales taxes for part of the income tax but also a policy of concentrating tax reductions on the income tax and of increasing the fraction of total revenue raised by state and local governments. Since state and local governments use the income tax far less than the federal government does, an enlargement of their share in total taxation is expected to reduce over-all progressivity.

Uncommitted citizens may find it easier to pass judgment on tax programs if the question of progressivity is more sharply separated from the choice of tax form and the relative size of federal and state-local revenues. The income tax, though historically an instrument of progressivity, allows an infinite choice of rate schedules. Any agreed reduction of tax progressivity could be achieved by modification of income tax rates and exemptions. It would even be possible to discard progressivity by eliminating rate graduation and personal exemptions. The adaptability of the income tax to the desired degree of progressivity is one of its great strengths. Advocates of indirect taxation as a means of reducing progressivity seem to concede that their objective would not win public support if explicitly presented in the form of a revision of income tax rates.

The division of fiscal resources between levels of government is less easily separated from the question of progressivity, given the practical limitations on state-local income taxes, but flexibility can be attained through grants-in-aid and tax credits. The tax-credit idea contemplates allowing persons who pay state income taxes to deduct them from their federal income tax liability, within limits, rather than treating the state taxes as personal deductions from adjusted gross income (AGI), as at present. The purpose would be to overcome interstate tax competition and to offer a special inducement to state income taxation together with a conditional decrease in the federal income tax.[2]

The Revenue Act of 1964, by cutting individual and corporate income tax rates while leaving excise taxes and social security taxes unchanged, somewhat reduced over-all progressivity and probably weakened support for a more drastic realignment of taxes. But the rate reductions were not as deep as many critics had hoped and did not satisfy those who believe that the United States relies too heavily on progressive taxation. Although there may be a pause, attacks on progressivity can be expected to be resumed.

Those who wish to lessen or eliminate tax progressivity argue that graduated income taxation impedes economic growth and efficiency. The extent to which fear of economic harm is well founded is debatable, partly because of analytical difficulties and partly because the U. S. income tax is actually much less progressive than the nominal rates suggest. Empirical evidence is lacking, but deductive reasoning confirms the apprehension that tax progressivity may have an economic cost. It shows that a person who has to pay a given amount of tax would be more likely to be discouraged from working and investing when faced by graduated rates than when taxes are proportional or regressive. This generalization, though significant, is of uncertain value for policy-making because it does not allow for possible differences in attitudes of high income groups and low income groups, who are differently affected by progressive and regressive taxes, and because it does not tell whether the effects of progressivity are great or small.

Any reduction in tax progressivity, especially the substitution of indirect consumption taxes for the income tax, would tend to in-

[2] See James A. Maxwell, *Tax Credits and Intergovernmental Fiscal Relations* (Washington: Brookings Institution, 1962).

crease, to some degree, the amount of personal saving out of any given total personal income. The available evidence suggests that the effect on saving of a reduction in tax progressivity would be small; the influence of a switch from income taxation to consumption taxes is conjectural.

An increased propensity to save permits more rapid economic growth because it allows greater capital formation, but it does not assure faster growth. An attempt to save more may depress economic activity when output is being limited by inadequate demand rather than scarcity of capital. Although it would always be possible to overcome demand deficiencies, and thus prevent abortive saving, by sufficiently vigorous fiscal and monetary policy, this kind of policy remains an aspiration rather than a firm basis for planning. Statistical studies, moreover, indicate that even large increases in net saving may bring rather small increases in economic growth. Probable effects on personal saving are not, in my view, a convincing reason for partially replacing the income tax with indirect consumption taxes or for experimenting with a personal expenditure tax.

Goals and Reforms

In appraising the income tax or any other tax, it is well to recognize that the separate desiderata are to some extent competing. Equity and progressivity have a cost in complexity and administrative difficulty and also may have an economic cost. While my judgment is that these conflicts are less acute than has often been implied, so long as no one objective is pursued to extreme lengths, their existence should not be denied. Policy differences often reflect unstated opinions concerning priorities of objectives and the terms of exchange between them.

The individual income tax compares favorably with other taxes but should not be regarded as a modern single tax. The corporation income tax, estate and gift taxes, and special-benefit excises have well-established and well-deserved places in the revenue system. Sole reliance on the individual income tax would magnify its shortcomings, which even now are serious enough to call for remedial action.

An income tax reform that would contribute greatly to equity is more effective taxation of capital gains, accompanied by more liberal treatment of capital losses. Since capital gains are not clearly distinguishable from other income, their preferential taxation conflicts with the ability-to-pay principle and invites taxpayers to rearrange their affairs to take advantage of the low rates. The economic effects of the present provisions are partly desirable and partly undesirable and, on balance, ambiguous. The goal, in my opinion, should be full taxation of gains and full deduction of losses, with proration to avoid discrimination against investors whose gains or losses accrue over several years and with constructive realization of gains on assets transferred by gift or death. Short of sweeping reforms, worthwhile revisions could be made by narrowing the applicability of preferential rates for capital gains.

The definition of taxable income should be rationalized by the elimination of unjustifiable exclusions and personal deductions and the addition of one or two new deductions. Some progress was made in the Revenue Act of 1964 by the limitation of the sick-pay exclusion and deductions for taxes paid and casualty losses.

Several items now omitted from AGI might justifiably be included. In declining order, considering both importance and feasibility of assessment, they are as follows: (1) capital gains constructively realized by transfer of property by gift or at death; (2) interest on state and local government securities; (3) one-half of old-age and disability benefits under Old-Age, Survivors, and Disability Insurance and Railroad Retirement; (4) imputed net rent of owner-occupied dwellings; (5) employer contributions to the cost of all life, accident, health, and medical insurance for employees; (6) the part of sick pay that is still excluded from AGI; and (7) policyholders' interest income from life insurance reserves.

In order to define net income more accurately, the following seem desirable: (1) current deductions or amortization allowances for students—but not for their parents—for certain out-of-pocket costs of college, university, vocational, and technical education; (2) a small special deduction or earned income credit for all employed persons or for working wives only; and (3) stricter limits on the deductibility of travel and entertainment expenses by self-employed persons, together with the inclusion in taxable income of employees of reimbursements for expenses similar to those that would not be deductible by self-employed taxpayers.

Deductions for interest paid, casualty losses, and property taxes and most other taxes should, in my opinion, be restricted to items connected with the production of taxable income. However, in the interest of harmonious intergovernmental relations and the fiscal strength of the states, the personal deductions should be continued for state-local income taxes and broad sales taxes. If these revisions were made, homeowners would be allowed to deduct mortgage interest and property taxes only if imputed net rent were included in gross income for tax purposes.

Personal deductions for medical expenses and philanthropic contributions are justifiable; however, I think that consideration should be given to the restriction of the deductions to expenditures or gifts exceeding routine amounts. This would involve the restoration of the floor for medical expenditures to a level nearer to average outlays and the adoption of a floor for philanthropic contributions that would make contributions deductible only to the extent that they exceed a certain percentage of income. The ceiling on the deduction for contributions could appropriately be removed, provided the treatment of gifts of appreciated property and other gifts were equalized.

These revisions would broaden the tax base, but they do not go as far as several tax specialists have proposed. Specialists have rightly sounded the alarm about the erosion of the tax base and have stimulated discussion and a little legislative action to restore items to the base. Continued attention to these problems is desirable. While exclusions and personal deductions should always be skeptically viewed, a number of them, in my judgment, satisfactorily serve valid social purposes. Certain exclusions, though questionable, should be left undisturbed because it would be too costly or inconvenient to end them. New deductions should be introduced where needed to cover costs of earning income.

The reform of the exclusions and deductions and full taxation of capital gains would greatly increase the potential yield of the income tax. This would allow substantial reductions in tax rates without loss of revenue. The tax cuts could be allocated in many ways, depending on how they were divided between the individual income tax and the corporation income tax and the excises and how the individual income tax reductions were distributed among brackets. If structural reforms were combined with a compensating change in individual income tax rates equal to the same fraction in all brackets, progressivity would be enhanced; if the objective were to preserve the existing degree of progressivity, statutory rates would have to be cut much more deeply in the upper brackets than in the lower brackets. This is true because the exclusions, deductions, and capital gains provisions diminish effective rates more in upper brackets than in lower brackets. The revisions would narrow the gap between nominal and effective rates and between marginal and average rates, with beneficial effects on public understanding and economic incentives. In my opinion, the same income tax rate schedule should apply to married couples and single persons, thus further narrowing the differences between nominal and effective rates and reducing the relative tax load of single people.

The rise in consumer prices and the growth of average income seem to justify an increase of personal exemptions for single persons and a smaller increase for married couples. Exemptions for dependent children are already relatively more liberal than those for adults. While the adoption of the minimum standard deduction in the Revenue Act of 1964 has diminished the urgency of revising personal exemptions, it does not seem to be a satisfactory permanent solution.

Experience has repeatedly shown that it is hard to muster decisive support for tax reforms that withdraw preferential treatment from even a small minority of taxpayers. A fight must be waged merely to prevent the introduction of new preferences whenever tax legislation is before Congress. A great part of the difficulty is due to the complex nature of tax problems and the lack of understanding of them. Legislators and the public need to be better informed about taxation, if reform proposals are to be more favorably received. Leadership must come from the executive branch of the government which, because of its technical resources and the President's national constituency, can take a broad view of the public interest. It would be over-optimistic to expect a sweeping reform that would resolve all outstanding issues at once. But gradually, with patience and energy in the study of taxation, in the dissemination of research results, and in persuasion, income tax reforms can be achieved and a good tax made better.

APPENDIXES

APPENDIX A

Tables on Yield and Coverage, Deductions, and Rates

TABLE A-1. Federal Receipts by Source, 1914-63[a]

(Averages for fiscal years ending June 30, in millions of dollars)

Period	Total Receipts	Individual Income Tax	Corporate Income and Excess Profits Taxes	Excises and Customs[b]	Employ-ment Taxes	Estate and Gift Taxes	Other Receipts[c]
1914–16	738	46[d]	46[d]	582	—	—	64
1917–20	4,159	764[d]	1,646[d]	1,188	—	60	502
1921–29	4,189	953	1,186	1,299	—	108	641
1930–40	4,425	789	881	1,747	231	211	566
1941–45	29,477	9,842	9,242	4,574	1,431	482	3,905
1946–49	43,500	17,211	10,319	7,684	2,150	777	5,359
1950–59	69,605	29,295	18,541	10,207	5,998	1,022	4,543
1960–63	100,981	43,803	21,138	13,424	12,724	1,921	7,971

[a] Total Treasury receipts, 1914-33, excluding trust account receipts for 1931-33 (U. S. Bureau of the Census, *Historical Statistics of the United States, 1789-1945,* pp. 295-96, 304); cash receipts from the public, 1934-63, which are net of tax refunds. For 1934-47, the data are unpublished statistics compiled by the U. S. Bureau of the Budget from its records, the *Treasury Bulletin,* and *Annual Report of the Secretary of the Treasury.* Although the totals are expressed in millions, the 1934-47 figures may not be precise to that level of significance because adjustments were made for major intragovernmental transactions only; additional adjustments might be appropriate for some of the items included in "other receipts." For 1948-63, the data are from *The Budget of the United States Government for the Fiscal Year Ending June 30, 1959,* p. 879; *ibid., 1965,* p. 460.

[b] Includes capital stock tax.

[c] For 1934 and later years, includes veterans life insurance premiums (and National Service Life Insurance beginning 1942), unemployment insurance deposits by states, and other budget and trust receipts.

[d] For fiscal years 1914-15 and 1917-24, total income and profits taxes were allocated between individuals and corporations on the basis of liabilities of preceding calendar years (*Historical Statistics, 1789-1945,* pp. 307-08).

TABLE A-2. Percentage Composition of Federal Receipts, 1914-63[a]

(Averages for fiscal years ending June 30)

Period	Total Receipts	Individual Income Tax	Corporate Income and Excess Profits Taxes	Excises and Customs	Employment Taxes	Estate and Gift Taxes	Other Receipts
1914–16	100.0	6.2	6.2	78.9	—	—	8.7
1917–20	100.0	18.4	39.6	28.6	—	1.4	12.1
1921–29	100.0	22.8	28.3	31.0	—	2.6	15.3
1930–40	100.0	17.8	19.9	39.5	5.2	4.8	12.8
1941–45	100.0	33.4	31.4	15.5	4.9	1.6	13.2
1946–49	100.0	39.6	23.7	17.7	4.9	1.8	12.3
1950–59	100.0	42.1	26.6	14.7	8.6	1.5	6.5
1960–63	100.0	43.4	20.9	13.3	12.6	1.9	7.9

[a] Derived from Table A-1. Footnotes for that table also apply here.

TABLE A-3. Number of Taxable Individual Income Tax Returns and Population Covered by Them, 1918-60

(Averages for calendar years, in thousands)

Period	Number of Taxable Returns[a]	Number of Taxpayers and Dependents Covered by Taxable Returns[b]	Total Population[c]	Percentage of Total Population Covered by Taxable Returns
1918–20	4,381	9,983	105,360	9.5
1921–29	3,158	5,996	115,467	5.2
1930–40	2,879	5,111	127,505	4.0
1941–45	34,073	78,279	137,178	57.1
1946–49	37,884	82,969	145,902	56.9
1950–59	44,354	112,735	164,744	68.4
1960	48,061	132,038	180,676	73.1

[a] Figures for 1918-36 include taxable fiduciary returns. From U. S. Treasury Department, Internal Revenue Service, *Statistics of Income*, selected volumes.

[b] 1918-57, from Lawrence H. Seltzer, *The Personal Exemptions in the Federal Income Tax* (forthcoming study of National Bureau of Economic Research, draft manuscript); 1958-60, from *Statistics of Income*, annual volumes, with 1958 figure adjusted by interpolation to exclude additional exemptions for the aged and blind.

[c] Includes armed forces overseas. From U. S. Bureau of the Census, *Statistical Abstract of the United States, 1963*, p. 5. Alaska and Hawaii included beginning in 1940.

TABLE A-4. Personal Income, Adjusted Gross Income, and Taxable Income, Selected Years, 1918-60

(Money amounts in billions of dollars)

Year	Personal Income[a]	Adjusted Gross Income[b]		Taxable Income[b]	
		Amount	Percent of Personal Income	Amount	Percent of Personal Income
1918	$ 62.5[c]	$ 50.3	80.5	$ 8.1	13.0
1926	79.5	69.4	87.3	11.2	14.1
1939	72.9	64.7	88.8	8.3	11.4
1945	171.2	139.6	81.5	57.1	33.4
1950	228.5	202.1	88.4	84.3	36.9
1960	401.3	349.0	87.0	171.5	42.7

[a] 1918 and 1926, Raymond W. Goldsmith's estimates, from U. S. Bureau of the Census, *Historical Statistics of the United States, Colonial Times to 1957*, p. 139; 1939 and later, estimates of Office of Business Economics, U. S. Department of Commerce, from *Economic Report of the President, January 1963*, p. 187.

[b] AGI includes estimated amount not reported on tax returns. 1918, 1926, and 1939, from C. Harry Kahn, *Personal Deductions in the Federal Income Tax* (Princeton, N. J.: Princeton University Press for National Bureau of Economic Research, 1960), p. 18; 1945 and 1950, from Joseph A. Pechman, "What Would a Comprehensive Individual Income Tax Yield?" in *Tax Revision Compendium*, House Ways and Means Committee (1959), Vol. 1, pp. 256, 258; 1960, Table A-5. Includes taxable fiduciaries for 1918, 1926, and 1939 but not for later years.

[c] Average of 1917-21.

TABLE A-5. Derivation of Adjusted Gross Income from Personal Income, 1960[a]

(In billions of dollars)

1. Personal income		401.3
Deduct: Receipts included in personal income but not in AGI		70.1
2. Social insurance benefits	18.1	
3. Direct relief	3.2	
4. Military pensions and disability payments and certain veterans' benefits	3.8[b]	
5. Other government and private transfer payments	3.7	
6. Employer contributions to private pension and welfare funds	8.6	
7. Food, lodging, and clothing furnished employees	2.0[c]	
8. Nontaxable military pay and allowances	2.1	
9. Imputed net rent of owner-occupied dwellings	6.8	
10. Imputed interest	11.1	
11. Food and fuel produced and consumed on farms	1.3	
12. Tax-exempt interest, excludable dividends, and excludable sick pay	1.9	
13. Property income of nonprofit organizations and undistributed income (other than capital gains) of fiduciaries	3.7	
14. Miscellaneous	3.8[d]	
Add: Receipts included in AGI but not in personal income		17.8
15. Personal contributions for social insurance	9.2	
16. Annuities and pensions reported on tax returns	1.6	
17. Miscellaneous income reported on tax returns	1.3[e]	
18. Net gain from sale of capital assets and other property reported on tax returns	6.0	
19. Deduction for net operating loss carryover and depletion	−0.4	
20. Adjusted gross income		349.0

[a] Derived from *Survey of Current Business,* May 1963, July 1962, July 1963.

[b] Government transfer payments for military pension, disability, and retirement payments plus readjustment, self-employment, and subsistence allowance to veterans (*Survey of Current Business,* July 1963, p. 26) minus military retirement pay (*The Budget of the United States Government for the Fiscal Year Ending June 30, 1962,* Appendix, p. 498).

[c] Includes standard clothing issued to military personnel.

[d] Includes value of change in farm inventories, accrued interest on U. S. government bonds, capital gains distribution by investment companies, part of "other labor income," and part of income in kind and imputed income.

[e] Includes items such as alimony received, prizes, awards, sweepstakes winnings, gambling profits, recovery of bad debts and taxes deducted in prior years, and insurance received as reimbursement for medical expenses deducted in a previous year. See U. S. Treasury Department, *Statistics of Income, Individual Income Tax Returns, 1960,* p. 25.

TABLE A-6. Difference Between Adjusted Gross Income and Taxable Income, 1939 and 1960

(In billions of dollars)

Item	1939[a]	1960[b]
1. Adjusted gross income	64.7	349.0
2. Deduct: AGI of nontaxable individuals	43.4	51.8[c]
3. Amount unexplained	3.8	
4. Equals: AGI on taxable returns	17.5	297.2
5. Deduct: Personal deductions[d]	1.7	44.5
6. Personal exemptions[d]	6.6	81.2
7. Earned income credit[d]	0.9	—
8. Equals: Taxable income	8.3	171.5

[a] C. Harry Kahn, *Personal Deductions in the Federal Income Tax* (Princeton, N. J.: Princeton University Press for National Bureau of Economic Research, 1960), p. 18. Includes taxable fiduciaries.
[b] Table A-5 and *Survey of Current Business*, May 1963, p. 3.
[c] Of this total, $18.3 billion was reported on nontaxable returns.
[d] On taxable returns.

TABLE A-7. Percentage of Returns with Particular Deductions, by Adjusted Gross Income Classes, Taxable Individual Returns with Itemized Deductions, 1960[a]

AGI Class ($000)	Interest Paid	Medical Expenses	Contributions	Taxes
Under 2	34.3	61.0	89.3	92.4
2–3	51.9	68.0	93.1	96.2
3–5	70.9	67.1	95.2	98.4
5–10	87.3	59.6	97.7	99.5
10–25	85.4	45.0	98.9	99.7
25–50	70.5	30.0	98.8	99.3
50–100	67.6	29.7	98.8	99.3
100–500	69.5	36.6	99.0	99.5
500 and over	73.0	35.1	98.8	99.1
All classes	79.5	58.8	96.8	98.9

[a] Derived from U. S. Treasury Department, *Statistics of Income, Individual Income Tax Returns, 1960*, p. 55.

TABLE A-8. Selected Personal Deductions by Adjusted Gross Income Classes, Taxable Individual Returns with Itemized Deductions, 1960[a]
(In percent of AGI on taxable returns with itemized deductions)

AGI Class ($000)	Total Itemized Deductions	Interest Paid	Medical Expenses	Contri- butions	Taxes	Other Itemized Deductions
Under 2	25.4	2.1	7.3	5.9	6.5	3.8
2–3	23.7	2.9	6.5	5.1	6.0	3.2
3–5	21.7	4.3	4.8	4.2	5.8	2.8
5–10	19.5	5.4	2.7	3.3	5.8	2.3
10–25	16.8	4.2	1.7	3.2	5.6	2.0
25–50	14.8	2.7	1.1	3.5	5.5	2.0
50–100	15.5	2.6	0.9	4.2	5.4	2.4
100–500	20.2	3.0	0.5	7.8	5.7	3.2
500 and over	21.6	2.2	0.1	12.4	4.5	2.4
All classes	18.7	4.5	2.5	3.6	5.7	2.3

[a] Derived from U. S. Treasury Department, *Statistics of Income, Individual Income Tax Returns, 1960,* p. 55.

**TABLE A-9. Individual Income Tax Rate Schedules,
Selected Years, 1936-65**[a]

(In percent)

Taxable Income ($000)[b]	1936–39[c]	1944–45	1946–47[d]	1948–49[d]	1952–53	1954–63	1964	1965
Under 0.5	⎰ 4	23	19.0	16.6	22.2	20	⎰ 16.0	14
0.5– 1.0							16.5	15
1.0– 1.5							17.5	16
1.5– 2.0	⎱						⎱ 18.0	17
2.0– 4.0	4	25	20.9	19.4	24.6	22	20.0	19
4.0– 6.0	8	29	24.7	22.9	29.0	26	23.5	22
6.0– 8.0	9	33	28.5	26.4	34.0	30	27.0	25
8.0– 10.0	10	37	32.3	29.9	38.0	34	30.5	28
10.0– 12.0	11	41	36.1	33.4	42.0	38	34.0	32
12.0– 14.0	12	46	40.8	37.8	48.0	43	37.5	36
14.0– 16.0	13	50	44.6	41.4	53.0	47	41.0	39
16.0– 18.0	15	53	47.5	44.0	56.0	50	44.5	42
18.0– 20.0	17	56	50.4	46.6	59.0	53	47.5	45
20.0– 22.0	19	59	53.2	49.3	62.0	56	50.5	48
22.0– 26.0	21	62	56.0	51.9	66.0	59	53.5	50
26.0– 32.0	23	65	58.9	54.6	67.0	62	56.0	53
32.0– 38.0	25	68	61.8	57.2	68.0	65	58.5	55
38.0– 44.0	28	72	65.6	60.7	72.0	69	61.0	58
44.0– 50.0	31	75	68.4	63.4	75.0	72	63.5	60
50.0– 56.0	⎰ 35	78	71.2	66.0	77.0	75	66.0	62
56.0– 60.0	⎱ 39							
60.0– 62.0	⎰ 39	81	74.1	68.6	80.0	78	68.5	64
62.0– 68.0	43							
68.0– 70.0	⎱ 47							
70.0– 74.0	⎰ 47	84	77.0	71.3	83.0	81	71.0	66
74.0– 80.0	⎱ 51							
80.0– 90.0	55	87	79.8	73.9	85.0	84	73.5	68
90.0–100.0	59	90	82.6	76.6	88.0	87	75.0	69
100.0–136.7	⎰ 62	92	84.6	⎰ 78.3	90.0	89	76.5	70
136.7–150.0	⎱			⎱ 80.3				
150.0–200.0	64	93	85.5	81.2	91.0	90	76.5	70
200.0 and over[e]	f	94	86.4	82.1	92.0	91	77.0	70

a Compiled from U. S. Treasury Department, *Statistics of Income*, annual volumes; *The Federal Revenue System: Facts and Problems, 1961*, Joint Economic Committee, 87 Cong. 1 sess. (1961), p. 208; and Revenue Act of 1964 (P.L. 88-272). Rates apply to calendar years shown. Rates for 1940-43 and 1950-51 were between those for adjacent periods.

b Surtax net income prior to 1954. For 1948 and later years, the rate brackets for husbands and wives filing joint returns are twice as wide as those shown, which apply to single persons and separate returns of husbands and wives. For 1952 and later years, separate schedules are applied to unmarried heads of households, providing approximately one-half the benefits of income splitting by husbands and wives.

c Does not reflect earned income credit, which reduced rates shown by a maximum of 0.4 percentage points up to a net income of $14,000.

d After reductions from tentative tax.

e Subject to maximum effective rate limitations as follows: 1944-45, 90 percent; 1946-47, 85.5 percent; 1948-49, 77 percent; 1952-53, 88 percent; 1954-63, 87 percent.

f Range of 66 percent to a maximum of 79 percent on surtax net income in excess of $5 million.

TABLE A-10. Influence of Various Provisions on Effective Rates of Individual Income Tax: Taxable Returns, by Total Income Classes, 1960[a]

(In percent of total income)

Total Income Class ($000)	Nominal Tax[b]	Reduction Due to				Actual Tax[d]
		Personal Exemptions	Deductions[c]	Capital Gains Provisions	Income Splitting	
	(1)	(2)	(3)	(4)	(5)	(6)
Under 1	20.0	14.5	2.1	—	—	3.4
1–2	20.0	9.5	2.5	—	—	8.0
2–3	20.4	8.9	2.7	0.1	—	8.7
3–4	20.9	8.4	3.0	0.1	—	9.4
4–5	21.6	8.6	3.2	0.1	—	9.6
5–6	22.4	8.8	3.5	0.1	0.2	9.8
6–7	23.2	8.7	3.7	0.1	0.4	10.3
7–8	24.1	8.1	4.0	0.1	0.6	11.3
8–9	25.0	7.7	4.2	0.2	0.9	12.0
9–10	26.0	7.4	4.5	0.1	1.3	12.7
10–15	28.4	6.7	4.9	0.4	2.1	14.2
15–20	33.7	6.1	6.0	1.1	3.9	16.4
20–25	38.4	5.6	7.0	1.8	5.4	18.3
25–50	46.4	4.3	8.3	2.8	7.7	22.9
50–100	59.6	2.6	10.5	7.7	8.1	30.1
100–150	70.9	1.6	13.5	15.0	6.6	33.3
150–200	76.4	1.1	14.6	22.2	5.3	32.3
200–500	82.4	0.6	15.0	29.6	3.3	32.9
500–1,000	86.8	0.3	12.4	41.8	1.3	30.2
1,000 and over	87.0	0.1	10.6	45.5	0.3	29.8
All classes	28.1	7.5	4.6	1.2	1.6	13.1

[a] Total income is AGI + excluded portion of net realized capital gain or loss + excludable sick pay + excludable dividends. Derived from 1960 Tax File (sample of individual income tax returns for 1960; see footnote 2, Chapter VII).

[b] Rate schedule for single persons applied to total income.

[c] Personal deductions plus dividend exclusion and sick-pay exclusion.

[d] Actual tax after the dividends received credit and foreign tax credit, which are not shown separately here.

TABLE A-11. Average and Marginal Rates of Individual Income Tax: Taxable Individual Returns, by Adjusted Gross Income Classes, 1960[a]

(In percent of adjusted gross income)

AGI Class ($000)	Average Rate	Marginal Rate[b]
	(1)	(2)
Under 1	3.4	18.0
1–2	8.0	18.2
2–3	8.7	18.5
3–4	9.5	19.2
4–5	9.7	19.3
5–6	9.9	19.8
6–7	10.4	20.1
7–8	11.5	20.7
8–9	12.2	21.2
9–10	12.9	21.4
10–15	14.5	24.3
15–20	17.2	29.4
20–25	19.4	34.0
25–50	24.6	43.9
50–100	34.2	58.5
100–150	40.4	66.1
150–200	42.8	68.3
200–500	44.6	68.7
500–1,000	46.6	62.4
1,000 and over	48.3	60.3
All classes	13.4	20.5

[a] Derived from 1960 Tax File (sample of individual income tax returns for 1960; see footnote 2, Chapter VII).

[b] Computed on $1 of additional AGI.

Notes to Chapter III

Equal-Yield Rates of Income and Expenditure Tax

For equal-yield taxes,

$$t_e C = t_y Y,$$

where t_e is the expenditure tax rate, C is personal consumption when the expenditure tax is employed, t_y is the income tax rate, and Y is personal income. C may be stated as

$$C = c(Y - t_e C),$$

where c is the fraction of income, net of tax, which is consumed with the expenditure tax in effect. Since equal yields are assumed, $t_y Y$ may be substituted for $t_e C$ in the consumption equation:

$$C = c(Y - t_y Y) = c(1 - t_y)Y.$$

When the last expression is substituted for C in the first equation, the requirement for equal yields becomes

$$t_e[c(1 - t_y)Y] = t_y Y,$$

which reduces to

$$t_e = t_y/[c(1 - t_y)].$$

When there is zero saving, $c = 1$ and equal-yield tax rates are

$$t_e = t_y/(1 - t_y).$$

The foregoing is based on a paper by A. R. Prest, "The Expenditure Tax and Saving," *Economic Journal,* Vol. 69 (September 1959), pp.

483-89. See also Prest's book, *Public Finance in Theory and Practice* (London: Weidenfeld & Nicolson, 1960), pp. 48, 79-82.

Reward for Saving-and-Investing under Income Tax and Expenditure Tax

Under the income tax, when one saves an amount S he gives up current consumption of that amount and by investing at the market rate of interest, r, can obtain a gross yield of rS, which is reduced by the tax to $(1 - t_y)rS$. In relation to the amount of consumption forgone, the rate of net yield is $(1 - t_y)r$.

Under the expenditure tax, when one saves S he also avoids (or postpones) tax; $S = C' + t_eC' = C'(1 + t_e)$, where C' is the current consumption forgone and t_eC' the tax avoided or postponed. $C' = S/(1 + t_e)$. The saver can obtain an annual yield of rS, from which he can consume $rS/(1 + t_e)$. In relation to the amount of consumption earlier forgone, the additional annual consumption is

$$\frac{rS/(1 + t_e)}{S/(1 + t_e)} = r.$$

Thus the reward for saving-and-investing, in relation to the amount of consumption forgone, is equal to the market rate of interest, under the expenditure tax as it would be in the absence of taxation.

This is the conclusion reached by Nicholas Kaldor *(An Expenditure Tax* [London: Allen and Unwin, 1955], pp. 81-87) and Prest *(Economic Journal,* Vol. 69, pp. 483-84).

Response of Saving to Changes in the Rate of Return

The response of saving to tax-caused changes in the rate of return obtained from real or financial investment is usually considered to be a matter of the interest elasticity of saving. Economists have long recognized that an increase in the market rate of interest may cause some individuals to save more in order to take advantage of the higher yield and others to save less because a smaller capital sum will satisfy their demands for retirement income and family security. The earlier tendency was to argue that an increase in saving was the usual response and that saving had positive interest elasticity, but there followed a period during which leading theorists took an agnostic position on the subject.[1] More recently, attempts have been made to re-establish the

[1] For selected citations, see my paper "Taxation of Saving and Consumption in Underdeveloped Countries," *National Tax Journal,* Vol. 14 (December 1961), p. 307 (Brookings Institution Reprint No. 55, 1962).

presumption that the interest elasticity of saving is positive.[2] Although I do not find the arguments wholly persuasive with respect to changes in the market rate of interest, I now think that when applied to the tax question they establish a reasonable presumption that the propensity to save will be greater under an expenditure tax than under an equal-yield income tax.

Hicks analyzes the effect of a change in the market rate of interest in the same way as a change in a commodity price, showing that it produces a substitution effect and an income effect *(Value and Capital,* pp. 232-35). The substitution effect of an increase in the interest rate is to lower the prices of future purchases relative to current purchases and hence is in the direction of increased saving. The income effect makes persons who plan to be lenders in the present and near future better off and will tend to induce them to spend more and save less. For lenders as a group, it is uncertain whether the substitution effect or income effect will dominate. For borrowers, the income effect is the opposite of that for lenders. Hicks believes that, in general, the positive and negative income effects will cancel out and that the substitution effect will dominate. Bailey's analysis of an arbitrary change in the interest rate with constant real resources is similar *(Journal of Political Economy,* Vol. 65, p. 280). My principal reservation about these analyses is that I do not think that positive and negative income effects can be expected to cancel out in any period in which the government and the central bank are significant net borrowers or lenders because, in my judgment, these institutions do not respond to the income effect in the same way as households.

Hicks' analysis does not indicate the effect on the average propensity to save of an increase or decrease in total taxation because, if taxpayers ignore the benefits from government expenditures, they will all experience a negative income effect when taxes rise and a positive income effect when taxes fall. But the analysis can be applied to the replacement of one tax by another. When an income tax is replaced by an equal-yield expenditure tax, there is a redistribution of current and expected after-tax income within the household sector, households with below-average ratios of consumption to income becoming better off and

[2] J. R. Hicks, *Value and Capital* (Oxford: Clarendon Press, 1939), pp. 232-35; Martin J. Bailey, "Saving and the Rate of Interest," *Journal of Political Economy,* Vol. 65 (August 1957), pp. 279-305; and Donald V. T. Bear, "The Relationship of Saving to the Rate of Interest, Real Income, and Expected Future Prices," *Review of Economics and Statistics,* Vol. 43 (February 1961), pp. 27-35. For a critical comment on Bailey's paper by James M. Buchanan and Bailey's reply, see *Journal of Political Economy,* Vol. 67 (February 1959), pp. 79-86.

those with above-average ratios becoming worse off. For the first group the income and substitution effects work in opposite directions, just as they do for an increase in the market rate of interest, but the second group suffers a loss of after-tax income equal to the gain of the first group and the income effects will cancel out if the two groups have similar psychologies. Allowance for possible differences between the attitudes of the two groups seems more likely to reinforce than to weaken the presumption that the substitution effects will dominate.

The conclusion is not vitiated by provisions for the deduction of interest paid from taxable income under the income tax and the exclusion of interest payments on consumer debt from taxable consumption under the expenditure tax. An income tax which allows the deduction is more favorable to dissaving through consumer borrowing than a tax which does not allow it; in this sense the deduction accentuates the substitution effect without eliminating the income effect. Under the expenditure tax, the exclusion of interest paid somewhat reduces the negative income effect on borrowers but does not eliminate it. The income effect would persist even if consumer debt could be contracted without payment of interest; fundamentally the negative income effect arises out of a redistribution of taxation between persons with different propensities to consume.[3]

[3] Michael A. Willemsen's argument on this point seems to me incorrect ("The Effect Upon the Rate of Private Savings of a Change from a Personal Income Tax to a Personal Expenditure Tax," *National Tax Journal,* Vol. 14 [March 1961], pp. 101-02), although his paper is a good treatment of the general subject.

Distribution of Taxes by Income Groups and Impact of Taxation on Saving

THE ESTIMATES OF TAX DISTRIBUTION and the impact of taxation on saving presented in Chapter IV are based mostly on survey data for 1950. However, the estimates relating to a tax on net worth (Chart 2) were derived from statistics of net worth in early 1950 of spending units classified by size of income in 1949. Certain later survey data are mentioned at the end of this appendix.

Basic Statistics

The basic data on money income, federal income tax liability, consumption expenditures, and saving in 1950 are from the Survey of Consumer Finances (SCF) sponsored by the Board of Governors of the Federal Reserve System and conducted by the Survey Research Center of the University of Michigan. Findings were published in the *Federal Reserve Bulletin,* August 1951 and September 1951. Additional details regarding disposable income and net saving appear in a paper by John B. Lansing and Harold Lydall ("An Anglo-American Comparison of Personal Saving," *Bulletin, Oxford University Institute of Statistics,* Vol. 22 [August 1960], p. 242). Later annual surveys do not give information on consumption expenditures and saving.

The data on net worth come indirectly from the SCF via estimates by Raymond W. Goldsmith published in *A Study of Saving in the*

United States, Vol. III (Princeton, N. J.: Princeton University Press, 1956) by Goldsmith, Dorothy S. Brady, and Horst Mendershausen.

The SCF data relate to "spending units," that is, to units consisting of all persons living in the same dwelling and belonging to the same family who pool their incomes to meet major expenses. Income is consumer money income before taxes, and consumption is money expenditures for consumer goods and services including durable goods except purchases of houses. Saving is conceptually equal to the difference between current money income and the sum of consumption expenditures and tax payments but in practice was estimated primarily from balance sheet data showing changes in asset holdings and debt. Capital gains and losses are excluded from income and saving. Federal individual income tax liability does not include tax attributable to net capital gains.

The statistics of net worth cover only selected items (see footnote to Appendix Table C-1). Items not included accounted for slightly over one-fifth of the estimated total value of household assets at the end of 1949. In addition, there are differences in estimated values of assets derived from the SCF and from other sources. Goldsmith's estimate of the total net worth of households derived from aggregate data is about 60 percent larger than the adjusted total which he derives from the SCF (*Study of Saving,* Vol. III, pp. 103, 107, 122, 126, *et passim*). It is not clear how the omissions and errors affect net worth in different income classes.

Effective Tax Rates

Effective rates of federal individual income tax in 1950 (Chart 2) were computed from estimates of income tax liability and money income by income deciles, which were derived from SCF data (see Appendix Table C-3). Estimates of money income by deciles were computed from published estimates of the percentage distribution of money income and aggregate money income. The percentage distribution of federal income tax liability by deciles was derived from estimates of mean tax liability and numbers of spending units by dollar income classes *(Federal Reserve Bulletin,* August 1951, pp. 921, 935) and from percentage distributions by quintiles *(ibid.,* September 1951, p. 1072). Interpolations for deciles were linear to the logarithms of cumulative percentage distributions of tax and number of units. Amounts of tax liability were computed from the percentages and estimated aggregate. These computations are subject to sizable rounding errors because of the form in which the SCF results are published.

The effective rates of the hypothetical flat-rate tax on consumption expenditures, which is assumed to replace the income tax, were obtained by (1) estimating consumption expenditures by income deciles in the absence of the income tax; (2) distributing in proportion to estimated consumption expenditures a consumption tax of $16 billion, which is approximately the SCF figure for 1950 federal individual income tax liability exclusive of tax attributable to net capital gain or loss; and (3) computing the ratio of the consumption tax to money income. Consumption expenditures in the absence of the income tax were estimated by increasing estimated actual consumption by an amount $(1 - s)T_y$, where s is the estimated marginal propensity to save from disposable income for the decile and T_y is the federal income tax liability. The derivation of s is explained below.

Effective rates of net worth tax by income quintiles and for the two highest income deciles were computed from distributions of (1) 1949 money income based on the SCF (Federal Reserve Bulletin, September 1951, p. 1074); and (2) net worth as of early 1950 obtained by linear interpolation from the logarithms of cumulations of Goldsmith's estimates of numbers and amounts by dollar income classes (Study of Saving, Vol. III, p. 122). The hypothetical flat-rate net worth tax is one

TABLE C-1. Money Income, Net Worth, and Flat-Rate Tax on Net Worth, by Money Income Quintiles and Deciles, 1949-50[a]

(In billions of dollars)

Money Income Quintile or Decile	Money Income (1)	Net Worth[b] (2)	Net Worth Tax[c] (3)
Lowest quintile	6.8	48.0	1.3
2d quintile	18.7	48.9	1.4
3d quintile	28.9	62.9	1.8
4th quintile	39.1	84.2	2.3
9th decile	25.5	70.2	2.0
Highest decile	51.0	223.6	6.2
Total	170.0	537.8	15.0

[a] Based on Raymond W. Goldsmith, Dorothy S. Brady, and Horst Mendershausen, A Study of Saving in the United States, Vol. III (Princeton, N. J.: Princeton University Press, 1956), pp. 122, 126; and Survey of Consumer Finances, Federal Reserve Bulletin, September 1951. Money income is that of 1949, net worth as of early 1950.

[b] Includes checking accounts, savings accounts in banks, postal savings, shares in savings and loan associations and credit unions, automobiles, owner-occupied homes and farms, equity in unincorporated businesses and closely held corporations, corporate stock, life insurance reserves, and reserves of contributory pension funds. All reported debts deducted. Does not include currency, bonds other than U. S. government issues, privately held mortgages, equity in government trust funds, personal trust funds, and consumer durables other than automobiles.

[c] Flat-rate tax that would yield the same fraction of money income as the federal income tax (exclusive of the tax attributable to net capital gains) yielded in 1950.

yielding the same fraction of 1949 consumer income as the income tax of 1950 yielded in 1950. The estimates of income, net worth, and net worth tax are summarized in Appendix Table C-1.

Saving Ratios

Estimates of mean disposable income and mean saving by money income deciles are from the paper by Lansing and Lydall. These estimates, together with computed average saving ratios, are shown in Appendix Table C-2 and are graphed in Chart 6. In drawing the saving curve, I omitted the figures that are bracketed in the table, those for the fifth and seventh deciles, because they seemed out of line with estimates for adjacent deciles. The curve was extrapolated beyond the highest observation by extending a straight line connecting the means for the two highest deciles.

TABLE C-2. Disposable Income and Saving, by Money Income Deciles, 1950[a]

Money Income Decile	Mean Disposable Income (1)	Mean Net Saving (2)	Average Saving Ratio (3)
Lowest	$ 479	$ − 426	− 88.9%
2d	1,112	− 45	− 4.0
3d	1,653	3	0.2
4th	2,121	22	1.0
5th	2,635	[− 22]	[− 0.8]
6th	3,089	112	3.6
7th	3,568	[256]	[7.2]
8th	4,122	310	7.5
9th	4,957	550	11.1
Highest	8,606	2,026	23.5

[a] Survey of Consumer Finances results, from John B. Lansing and Harold Lydall, "An Anglo-American Comparison of Personal Saving," *Bulletin*, Oxford University Institute of Statistics, Vol. 22 (August 1960), p. 242. Col. 3 derived.

Impact on Saving

The distribution of federal individual income tax liability (exclusive of the tax on net capital gains) and of flat-rate taxes on consumption and money income in 1950 is shown in Appendix Table C-3.

The table also shows estimates of the reduction of private saving attributable to the taxes. These estimates were derived by applying to

TABLE C-3. Estimated Reduction in Private Saving Due to Income and Consumption Taxes, by Money Income Deciles, 1950[a]

(In billions of dollars)

Money Income Decile	Money Income (1)	Tax Liability			Reduction in Saving		
		Federal Income Tax[b] (2)	Consumption Tax[c] (3)	Proportional Income Tax[c] (4)	Federal Income Tax[b] (5)	Consumption Tax[c] (6)	Proportional Income Tax[c] (7)
Lowest	1.8	—	0.4	0.2	—	0.3	0.1
2d	5.5	0.2	0.6	0.5	0.1	0.3	0.3
3d	9.2	0.3	0.9	0.8	—	0.1	—
4th	11.0	0.5	1.1	1.0	—	—	—
5th	14.6	0.7	1.4	1.3	0.1	0.1	0.1
6th	16.5	0.9	1.6	1.4	0.1	0.2	0.2
7th	20.1	1.4	1.8	1.8	0.3	0.3	0.3
8th	23.8	1.6	2.1	2.1	0.5	0.6	0.6
9th	27.5	2.0	2.3	2.4	0.8	0.9	0.9
Highest	53.1	8.4	3.8	4.6	3.4	1.5	1.9
Total	183.0	16.0	16.0	16.0	5.3	4.4	4.5

a. Based on Survey of Consumer Finances, *Federal Reserve Bulletin*, August and September 1951. For derivation of estimates, see text.
b. Excludes tax on net capital gains.
c. Flat-rate tax on all consumption expenditures or money income which is assumed to replace the federal individual income tax.

the tax distributions marginal saving ratios (marginal propensities to save) derived from the saving curve shown in Chart 6. The marginal saving ratios, which were calculated separately for each decile, represent the ratio of the change in mean net saving to change in mean disposable income over the range $(Y - T_y)$ to Y or $(Y - T_c)$ to Y, where Y is mean money income and T_y and T_c are, respectively, mean income tax and mean consumption tax liabilities. This procedure treats the income tax and the consumption tax in the same way on the assumption that both reduce real disposable income by the amount of the tax, regardless of whether the tax is paid direct to the government or indirectly in the form of higher prices.

An alternative approach would be to look on a permanent tax on consumption (either a fully shifted sales tax or a direct tax on personal expenditures) as a measure that reduces the purchasing power of all money income, including both the part of income that is spent immediately and that which is saved for future consumption. This would suggest that the levying of a consumption tax would reduce a nominal in-

CHART 6. Disposable Income and Net Saving, All Spending Units, 1950

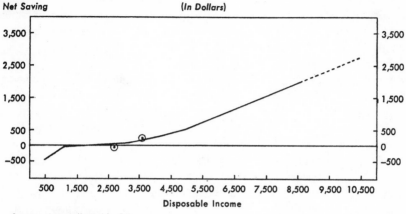

Source: Appendix Table C-2.

come of Y to $Y/(1 + t_c)$, where t_c is the consumption tax rate. When saving is positive, this approach will indicate a smaller real disposable income under a consumption tax than under an equal-yield income tax. Furthermore, if aggregate real consumption is an increasing function of aggregate real disposable income and saving is positive, this procedure will indicate that a consumption tax will reduce real consumption more (and saving less) than an equal-yield income tax,[1] whereas my procedure will indicate that the two forms of tax will have the same effects if they are distributed among income classes in the same proportions.

The choice between the two approaches involves theoretical issues and broader implications into which I do not wish to enter here; however, it does not greatly affect estimates of the kind described in this appendix. If disposable income under the consumption tax had been measured by the alternative method (by deflating total income by an index of the price of consumer goods and services) the estimates of the impact on potential saving would have been the same for the flat-rate consumption tax and the proportional income tax. As can be seen from Appendix Table C-3, the differences between the estimates for the two taxes made by my method are small.

[1] See E. Cary Brown, "Analysis of Consumption Taxes in Terms of the Theory of Income Determination," *American Economic Review*, Vol. 40 (March 1950), pp. 74-89; Challis A. Hall, Jr., *Fiscal Policy for Stable Growth* (New York: Holt, Rinehart and Winston, 1960), pp. 184-85.

Musgrave's Estimates

Richard A. Musgrave has made estimates of the impact of taxation on personal saving which are close to mine for the progressive income tax but which are substantially lower than mine for a proportional income tax or a flat-rate consumption tax ("Effects of Tax Policy on Private Capital Formation," in *Fiscal and Debt Management Policies,* Research Studies for the Commission on Money and Credit [Englewood Cliffs, N. J.: Prentice-Hall, 1963], pp. 45-142). Although he manipulates the statistics differently, his methods are broadly similar to mine and his estimates, like mine, are based on marginal propensities to save derived from the SCF data for 1950.

A difference between Musgrave's procedures and mine arises from our extrapolations of the saving curve for high income classes. Musgrave's extrapolation implies a rising marginal propensity to save beyond the highest observed value, whereas my linear extrapolation implies a constant marginal propensity to save in that range. The choice of extrapolation method has a significant effect on the estimates for the progressive income tax but affects the estimates for the other taxes less. For example, if Musgrave had used a straight-line extrapolation for income classes above $10,000, for which detailed observations were not available, his estimates and mine would show about the same number of percentage points of difference between the impact on saving of progressive, proportional, and regressive taxes. However, in that case Musgrave's estimates for all three taxes would be substantially lower than mine. Musgrave states that his procedure "is likely to overstate rather than understate the reduction in saving due to progression" (*ibid.,* p. 61). While I feel that my procedure is more likely to err in the opposite direction there is, I think, no satisfactory evidence on the point.

Expenditures Subject to Retail Sales Tax

Studies by Reed R. Hansen make it possible to estimate the fraction of total consumer expenditures in different income classes for items that are subject to a "typical retail sales tax." This tax is a "hypothetical one incorporating the provisions most commonly found in state retail sales tax laws in the United States of America."[2] Hansen classified consumer expenditures for various items as taxable or nontaxable according to the practice of the majority of states imposing a retail sales tax. In addition to his published estimates, Hansen generously made

[2] "Vertical and Horizontal Inequities Found in the Retail Sales Tax," in *Proceedings of Thirty-fifth Annual Conference of Western Economic Association,* 1960, p. 72.

TABLE C-4. Total Consumption and Taxable Consumption Under a "Typical Retail Sales Tax": All Families,[a] Large Cities of North, South, and West, 1950

Money Income Class	Ratio of Total Consumption to Money Income[b] (1)	Ratio of Taxable Consumption to Total Consumption[c] (2)
Under $1,000	2.044	0.656
$1,000–1,999	1.134	0.688
2,000–2,999	1.009	0.704
3,000–3,999	0.960	0.719
4,000–4,999	0.928	0.727
5,000–5,999	0.881	0.737
6,000–7,499	0.826	0.732
7,500–9,999	0.776	0.728
10,000 and over	0.580	0.733

[a] Includes single persons.

[b] Derived from survey data, U. S. Bureau of Labor Statistics and Wharton School of Finance, University of Pennsylvania, *Study of Consumer Expenditures, Incomes, and Savings* (Philadelphia: University of Pennsylvania, 1956), Vol. 1, pp. 10-11.

[c] Derived from Reed R. Hansen, "An Empirical Analysis of the Retail Sales Tax with Policy Recommendations," *National Tax Journal*, Vol. 15 (March 1962), pp. 1-13, and Hansen's worksheets and supplementary computations.

available his worksheets and certain supplementary computations.

The ratios shown in Appendix Table C-4 relate only to families (including single persons) in large cities. They were derived from survey data of the U. S. Bureau of Labor Statistics and Wharton School of Finance and from Hansen's estimates. Column 1 was obtained by combining ratios for the three regions with weights proportional to the sample numbers in each income class. Column 2 was derived by multiplying the ratio of taxable consumption to income (as estimated by Hansen) by the ratio of money income to total consumption (the reciprocal of column 1). Hansen's summary ratios for each income class were computed by weighting ratios for families of different sizes and for the three regions by sample numbers.

Studies by David G. Davies, also based on 1950 survey data, show that under both the California and Ohio sales taxes the ratio of taxable consumption to total consumption at first rises with income, then remains approximately constant over a considerable range of income, and rises again in the income class $10,000 and over.[3] Except for the rise

[3] "The Relative Burden of Sales Taxation: A Statistical Analysis of California Data," *American Journal of Economics and Sociology*, Vol. 19 (April 1960), p. 290; "Progressiveness of a Sales Tax in Relation to Various Income Bases," *American Economic Review*, Vol. 50 (December 1960), p. 990.

of the ratio in the highest income class, Davies' findings agree generally with those presented in Appendix Table C-4.

Later Survey Data

Survey data on net worth in early 1962 in relation to consumer income in 1961 were published after the completion of the estimates reported above.[4] The curve relating net worth to money income has the same general shape as that for 1949-50; however, the ratio of net worth to money income is lower in 1960-61.

The Bureau of Labor Statistics (BLS) has recently published summary data from a field survey of money income and expenditures of urban consumers in 1960-61.[5] The BLS data cannot be directly compared with the SCF statistics for 1950 since the BLS survey did not cover the rural population, comprising about 30 percent of the total; there are also differences in definitions and in classification of the statistics. Compared with a BLS survey for 1950,[6] the 1960 survey shows lower average ratios of consumption to money income. However, the shape of the curve depicting the ratio of consumption expenditures to disposable money income, by income deciles, in 1960 is similar to that of the curve for 1950, and the implied marginal propensity to consume for all urban families and single individuals appears to be about the same in 1960 as in 1950 (calculated by weighting the implied marginal propensities to consume in income classes by disposable income). This comparison, therefore, is consistent with the hypothesis that the estimates for all consumers based on the 1950 SCF may be applied to later years.

[4] George Katona, Charles A. Lininger, and Richard F. Kosobud, *1962 Survey of Consumer Finances,* Monograph 32, Survey Research Center, Institute for Social Research, University of Michigan (Ann Arbor, Mich., 1963).

[5] U. S. Bureau of Labor Statistics, *Consumer Expenditures and Income, Urban United States, 1960-61,* BLS Report No. 237-38 (April 1964).

[6] *Study of Consumer Expenditures, Incomes, and Savings,* Wharton School of Finance and Commerce, University of Pennsylvania, Vol. XVIII (Philadelphia: University of Pennsylvania, 1957).

Limitations of Statistics
on Size Distribution of Income

THERE ARE REASONS for believing that the available statistics understate the income share of top income groups. It is also possible that
they exaggerate the reduction over time in the share of income received
by these groups.[1]

The most obvious shortcoming of the statistics for purposes of evaluation of the income tax is the omission of capital gains and losses. While
comprehensive adjustments to take account of capital gains and losses
(or net capital gains, that is, gains minus losses) are not available, an
impression of the possible importance of this kind of income can be
obtained from Appendix Table D-1. These figures indicate that the
inclusion of realized net capital gains would have substantially increased the income share of the top 5 percent in 1929 and would have
increased their share by smaller amounts in 1936-37, 1944, and 1958.
The pairs of estimates for 1929, 1935-36, and 1944, however, are not

---

[1] For critiques of the statistics, see George Garvy, "Functional and Size Dis-
tributions of Income and Their Meaning," *American Economic Review*, Vol. 44,
Papers and Proceedings (May 1954), pp. 242-47; Robert J. Lampman, "Recent
Changes in Income Inequality Reconsidered," *American Economic Review*, Vol. 44
(June 1954), pp. 254-67; Joseph A. Pechman, "Comment," in *Studies in Income and
Wealth*, Conference on Research in Income and Wealth, Vol. 23 (1958), pp. 107-15;
Selma F. Goldsmith, "Changes in the Size Distribution of Income," *American Eco-
nomic Review*, Vol. 47, Papers and Proceedings (May 1957), pp. 511-18; Gabriel
Kolko, *Wealth and Power in America* (New York: Praeger, 1962), pp. 13-29.

**TABLE D-1. Realized Net Capital Gains and Income Share
of Top 5 Percent, 1929, 1935-36, 1944, and 1958**

Item	1929	1935–36	1944	1958
1. Net capital gains reported on tax returns (billions)[a]	$ 2.9	$ 0.2	$ 1.6	$ 8.5
2. Line 1 as percent of total family personal income plus line 1[b]	3.3%	0.3%	1.1%	2.4%
3. Income share of top 5 percent of population, Kuznets[c]				
a. Basic variant	26.4%	24.0%	16.6%	..
b. Basic variant adjusted to include realized net capital gains	30.0%	24.6%	17.4%	..
4. Income share of top 5 percent of consumer units, OBE[d]				
a. Family personal income	30.0%	26.5%	20.7%	19.9%[e]
b. Family personal income + realized net capital gains	..	..	..	20.3%

[a] Net gain realized from sales of capital assets and other property, at 100 percent; 1929, 1935-36, and 1944 from Lawrence H. Seltzer, *Nature and Tax Treatment of Capital Gains and Losses* (New York: National Bureau of Economic Research, 1951), p. 367; 1958, estimate by Seltzer published in *The Uses of Economic Research*, Forty-third Annual Report of National Bureau of Economic Research (New York, May 1963), p. 89. Taxable fiduciaries are included for all years except 1958.

[b] Based on estimates of family personal income from Selma F. Goldsmith, George Jaszi, Hyman Kaitz, and Maurice Liebenberg, "Size Distribution of Income Since the Mid-Thirties," *Review of Economics and Statistics*, Vol. 36 (February 1954), p. 3; U. S. Department of Commerce, Office of Business Economics, *Survey of Current Business*, April 1958, p. 15, April 1963, p. 15.

[c] Simon Kuznets, *Shares of Upper Income Groups in Income and Savings* (New York: National Bureau of Economic Research, 1953), p. 599.

[d] Except for 1958, from U. S. Bureau of the Census, *Historical Statistics of the United States, Colonial Times to 1957*, p. 166; 1958, lines 4a and 4b, from *Survey of Current Business*, May 1961, p. 14.

[e] This estimate has subsequently been revised to 20.0 percent (*Survey of Current Business*, April 1963, p. 18); presumably the figure in line 4b would be increased to 20.4 percent if correspondingly revised.

fully comparable with the 1958 pair and seem to indicate more difference between the income shares of the top 5 percent, including and excluding realized net capital gains, than would estimates made in the same way as those for 1958.[2]

Another shortcoming of the personal income statistics that is often

---

[2] The 1958 figures are estimates of the Office of Business Economics (OBE), U. S. Department of Commerce; they allow for reranking of units when net capital gains are included in income; Kuznets' estimates for the earlier years do not provide for reranking. My own estimate for 1958, which I believe to be comparable to Kuznets' earlier estimates, although not identical in technique, indicates that, if realized net capital gains are added to family personal income as estimated by OBE, the income share of the top 5 percent is raised by 1.6 percentage points rather than 0.4 percentage point. My estimate, derived from *Statistics of Income*, ranks income recipients by adjusted gross income rather than family personal income and does not allow for reranking.

mentioned is the omission of retained profits of corporations. If, however, capital gains are taken into account, the addition of retained profits as well would involve double counting, since a large part of capital gains reflects retained profits.

The reliability of the personal income statistics as measures of real income has been progressively impaired by the increasing participation of married women in work outside the home and the decline in the value of home production, which causes measured income to rise more rapidly than real income. On the other hand, the growth of expense accounts and fringe benefits that are not included in current personal income has the opposite effect. Although data are not available on which to base adjustments for these factors, it is apparent that their influence is not confined to either upper or lower incomes. Liberal expense accounts may be mainly a high-income perquisite, but other fringe benefits extend to the lower ranks. Allowance for the earnings of working wives appears to raise the income share of middle and upper-middle income groups but probably does not increase the share of the highest income group.[3] Although it seems likely that the failure to allow for the substitution between measured and unmeasured income causes an overstatement of changes in the degree of inequality, the size of the error is unknown.

Division of property among family members can reduce the apparent concentration of income without equally affecting the distribution of welfare and economic power. In principle, the statistics on which primary reliance has been placed in Chapter X should not be affected by transfers between husbands and wives and parents and children living in the same household, since an attempt is made to consolidate the incomes of all members of the household. Owing to statistical difficulties, this consolidation may be incomplete or inaccurate. Even with full adjustment for transfers within households, transfers of income-producing property between households, as between parents and married children or between grandparents and grandchildren, will cause a statistical reduction in income inequality which may exaggerate the real change. These transfers may be motivated in considerable part by the desire to avoid income and estate taxes.

In appraising the importance of the various limitations of the statistics, it is well to remember that large dollar corrections would have to be made to have a great effect on income shares. At recent income levels, a correction of almost $4 billion would be required to change

[3] See James Morgan, "Anatomy of Income Distribution," *Review of Economics and Statistics*, Vol. 44 (August 1962), p. 270; Herman P. Miller, *Rich Man, Poor Man* (New York: Crowell, 1964), pp. 188-92.

an income share by 1 percentage point. Therefore, in order to show that
no reduction occurred in the income share of the top 5 percent of consumer units between 1929 and 1960, it would be necessary to demonstrate that at least another $40 billion of economic income should be
added to the estimated $75 billion received by the group in 1960.[4]
This figure is a minimum because it makes no allowance for possible
corrections of the 1929 estimates or the estimate for the lower 95 percent in 1960.

[4] For a similar argument, see Selma F. Goldsmith, *American Economic Review,* Vol. 47, Papers and Proceedings, p. 514. The before-tax share of the top
5 percent fell by 10.4 percentage points between 1929 and 1960 (Table 26).

Estimates Relating to
Built-in Flexibility

Taxable Income and Marginal Tax Rate: Structural Estimates

The relation between taxable individual income (*TI*) and GNP was measured by a linear regression covering the period 1950-60:

$$TI_t - TI_{t-1} = \$0.61 \text{ billion} + 0.381 \ (\text{GNP}_t - \text{GNP}_{t-1}).$$
$$(0.049) \qquad r^2 = 0.845$$

The subscripts *t* and *t* − 1 refer to time measured in years. The standard error of the regression coefficient is shown in parentheses. The data are from the same sources as Table 28.

If the regression is based on the original data (1949-60), rather than first differences, the equation is

$$TI = - \$33.12 \text{ billion} + 0.407 \text{ GNP}.$$
$$(0.011) \qquad r^2 = 0.992$$

The first-difference form is considered preferable because it is less influenced by the common trend (collinearity) of *TI* and GNP.

After inspection of Table 28 and the computation of linear regressions, I concluded that the marginal tax rate on taxable income was approximately 23.0 percent in the years 1954-60, when the statutory rate schedule was constant. The following regression coefficients were obtained for the period 1954-60:

$T_t - T_{t-1}$ on $TI_t - TI_{t-1}$ 0.236

T on TI 0.230

345

where T is federal individual income tax liability, and the other symbols have the meaning defined above.

Alternative Structural Estimates

I also experimented with structural estimates based on statistics that exclude capital gains and losses and the tax attributable to them and on per capita statistics of income and tax liabilities. While the alternative estimates might be supported on behavioral grounds, I considered them mainly as possible refinements in the measurement of built-in flexibility of aggregate tax liability with respect to aggregate income.

Since realized capital gains are highly volatile and may not be closely related to the general business cycle, they may obscure the relationship between ordinary income and ordinary tax liabilities.[1] My calculations, however, indicate that the exclusion of net realized capital gains (as reported on tax returns) and the tax attributable to them would have little effect on the estimate of built-in flexibility. The coefficient of first differences of TI' on first differences of GNP (1950-60) is 0.373, where TI' is taxable income excluding net capital gains. The marginal tax rate exclusive of the tax attributable to capital gains (1954-60) is 0.230 when computed from first differences of tax liability and TI'.[2]

Per capita estimates may be useful because they isolate the influence of population growth, which affects the number of personal exemptions and other variables. A priori, one would expect the marginal ratio of TI to GNP to be higher when measured on a per capita basis than when measured with respect to aggregates. My calculations, however, did not confirm this expectation. A linear regression of first differences of TI/P on first differences of GNP/P (1950-60) yielded a coefficient of 0.380, which is virtually identical with the coefficient for first differences of aggregates. (In these calculations, P is midyear population, including members of the armed forces overseas.) The coefficient for first differences of T/P on first differences of TI/P is 0.234 (1954-60).

Another approach, which I have not explored, though I believe it worthy of further consideration, is to base the estimates of built-in flexibility on cross-section data.[3] It should be noted in this connection that

[1] Wilfred Lewis, Jr., *Federal Fiscal Policy in the Postwar Recessions*, Studies of Government Finance (Washington: Brookings Institution, 1962), pp. 38-39, 49-50.

[2] Estimates of TI' and the tax attributable to net capital gains are from Lewis, *Federal Fiscal Policy*, p. 284, and U. S. Treasury Department, *Statistics of Income, Individual Income Tax Returns, 1960*, pp. 76-77, with 1960 tax liability on capital gains estimated by Lewis' method.

[3] An example of a study using both time-series and cross-section estimates is A. R. Prest, "The Sensitivity of the Yield of Personal Income Tax in the United Kingdom," *Economic Journal*, Vol. 72 (September 1962), pp. 576-96.

estimates of the marginal tax rate at any moment of time, such as those reported in Chapter IX, are not directly applicable to measurement of built-in flexibility because they do not allow for changes in income distribution and in the number of persons filing returns that may accompany fluctuations in aggregate income.

Historical Estimates, Individual Income Tax

The historical estimates of the built-in flexibility of the individual income tax appear in Appendix Tables E-1 and E-2. In these tables ΔGNP is the change in gross national product, ΔTI the change in taxable income, $\Delta TI'$ the change in taxable income excluding net capital gains, ΔT the change in federal individual income tax liabilities at con-

TABLE E-1. Historical Built-in Flexibility of Federal Individual Income Tax Liability at Constant (1954-60) Statutory Rates, Selected Periods, 1949-60, Annual Data[a]

Period and Description	$\Delta TI/\Delta GNP$	$\Delta T/\Delta TI$	Built-In Flexibility $(\Delta T/\Delta GNP)$
Including net capital gains and tax attributable to them			
Expansion, 1949–53	0.409	0.212	0.087
Recession, 1953–54	0.140	b	b
Expansion, 1954–57	0.426	0.227	0.097
Recession, 1957–58	b	1.250	b
1958–60	0.384	0.230	0.088
	$\Delta TI'/\Delta GNP$	$\Delta T'/\Delta TI'$	$\Delta T'/\Delta GNP$
Excluding net capital gains and tax attributable to them			
Expansion, 1949–53	0.405	0.209	0.085
Recession, 1953–54	0.667	0.092	0.061
Expansion, 1954–57	0.425	0.227	0.096
Recession, 1957–58	b	0.412	b
1958–60	0.370	0.222	0.082

[a] For explanation of symbols and computation methods and sources of data, see appendix text.
[b] Not computed because of different signs.

stant (1954-60) statutory rates, and $\Delta T'$ the change in liabilities excluding the tax attributable to net capital gains, changes being measured as the difference between the values for the initial and terminal years or quarters. The data sources are those listed for Table 28 plus U. S. Department of Commerce, Office of Business Economics, *U. S. Income and Output* (1958), and Lewis, *Federal Fiscal Policy*, pp. 284, 290.

TABLE E-2. Historical Built-in Flexibility of Federal Individual Income Tax Liability at Constant (1954-60) Statutory Rates, Selected Periods, 1949-58, Quarterly Data[a]

(Quarterly estimates at seasonally adjusted annual rates)

Period	Built-in Flexibility ($\Delta T / \Delta GNP$)	
	Including Tax Attributable to Net Capital Gains	Excluding Tax Attributable to Net Capital Gains
Expansion:		
1949–II to 1953–II	0.082	0.080
Recession:		
1953–II to 1954–II	0.020	0.071
Expansion:		
1954–II to 1957–III	0.097	0.096
Recession:		
1957–III to 1958–I	0.104	0.110

[a] For explanation of symbols and computation methods and sources of data, see appendix text.

Quarterly estimates of T' at seasonally adjusted annual rates are from Lewis, p. 288. In order to obtain quarterly estimates of T, I added back Lewis' estimates of liability attributable to net capital gains for the year, allocating the annual total among quarters by reference to Standard & Poor's composite stock index.

The erratic results obtained for the 1957-58 recession in the computations using annual data may be due largely to the brevity and mildness of the recession. Between 1957 and 1958, GNP in current prices increased slightly and personal income rose 2.5 percent, despite the recession, while TI and TI' declined slightly. From 1953 to 1954, TI declined slightly while estimated T rose slightly. These estimates are affected by the insensitivity of annual data and possibly by inaccuracies in adjusting for the 1954 changes in the tax law. Estimates obtained from the ratios of small changes in large aggregates are suspect because they are heavily influenced by minor disturbances that are not taken into account. The estimates for the expansions are less erratic because longer periods and larger changes are involved.

Earlier Estimates of Built-in Flexibility and Elasticity of Individual Income Tax

BUILT-IN FLEXIBILITY. Lewis presents historical estimates of built-in flexibility of federal individual income tax liability excluding the tax attributable to net capital gains for selected recession and recovery periods 1948-59 on the basis of his seasonally adjusted quarterly estimates of tax accruals and for 1960-61 on the basis of national income and product account estimates (*Federal Fiscal Policy,* p. 47). His estimates for the 1953-54 and 1957-58 recessions are close to comparable ones shown in my Appendix Table E-2. His recovery periods are briefer than the expansion periods shown in my table, and his estimates of built-in flexibility in recovery periods are somewhat lower than my estimates for the complete expansions from trough to peak.

Ando and Brown estimated the built-in flexibility of the individual income tax under 1959 rates and other conditions at 14 percent with respect to personal income on an annual basis and at 11 percent on a quarterly or monthly basis. Using an estimate of the short-run relationship between personal income and GNP for the period 1947-60, they translated their quarterly estimate into a figure of 6 percent with respect to GNP. See Albert Ando and E. Cary Brown, "Lags in Fiscal Policy," in *Stabilization Policies,* Research Studies for the Commission on Money and Credit (Englewood Cliffs, N. J.: Prentice-Hall, 1963), pp. 102, 106. Earlier estimates by Brown appear in his paper, "The Personal Income Tax as an Automatic Stabilizer," in House Ways and Means Committee, *Tax Revision Compendium* (1959), Vol. 3, pp. 2357-62.

Cohen derived separate measures of built-in flexibility of individual income tax liability for each of several years and summarized his results in the form of weighted averages. At 1954 statutory rates, he estimated built-in flexibility with respect to total AGI at 12.9 percent in 1949-53 and 14.6 percent in 1954-57, attributing the difference to a change in the distribution of taxable income. See Leo Cohen, "A More Recent Measurement of the Built-in Flexibility of the Individual Income Tax," *National Tax Journal,* Vol. 13 (June 1960), p. 126; for earlier estimates by Cohen, see "An Empirical Measurement of the Built-in Flexibility of the Individual Income Tax," *American Economic Review,* Vol. 49, Papers and Proceedings (May 1959), pp. 532-41. Over the period 1949-57, total AGI tended to change from one year to the next by 56 percent of the change in GNP.[4] Hence Cohen's estimates imply built-in flexibility with respect to GNP of 7.2 percent in 1949-53 and 8.2 percent in 1954-57.

[4] My estimate, based on a linear regression of first differences, 1950-57, using estimates of total AGI, including AGI not reported on tax returns, by Joseph A. Pechman from his paper "What Would a Comprehensive Income Tax Yield?" in House Ways and Means Committee, *Tax Revision Compendium* (1959), Vol. 1, p. 256.

Pechman estimated built-in flexibility of individual income tax liability with respect to total AGI at 17.0 to 18.0 percent at 1953 tax rates and at 15.0 to 16.0 percent at 1954 rates. See Joseph A. Pechman, "Yield of the Individual Income Tax During a Recession," *National Tax Journal,* Vol. 7 (March 1954), pp. 1-16, and (slightly revised) in *Policies to Combat Depression,* Conference of Universities-National Bureau of Economic Research Committee for Economic Research (Princeton, N. J.: Princeton University Press for National Bureau of Economic Research, 1956), pp. 123-45. On the basis of the 56 percent marginal ratio of AGI to GNP mentioned above, Pechman's figures imply built-in flexibility with respect to GNP of 9.5 to 10.1 percent at 1953 tax rates and 8.4 to 9.0 percent at 1954 rates.

Clement estimated built-in flexibility of the withheld portion of federal individual income tax collections, at 1957 statutory rates (which were the same as 1954 rates), at 11.4 percent with respect to national income during expansions and 13.8 percent during contractions. His estimates were based on seasonally adjusted quarterly statistics. See M. O. Clement, "The Quantitative Impact of Automatic Stabilizers," *Review of Economics and Statistics,* Vol. 42 (February 1960), pp. 56-61.

ELASTICITY. Lewis estimated the elasticity of federal individual income tax yield, with respect to personal income (*PI*), at constant 1954-60 tax rates, at 1.25 or more, "measured for comparable stages of the cycle in order to approximate stable growth conditions. . . ." See Wilfred Lewis, Jr., "The Federal Sector in National Income Models," in *Studies in Income and Wealth,* Conference on Research in Income and Wealth, Vol. 28 (Princeton, N. J.: Princeton University Press for National Bureau of Economic Research, 1964), p. 237.

Brown and Kruizenga estimated the elasticity of *TI* with respect to *PI* at 1.4 at 1953 income levels. See E. Cary Brown and Richard J. Kruizenga, "Income Sensitivity of a Simple Personal Income Tax," *Review of Economics and Statistics,* Vol. 41 (August 1959), p. 268. Over the range in which the marginal tax rate with respect to *TI* is approximately constant, the elasticity of tax liability is approximately equal to the elasticity of *TI*.

Writing in 1945, Musgrave estimated the yield elasticity of the individual income tax at 1945 rates and exemptions at 2.2 with respect to GNP. See Richard A. Musgrave, "Federal Tax Reform," in *Public Finance and Full Employment,* Postwar Economic Studies No. 3, Board of Governors of the Federal Reserve System (1945), p. 42. Musgrave's estimate was based on prewar data.

In the long run, elasticities with respect to *PI* and GNP should be approximately equal, inasmuch as there seems to be no pronounced trend in the ratio of *PI* to GNP. In the short run, however, the marginal ratio of *PI* to GNP seems to be lower than the average ratio, that is, the year-to-year change in *PI* seems to be less than would be expected solely on the basis of the average ratio. For the period 1950-60, I estimate the marginal ratio of *PI* to GNP at 48.7 percent (from a linear regression of first differences of *PI* on first differences of GNP), whereas the average ratio for these years was 79.4 percent. If my estimate of the marginal ratio of *PI* to GNP is correct, an elasticity of 1.25 with respect to *PI* implies a short-run elasticity with respect to GNP of only 0.8 at 1960 income levels, and an elasticity of 1.4 with respect to *PI* is equivalent to a short-run elasticity of 0.9 with respect to GNP.[5] On the other hand, a short-run elasticity of 1.1 with respect to GNP, which is my estimate for federal individual income tax liabilities at 1954-60 statutory rates and 1960 income levels, is equivalent to a short-run figure of 1.8 with respect to *PI*.

Corporation Income Tax

The historical estimates of built-in flexibility of the corporation income tax are summarized in Appendix Table E-3. For the expansion periods, the first figure given covers the same number of quarters as the preceding recession whereas the second figure covers the whole expansion.

The estimates should be regarded only as rough approximations owing to the lack of full correction for statutory changes in the corporate tax. The basic rates of the federal corporation income tax were the same throughout the period, but the tax was modified in certain other respects. The most important revision was the liberalization of depreciation allowances in 1954. This reduced profits, as reported for tax purposes and as shown in the national income accounts, but did not modify the effective rate of tax on reported profits. No allowance was made for the change in depreciation methods or for minor revisions that also tended to reduce corporate taxes.[6] An adjustment was made to reflect the expiration of the excess profits tax at the end of 1953.

[5] Elasticity with respect to *PI* is $\Delta T/T \cdot PI/\Delta PI$. Multiplying by $\Delta PI/\Delta GNP$ and dividing by PI/GNP gives $\Delta T/T \cdot GNP/\Delta GNP$, which is elasticity with respect to GNP. In 1960, $PI/GNP = 0.80$.

[6] For a summary of several of the revisions, see *Annual Report of the Secretary of the Treasury, 1954*, pp. 247, 256-73.

TABLE E-3. Historical Built-in Flexibility and Elasticity of Federal Corporation Income Tax at Constant Statutory Rates, 1953-61[a]

(Quarterly estimates at seasonally adjusted annual rates, national income accounts basis)

Period	$\Delta CP/\Delta GNP$	$\Delta CT/\Delta CP$	Built-in Flexibility $(\Delta CT/\Delta GNP)$	Elasticity[b]
Recession:				
1953–II to 1954–II	0.818	0.395	0.323	6.6
Expansion:				
1954–II to 1955–II	0.279	0.400	0.111	2.3
1954–II to 1957–III	0.117	0.390	0.046	1.0
Recession:				
1957–III to 1958–I	0.721	0.423	0.305	7.5
Expansion:				
1958–I to 1958–III	0.390	0.454	0.177	4.7
1958–I to 1960–II	0.178	0.472	0.084	2.1
Recession:				
1960–II to 1961–I	1.864	0.478	0.892	22.5
Expansion:				
1961–I to 1961–IV	0.278	0.471	0.131	3.3

[a] Symbols: ΔCP = change in corporate profits before taxes; ΔGNP = change in gross national product; ΔCT = change in federal corporation income tax accruals (excess profits tax not included).
Calculations are based on estimates of U. S. Department of Commerce, Office of Business Economics: *U. S. Income and Output* (1958) and *Survey of Current Business*, July 1962, July 1963.
[b] Elasticity is $\dfrac{\Delta CT}{CT^*} \div \dfrac{\Delta GNP}{GNP^*}$, where CT* and GNP* are arithmetic means of the values for the beginning and ending quarters of the periods.

Elasticity of Retail Sales Tax

At 1960 income and consumption levels, the short-run elasticity of consumption with respect to GNP appears to have been less than 0.5.[7] While a federal retail sales tax would be imposed mainly on consumption

[7] $E = [c(\Delta PI - \Delta T - \Delta D)/\Delta GNP]\,(GNP/C)$
where E is elasticity of consumption with respect to GNP, c is the marginal propensity to consume out of disposable income, ΔD is the increase in personal taxes other than the federal individual income tax (mainly state-local income taxes and estate and gift taxes), C is consumption expenditures, and the other symbols have the meaning defined earlier in this appendix. Using the value for c estimated below and assuming that $\Delta D/GNP = 0.018$, the numerical estimate for 1960 is
$$E = .812\ (.487 - .087 - .018)\ 1.53 = 0.47.$$

goods, many consumption expenditures would be omitted from the base and some nonconsumption items might be taxed.[8] The yield elasticity of the tax cannot be closely estimated without detailed assumptions regarding its coverage and statistical studies of the behavior of expenditures on the taxed items, a task which I have not attempted. Nevertheless, I think it is highly likely that the short-run elasticity of yield of a broad retail sales tax would be below unity; the figure might be far less than 1.

Marginal Propensity to Consume

The short-run marginal propensity to consume was estimated from a linear regression for the period 1948-62:

$$C_t - C_{t-1} = \$0.41 \text{ billion} + 0.812 \ (Y_t - Y_{t-1})$$
$$(0.110) \qquad r^2 = 0.681$$

where C is personal consumption expenditures and Y is personal disposable income, both in constant (1954) dollars, and t is time measured in years. Data are from OBE estimates from *Survey of Current Business,* July 1963. A marginal propensity to consume close to 0.9 and a much higher r^2 are obtained if the regression is based on the original data, but the first-difference form is considered a better estimate of the short-run marginal propensity to consume because it is less influenced by the common growth trend of consumption and disposable income.

Consumption Multiplier

The consumption multiplier, on GNP, may be approximated as

$$m = \frac{1}{1 - (1 - a - b - d)c},$$

where m is the multiplier, a is the marginal ratio of PI to GNP, b is built-in flexibility of the federal individual income tax with respect to GNP, d is built-in flexibility of personal taxes other than the federal individual income tax, and c is the marginal propensity to consume out of disposable personal income.

The short-run relations estimated or assumed above are $a = 0.487$, $b = 0.087$, $d = 0.018$, and $c = 0.812$. These figures indicate a multiplier of 1.49. In the absence of the federal income tax, b would be zero and the value of m would be 1.67.

[8] See paper by Douglas H. Eldridge in *The Role of Direct and Indirect Taxes in the Federal Revenue System,* A Conference Report of the National Bureau of Economic Research and the Brookings Institution, Studies of Government Finance (Princeton, N. J.: Princeton University Press, 1964), p. 141 ff; also Appendix C.

The long-run values of a, b, and c are higher than their short-run values. On the basis of long-run relations, m would be higher than the figure given above, and the inclusion or exclusion of b in the calculation would have more effect on the value of m.

While simple multiplier calculations of this kind shed light on the stabilizing power of built-in flexibility, they are of limited usefulness. The behavioral relations on which the calculations rest may not be properly measured or may be unstable, and the analysis does not deal adequately with the time dimension of economic fluctuations. From the policy point of view, it is also important to recognize that any tax that might be substituted for the individual income tax would almost certainly have positive built-in flexibility and hence would also act as a stabilizer.

Index*

Ability to pay. *See* Taxpaying capacity

Accrued-income tax concept: administrative difficulties in, 29; items entering into assessment of, 29

Adjustment gross income (AGI), 33-34, 99, 100, 104, 105, 107-10, 112, 114, 116, 118, 119, 121, 122, 130, 131, 133, 137, 138, 147, 149, 151-53, 157, 158, 160, 161, 164, 165, 173, 176, 179, 180, 185, 202-3, 223, 226, 228, 229n, 233, 235, 237, 239, 311, 313

Administration of income tax: complex procedures of, 73, 198; costs of, 33, 34; difficulties of assessments, 28-34; theoretical issues of "capital" definitions in, 30

After-tax distribution of income, 262-85

Age 65 or over: deductions for medical expenses, 166; exclusion from AGI of gain on sale of residence, 185; exemptions for, 223, 227, 233-34, 258

AGI. *See* Adjusted gross income

Aid to dependent children, 226

Alcoholic-beverage taxes, 36, 63, 176

Alternative taxes: choice of in influence on saving, 44; compared with income tax, 38, 151; fairness of, 12; possible combination of with income tax, 25; as substitutes for income tax, 5, 7-8, 17. *See also* Expenditure tax; Wealth tax

Ando, Albert, 292n, 304n

Andrews, F. Emerson, 172n

Ashley, W. J., 25n

Atkinson, Thomas R., 277, 278n

Australia: income taxes used in before 1913, 1

* References to tables and charts are in italics.

Averaging of fluctuating incomes: advantage of, 255; "averageable income" defined, 251; base period for, 251; persons benefiting from, 252-53; tax computation in, 252; weaknesses of plan for, 254, 259

Becker, Gary S., 86

Before-tax distribution of income, 262-85, *270, 271;* historical changes in, 269-79

Blakey, Gladys C., 8n

Blakey, Roy G., 8n

Blind taxpayer or spouse: exemption for, 223, 233-34, 258

Blum, Walter J., viii, 17n, 309n

Bodkin, Ronald, 304

Bollinger, Lynn L., 52n, 137n, 205n, 213n

Bonuses, 101

Borrowing: anticipatory consumption financed by, 41; for educational purposes, 91; in undertaking business ventures, 46-47; yield of assets financed by, 158

Brady, Dorothy S., 135n, 249n

Brazer, Harvey E., 54n, 231n

Break, George F., 21n, 54n, 55, 56, 101n

British Commonwealth: deduction in for housewives' costs due to outside jobs, 257; earned-income credit allowed in, 255; income-equalizing effect of tax in, 268; income splitting not allowed in, 247; "vanishing" exemption used in several countries of, 229. *See also* Great Britain

Brittain, John A., viii, 277n, 298, 299

355